AFE 0894

D0215172

TEACHING TODAY

An Introduction to Education

Fifth Edition

TEACHING TODAY

An Introduction to Education

DAVID G. ARMSTRONG
Texas A & M University

KENNETH T. HENSON
Eastern Kentucky University

TOM V. SAVAGE
California State University, Fullerton

Merrill,
an imprint of Prentice Hall
Upper Saddle River, New Jersey   Columbus, Ohio

Library of Congress Cataloging-in-Publication Data

Armstrong, David G.
    Teaching today: an introduction to education/David G. Armstrong, Kenneth T. Henson, Tom V. Savage. —5th ed.
        p. cm.
    "Formerly titled, Education: an introduction."
    Includes bibliographical references and index.
    ISBN 0-13-382177-3
    1. Teaching—Vocational guidance—United States. 2. Education—Study and teaching—United States. 3. Public schools—United States. I. Henson, Kenneth T. II. Savage, Tom V. III. Armstrong, David G. Education, an introduction. IV. Title.
    LB1775.2.A75   1997
    371'.01'0973—dc20   96-20386
                                                        CIP

Cover art: Detail of the 1995 untitled mixed media painting by Randy Henson, photographed by Sharon K. Henson
Editor: Debra A. Stollenwerk
Production Editor: Mary M. Irvin
Photo Researcher: Anthony Magnacca
Design Coordinator: Julia Zonneveld Van Hook
Text Designer: Susan Frankenberry
Cover Designer: Proof Positive/Farrowlyne Assoc.
Production Manager: Pamela A. Bennett
Electronic Text Management: Marilyn Wilson Phelps, Matthew Williams, Karen L. Bretz, Tracey Ward

This book was set in Schneidler and Humanist by Prentice Hall and was printed and bound by R. R. Donnelley/VA. The cover was printed by Phoenix Color Corp.

© 1997 by Prentice-Hall, Inc.
Simon & Schuster/A Viacom Company
Upper Saddle River, New Jersey 07458

Earlier editions entitled *Education: An Introduction* © 1993, 1989, 1985, 1981 by Macmillan Publishing Company.

Photo credits: Scott Cunningham/Merrill/Prentice Hall: 3, 20, 102, 115, 142, 174, 186, 197, 200, 214, 223, 236, 290, 306, 311, 314; Andy Brunk/Merrill/Prentice Hall: 9, 244; Anthony Magnacca/Merrill/Prentice Hall: 33, 179, 263; Robert Vega/Merrill/Prentice Hall: 36; Anne Vega/Merrill/Prentice Hall: 43, 77, 81, 149, 209, 350; Barbara Schwartz/Merrill/Prentice Hall: 53, 96, 106, 255; Ulrike Welsch: 67; Bruce Johnson/Merrill/Prentice Hall: 71, 322; KS Studios/Merrill/Prentice Hall: 85, 166, 278; Bettmann Archive: 122, 127, 129, 155, 231; Gale Zucker: 216; Red Morgan/Time Magazine: 265; Jean Claude LeJeune: 273; Merrill/Prentice Hall: 331; Carolyn Salisbury/NEA: 344

Printed in the United States of America

10 9 8 7 6 5 4 3

ISBN: 0-13-382177-3

Prentice-Hall International (UK) Limited, *London*
Prentice-Hall of Australia Pty. Limited, *Sydney*
Prentice-Hall of Canada, Inc., *Toronto*
Prentice-Hall Hispanoamericana, S. A., *Mexico*
Prentice-Hall of India Private Limited, *New Delhi*
Prentice-Hall of Japan, Inc., *Tokyo*
Simon & Schuster Asia Pte. Ltd., *Singapore*
Editora Prentice-Hall do Brasil, Ltda., *Rio de Janeiro*

Teaching Today: An Introduction to Education is a comprehensive treatment of education and teaching. It provides a solid grounding in the intellectual foundations of the field, results of research, and current issues. We have provided many opportunities for users of the book to reflect, analyze, and decide. We think the book will develop your decision-making skills. This is something we value. And we hope it is something you as future teachers will prize, as well. Good luck!

Previous editions of this text have been used successfully in undergraduate and graduate courses. We have designed the book for use in introduction to education classes, introduction to teaching classes, general education classes, foundations of education classes, issues in education classes, and problems in education classes. Some content has relevance for inservice work with teachers and as a valuable professional reference for the career educator.

ORGANIZATION OF THE TEXT

We believe teachers should design their own courses and not be bound by the order of presentations of chapters in their textbooks. We also feel that this is how instructors should use our book. We have organized the book in a way that makes sense to us, but we recognize that others will want to follow a different sequence of chapters, and we encourage them to do so. Chapters have been written so that each is freestanding, that no chapter is a prerequisite to understanding content introduced in another.

In preparing this text, we decided to organize content under four major headings. These headings establish a general context for the related chapters. We begin with a section titled "Trends and Realities." Chapter 1 introduces a selection of important issues facing educators today. Chapter 2 takes a more detailed look at what teaching is like in today's schools. Management and discipline continue to be issues of great concern to newcomers to our profession. For this reason, we treat this issue early in the text, in Chapter 3. Chapter 4 focuses on patterns of instructional organization in the schools. We find that many beginning teachers have thought little about the many categories of employees in schools. Information about this issue and about patterns of school organization is treated in Chapter 5.

The second section, "Contexts for Teaching," is designed to provide prospective teachers with an understanding of some characteristics and constraints they will find in today's classroom. Chapter 6 develops themes related to the international roots of American education. Chapter 7 introduces some philosophical perspectives that are reflected in attitudes toward school programs. This chapter is designed to help newcomers understand that not all people they will encounter will define "good education" in the same way. Chapter 8 introduces issues associated with the important impact of groups to which learners belong on their values and attitudes toward teachers and schools. Finally, Chapter 9 highlights important technological changes in education, with particular references to the World Wide Web of the Internet as an information source.

The third section, "Today's Diverse Learners," describes the great diversity of young people in today's schools. Chapter 10 profiles the range of learners in the schools, with particular attention to characteristics of young people in different age groups. Chapter 11 provides detailed information about the changing demographic characteristics of the schools, particularly regarding the rapidly increasing numbers of learners from minority cultural and ethnic groups. This chapter also introduces issues associated with gender equity. We live in a particularly litigious time. The final chapter in this section, Chapter 12, focuses on important issues associated with legal rights and responsibilities of learners.

The fourth section, "Teachers and Their Work," includes chapters addressing issues having to do with various dimensions of teachers' professional lives. We are strongly committed to the view that teaching practices can be improved through careful research. Chapter 13 introduces key findings of leading teacher-effectiveness researchers. Chapter 14 promotes the importance of individual classroom teachers doing research of their own design in their own classrooms. Chapter 15 introduces information about important legal issues facing teachers, with special reference to key court cases. The final chapter, Chapter 16, introduces both general teachers' organizations and specialty teachers' organizations.

CHAPTER FEATURES

Each chapter in the fifth edition of *Teaching Today: An Introduction to Education* includes

- *bulleted objectives* to help focus attention on key chapter content
- *an introduction* to establish a clear context for the content to follow

- *critical incidents* to prompt reflective thinking about typical issues and situations that confront teachers every day
- *boxes, figures, or tables* that raise important issues for student comment and consideration or that introduce important supplementary information
- *key ideas in summary* to review critical aspects of chapter content succinctly and efficiently
- *review and discussion questions* to provide students with opportunities to check their own learning and extend their thinking powers
- *ideas for field experiences, projects, and enrichment* to suggest opportunities for extending and applying chapter content
- *references* to indicate to students where they might find some of the original materials consulted by the authors

NEW TO THIS EDITION

The fifth edition contains much new content, including

- a new chapter on "Teachers as Researchers"
- a new chapter titled "How Groups Affect Learners"
- greatly expanded coverage of technology, focusing particularly on uses of the World Wide Web of the Internet in public schools
- extensive coverage of the Goals 2000 initiative
- treatment of trends such as "systemic reform," "school choice," "charter schools," "full service schools," "magnet schools," "voucher plans," and "school-business partnerships"
- discussion of the National Board for Professional Teaching Standards
- expanded and updated coverage of issues related to multicultural (including gender equity) and bilingual education
- increased coverage of issues related to management and discipline
- comprehensive treatment of results of teacher-effectiveness research
- thorough discussion of legal issues affecting teachers and learners
- "critical incidents" in each chapter to promote reflective thinking on real issues teachers face
- extensive updating of content in all chapters

SUPPLEMENTS TO THE TEXT

Continuing the pattern established in previous editions of *Teaching Today: An Introduction to Education*, an instructor's guide has been prepared. It has been completely revised for this edition and includes

- overviews of the chapter content
- alternative ideas for sequencing courses using this text

- suggested activities
- a collection of questions suitable for quizzes and tests, with accompanying keys

The test items are also available in a disk format configured for use in either Apple-based or DOS-based computers.

ACKNOWLEDGMENTS

We want to conclude by recognizing some incredibly patient and tolerant people who helped with the development of the fifth edition of. We would like to thank Grace Burton, University of North Carolina, Wilmington; Leslie Owen Wilson, University of Wisconsin, Stevens Point; Sister Judith Costello, Regis College; Margaret Laughlin, University of Wisconsin, Green Bay; and Anne Russ, Wells College. The editor for this project, Debbie Stollenwerk, gave long hours to this project, and her suggestions added immeasurably to the substance and coherence of the final version. Finally, our spouses deserve special thanks for their support while we were working on this revision.

Wags sometimes comment that the United States and the United Kingdom are divided by a common language. Similarly, we educators are "divided" by a profession that provides a forum for disputes as much as it gives us a set of common purposes. Our individual perspectives are wide-ranging, and the contexts within which we work are incredibly varied. This book aims to help you understand our profession's diversity (including some raging disputes that now engage us) as well as the special "professional glue" that binds us together.

As you read this book and begin preparing for your career in education, we ask you to begin by "unlearning" some important lessons. These lessons or perspectives may be ones you don't even know you have acquired. These are the comfortable "truths" of personal experience, particularly the personal experiences you have had as a learner in the schools.

Your recollection of what went on in schools you attended may be sound. We do not mean to challenge the accuracy of your understanding of your own school experiences. Though many people recall "slices of past life" that collectively are a misrepresentation of what really happened, we accept that you may be an exception. What we want you to do, though, is avoid generalizing from your own school experiences to schooling and education in general. In our years of working with prospective teachers, one of the biggest barriers we have had to overcome is the tendency of newcomers to expect the school environment where they will be working to be essentially the same as the one they remember from their own school years. Untrue. Erase that idea. *Expect* sharp and sometimes surprising differences.

Schools where you will do preservice field experience work, including student teaching, and the school where you will begin your teaching careers may have little in common with the mental picture you now have of the world of public education. Some of you may be comfortable with differences you experience. Others of you may be uncomfortable. We want to make a comment or two to some of you who may be distressed by what you encounter.

First of all, you need to understand that the diversity among schools today is probably greater than it has ever been. If conditions at a school where you initially find work do not please you, you may be able to find another one where patterns are more to your liking. Second, teachers today are expected to participate in shaping the environment of the school where they work. If conditions are not what you think they ought to be, you have an obligation to try to change them.

Though differences among schools today are profound, there are threads that draw together members of our profession. Most of us work in fairly large institutions that also employ other professionals. We are in a public service enterprise. People we work with have college degrees. We are committed to helping new generations of young people take their place in our society.

What kind of a person succeeds in teaching today? There is no definitive answer to this question. However, if schools today were in the habit of putting up signs to attract prospective employees, lots of them might read: "Wanted: Teachers Who Lead." If you are looking for an occupation that is sheltered from the frustrations of contemporary life, teaching is not for you. If you expect to avoid making major policy decisions and just want to be left alone to "work with the kids," teaching is not for you. If you expect to be through with your own learning and professional development once you qualify for a teaching certificate and obtain a job, teaching is not for you.

Teachers today are expected to be proactive leaders. Many are active in the political process, particularly in lobbying efforts designed to win support for legislation to improve public education. New school leadership approaches, often referred to as "site-based management," require teachers to participate in decisions about curricula, graduation requirements, attendance policies, budgets, and other issues that used to be the exclusive responsibility of school administrators. Teachers increasingly are doing research in their own classrooms directed at improving instruction. They are taking the lead in utilizing the incredible intellectual resources available on the World Wide Web of the Internet to provide better programs for students.

Teachers who lead expect challenges to their decisions. There is much debate today about what goes on in schools. Virtually anything a teacher decides to do may lead to a confrontation. So how do you prepare for this kind of a role? Nobody has all the answers to this question, but certainly you need to develop a solid grasp of academic subject matter and research results related to effective classroom practice. This kind of a data base provides you some intellectual legs to stand on. You should strive, too, to develop your written and oral communication skills. The power of your ideas, alone, will not carry the day. But if you are "good on your feet" and can speak your thoughts forcefully, and if you can write clear, logical responses to concerns, chances are that you will fare well in your role as a teacher-leader.

The "professional life space" of a teacher today may last as long as 45 years. This means that you will need to keep learning and adapting in response to changing conditions in the schools. Information we provide in this text is designed to provide you with an "effective initial launch" into the profession. We believe ideas you will find here will allow you to have a satisfying and successful beginning.

D.G.A.
K.T.H.
T.V.S.

3

Classroom Management and Discipline   50

4

The Curriculum   75

11

Multiculturalism 230

12

Learners' Rights and Responsibilities 251

16

Professional Groups 341

Author Index 361

Subject Index 365

TEACHING TODAY

*An Introduction
to Education*

Trends and Realities

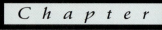

1

Challenges Facing Today's Schools

OBJECTIVES

- Identify the responsibilities of schools as developers of social capital.

- Recognize characteristics of systemic reform.

- Point out key provisions of the Goals 2000 legislation.

- Describe activities of the National Board for Professional Teaching Standards, and discuss some issues associated with national certification of teachers.

- Explain responses to the idea of school choice, including voucher plans, open-enrollment plans, magnet schools, and charter schools.

- Describe some alternative approaches to school-business partnerships.

- Point out some reasons there is a growing interest in establishing full-service schools.

- Suggest questions that might be used as a focus for a personal professional development plan.

Schools play many roles. They transmit academic content from one generation to another. They provide opportunities for learners to develop useful interpersonal relations skills. They help young people prepare for the world of work. Perhaps most significant of all, schools nurture development of social capital.

Social capital refers to the propensity of people to work cooperatively and voluntarily in groups and organizations that include individuals who are not members of their own families. The willingness of Americans to join and participate actively in voluntary groups has long been recognized as one of our nation's strengths. Alexis de Tocqueville, who traveled in the United States in the 1830s, was struck by this behavior of Americans—something he noted that differed markedly from prevalent social practices in Europe.

Our society's large supply of social capital has allowed us to take maximum advantage of individual talents. As a result, our businesses, governments, and social service organizations have been able to draw on the expertise of extraordinarily bright and gifted people. Social capital has ensured a continuity in our private and public institutions, which is in sharp contrast with circumstances in some other parts of the world.

In China, for example, social and business organizations have been built largely around families, which has made it particularly difficult for large-scale enterprises to be maintained across generations. Although expertise within a given family may exist for a few years, once the leaders die, there may not be similarly talented members within the same family group to take their places. In China, there has been little tradition of seeking professional managers outside the ranks of the family controlling the enterprise. This varies significantly from our American practice of voluntary, non-family-based organizations in which professional managerial talent is the norm and it is common practice to go outside of the organization to find new leadership talent when the need arises.

The success of our system depends on a willingness of people to work together voluntarily and to subordinate at least some personal priorities for the good of the group. Some people feel this type of commitment is not as strong today as it once was. There are fears that a diminished stock of social capital may undermine our way of life. Francis Fukuyama (1995), a prominent social commentator, argues that "our preoccupation with the lonesome individual and his or her absolute sphere of autonomy has weakened all forms of group life" (p. 5).

Fukuyama (1995) notes several threats to our stock of social capital. First of all, recent economic dislocations such as large downsizing of basic industries have uprooted many people from their traditional places of residence. Unexpected and unwelcome moves have diminished people's willingness to establish strong voluntary ties with groups such as churches, PTAs, political associations, and social organizations. Also, the electronic revolution that has furnished our homes with televisions, VCRs, and modem-equipped computers has made it convenient for us to spend our leisure hours at home rather than in public gathering places such as court house squares and parks. Finally, there has been a movement in recent years toward hard-nosed defense of individual rights (ranging across themes from gun control to euthanasia) that has made us increasingly less inclined to accept compromises in the name of the good of the larger community.

Evidence abounds that our nation's social fabric is being strained. Crime rates are up. Families experience severe difficulties. Economic uncertainty unsettles many of our citizens. Our faith in our fellow citizens is not what it once was. A survey taken in 1960 revealed that 58 percent of respondents answered yes to the question, "Can most people be trusted?" In 1993, only 37 percent responded yes to the same question (Fukuyama, 1995). These results underscore the responsibility our schools have to provide programs that strike an acceptable balance between our need to develop learners' individual characteristics and our need to develop citizens who will willingly associate with, trust, and support others.

Teachers for the new century must be willing to engage others in the debates that are now under way and that promise to continue regarding what schools should do. Those who join the fray will exert a professional influence on their own conditions of practice. All who stand back will find themselves working in school environments that may be far from what they would like. As we look forward to the next decade in education, the one certainty is that there will be changes. In this chapter, we introduce some challenges to present practices that are already under way.

SYSTEMIC REFORM

A key event in the present wave of educational change occurred in 1983 with the publication of *A Nation at Risk: The Imperative for Educational Reform* (National Commission on Excellence in Education, 1983). This document detailed potential long-term threats to our country that logically might follow declines in test scores and high drop-out rates. This report and many others that followed its publication proposed that schools could be "made better" by increasing the rigor of academic programs, stiffening requirements for teacher preparation, and introducing more sophisticated managerial practices into school management.

BOX 1-1

Quality of Local Schools

Public opinion surveys regularly find that people rate their local schools higher than they rate schools in general. This may result from media coverage that highlights exceptionally bad school situations, or it may simply be a matter of people being more willing to believe that what they know well is "good" and to believe what they do not know well is "suspect" or "bad." Other explanations might also explain the tendency of Americans to look kindly at their own local schools.

What Do You Think?

1. What were the best features of the schools you attended?
2. In general, do you think your teachers were competent?
   What are some weaknesses of schools you attended?
3. Think about general criticisms you have heard about American schools. Could any of these logically be applied to schools you attended?
4. Why do you think we tend to think schools in our local areas are better than American schools in general?

The reform efforts of the 1980s led to calls for schools to present more public information about how well learners were doing. This kind of pressure greatly increased the use of standardized tests and wider reporting of scores. Although low test scores often were perceived to be indicative of problems in particular schools, by themselves, the scores explained little about causes of particular difficulties. Neither did they ensure that resources would be diverted to schools where learners were experiencing problems nor that innovative new instructional techniques would be used to assist low-scoring learners. The emphasis on standardized testing by itself was found to have little impact on learners' achievement.

In response to this situation, those interested in improving the schools increasingly have come to recognize that many variables affect learners' performance. More people are coming to believe that changes likely to produce beneficial results must attack a number of problem areas at the same time, including outdated administrative arrangements, inappropriate instructional materials, kinds of family support provided to learners, authority given individual teachers to make decisions about how to teach their own learners, and the general nature of the school environment. The term that is being applied to the effort to effect these multivariable changes is *systemic reform*. Many systemic reform efforts include attention to the following:

- developing "learning communities"
- an emphasis on "outcome goals"
- decentralized school management
- redesigned teacher responsibility and compensation schemes

Developing Learning Communities

Specialists who have studied organizations have found that those that prosper avoid complacency (Shaffer & Amundsen, 1993). More specifically, they engage in ongoing challenges to their operating assumptions, and they involve employees at all levels in examining present practices with a view to providing better alternatives. Today, leaders in education increasingly recognize that schools must become learning organizations or communities. Schools should engage in careful study of present practices, involve many different kinds of people in decision making, and courageously implement instructional and managerial practices that are quite different from what many of us experienced as clients of the schools (Henson, in press).

Learning communities are proactive. They embark on change in anticipation of problems rather than in response to concerns raised by others. Traditionally, school practices have been slow to change. When changes have come, they have resulted because external pressures have been brought to bear. Schools that reconstitute themselves as learning communities and actively involve parents, teachers, administrators, support staff members, learners, and community members in the decision-making process may be able to modify deficient practices more quickly and, thereby, avoid the kinds of negative comments that dissatisfied groups have often directed at schools in the past.

Outcome Goals

The emphasis on outcome goals represents a shift away from a focus on "inputs." In the past, for example, comparisons among schools were sometimes made using such evidence as the number of computers in the classrooms, the percentage of teachers with advanced degrees, and the availability of recently published texts and other instructional materials. The problem with information about these inputs is that it tells us nothing about what learners are gaining from their experiences in schools that "look good" when input criteria are used. Outcome goals refocus on learners and what they understand from our instruction.

Part of the effort to focus on outcome goals has been directed at identifying high-quality curriculum standards for all subject areas. Among excellent work in this regard has been that done by the National Councils of Teachers of Mathematics and the National Council for Geographic Education. New curriculum standards developed by these groups are now being reflected in published material, and efforts are under way to prepare teachers to emphasize the new upgraded standards in their instruction. Many other professional groups are also working to upgrade curriculum standards in their respective subject areas.

We also are witnessing an emphasis on more rigorous kinds of assessment procedures. In general, evaluation techniques that require learners to demonstrate sophisticated thinking skills are replacing older forced choice techniques such as true-false and matching tests that lack the capacity to assess higher-order learning. One approach to evaluating learners' performances that is now attracting much interest is *authentic assessment* (Wiggins, 1989; Spady, 1994).

Authentic assessment requires learners to demonstrate what they have learned in a way that has much in common with how a proficient adult might deal with the content that has been learned. In a traditional class, for example, we might ask learners to write an essay about possible consequences of locating a new factory close to a residential neighborhood. In authentic assessment, we might ask the student to provide documentation and testimony to a committee playing the role of a zoning board (and we might actually invite a zoning board member or two to participate in the exercise).

Decentralized School Management

In the past, some efforts to improve the quality of our schools have been stifled because highly centralized administrative arrangements in school districts have not responded well to conditions faced by principals and teachers at individual schools. To remedy this situation, many supporters of systemic reform favor decentralizing decision-making power. The idea is to greatly expand the authority of teachers and administrators at the individual building level to make all kinds of decisions related to the operation of the school. The term *site-based management* is one that increasingly is used to describe the decentralization of decision-making power to professionals at the individual school level.

The idea of site-based decision making is to trust critical decisions to the people who will actually be delivering educational services to learners. Often a team

Members of this school staff are discussing a transition to a site-based management plan, which would place greater decision-making power in the hands of teachers actually delivering instructional services.

approach is used. Leadership team members from an individual school may include teachers, administrators, parents, representatives from the local community, and a few learners. More and more frequently, site-based leadership teams are being given authority over such issues as budgeting, personnel selection, school curriculum, and in-service planning. Those of you who are preparing for careers as teachers need to think about getting some expertise in areas related to school budgets, community relations, state curriculum guidelines, and personnel selection and hiring. Teachers today are assuming responsibilities that go well beyond their traditional role as instructors.

Redesigned Teacher Responsibility and Compensation Schemes

The expansion of teachers' responsibilities that has been encouraged by the trend toward site-based management has led to new interest in the old idea of *differentiated staffing*. Differentiated staffing refers to the idea that not all teachers should have exactly the same set of responsibilities. For example, teachers who become particularly good at working with student teachers might be allocated some time to work exclusively with a group of these potential members of the profession.

Others who are especially adept at wrestling with issues associated with school budgets might be allocated time to work out alternative financial scenarios for presentation to the school's management team. Still others might have quasi-administrative roles requiring them to mentor and assist teachers who may be experiencing either professional or personal difficulties.

What we could call the "professional life space" of a teacher may last 40 or more years. Traditionally, formal preparation has ended at the very beginning of this period of time. Even though some staff development experiences often have been required for teachers to remain in good standing, there usually has not been an expectation that teachers' breadth of expertise will be much different in the middle or the end of their teaching careers than it is at the beginning. Differentiated staffing challenges this pattern. It assumes that teachers will grow in terms of what they can do as they mature in the profession. As this happens, they will be assigned new and more challenging roles. It is thought that this strategy will help keep bright people in the profession by providing them with new responsibilities as their expertise warrants. Differentiated staffing can be an antidote to teacher boredom and burnout.

In part, successful differentiated staffing requires that teachers who perform more challenging roles receive some kind of recognition. In some places, titles such as lead teacher, teacher curriculum specialist, and team leader are used to denote those individuals who have earned the right to play specialized roles. Increasingly, we are seeing efforts to provide additional compensation to teachers who have been assigned to discharge special responsibilities.

Various compensation schemes have been devised. These differ somewhat from traditional merit pay plans, which provided salary supplements for teachers who were identified as being outstanding faculty members. The idea was to provide extra compensation to these "good" teachers with a view to keeping them in the classroom. The pay was not usually tied to any special, nontraditional responsibilities.

Merit pay plans generally have not been popular with teachers. There have often been suspicions that individuals identified as meritorious were selected because of their personal compatibility with raters rather than because they were more effective practitioners than others. Compensation plans associated with differentiated staffing have been somewhat less controversial. This is because the additional money is paid because individuals have met specific, demanding responsibilities. These responsibilities clearly go well beyond those demanded of typical classroom teachers; hence, there has not been so much concern that personality factors have played a role in the decision to award these increases as has been the case in many traditional merit play plans.

GOALS 2000

Many efforts to improve our schools today are tied to some important federal legislation. This includes the *Goals 2000: Educate America Act of 1993* and a related piece of legislation, the *National Skills Standard Act of 1993*. Goals 2000 supports a systemic approach to educational reform. It is designed to encourage communities to align all components of their school system to help learners master content and graduate as contributing citizens who are ready to go to work or are prepared to enter our colleges and universities. It calls for a concurrent focus on school curricula, textbooks, instructional practices, technology, assessment, community involvement in decision making, and professional school management and governance. The legislation establishes a National Goals Panel that is charged with reporting on progress toward achieving goals related to these eight areas:

1. *Readiness for school:* By the year 2000, all children in America will start school ready to learn.
2. *High school completion:* By the year 2000, the high school graduation rate will increase to at least 90 percent.
3. *Student achievement and citizenship:* By the year 2000, American students will leave grades four, eight, and twelve having demonstrated competency in challenging subject matter including English, mathematics, science, history, and geography; and every school in America will ensure that all students learn to use their minds well, so they may be prepared for responsible citizenship, further learning, and productive employment in our modern economy.
4. *Teachers' professional development:* By the year 2000, the nation's teaching force will have access to programs for the continued development of their professional skills and the opportunity to acquire the knowledge and skills needed to instruct and prepare all American students for the next century.
5. *Science and mathematics:* By the year 2000, U.S. students will be first in the world in science and mathematics achievement.
6. *Adult literacy and lifelong learning:* By the year 2000, every adult in America will be literate and will possess the knowledge and skills necessary to compete in a global economy and exercise the rights and responsibilities of citizenship.
7. *Safe, disciplined, and drug-free schools:* By the year 2000, every school in America will be free of drugs and violence and will offer a disciplined environment conducive to learning.
8. *Partnerships:* By the year 2000, each school will promote partnerships that will increase parental involvement and participation in promoting the social, emotional, and academic growth of children.

This legislation encourages states and local communities to voluntarily adopt these goals and to take action in support of them. Many states and communities have acted to do this. However, not all Americans support this effort. Even though the goals themselves and the academic standards being developed in support of them are voluntary, some critics allege that this legislation represents an effort to nationalize education. Education, they argue, has traditionally been a state and local matter and the federal government should play a very minor role in determining what good schooling is all about.

Supporters of Goals 2000 counter that historically there has been no serious attention paid to developing standards for schools that describe intended learning outcomes. They suggest that performance standards developed by the best minds in the nation will impose nothing on individual states and school districts. Rather, they will be models that the states and districts may choose to adopt, modify, or reject. There is no intent at all to impose rigid, uniform standards on the nation as a whole.

NATIONAL BOARD FOR PROFESSIONAL TEACHING STANDARDS

Early versions of the Goals 2000 legislation did not address the issue of teacher preparation and the quality of the teaching force. The decision to add the goal related to teachers' professional development may have been influenced by some work initiated by the Carnegie Forum on Education and the Economy. Based on recommendations of this group, a National Board for Professional Teaching Standards (NBPTS) was established in 1987. The board is governed by 63 people representing teachers, administrators, members of the public, and other stakeholders in education. Most members are teachers. NBPTS is a private, nonprofit group. Financial support comes from foundations, grants from large businesses, and federal funding sources.

NBPTS attempts to identify high and rigorous standards regarding what teachers should know and be able to demonstrate to help learners achieve. The group is working on developing a process that will issue National Board certificates to teachers who meet these rigorous standards. Candidates for these certificates will be observed both in actual classroom teaching situations and at special assessment centers (Baratz-Snowden, 1992).

National Board certificates will not replace teaching credentials, certificates, or licenses issued by states. State certificates typically indicate that individuals have met minimum requirements necessary to work with learners in the classroom. National Board certificates will recognize people who have met much higher standards. State certificates signal that holders have met requirements established by a single state. National Board certificates will verify that holders have met a standard of excellence that will be applied uniformly to applicants from all over the country. In essence, the idea is that National Board certificates will provide school districts throughout the country with evidence that holders are outstanding classroom practitioners.

It is envisioned that there will be a number of categories of National Board certificates (Baratz-Snowden, 1992):

- Early Childhood (ages 3–8) — generalist
- Middle Childhood (ages 7–12) — generalist, English language arts, mathematics, science, social studies/history
- Early and Middle Childhood (ages 3–12) — art, foreign language, guidance counseling, library/media, music, physical education/health
- Early Adolescence (ages 11–15) — generalist, English language arts, mathematics, science, social studies/history
- Adolescence and Young Adulthood (ages 14–18+) — English language arts, mathematics, science, social studies/history

- Early Adolescence through Young Adulthood (ages 11–18+) — art, foreign language, guidance counseling, library/media, music, physical education/health, vocational education

At the present time, work is being completed on establishing standards related to each of these certificates. It is anticipated that the full system of National Board certification will be operational by school year 1998–1999.

The idea of National Board certification has attracted some of the same kinds of controversies that have surrounded discussions of the Goals 2000 legislation. The idea of national certification runs counter to our long-standing practice of certifying teachers at the state level. Even though National Board certification is not intended to replace state certification, some critics allege that it is a first step in that direction. Supporters point out that the high standards that will be reflected in the NBPTS requirements will prompt states to impose more rigorous certification requirements and that this trend will, in time, improve the quality of teachers in all of our nation's classrooms.

SCHOOL CHOICE

Another thread running through the fabric of school reform discussions is the idea of school choice, which allows parents and learners to choose from among a variety of schools. School choice is in contrast to traditional practices that obligate children to attend schools lying within attendance zones prescribed by local school districts. Proponents of school choice point out that learners have many different needs. They also note that views of parents about what constitutes "good school practice" vary tremendously. It is unlikely that any one school lying within a single attendance zone can accommodate wishes of all parents and characteristics of all learners living within the zone. School choice allows parents and learners to consider many different schools and to select one that they believe represents a best fit with priorities of each family.

A number of benefits have been claimed for school choice policies. Among claimed pluses for these policies are the following (Wells, 1990):

- School choice policies have the potential to allow learners from low-income families to avoid mediocre, overcrowded inner-city schools.
- Families' interest in education may increase because they play an active role in selecting schools their children attend.
- Competition among schools to attract learners may result in a general improvement in the quality of all schools.
- Children attending schools that have been selected from among several alternatives potentially will find themselves in learning environments better matched to their needs than schools within their traditional mandatory attendance areas.

A variety of approaches to school choice has been tried in various parts of the country. These include voucher plans, open enrollment plans, magnet schools, and charter schools.

Voucher Plans

In a *voucher plan*, tax money is provided to parents that they can use to pay for the education of their children at a school of their choice. One possible scenario is that if a state pays individual schools $4,500 per year for each child in attendance, a parent will receive a voucher in this amount for each school-aged child in the household. Once the parent decides what school the child will attend, this voucher is turned over to officials at that school. The officials deposit the money in the school's account and use it as part of the school's instructional and operational budget.

The voucher plan is an idea that has been discussed for many years. Supporters believe it will promote healthy competition among schools. School programs will improve as administrators and teachers work to attract additional learners. Some critics suggest that voucher plans have no provision for helping schools that are not perceived to be good and that might fail to attract learners. Such schools may become worse, because as learners and their support vouchers depart for other schools, the deserted schools will have to deliver instructional services with less money than they had before. Although leaders in such schools may want to do a better job, they will lack the financial resources to make needed improvements.

There also have been concerns about whether voucher plans will serve the needs of learners from economically impoverished families. If a selected school is out of a learner's usual attendance zone, transportation to the school may be expensive or highly inconvenient. Well-to-do families may be able to drive their children to these schools; less affluent families may not be able to. If students must rely on public transportation, families may find it difficult to handle the added expense. Some voucher plans that have been proposed make special financial provisions to help parents who may have concerns about transporting their children to these schools.

There are relatively few voucher plans in place at the present time. Most of them require parents to spend their vouchers at public schools. An interesting exception is a program in Milwaukee. In existence since 1990, this program is designed to make it possible for learners from economically impoverished families to use vouchers to pay tuition at private schools. The program is limited to no more than 1.5% of the total student population of the Milwaukee Public Schools. In school year 1994–1995, learners in the program were enrolled in 12 Milwaukee private schools. Each of these schools received approximately $3,200 for each enrolled learner (Witte & Thorn, 1994).

Participants in the Milwaukee program have come mostly from single-parent, economically deprived families. Parents of these children tend to have high educational expectations for their daughters and sons. Academic achievement results of learners in the private schools, as measured by standardized test scores, have not differed from scores of similar learners who have remained in the Milwaukee Public Schools. Surveys of parents of these learners, however, indicate that they are much more pleased with the experiences of their children in the private schools than they were when their youngsters had been learners in the public schools (Witte & Thorn, 1994).

Open Enrollment Plans

Open enrollment plans vary from voucher plans in that they do not issue tax funds directly to parents. Rather, a system is established that permits parents to select the school their child wishes to attend. The child attends that school, and the state, with the advice of the local district, sees to it that support money is diverted to the budget of the chosen school. Most open enrollment plans limit learners' choices to schools within a given school district. A few allow learners to cross district lines. Minnesota, for example, has a law that allows a learner to enroll in any school in any school district in the state.

Sometimes open enrollment plans are described as "controlled choice" plans. Even though these plans place great stock in parental preferences in assigning learners to individual schools, other considerations do come into play, and the central school district administrators retain some final control over assignment of pupils and students to particular schools. Typically there are provisions that allow administrators to ensure that acceptable racial balances will be maintained in individual schools.

The number of learners in open enrollment districts who have chosen to attend schools outside of their normal attendance zones has varied from place to place. In Minneapolis relatively few learners have elected to do so (Rubenstein, 1992), but there is evidence that in some places these programs are providing benefits to young people from economically impoverished families. For example, scores on tests of reading proficiency have risen four-fold in New York City's District 4 since an open enrollment policy was instituted (Wells, 1990).

Supporters of open enrollment have suggested that this policy will encourage parents to look carefully at the quality of academic programs in individual schools. The idea is that they will choose to send their children to those schools that they believe provide more rigorous learning experiences for their sons and daughters. Critics point out that some parents have chosen schools for reasons having little to do with the quality of the educational program. It is alleged that some children are placed in individual schools because the schools are closer to where parents work than the school in the traditional attendance zone. There also are suspicions that a few parents have chosen school A over school B because of a feeling their athletically inclined son or daughter could make the team easier at A than at B.

Magnet Schools

Magnet schools, most of which are secondary schools, are located within a single school district and draw learners from throughout the district. Many large cities, including Houston, Chicago, Boston, New York, and Philadelphia, have had magnet schools for many years. Often individual magnet schools have a specific theme for which they are especially well known; for example, there may be a magnet school specializing in the sciences or one specializing in the performing arts. In addition to serving the special interest of learners they enroll, they also provide urban school districts with a means of achieving acceptable levels of racial integration. Integration in magnet schools can be accomplished because, unlike zones drawing on learners living in residential areas that may not have racially mixed populations, magnet schools enroll learners from all residential areas in a city.

Magnet schools have provided outstanding learning experiences for many of the students they enroll. They are not without their problems, however. The issue of transportation is a particular concern. Some critics allege that transportation problems facing learners from economically impoverished families have made it easier for learners from more affluent families to attend magnet schools. (In many districts, transportation subsidies of some kind are provided to learners from low-income families in response to this problem.)

Admission to many magnet schools requires a record of excellent academic performance in schools previously attended. Some argue that this results in a skimming of the learner population that deprives other schools in the district of much needed academic talent. Further, there have been suspicions that magnet schools have received funding at levels that have placed other schools in their districts at a disadvantage.

Charter Schools

A school choice option that has become popular in the 1990s is the *charter school*. Supporters of charter schools believe that problems most public schools face today are closely associated with excessive regulation from state and local authorities. Charter schools are schools that are exempted from important rules to provide for more flexibility of operation and management. These schools typically pursue a specific set of objectives that are approved by the chartering agency, typically an arm of state government.

Supporters of charter schools make some arguments that are similar to those favoring voucher plans and open enrollment plans. It is hoped that, freed from regulatory burdens, charter schools will develop outstanding instructional programs that will become models for other schools to emulate. Charter schools can be set up to meet special needs of particular categories of learners. In California, for example, charter schools have been created specifically to help Hispanic learners who don't know English.

Many arguments have been made both in support of and in opposition to charter schools (Rael, 1995). Some people argue that charter schools are cost-effective. This is true because they do not have to put up with the bureaucratic inefficiencies characterizing typical public schools. Supporters also contend that outstanding teachers who are frustrated by constraints imposed on them in most public schools will be attracted to charter schools and that they will introduce exciting, innovative kinds of instruction.

Detractors point out some negatives associated with charter schools. Among other things, they suggest that they have the potential to divert money away from schools already in existence. Any improvements in education that are seen at a charter school may come at the expense of a decrease in quality at other schools. Others argue that bureaucratic constraint as an obstacle to innovation in existing

Is *My* Subject a Frill?

My name is Sook-ja Kim. I'm about eight months through my second year of teaching at Centennial Middle School. My major responsibility is directing the school orchestra and teaching orchestra classes. For the most part, I have had a great experience.

Last month, I took my students on a two-day trip to the state orchestra competition. It was held in the state capital, about 100 miles away. My students raised money for the trip, and we had plenty of parents along to help. These kids had really worked hard for this contest experience, and I was absolutely thrilled when we received a "1" rating, the highest awarded in our state.

As soon as the award ceremony was over, I hurried back to the hotel and called my principal. She was delighted at the good news. Centennial's orchestra had never before received such a high rating. In fact, the principal was so excited that she immediately called the superintendent. It turns out that our superintendent has been concerned for some time that our district's music program was not as strong as it should be, and the news about our 1 rating was very welcome.

A few days after I returned to school, I got a nice letter from the superintendent congratulating me and all of the kids in the orchestra for their hard work. The letter went on to invite me to a school board meeting where I was to receive some public congratulations for the honor brought to the district by our orchestra's high rating. The school board meeting was last night.

It was fairly late into the evening when the board president asked me to stand. Some very nice words were said about what had been accomplished by the Centennial orchestra kids, and some warm comments were made to me about how much the district appreciated what I had accomplished in just two years in the district. At the conclusion of these remarks, each member of the school board came over to shake my hand. I felt I had arrived at some kind of professional pinnacle.

The next item on the agenda was an open forum for citizens' comments. The first speaker deflated my fine feelings in a hurry. He said that the school district was spending entirely too much money on frivolous nonacademic subjects such as music. He said that he and other people in the district were "sick and tired" of not being able to hire high school graduates who could write a grammatical sentence or make accurate change. He indicated that the two days my orchestra kids had spent participating in the state contest had robbed them of two days of serious instruction in English and mathematics. He said this kind of thing provided just one more reason in support of an effort he and another group of citizens were mounting to start a charter school that would focus on what he called serious academics.

I left the meeting feeling depressed. I've worked so hard this year, but now I know that there are people in town who think my entire function is unnecessary. I have a really bad taste in my mouth about this. I just don't know what I'm going to do.

What are differences in how Sook-ja Kim probably describes "excellence" in school programming and how the person who spoke at the school board meeting describes it? What do these differences say about what is important to each? What do you think Sook-ja should do next? Do the school principal and the superintendent have roles to play here? If so, what are they? What advice would you give to this teacher? Do you think other teachers have faced similar circumstances? If you know of any particular instances, how did these teachers resolve their difficulties? How might other schools in this district be affected if a charter school focusing on "serious academics" is established?

public schools has been overstated by charter school supporters. They point out that many innovative schools exist that have not asked for the kinds of relief from existing state and local regulations that have been given to charter schools.

Charter schools are too new for there yet to be an extensive body of research with findings related to their effectiveness. By the middle 1990s, about three-fifths of the states had approved or were strongly considering legislation authorizing establishment of charter schools (Mauhs-Pugh, 1995). Enabling legislation in many places put some limits on kinds of schools that could be chartered and numbers of such schools that could be authorized (Roda, 1995). For example, Arizona legislation allows the approval of no more than 50 charter schools each year. Colorado law states that no more than 50 may be in existence at any one time. In California, no more than 100 charter schools can be created, with a further provision that no more than 10 can be established in any single school district (Sinis & Roda, 1995).

Although interest in charter schools remains high, these schools are not yet being established in large numbers even in states that have approved enabling legislation. Specifics in individual state legislation account for some of this slow growth. For example, in Kansas and New Mexico, a charter school must make a separate request for every regulation it wishes to have waived. In states such as Georgia and Wisconsin, applications for charter schools have to be initiated by local school boards. These may be composed of people who have few quarrels with many existing regulations and school practices. Still other states require that charters be issued only to existing public schools so that scarce educational dollars are not encumbered to build new schools (Eggleston, 1995).

Despite some problems supporters have experienced in states where charter schools have been authorized, strong interest continues in this approach to school choice. For example, the U.S. Department of Education has established a "Charter School Demonstration Program" that is designed to generate and disseminate knowledge about how effective charter schools operate. Discussion of charter schools seems certain to be a hot topic among educators for the remaining years of the century.

SCHOOL-BUSINESS PARTNERSHIP PROGRAMS

Because our entire society benefits when learners have productive experiences in school, many outside our profession have a keen interest in what goes on in the schools. This interest has led to many efforts over the years to establish partnerships of various kinds between public schools and other agencies and organizations. For example, many colleges and universities around the country have linked with specific schools for the purpose of helping them develop academic programs that will adequately prepare graduates for the demands of higher education. In some places, social agencies have established ties with schools that are designed to make their services more readily available to learners. (More about this kind of cooperative activity is introduced in the next section, which focuses on full-service schools). In recent years, corporations and businesses of all kinds have actively sought to establish formal partnership arrangements with schools.

One important effect of the interest of business in the schools has been the establishment of *tech prep programs* throughout the country. Tech prep programs came about because there were fears that many efforts to reform the schools were promoting academic experiences having little practical value to students once they left school. Tech prep programs for the most part are 2 + 2 models, which means that they focus on the last two years of high school and two additional years of training, most often in community and junior colleges.

The intent of tech prep programs is to provide rigorous, integrated experiences that will smooth the transition from school to the world of the contributing adult citizen. To this end, the Carl D. Perkins Vocational and Applied Technology Act of 1990 defines tech prep as a program that (1) leads to an associate degree or two-year certificate, (2) provides technical preparation in at least one field of engineering technology, applied science, mechanical, industrial, or practical art or trade, or agriculture, health, or business, (3) builds student competence in mathematics, science, and communication (including applied academics) through a sequential course of study, and (4) leads to placement in employment.

Proliferation of programs designed to foster school programs that help students make a smooth transition to the workplace led to passage of the federal School-to-Work Opportunities Act in 1994. This act provides grants to states and communities to develop systems and partnerships designed to better prepare young people for additional education and careers. The intent is for students to experience the workplace as an active learning environment and to ensure that they see relationships between what they experience in school and what they will need to know to earn a living.

Business interest in school programs has taken many forms other than supporting legislation such as the Carl D. Perkins Act and the School-to-Work Opportunities Act. In some cases, schools have been helped in somewhat indirect ways. For example, companies have initiated child-care services and programs for employees that have encouraged them to play active roles in their children's education. Often these initiatives have offered employees flexible work schedules to enable parents to visit schools during the day.

Other business-school partnerships have been much more ambitious and have encouraged partnerships as a way of improving entire systems of schools. One of the most notable efforts has occurred in Kentucky where leaders of The Business Roundtable, which is a national group including chief executive officers of 200 of the nation's largest corporations, have established The Partnership for Kentucky School Reform. This coalition of people from business, government, labor, and education has been formed to support efforts to reform and improve public education throughout the state of Kentucky. The Partnership for Kentucky School Reform has undertaken a number initiatives. Among them are:

- *The Kentucky Educational Reform Act Bus Exhibit:* This is a school bus that travels throughout the state and features information about efforts to improve public school education in Kentucky.
- *A resource center:* This is a collection of present and historical information about educational reform.
- *A speakers bureau:* This provides names of people who are willing to talk to groups about school reform issues.

- *An 800 telephone line:*   This is a phone number people can call for information about school reform initiatives.
- *Business initiatives:*   This is a program that reaches out to businesses throughout the state to encourage them to get involved in supporting school improvement efforts.
- T^2 — *Teachers to the Power of Two:*   This is a joint arrangement between the Kentucky Education Association and the Partnership for Kentucky School Reform that is designed to help teachers learn about implementing reform proposals by learning about them from other teachers.
- *Professional development:*   The Partnership for Kentucky School Reform has developed a set of recommendations designed to provide future Kentucky teachers with the best possible preservice training and present teachers with the finest staff-development opportunities.

If you are interested in additional information about The Partnership for Kentucky School Reform, contact:

The Partnership for Kentucky School Reform
P.O. Box 1658
Lexington, Kentucky 40592

These business and school leaders are working together to identify ways in which a school-business partnership might be established. The aim of such programs is to make school programs better.

Some business-school partnerships have been developed between businesses and a single school. For example, at Everett Elementary School in Lincoln, Nebraska, a program called Ventures in Partnerships has been established. Among other things, this involves a "school buddies" program for children who have been identified as being at risk. Many buddies come from businesses who have agreed to be involved in the program. The idea is to provide at-risk learners with some attention from a caring, supportive adult. The buddies come to school and get involved in such things as eating lunch with their assigned child, participating with the child during recess, and talking about school work. Some participating firms send letters to the child commending such things as good classroom performance and perfect attendance.

Interest in business-school partnerships is increasing, but not everyone agrees that they are a good idea. There are fears that some businesses are not so much interested in helping children as they are in promoting their own products. Supporters argue that schools can develop guidelines to prevent this sort of thing from happening and that it is in the interest of educators to encourage an interest in public education of people outside of the profession. Discussions about this issue are continuing.

FULL-SERVICE SCHOOLS

Individual human services professions that serve our nation's education, health, legal, and social support needs have developed huge bodies of sophisticated knowledge over the past half century. Training of specialists in these professions has never been better. What has not happened is to bring these professions together in ways that build on strengths of each and that bring their diverse understandings to bear on common problems. This is particularly true in the public education arena. Difficulties children face cannot neatly be sorted into categories labeled educational problems, health problems, legal problems, and social problems. What children experience as individuals are difficulties that cross all of these lines.

Full-service schools are beginning to emerge that attempt to bring all human-support activities together under one roof. The need to do this was recognized over 20 years ago when the Bicentennial Commission of the American Association of Colleges of Teacher Education devoted fully 40 pages to the need to link education and human services (Howsam, Corrigan, Denemark, & Nash, 1976). More recently, the Children's Defense Fund in *The State of America's Children* (1994) highlighted the intractability of problems facing our young people and the need to engage multiple human services professions in the effort to solve them.

Many full-service schools have been established to help learners from economically or educationally impoverished backgrounds. There is evidence that some families in these circumstances are unable to take advantage of some of the support services various social agencies provide. When these services are gathered together in one place, the school, access becomes more user-friendly. Full-service schools are in operation in many parts of the country. The Options School in McAllen, Texas, has social workers, nurses, and various other social service professionals on hand as well as classroom teachers. Students there receive specialized job training in addition to their regular academic classes (Stallings, 1995).

In New York City, IS 218 is a full-service school that opened as a result of a special partnership between the Children's Aid Society, the New York City Board of Education, and the Board of Community College School District Six. The school offers a number of support services not found in most schools. For example, there are dental and health clinics located inside the front door. Social services offices that can easily be accessed by learners, their families, and residents living close to the school are located nearby. IS 218 is open 15 hours a day, 6 days a week, year round. Over a thousand parents are involved in courses and workshops the school makes available. In a recent year, IS 218 had the highest attendance rates of any school in its district. Academic achievement scores of its learners were higher than those of comparable young people in schools lacking the full complement of IS 218 services (Stallings, 1995).

Some critics of full-service schools argue that they are attempting to usurp responsibilities that properly belong to families. Supporters contend that families play important roles in determining what goes on in these schools and that learners who are enrolled simply would not be able to access many services were they not available at the school site. At the present time, many national organizations representing the interests of different human-support services organizations are expressing interest in expanding the number of full-service schools (Corrigan & Udas, 1996). Any expansion will have implications for training of future social service professionals.

Traditionally, prospective teachers have been introduced to information about such issues as learning styles, instructional design, psychological development of young people, classroom management, assessment of learners, administrative arrangements of schools, and so forth. Very little time has been spent focusing on content related to public health, social work, law enforcement, and other areas that have always been discharged by social service professionals working in other settings.

Increasingly, leaders in the human services professions are coming to agree that social service professionals should be doing more cooperative and collaborative work. In settings such as full-service schools, human support professionals with expertise in many different service areas come together. For maximum benefits to accrue to learners, it makes sense for professionals from different human services areas to know something about what one another do. This has led to recommendations for cross-professional training. For example, prospective teachers ought to have at least some formal exposure in their preparation programs to content related to what pediatricians, social workers, law enforcement officials, and public health workers do. Similarly, training programs for these professionals should expose them to at least some of the kinds of training that typically is provided to beginning teachers. Today, a number of colleges and universities around the country are beginning to provide some cross-professional training to prospective teachers (Corrigan & Udas, 1996). It seems likely that more will be doing so in the future.

CHALLENGES AND PROSPECTIVE TEACHERS

We have introduced in this chapter just a few challenges facing our profession. These issues represent a sample of the many ideas that are now percolating within the education community as we work to make our schools better. We think this is a particularly fine time for new people to be going into education. Interest in improving the schools is widespread, and as indicated by some of the discussion in this chapter, we are well beyond the point of talking about what "might" be done. New kinds of schools and new instructional approaches are already in place that differ in important ways from traditional ways of organizing and instructing young people. There is a wonderful opportunity for bright new professionals to influence our country's educational future.

As you look forward to joining our ranks, we urge you to engage in a personal professional development program that goes beyond what you will be able to take away from your courses and your field work in the schools. Read widely, talk to people in the field, ask questions. Think about your own responses to questions such as these:

- What are some reasonable learning outcomes for pupils and students in areas I want to teach, and what might I do to measure them?
- What can I do to prepare myself to participate in making management decisions as a member of a school leadership team that might include administrators, other teachers, parents, and community members?
- What should I learn about other human service professions and how their services can best be accessed by my learners and their families?
- What valuable new knowledge might I apply to my own teaching situation from experiences of charter schools and voucher plans?
- How can links be established between schools and businesses in ways that promote legitimate educational interests but do not allow for a co-option of the school program?

These focus questions touch on just a few areas we believe might be of interest to beginning teachers. We well might have included others related to such issues as multiple intelligences, approaches to preparing for instruction, and managing learners. However, we feel these issues are treated more frequently in many preparation programs than is information related at least to some of the questions we decided to include.

In this text, we attempt to provide some information that we believe will ease the transition from college and university student to professional teacher. We hope that this material, taken together with what you derive from your personal professional development program, will ease your entree into the profession. We look forward to having you.

• Key Ideas in Summary

- One key obligation of schools is to help build our nation's store of social capital. Social capital refers to people's willingness to work cooperatively and voluntarily with groups and organizations that include individuals who are not members of their own family. This commitment to work with and support others is thought to have contributed importantly to the development of our country.

- Change is afoot in education. Proposals for doing things in different ways come from many quarters. It behooves people thinking about entering teaching to become familiar with school reform initiatives and to become part of the national discussion related to this important issue. Those who become involved may affect the direction of change; those who don't may find themselves working in school environments that are shaped in ways that dismay professional educators.

- Because problems of schools are so complex, many critics of present practices are convinced that the only successful reforms will be those that will attack many variables at the same time. This effort is known as systemic reform. Many systemic reform efforts include a concern for developing schools that are learning communities, an emphasis on outcomes of education rather than inputs, an emphasis on decentralized school management, and an emphasis on redesigned teacher responsibility and compensation schemes.

- The Goals 2000: Education America Act of 1993 is important federal legislation that supports a systemic approach to educational reform. It seeks to encourage localities throughout the nation to align all components of their school system to help learners master content and graduate as contributing citizens. It has established goals in these eight areas: (1) readiness for school, (2) high school completion, (3) student achievement and citizenship, (4) teachers' professional development, (5) science and mathematics achievement, (6) adult literacy and lifelong learning, (7) safe, disciplined, and drug-free schools, and (8) partnerships.

- The National Board for Professional Teaching Standards (NBPTS) is attempting to identify high and rigorous standards regarding what teachers should know and be able to demonstrate to help learners achieve. There are plans for NBPTS to issue National Board certificates to teachers meeting appropriate standards. These certificates will not replace local certificates but rather will be recognitions for outstanding teachers who have met extraordinarily high national standards of excellence. The certification plan is expected to be in operation by school year 1998–1999.

- An important idea running through discussions of school improvement is school choice. School choice allows parents and learners to select a school from among a number of alternatives. This represents a change from traditional arrangements where learners were assigned to specific schools based on their home addresses. Among school choice approaches that have been tried are voucher plans, open enrollment plans, magnet schools, and charter schools.

- Many businesses and corporations have been interested in improving the quality of public education. This interest has been reflected in a number of ways. Private sector support has been an important factor in supporting the spread of tech prep programs. These are programs designed to integrate training during the last two years of high school and two years in a post-high-school institution, typically a community or junior college. The idea is to provide rigorous academic work that is tied in practical ways to the demands these young people will face at the end of the program. In addition to their support of tech prep, businesses have also been involved in many other kinds of partnerships with schools. These range from efforts to improve the quality of education within an entire state to efforts centered on a single school.

- Many different professions are involved in important human service activities. In addition to education, these include professionals trained in health care, social welfare, law, and law enforcement. There is evidence that professionals in these respective areas do not know much about what professionals in other human services areas are doing. Further, some people in our society find it difficult to access all of the human services to which they are entitled. One response to this problem has been the establishment of full-service schools. These schools bring together at a common location professionals from a variety of human service professions. They encourage communication among professionals from different human service backgrounds and make it easier for learners and their families to access their expertise.

- Professional courses and field experience opportunities are important contributors to the development of prospective teachers. However, it also makes sense for individuals planning to go into teaching to develop personal professional development plans. A series of focus questions can be developed to guide reading, interviews, and other actions taken to broaden understanding of the many issues facing educators today.

• Review and Discussion Questions

1. What is the importance of having schools that seek to develop social capital?
2. What are some components of systemic reform, and why do its supporters believe this kind of reform is necessary to improve our schools?
3. How does site-based decision making differ from more traditional patterns of school governance? Do teachers who will be working in such environments need skills that differ from teachers who work in schools featuring more traditional kinds of management?
4. The Goals 2000: Educate America Act has vocal admirers and detractors. What are some positions taken by supporters and opponents? What impact do you think this legislation will have on our schools and why?
5. Some critics of the National Board for Professional Teaching Standards are concerned that National Board certification is a first step toward moving certification authority from the states to the federal government. Suppose this were to happen. Would this have good or bad effects on the effort to make our schools better?
6. What are voucher plans? Suppose a voucher system were in place everywhere. What changes would there be in how schools operate? What would be some problems teachers and administrators might face? Would such a policy improve our schools? Why or why not?
7. Proponents of charter schools argue that existing state and local regulations are important barriers to educational reform. How valid are these arguments? What do you see as strengths and weaknesses of points made by those who would like to see more charter schools?

8. Should business-school partnership programs be encouraged? What negatives and positives might be associated with an effort to dramatically increase the number of such relationships?

9. Full-service schools attempt to bring together at one place a range of educational, health, legal, and social welfare services. Professionals from these various human-support services organizations work cooperatively to help learners and their families. How do you feel about such arrangements?

10. Today many different approaches to delivering educational services to the young are being tried. We are in the middle of an effort to reform American education that has been accelerating rapidly since the middle 1980s. How do you think some changes you already know about might change teacher preparation programs in the future? What are some things you can be doing to prepare yourself for the educational world of the twenty-first century?

• Ideas for Field Experience Projects and Enrichment

1. In a few places around the country, local citizens have lost so much faith in the abilities of public school officials to manage local school programs that they have turned over operation of their schools to private corporations or to a local university. The term *contract school* sometimes is applied to a school that has been placed under the authority of this kind of external contracting agency. In essence, the private corporation or university contracts with the local citizens to improve the quality of educational services. Do some reading about how these arrangements have worked out. Prepare a report to share with others in your class.

2. The majority of states either now have or are now considering legislation allowing the establishment of charter schools. If your state has or is considering such legislation, find out what requirements must be met to establish a charter school. If your state legislature has not considered this issue, gather information about the situation in a neighboring state. Prepare a short paper in which you make reference to such issues as (1) kinds of groups that can request authority to establish a charter school, (2) limitations on numbers of charter schools that can be established, and (3) provisions relating to funding of charter schools.

3. Attempts to establish full-service schools have sometimes been thwarted because of objections from parents who do not want public health officials and social welfare officials working with their children. They are concerned that some information may be disseminated to their children about issues such as birth control that are inconsistent with values taught at home. Organize a debate on this topic: "Resolved that full-service schools are a threat to the authority of the family."

4. Ask your instructor if there have been efforts to decentralize decision making in your area through such mechanisms as site-based management. If this has been done, interview some teachers who are participating as members of school leadership teams. Ask them whether they were prepared for these kinds of management responsibilities when they were preparing to become teachers. What advice do they wish to share with future teachers who might find themselves working in schools with site-based management?

5. Help organize a panel of six to eight teachers from local area schools. Ask them to comment on the kinds of things they do every day for which they had little formal preparation. Take notes on their remarks and consider them as bases for some questions you might wish to pursue as part of your personal professional development plan.

• References

Baratz-Snowden, J. (November, 1992). National Board for Professional Teaching Standards — update. *ERIC Digest.* (ED 351336)

Children's Defense Fund. (1994). *The state of America's children yearbook 1994: Leave no child behind.* Washington, DC: Author.

Corrigan, D., & Udas, K. (1996). Creating collaborative, child and family centered, education, health, and human services systems. In J. Sikula, T. Buttery, & E. Guyton (Eds.). *Handbook of research on teacher education* (pp. 893–921). New York: Macmillan Publishing.

Eggleston, L., Jr. (1995). Why no charter schools have been formed in some states that have passed legislation. In T. J. Mauhs-Pugh (Ed). Charter schools 1995: A survey and analysis of the laws and practices of the states. *Education Policy Analysis Archives*, 3(12). Available Internet URL. http://infor.asu.edu/asu-cwis/epaa/welcome.html

Fukuyama, F. (1995, July 30). Rights revolution undercutting America's sense of community. *The Houston Chronicle.* pp. C1, C5.

Henson, K. T. (in press). *Instructional supervision.* New York: HarperCollins.

Howsam, R. B., Corrigan, D. C., Denemark, G. W., & Nash, R. J. (1976). *Educating a profession: Relating to human services education.* Washington, DC: American Association of Colleges for Teacher Education.

Mauhs-Pugh, T. J. (Ed). (1995). Charter schools 1995: A survey and analysis of the laws and practices of the states. *Education Policy Analysis Archives*, 3(12). Available Internet URL. http://infor.asu.edu/asu-cwis/epaa/welcome.html

National Commission on Excellence in Education. (1983). *A nation at risk: The imperative for educational reform.* Washington, DC: U.S. Department of Education.

Rael, E. J. (1995). A summary of arguments for and against charter schools. In T. J. Mauhs-Pugh, (Ed). Charter schools 1995: A survey and analysis of the laws and practices of the states. *Education Policy Analysis Archives*, 3(12). Available Internet URL. http://infor.asu.edu/asu-cwis/epaa/welcome.html

Roda, K. (1995). Obstacles. In T. J. Mauhs-Pugh (Ed). Charter schools 1995: A survey and analysis of the laws and practices of the states. *Education Policy Analysis Archives*, 3(12). Available Internet URL. http://infor.asu.edu/asu-cwis/epaa/welcome.html

Rubenstein, M. C. (1992). *Minnesota's open enrollment option.* Washington, DC: U.S. Department of Education, Office of Policy and Planning.

Shaffer, C. R., & Amundsen, K. (1993). *Creating community anywhere.* New York: Jeremy P. Tarcher/Putnam Sons.

Sinis, P., & Roda, K. (1995). California. In T. J. Mauhs-Pugh (Ed). Charter schools 1995: A survey and analysis of the laws and practices of the states. *Education Policy Analysis Archives*, 3(12). Available Internet URL. http://infor.asu.edu/asu-cwis/epaa/welcome.html

Spady, W. G. (1994). Choosing outcomes of significance. *Educational Leadership, 51*(6), 18–22.

Stallings, J. (1995, April). *Ensuring teaching and learning in the 21st century.* Presidential address at the annual meeting of the American Educational Research Association, San Francisco.

Wells, A. S. (1990, March). *Public school choice: Issues and concerns for urban educators.* ERIC/CUE Digest, No. 63. (ERIC Clearinghouse on Urban Education No. ED 322275)

Wiggins, G. (1989). A true test: Toward more authentic and equitable measurement. *Phi Delta Kappan, 70*(9), 703–713.

Witte, J. F., & Thorn, C. A. (1994, December). *Fourth-year report: Milwaukee Parental Choice Program.* Madison, WI: University of Wisconsin, Department of Political Science and the Robert La Follette Institute of Public Affairs.

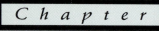

2

Teaching in an Age of Change

OBJECTIVES

- Describe how changes in society influence education.
- State alternative views concerning needed reform of schools.
- List examples of changes that have already been implemented in some schools.
- Describe how changes in the learner population are leading to changes in education.
- State alternative views relating to multicultural and bilingual education.
- Define what is meant by "full inclusion."
- Point out some implications of "constructivism" for educational practice
- Describe what is meant by "multiple intelligence."
- Identity some factors that contribute to the complexity of teaching.

How do you react to change? Do you find it exciting or threatening? Do you feel most comfortable when following tradition, or do you become energized doing something different? As you contemplate a career in education, you need to consider your responses to these questions because education is a field undergoing tremendous change. Some of these changes were discussed in Chapter 1.

Among changes under discussion are new proposals for the length of the school year, the length of the school day, the content of the curriculum, the choices parents have in where they send their youngsters, the control of the school district, the power of the local school and the parents, the way teachers are educated, the contracts under which teachers work, the dress and conduct of the learners, and the organization of the school by grade levels and subjects. Rationales for these changes vary.

Some people believe that schools fail to adequately prepare young people for the demands of present-day life; they argue that significant, even revolutionary changes in our schools are required. Others believe that the schools have drifted off course and that we educators must be directed to return to more traditional methods of teaching learners and organizing schools. Still others have identified additional causes for difficulties facing education today, and they have committed to specific remedies to cure these ills. What is clear from this confusion is that schools are under great pressure to change and that you, as an educator, will be forced to consider many different alternatives that are presented as solutions.

All of this means that teachers today have to work hard to stay informed if they hope to make intelligent choices from a bewildering array of proposals to fix education. In this chapter, we introduce some of the forces leading to change in education and also provide a brief glimpse of a teacher's day at school.

WHY THERE IS NO CONSENSUS ABOUT WHAT SCHOOLS SHOULD DO

Education is an important component of the health and vitality of any community and nation. Because of this, the quality of education is often the topic of heated debate. Some parents and adults think that schools were better in the past. Many politicians are quick to call for a return to the basics and ascribe a variety of social ills to a loss of direction and educational fads. On the other hand, there are those who claim that education is not changing fast enough to keep up with the rapid rate of change in the world. They claim the problems in education are related to irrelevant and obsolete curricula and methods. In truth, there is no consensus regarding educational goals and the methods of attaining them. The debate is further compounded by the difficulty of measuring the success of American schools. It often seems as if all Americans are self-proclaimed experts when it comes to education, and many can cite some type of evidence to support a particular claim.

Because the world is constantly changing, education cannot stand still. As you prepare to enter our profession, you need to recognize that dealing with change will be one of the constants of your life as an educator. Sections that follow introduce some issues associated with change you will encounter as a teacher.

Let Me Teach

Laura Jacobs is a college senior. She has been frustrated in her attempts to fit in all of the requirements for graduation with the extra courses required for her teaching certificate. Until yesterday, she had pretty well reconciled herself to spending a least one extra semester to meet all of the requirements. She brightened last night when her eyes fell on a headline in the local paper, "Governor Proposes Change in Teacher Education."

The article described the governor's frustration with the low scores of public school students on the most recent administration of standardized tests. She said the "obvious remedy" was putting teachers in the classroom who had more academic preparation in the subjects they were teaching. The governor went on to take note of recent cutbacks in the defense and aerospace industries. There were, she claimed, a large number of individuals with a rich background in math and science who could make an excellent contribution to solving the current education crisis. The governor fumed that present regulations would require any of these people who might be interested in teaching to go back to college to take a lot of "meaningless education courses." The governor announced that she was sending the legislature a proposal to scrap many course-related requirements for teacher certification — a move, she said, that would get some "really high quality people in our classrooms in a hurry."

Laura put down the paper and thought to herself, That really makes sense. I hope the legislators will move on this idea in a hurry. It would really help me. I don't need to take all of these education courses. I *know* how to teach. In fact, I've known how for years. I've always watched my favorite teachers carefully, and I'm sure I can do what they did. I especially remember Ms. Edwards. When I was in high school, she really turned me on to academics and got me interested in learning. Thanks to her, I went on to college, and I'm pretty proud of how well I've done. I know I've learned information far beyond what elementary kids will need to know.

Friends who are teaching tell me that wonderful teacher's guides are provided with all of the textbooks. They should help me plan. I also know about working with children. In addition, I've had lots of experience working at the YWCA, and I've done lots of baby-sitting. What more do I really need? How hard can it be to teach kids that two times two is four or that "cat" is spelled c-a-t? I feel I'm ready to go to work right now. These education courses are only going to waste my time. Maybe there are some people who need them, but I don't. I want to get out there and start teaching. I hope the governor's idea becomes law so I can avoid these required courses, go to work, and finally start making some money.

What are some assumptions the governor makes about characteristics of good teachers? How realistic are these? If the governor's proposals become law, what are the prospects that high numbers of talented new people will enter the teaching profession? On what do you base your conclusion?

What is your reaction to the points Laura makes? Is there specialized knowledge needed by people who are preparing to teach? Do you think most people have had so much experience as learners themselves that they already know how to teach? What assumptions is Laura making about the role of a teacher? Do you think that reducing requirements for certification would be an incentive for academically talented individuals to enter teaching? How do you react to her modeling her teaching after a favorite teacher in the past? Does Laura seem to be inferring that the challenges of teaching are constant and do not change over time? What general advice would you give to Laura?

CHANGES IN SOCIETY

As we look forward a few years to the new century, we find ourselves in a world where the rate of change is accelerating. Political changes, for example, both international and domestic, challenge many of our traditional assumptions about how the world is. On the home front, who a decade or two ago would have predicted the Republican party would be stronger in the South than the Democratic party? Who would have predicted serious assaults on affirmative action and other civil rights legislation? Internationally, who 25 years ago would have thought such places as South Korea, Taiwan, and Singapore would provide serious competition to American industries? Who even a dozen years ago would have imagined a world where there was no Soviet Union?

Breaks with familiar patterns and shattering of traditional assumptions have had social consequences. In this country, traditional institutions such as the family are at risk. Today, about half of all marriages end in divorce. Changes have led to reconsideration of what constitutes morality and how we should define right and wrong. These changes have led to great social stresses. It has become increasingly difficult to find consensus on critically important issues. Some people believe we are experiencing more social fragmentation than we have ever before endured as a people, fragmentation that is reflected in increasing incidences of terrorism, gang violence, and a general rise in levels of incivility.

As these problems continue to mount, ever more people look to the schools for help. The difficulty is that there is little agreement regarding what schools should do. Because of this division of opinion, we educators cannot assume that proposals we suggest will automatically be endorsed by the communities we serve. To expect an easy consensus to form in support of our professional decisions is to ignore the sometimes bitter divisions that define the reality of the contemporary world.

DEBATES ABOUT HOW TO MAKE SCHOOLS BETTER

Proposals to improve education have come from many different groups within society. These run the gamut from a total replacement of the existing system to a return to schools as they existed a couple of decades ago. Some of those proposing change forget that schools in the "good old days" were also criticized and that things might not have been quite as wonderful then as people like to imagine they were (Coontz, 1992). Contemporary education must address the realities of today, not an idealized and romanticized image of the past.

Other reformers claim that schools as we now know them are obsolete. They claim that the basic assumptions and organizational framework controlling education derive from an obsolete industrialized model of production that must be replaced. This model is based on an efficiency scheme developed to improve assembly-line production (Levin, 1994). Standardization is a hallmark of this model. Schools were standardized so that learners could move from one school to another with little or no difficulty. Learners were organized into same-grade-level or same-subject classes. The curriculum was standardized, all classrooms used the same textbooks, and standardized achievement tests were used to make sure learners had mastered the content of the curriculum before they moved on. The assumption was that if the raw materials (the learners) were subjected to the same treatment (curriculum and instruction), the result would be a standardized product that would meet quality control standards (a good test score).

Learners were given little or no input into the educational process because they were simply raw materials to be molded into an appropriate form. Overseers (school administrators) were there to manage and observe the practices of the workers (teachers) to make sure that they were following accepted procedures. This approach assumed a consensus regarding what the final product should be and that standardized tests were valid measures of that product.

This model never worked well. Not all learners learned the same content at the same pace or had the same motivations. In education, there is a problem defining "raw material" and who is "producing." Are the learners the raw materials being processed, or are they the workers producing learning? Learners play a much more important role than simply serving as raw material to be transformed. If any transformation is to take place, learners must be involved in the process and must choose to make the transformation. Thus educational production is far different than factory production (Levin, 1994). Learners have individual differences in motivations, aspirations, and abilities. They are not the same, and the same type of process will not transform all of them in the same way.

Another problem relates to determining the outcomes of the process. An assumption that guided much past educational practice was that the "product" of public schools should be learners who were prepared for entry into college; however, the majority of the learners graduating from the public school system did not enter college. Many of those who did not have college as a goal or who had learning difficulties either dropped out or were forced out. Our fascination with efficiency and standardized production often blinded policymakers to these problems.

As it became clear that society could no longer afford to allow large numbers of learners to drop out of school or fail, serious questions were raised. What should be the purposes of education? Should it be to prepare individuals for college, for a vocation, or for their roles in a democratic society? Who should be educated? Should all learners be required to attend the same type of schools? Who should have control over the conduct of the schools? What quality standards should be applied to judge the success of the system?

As individuals have answered these questions in different ways, different proposals for change have emerged. Some of the proposals reflect an acceptance of the industrial model and call for changes that would lead to more standardization. There are calls for national curriculum standards, national accreditation standards, and standardized tests that all learners must pass in order to graduate (Cohen, 1995; Jennings, 1995). Some states have experimented with statewide teacher evaluation systems in an attempt to standardize instruction .

Others think that this is the wrong approach (Moffett, 1994; Eisner, 1995; Smith, 1995). These individuals have a completely different set of recommendations concerning what needs to be done to improve education. They are concerned that basing current practices on a faulty model of education will lead to more serious problems rather than solutions.

The School Board meeting often is the place where people with differing views about what constitutes "good" education come together to debate their positions.

It has been pointed out that modern business has moved beyond the industrial model. Today, emphasis is placed on problem solving and critical thinking and teamwork. Therefore, schools need to emphasize more cooperation and higher-level thinking while decreasing rote memory and competition among individuals.

In general, it is safe to say that most of us in the profession today understand that learners are not simply raw materials we can shape in particular directions. Each learner brings a prior set of understandings and unique abilities and motivations to the classroom. Education is not a set of "truths" that can be stamped into the minds of learners. Each person processes information and constructs his or her own meaning of the information based on prior experience. Simply subjecting all learners to the same processes and the same information does not mean that they will all develop the same understandings and the same values.

EXAMPLES OF CHANGES THAT HAVE BEEN IMPLEMENTED

There are many educational changes that are beginning to appear as a result of these changed perceptions. Rather than placing all learners of the same age in one grade, multigrade classrooms are appearing. The curriculum is placing more emphasis on thinking and problem solving rather than rote memorization. Learners are being challenged to share their understanding and knowledge constructions rather than being asked to memorize and repeat the conclusions of others. There is more focus on active learning and allowing learners to develop and share their unique talents and abilities in cooperative groups rather than in individual competition. Less emphasis is being placed on everyone reading the same textbook and doing the same assignments.

New electronic technologies such as computers are providing learners with opportunities to gather and use information in creative ways. Assessments of learner achievements are beginning to turn away from standardized assessments to alternative forms of assessment such as performance assessments and portfolios whereby learners have more choice in sharing what they have learned and what they think is important.

Some proposals for changing the educational system to meet the new attitudes and perceptions of society were discussed in Chapter 1. They include school choice options such as charter schools, voucher plans, open enrollment plans, and magnet schools. One variation of the magnet school concept has been the "fundamental" school. These schools reflect a back-to-basics approach to education. The emphasis is on learning fundamental skills and knowledge. Parents throughout the district can elect to send their children to these schools, which have been very popular with parents in areas where they have been developed.

These changes signal important changes in our roles as classroom teachers. The familiar lineup of desks and textbooks, the comfortable schedule of separate subjects taught at specific times of the day, and standing in front of the class dispensing knowledge are missing. What we need to know and do to be a good teacher is something that is very much open to professional and public debate.

DEBATES ABOUT RESPONSES TO A CHANGED LEARNER POPULATION

Something that has profound implications for teaching is the change in the characteristics of the population served by the schools. It is not uncommon for contemporary schools to have numerous learners attending schools from homes where the primary language spoken is not English. For example, one quarter of the total enrollment in California in 1995 were limited English proficient learners (Schnalberg, 1995). It is a tremendous challenge to provide an environment where these learners can achieve success and where there are open lines of communication between educators and parents. (For additional information about characteristics of pupils and students, see Chapter 10.)

Accommodating this diversity in the classroom has led to several important changes. Many schools have bilingual programs where learners are taught in their native language for at least a portion of the day. Teachers have had to learn new skills for teaching this linguistically diverse learner population. There has also been a major emphasis on multicultural education that emphasizes the cultural heritage of a variety of groups, not just that of white, Anglo America. Both of these trends have resulted in heated debate about the appropriateness of teaching in languages other than English and about including multicultural content in the curriculum. (For more information about bilingual education, see Chapter 11.)

James Banks (1994) states that the growing ethnic diversity of the nation requires rethinking the curriculum in schools. He points out the need for all learners to develop multicultural perspectives and states that the curriculum ought to describe the ways different cultural groups have interacted with and influenced Western civilization. Accordingly, we need to teach learners that knowledge is a social construction that reflects the biases and perspectives of the people who construct it. Thus, rather than a place where the perspectives and knowledge of different groups is excluded, the classroom should be a place where multicultural debates about knowledge occur. Rather than being divisive, Banks claims that the goal of multicultural education is to reduce race, class, and gender divisions in the world.

Multicultural education has had considerable impact on education. Most textbooks now include multicultural content and many states mandate the inclusion of multicultural content in the curriculum. (For additional information, see Chapter 11.) However, not everyone supports the idea that more multicultural perspectives should be provided in school curricula.

Critics of multicultural education worry that, at best, the multicultural content replaces important substantive content in the curriculum or, at worst, tears down the basic values of our national heritage and leads to national disunity (Schlesinger, 1995). These critics are concerned that traditional Western writers such as Shakespeare will be eliminated from the curriculum and the teaching of history will be distorted. The debate in the middle 1990s regarding proposed standards for the teaching of history centered on the place of multicultural perspectives in the history curriculum.

Similar debates regarding bilingual education abound. Advocates of bilingual education contend that the education of learners should not be delayed until they acquire language proficiency. The Bilingual Education Act of 1968 was developed as a program to help learners begin their study of major subjects in languages other than English (Ravitch, 1995). Another argument for bilingual education is that learning in one's primary language improves the feeling of self-worth and helps to develop an understanding of one's own culture (Macedo, 1995).

Critics contend that the effectiveness of bilingual education has not been validated (Ravitch, 1995). They contend that language is an important means by which national unity is maintained. The high costs of bilingual education are cited, and it is claimed that the educational opportunities of the language minority learners are harmed by delaying their learning of English. Critics contend that the most effective language instruction programs are total immersion programs (Ravitch, 1995). This controversy over bilingual education has given rise to an effort to have English declared to be the official language of the United States. Some supporters of this idea would like to take money currently spent on bilingual education and reallocate it to pay for total immersion programs for non–English speaking learners.

Another type of diversity relates to the inclusion of learners with a range of mental and physical challenges in the typical classroom. For many years, the traditional education practice was to separate these learners in special education classrooms. A concern about the appropriateness of this practice led to legislation mandating the mainstreaming of some of these learners into regular classrooms. In recent years, this has led to what is termed *full inclusion*, which virtually eliminates

More and more classrooms include learners whose first language is not English. Bilingual education programs have been developed to serve their needs. Not everyone agrees that this is a good approach.

special education classrooms and places all learners in regular classrooms. Special education teachers work with the regular teachers in designing and delivering instruction to these learners. (For additional information about special learners, see Chapter 10.)

Advocates of full inclusion claim benefits for all learners. They claim that full inclusion is basically a moral issue. Disabled learners have the right to "belong" and be educated with others (Arnold & Dodge, 1995). Segregating them into special education classes is an immoral practice that leads to exclusion and feelings of inferiority. On the other hand, when all learners are in the regular classroom, those without disabilities develop an understanding and appreciation for individuals with disabilities.

Others, however, are concerned that the regular classroom does not provide an environment that is beneficial to all disabled learners (Kauffman, Lloyd, Baker, & Riedel, 1995). They point out that, ideally, the resources are supposed to follow the fully included youngster into the classroom and provide services that will help the learner. However, full inclusion may become a way for school districts to save money by cutting those resources (Shanker, 1995). In addition, learners with severe behavior problems can disrupt the learning of other learners in the classroom. At a time when schools are being challenged to increase the achievement of all learners, some question whether full inclusion is compatible with this goal (Shanker, 1995).

CHANGES IN THEORIES OF TEACHING AND LEARNING

Learning is the major focus of education. How learning takes place has been a topic of interest for centuries. There is still much that we don't know about the human brain and how learning happens. As additional research is conducted, theories on how learning occurs and how teachers can best facilitate learning continue to change and evolve. These theories are then translated into teaching approaches. In recent years, new perspectives on how individuals learn and the nature of intelligence have influenced educational practice.

Constructivism

Many changes in education are related to a revolution taking place in learning that is called *constructivism* (Slavin, 1994). Constructivism is based on the principle that individuals cannot simply be given knowledge. Rather, learners must construct knowledge through interacting with the world around them. Their constructions of knowledge are rooted in their prior knowledge. Knowledge grows as people compare new information to what they already know. The theory holds that the mind constantly looks for patterns and tries to resolve discrepancies. The social and cultural context within which learning takes place also plays an important part in what is constructed or learned.

There are several important implications of constructivism. One is that the conditions that best facilitate learning are what might be described as "top-down" (Slavin, 1994). This means it is best to provide the learner with more complex, complete, and "authentic" problems. The teacher then provides guidance to help the learners learn what they need to know to solve the problem. This contrasts with more traditional approaches that introduce learners to small pieces of information that, in time, are put together into more meaningful wholes.

For example, a traditional approach to teaching elementary children arithmetic features lessons requiring them to memorize multiplication tables. The expectation is that this information will prove useful to learners at a later time when they have a need to apply these skills to solve problems that are important to them. By way of contrast, a constructivist approach to teaching multiplication tables begins by presenting learners with a problem that requires multiplication skills for its solution. The teacher and learners together consider what is needed to solve the problem, and the teacher works with class members as they begin noting patterns and developing a generalized understanding of how multiplication processes work. The idea is to teach multiplication in the context of "real" problems when this skill is needed by the learner.

In the same vein, constructivist approaches to teaching topics such as punctuation and spelling are embedded within larger, story-writing activities that provide learners with a real need to have mastered this kind of content. This general approach has led to a technique that is commonly referred to as *whole language* instruction, which features lessons in which reading, writing, speaking, and listening are taught as a whole process to be learned together. Youngsters in the earliest grades write stories using "invented spelling" and then read them to others. The focus is on encouraging learners to use language, to look for patterns, and to learn writing conventions as they are needed.

Another assumption of constructivism is that the learners need to be actively involved in the learning process. They must actively seek solutions and share ideas. Because the social and cultural context is important, and because it is not likely that any one learner can find a solution working alone, learners often work in pairs or small groups. As a result, lessons built around constructivist principles feature considerable noise and movement.

Constructivism has also changed the way educators think about assessment. Rather than giving a standardized test designed to measure how well learners can repeat what they have been told, new assessment procedures actively involve the learner in sharing and discussing what they have discovered and learned.

Multiple Intelligences

Another important thrust that has changed the way many teachers design teaching is in the area of the nature of intelligence. Throughout history, there have been debates focusing on the question of whether intelligence is a single ability or many separate abilities (Woolfolk, 1995). Traditionally, educators have generally operated on the assumption that intelligence is a single trait that affects all cognitively oriented tasks and that it can be measured by an IQ test. Thus an intelligent person, although experiencing somewhat different problems in dealing with individual tasks, still has been assumed to have potential for success in dealing with most academic situations.

In recent years, there has been growing support for the view of *multiple intelligences*. Howard Gardner (1993) has proposed that there are at least seven distinct and separate kinds of intelligences:

- logical-mathematical
- linguistic, musical
- spatial
- bodily-kinesthetic
- interpersonal
- intrapersonal

Thus, an individual who is gifted in the area of logical-mathematical intelligence quickly discerns logical and mathematical patterns. On the other hand, a person gifted in the area of interpersonal intelligence recognizes and responds appropriately to the moods, temperaments, and motivations of others.

Another influential theorist in the area of multiple intelligences is Robert Sternberg (1990), who has proposed a triarchic theory of intelligence. The three types of intelligences he espouses are:

- componential
- experiential
- contextual

Componental intelligence refers to the ability to acquire information by separating the relevant from the irrelevant, to think abstractly, and to determine what needs to be done. *Contextual intelligence* refers to the ability to adapt to new experiences and to solve problems in a specific situation or context. *Experiential intelligence* refers to the ability to cope with new experiences by formulating new ideas and combining unrelated facts to solve new problems. This involves two characteristics: (1) having insight or the ability to deal effectively with novel situations and (2) having *automaticity*, the ability to quickly turn new solutions into routine procedures (Woolfolk, 1995).

Multiple intelligence theories have several important implications for teachers. Perhaps the most important is the need for us to avoid labeling learners according to their IQ scores. We need to understand that there may be numerous ways that individuals can be "gifted." Another implication is that the school curriculum needs to be varied in order to excite and challenge the different types of intelligences. Finally, the possibility of different types of intelligences has implications for the way material is presented to learners. Learning tasks should not focus just on the acquisition of information but also provide opportunities for learners to use creativity when solving new problems and adapting to different situations or contexts.

CHANGE AND PROSPECTIVE TEACHERS

The reality that change is a constant of educators' lives underscores the need for people who are entering the profession to commit to lifelong learning. A staggering number of changes are already affecting school curricula, instructional practices, and organizational patterns. Pressures for additional changes come from dozens of

---

**BOX
2-1**

Are There Multiple Intelligences?

Not everyone agrees with the concept of multiple intelligences. Critics of the idea of multiple intelligences point out that although there are individual differences in ability, individuals who tend to be good in one area are usually talented in other areas as well. This, they argue, is an indication that there is a single, common factor of intelligence.

What Do You Think?

1. Do you agree or disagree with the idea of multiple intelligences?
2. What evidence or experiences do you have that would support one view or the other?
3. How do you think the curriculum would need to change in order to support multiple intelligences?
4. Do you think that having multiple intelligences means that individuals who are gifted in one area should be allowed to focus on that area and not work in areas where they are not gifted?
5. How do you think schools, and society, would be different if everyone accepted the idea of multiple intelligences?

sources. All of these things mean that teachers need to be better informed and prepared than ever before. Business as usual is not an option. Those who are unable to adapt to change and controversy should consider another profession.

How do pressures influence teachers' daily lives in the classroom? In many ways. Some common patterns are introduced in the next section.

WHAT IS TEACHING REALLY LIKE?

We have observed an interesting phenomenon in our many years of working with people who are preparing to teach. These individuals have spent thousands of hours in classrooms under the guidance of a large number of different teachers. Some of them have been good, some not so good. Because of this experience, many prospective teachers are certain they *know* what it takes to be successful in the classroom. When some of these individuals first find themselves in the role of teacher, however, they are shocked to discover that teaching is quite different and more complex than they had imagined.

Although the performance of a teacher is very public and open to observation by learners and other interested individuals, there are many elements of good teaching that are not easy to see. Good teachers, like experts in other fields, make the public dimension of teaching appear easy. The handling of the less visible dimensions of teaching is often what separates the successful from the unsuccessful teacher.

Consider for a moment the public dimension of teaching. Doyle (1986) identified several features of the classroom that place pressure on the teacher and add great complexity to the task. These dimensions are:

- multidimensionality
- simultaneity
- immediacy
- unpredictability
- publicness
- history

Multidimensionality

There are multiple dimensions of any classroom that must be considered when teaching. As learners, many prospective teachers gave little thought to the complexity of managing a classroom. Teachers must accomplish a huge number of separate tasks. In addition to delivering instruction, these include grouping learners, keeping records, following a schedule, and managing materials. It is not uncommon for preservice teachers who have observed a teacher in action in a school classroom to ask, "How do you do all of that and still teach?"

Perhaps one of the largest challenges we face as teachers is responding adequately to the different kinds of learners in our classes. A typical class includes a wide range of individuals with different backgrounds, motivations, aspirations, needs, abilities, and learning styles. Some learners in the room will have the necessary prerequisite skills and abilities to achieve success on the assigned task; some will not. Some of the learners may have limited English proficiency, and many may come from cultural backgrounds very different from that of their teacher. Some of the learners will come to school ready to learn, and others will not. Some individuals will accept the task as important and interesting; others will not. Some may enter the room in poor health.

Inattention to the reality of the diversity within a classroom often leads to lesson failure. A novice observer may fail to see what the teacher has done to accommodate this diversity. The quality of these accommodations can spell the difference between success and failure for many learners. Teaching involves much more than merely standing in front of a group of learners and delivering information. It requires interacting and connecting with a diverse group of individuals with different interests and abilities.

Simultaneity

It should not be a revelation that many things are happening at once in the classroom. When in front of the classroom, we need to watch for indications of learner comprehension, interest, and attention. Learner answers and questions need to be attended to carefully for relevance, correctness, misconceptions, and signs of confusion. When providing assistance to one learner, the rest of the class must also be monitored. Interruptions and inappropriate behavior need to be dealt with, and one eye needs to stay on the clock.

In summary, we have to respond immediately to a number of stimuli. Inattention to any of them can spell disaster. Skilled teachers do so with a deceptive ease. Visitors to the classroom of this kind of professional may fail to observe the cues that are being used to orchestrate the many things that are occurring in the classroom. These actions become almost automatic for a good teacher; however, to an untrained observer, they may appear to be nothing more than random actions.

Immediacy

Not only do many things happen at the same time, classroom events must be dealt with immediately. We usually do not have the luxury of placing things on hold to be dealt with later. Teaching is a fast-paced activity that requires a large number of quick decisions. It simply does not work to tell a learner, "Just wait until I can figure out how to handle it." Good teachers are able to think on their feet and to make good decisions quickly.

Unpredictability

Unpredictability is a dimension of classroom interaction that experienced teachers often identify as a common characteristic of their classrooms. They frequently advise beginners to expect the unexpected. Classrooms are filled with young people whose reactions are not always predictable. We humans are not programmable computers who respond in consistent ways to similar situations. This is part of what makes teaching interesting. Individual learners and classes respond to the same stimuli in different ways. We need to be prepared to accept that a lesson that is a smashing success with one group of learners may be met with indifference by another.

Not only are learner responses unpredictable, distractions and interruptions occur with considerable frequency. An unexpected visitor, a call over the intercom, a fire drill, or a sudden change in the daily schedule are events that some teachers are convinced always occur during the most important part of a lesson.

The unpredictable dimension of instruction is one of which most observers are aware. It is often obvious when an unpredicted or unplanned event occurs. Usually, too, the response the teacher makes can easily be seen. What cannot be observed are the thought processes that a teacher uses in determining how to respond to these events. Often these thought processes are conditioned by the teacher's own philosophy and orientation to the profession. This means that different teachers respond to similar situations in various ways. For example, an unexpected response by learners might be interpreted by one teacher as an act of defiance that must be dealt with firmly, whereas another teacher might interpret the event as a lack of understanding that needs to be dealt with through communication and discussion.

Publicness

Classrooms are public places where the actions of the teacher and other learners are observed by a large number of individuals. Teachers are in a fishbowl where their every action is observed and analyzed. Learners are keen observers of what their teachers do, and it takes them only a few days to make personal decisions about what their teachers are "really like." The enthusiasm that a teacher displays about a subject, the way individuals are treated in the classroom, and the manner in which a teacher handles unexpected events communicate teacher values and priorities to a very aware learner audience.

History

Teachers generally meet learners five days a week for a semester or a year. The accumulation of this experience creates a class "history" or class "culture." The manner in which we relate to learners, plan instruction, and react to events and problems communicates a set of priorities and expectations for the learners. As a result, any single lesson or classroom event will be conditioned by these past events.

An observer may not realize that the effectiveness of an individual teacher action may not lie completely in that action. It may be a result of an accumulation of actions. Therefore, a quiet word to the class may have the effect of stopping inappropriate behavior in one class, whereas the same response by another teacher in another class is totally ignored. Therefore, new teachers who attempt to mimic the actions and responses of other teachers are often frustrated when their actions do not have the desired effect. They simply have not developed the same history or culture with the class as the person they are trying to emulate.

A DAY IN THE LIFE OF A TEACHER

The unobserved aspects of the public performance of the teacher are only one part of the teaching role that holds surprises for the beginning teacher. There are numerous aspects of teaching that simply cannot be experienced until one assumes the role of teacher. Many of these are not acquired during the student teaching phase of preparation programs. A common comment of new teachers is, "There is so much I didn't know."

Nonteaching Responsibilities

Unexpected aspects of teaching include such things as (1) the amount of planning and thinking required to produce a good lesson, (2) procedures for handling administrative duties such as record keeping and reporting grades, (3) planning and participating in events such as back-to-school night, (4) fulfilling noninstructional duties, (5) dealing with school politics, (6) participating in faculty meetings, (7) attending district-level meetings, (8) serving as a committee member at the building or district level, and (9) communicating with parents.

The types of activities in which teachers are involved vary according to the level that is taught and the nature of the school and the district. What might be an

It is common for teachers to have one or more non-instructional responsibilities as a normal part of their work load. Some of these duties carry extra compensation. Others do not.

issue in one school may not be an issue in another school. For example, the dynamics of one school may make an understanding of the power structure and the politics of the school critical for success. This may be much less critical in another setting. Secondary teachers may be expected to serve as advisors or sponsors to clubs and organizations or to assist at athletic events or social activities. Elementary teachers are more likely to find themselves serving as monitors on the playground during recess or in the lunchroom. Because these nonteaching duties can take considerable time, many school districts and teacher associations have negotiated what can be expected of a teacher in performing these duties.

There is really no way these site- and context-specific obligations can be taught in preservice programs. However, what you can do as a beginning teacher is to take time to carefully observe and diagnose the special characteristics of your own school and instructional setting. This kind of effort should provide you with excellent clues about the noninstructional duties that will contribute to your success as a teacher.

There are no ordinary days in teaching. Each day brings a different series of activities, questions, and events. Differences between communities and schools also make it difficult to capture the "reality" of a day in the life of a teacher. There are many realities. This point is often mentioned by experienced teachers who move from one school to another. They often comment on the surprising place-to-place differences they encounter.

In order to capture something of the flavor of a day in the life of a teacher, we observed an elementary teacher for a single day, which was chosen at random. Remember that this is only one snapshot of reality. Obviously other days for this teacher may be different. We certainly make no claim that this slice-of-life necessarily generalizes to teachers in other settings.

J. D. Smith's Day at School

Learners at J.D. Smith's elementary school are expected to arrive by 8:30 A.M. However, the day for J. D. and the rest of the teachers begins much earlier. At a minimum, school regulations require teachers to be present no later than 8:00 A.M. However, many teachers are there by 7:30 or earlier working on room decorations, preparing lessons, visiting the copying room to make handouts for learners, taking care of administrative work, and otherwise preparing for the instructional day. On this morning, J. D. spends time completing paperwork from the district personnel department relating to validation of summer-term courses taken at a local university.

J. D. learns that a parent has called the school. Her child is ill and will miss school for several days. J. D. has been asked to prepare assignments the parent can pick up and use with the child at home. The parent does not want her son to fall behind. Another surprise event this morning is the unexpected arrival of a parent of one of J. D.'s pupils. The parent is concerned about the youngster's progress. J. D. and the parent spend some time discussing the situation. Phone calls from parents, unexpected arrivals, and other early-morning events are typical of what J. D. encounters early each morning. On some days, there are scheduled early-morning meetings of the entire faculty. What all of this means is that days when J. D. has uninterrupted time in the early morning to work alone in the classroom are few.

We are visiting J. D. in early fall. This is the time of year when the district regularly schedules its annual Back-to-School Night. During this event, each teacher gives parents an overview of the curriculum and teacher expectations. J. D. knows that this explanation will need to be repeated at least twice because many parents with more than one youngster in school can visit at least two classrooms. On the other hand, J. D. does not have to engage in as much repetition as the secondary school teachers in the district who must prepare a brief overview for every period of the day. J. D. is expected to pay careful attention to the public relations importance of the Back-to-School event. Extra time will have to be spent making the classroom attractive. J. D. begins this before the start of the instructional day by putting up a bulletin board with samples of learners' work.

Learners arrive, and things begin to move quickly. J. D. moves the class smoothly through the topics taught during the first part of the morning. Class members stay on task, and things go well. Recess time arrives, and learners leave. J. D. quickly gathers up materials that have been used and puts them away. Then, after a quick check to make sure that the material needed for the rest of the morning is ready, it's time for a quick trip to the lounge for a cup of coffee and some conversation with other teachers.

Recess time passes quickly. J. D. and the other teachers position themselves in the hall outside their doors to monitor learners as they file back into the rooms. Several problems have occurred during the recess period. One of J. D.'s youngsters has a skinned elbow that needs attention. J. D. sends this child to the office. In times past, the school nurse would have handled this situation, but, because of budget cuts, a nurse is available in the building only for part of one day each week. In the absence of the nurse, the school secretary puts a bandage on the youngster's elbow.

J. D. also has to deal with a complaint brought by several learners who allege that some other youngsters were not behaving properly on the playground during recess. J. D. informs the complainants that the matter will be looked into. These assurances satisfy the complainants, and J. D. quickly puts the class to work. While learners are working independently, J. D. holds a brief conference with the learners involved in the recess incident. A warning in a firm tone of voice seems to achieve the desired outcome.

As the morning passes, some learners are having difficulty staying on task. Their attention span shortens as the day passes. In response to this situation, J. D. moves around the room working with different groups and refocusing learners' attention on what they are supposed to be doing. Lunch comes as a welcome break.

The lunch period begins with a trip to the cafeteria. J. D. briefly enjoys some light conversation and joking with other teachers over lunch. Then there is a trip to the mailbox nets where there are some announcements about Back-to-School Night that need to be sent home with the learners. J. D. finishes the lunch break by gathering a few things that will be needed for this afternoon's science lesson.

J. D. makes it back to the classroom before it is time for class members to return. Materials that are still out from the morning's work are cleaned up. J. D.

spends a few minutes reviewing plans for the afternoon. Needed materials are organized, and J. D. makes a few additional notes in the lesson plan book as reminders of things that need to be retaught or reviewed tomorrow.

J. D. is still making preparations for the afternoon when the bell rings and learners line up outside the classroom. The youngsters are still excited from lunch and a few minutes on the playground. They are talking loudly. To calm them down, J. D. has them go quickly to their seats and sit quietly. Then, a children's book is taken from the desk, and J. D. takes time to read a few pages. This is high-interest material, and there are some groans when the reading stops.

It is time for the next lesson. This lesson and those that follow go reasonably well, but the time from lunch until the close of the school day seems to pass more slowly. The class is more restless and less attentive. J. D. knows this is a typical pattern, and many of the afternoon lessons require active learner participation in the hope that this will keep them motivated and involved. A few minutes before the dismissal bell, J. D. stops instructional activities. Learner workers are asked to perform their duties. Books are replaced in the book shelves. Papers are collected. J. D. takes time to make last-minute announcements and to give reminders about homework. Papers that need to be sent home are distributed, and J. D. dismisses the class.

Today, J. D. has bus duty. After a hurried walk to the bus loading zone, J. D. monitors behavior of learners who ride buses and prepares to handle any problems that might occur. Once the buses leave, J. D. heads back to the classroom.

Back in the classroom, the first order of business is to gather the papers that need to be corrected. They are placed in a bag to be taken home. Next, J. D. begins to prepare for tomorrow. The sequence of lessons for the next day is reviewed. J. D. jots reminders about what is to be done tomorrow in the margins of the daily plan book. Then, it is time to create, gather, and organize supplementary material that will be used tomorrow. Some materials for tomorrow will require more time to develop. These are moved into the "take-home" bag. Over an hour has passed since the last learner boarded the bus. Finally, it is time for J. D. to lock the door and head home, carrying papers to be graded and lessons to be planned.

Teachers' Very Full Days

Each day in the life of a teacher is a busy one. Teachers do not show up with the learners and simply start teaching. A great deal of time must be spent planning and preparing for teaching. Although experienced teachers may not write out the complete lesson plans needed by beginners, successful teachers spend a considerable amount of time thinking about and planning their lessons. In addition, there are papers to grade, reports to be completed, records to be kept, faculty and committee meetings to attend, and special problems that need attention. These "extra" activities are especially frustrating to new teachers because they interfere with time needed to plan lessons and organize materials. They have to plan for new lessons for every period of the day for 180 days or more — an intimidating task.

As you prepare to enter the classroom, keep in mind that actual teaching is only one part of what you will do each day. Many other obligations will place a call on your time. Managing all of these responsibilities demands excellent organizational skills. On the other hand, these multiple challenges give our professional day a tremendously interesting and challenging variety. You will find few dull days!

• Key Ideas in Summary

- Because education is viewed as such an important societal institution, it is the subject of much debate and numerous proposals for change. Because there is no national consensus regarding the goals and purposes of education, there is no consensus regarding proposed changes.
- Schools exist as a part of society and as society changes, so do views regarding the role of education in society. There are those who are quick to blame schools for contributing to societal problems. Some see the problem as too much change, whereas others criticize school changes as moving too slowly.
- Some reformers are challenging the industrial model as a useful model for education to follow. They believe that many of the basic assumptions that guide educational practice need to be challenged.
- The characteristics of the learner population have changed dramatically in the past couple of decades. It is common to find classrooms with a diverse learner population that may include learners from a variety of cultures, learners who come from homes with primary languages other than English, and disabled learners.
- There continues to be changes in theories of teaching and learning. Especially important for the teacher is the development of the constructivist theory of learning. This theory has several profound implications for planning instruction and delivering content to learners.
- The notion that there are multiple intelligences rather than a single intelligence factor also has important implications for teaching. These implications have particular import for teachers who wish to develop instructional strategies that respond to individual intelligence types.
- Individuals preparing to teach often think they know precisely what a person needs to know and be able to do to be a teacher. They are often shocked to discover that teaching is much different than they expected. Some of the factors that make teaching more complex than many realize are its multidimensionality, simultaneity, immediacy, unpredictability, and publicness. Differing histories of individual classes also contribute to the complexity of the school environment.
- Because there are great differences in schools from place to place and by different levels, there is no one reality of teaching. However, observing the daily activities of a teacher can help individuals capture some of the feeling of what it means to be a professional educator.

• Review and Discussion Questions

1. What is your stand on change in education? Do you think the schools have changed too fast or too slowly?
2. What are examples of the industrial model as applied to education? Do you think this model is appropriate or outdated? Are there some aspects of this approach that can be salvaged, or does it represent too poor a fit with present realities to have any further use as a way of organizing schools and instruction?
3. Which proposals for change in education would you support? Which ones would you oppose?
4. How is today's learner population similar or different from what you experienced when you were in school?
5. What is your position on multicultural education and bilingual education? Are the benefits associated with these approaches worth the costs? Why or why not?
6. Why is it so difficult for an individual teacher today to know what people want from good teachers? How is it possible that there can be so many views regarding what should be going on in our schools?
7. What are the basic points of constructivist learning theory? In what ways would lessons developed according to a constructivist approach differ from those developed according to a more traditional planning scheme? What do you think about this theory?
8. What do you see as the implications of the multiple intelligence theory for teachers?
9. What are the dimensions of classroom teaching that make it so complex?
10. Which of the dimensions concern you most? Why?

• Ideas for Field Experiences, Projects, and Enrichment

1. Review the popular media for articles on education. What general patterns do you notice concerning proposed changes in education? Which proposals do you agree with and why?
2. Research the pro and con arguments related to one of the changes mentioned in the chapter, such as school choice, full inclusion, bilingual education, or multicultural education. Present your findings in a report to your class.
3. Interview a teacher and ask about the factors of multidimensionality, simultaneity, unpredictability, immediacy, and so forth. Ask how these factors influence this person's teaching. What advice does the teacher have for beginners who will be confronting these challenges for the first time?
4. Spend a day observing a teacher. Try to record the flow of activities and events in the classroom. If possible, choose a second teacher in a different school and at a different grade or subject. Compare the accounts. What patterns do you notice? What differences did you find?
5. Educators and others interested in the schools often make predictions about what teaching and learning will be like in the future. Look at some articles printed in professional journals such as *Phi Delta Kappan* between 1955 and 1965. What changes for the future were predicted in articles published during those years? How accurate were these predictions? Present your findings in a short speech to your class and develop some tentative explanations for predictions that failed to come true.

• References

Arnold, J., & Dodge, H. (1995). Room for all. In J. Noll (Ed.). *Taking sides: Clashing views on controversial educational issues* (8th ed., pp. 200–204). Guilford, CT: Dushkin.

Banks, J. (1994). *An introduction to multicultural education.* Boston: Allyn and Bacon.

Cohen, D. (1995). What standards for national standards? *Phi Delta Kappan, 76*(10), 751–757.

Coontz, S. (1992). *The way we never were.* New York: Basic Books.

Doyle W. (1986). Classroom organization and management. In M. Wittrock (Ed.). *Handbook of research on teaching* (3rd ed., pp. 392–431). New York: Macmillan.

Eisner, E. (1995). Standards for American schools: Help or hindrance. *Phi Delta Kappan, 76*(10), 758–764.

Gardner, H. (1993). *Multiple intelligences: The theory in practice.* New York: Basic Books.

Jennings, J. (1995). School reform based on what is taught and learned. *Phi Delta Kappan, 76*(10), 765–769.

Kauffman, J., Lloyd, J., Baker, J., & Riedel, T. (1995). Inclusion of all learners with emotional or behavioral disorders? Let's think again. *Phi Delta Kappan, 76*(7), 542–546.

Levin, B. (1994). Improving educational productivity: Putting learners at the center. *Phi Delta Kappan, 75*(10), 758–760.

Macedo, D. (1995). English only: The tongue-tying of America. In J. Noll (Ed.). *Taking sides: Clashing views on controversial educational issues*(8th ed., pp. 249–258). Guilford, CT: Dushkin.

Moffett, J. (1994). On to the past: Wrong-headed school reform. *Phi Delta Kappan, 75*(8), 584–590.

Ravitch, D. (1995). Politicization and the schools: The case of bilingual education. In J. Noll (Ed.). *Taking sides: Clashing views on controversial educational issues* (8th ed., pp. 240–248). Guilford, CT: Dushkin.

Schlesinger, A. (1995). The disuniting of America. In J. Noll (Ed.). *Taking sides: Clashing views on controversial educational issues* (8th ed., pp. 227–236). Guilford, CT: Dushkin.

Schnalberg, L. (1995, August 2). Board relaxes bilingual-ed. policy in California. *Education Week,* p. 1.

Shanker, A. (1995). Where we stand on the rush to inclusion. In J. Noll (Ed.). *Taking sides: Clashing views on controversial educational issues* (8th ed., pp. 205–211). Guilford, CT: Dushkin.

Slavin, R. (1994). *Educational psychology: Theory and practice* (4th ed.). Boston: Allyn and Bacon.

Smith, F. (1995). Let's declare education a disaster and get on with our lives. *Phi Delta Kappan, 76*(8), 584–590.

Sternberg, R. (1990). *Metaphors of mind: Conceptions of the nature of intelligence.* New York: Cambridge University Press.

Woolfolk, A. (1995). *Educational psychology* (6th ed.). Boston: Allyn and Bacon.

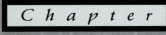
3

Classroom Management and Discipline

OBJECTIVES

- Point out the relationship between management and discipline.
- Identify the importance of space management.
- Describe time management.
- Define what needs to be considered when establishing the context for effective discipline.
- Describe what negotiation means in relation to discipline.
- Identify basic principles that need to be followed when responding to inappropriate behavior.
- List a range of alternative responses that can be used when responding to discipline problems.

To succeed in the classroom, we need to know how to manage learners and respond appropriately to their behavior. An inability to control the classroom is a major reason for teacher failure and dismissal. Well-meaning people who want to help beginners often willingly share a number of surefire prescriptions for success such as:

- Plan your lessons thoroughly.
- Love the students.
- Be enthusiastic.
- Don't smile until Christmas.
- Start off tough.
- Let them know you are the boss.

Although some of these statements may have an element of truth, they are inadequate for the complex task of managing the classroom. Yes, we do need to plan carefully, but even teachers who devote lots of time to planning lessons encounter discipline problems occasionally. Certainly, too, members of our profession who like young people and who approach life enthusiastically often do exceptionally well in the classroom. But these characteristics alone are no guarantee that classroom control and management problems will not surface from time to time.

The hard truth is that all teachers occasionally must contend with problems associated with learner misbehavior. There are no simple solutions to this challenge. However, there are some general principles that we can use to reduce the frequency of problem behavior. Part of our task as teachers involves helping young people learn appropriate behavior patterns. Because a well-managed classroom is an essential part of the classroom climate required for academic learning, we have a responsibility both to establish sound management procedures and to teach academic content (Savage, 1991). The two roles complement one another; good teaching helps prevent management problems, and sound management provides a context within which good teaching can occur.

Teacher-preparation programs often devote considerable time to acquainting prospective teachers with information related to good teaching. Classroom management, however, usually receives much less attention. This is because many instructors view management and discipline as dependent on personality traits and problem-solving skills that are difficult to teach. We do not agree. It is true that personality traits, such as a good dose of common sense and the ability to think on one's feet, are important in managing a classroom. However, we believe that there is a great deal that can be done to prepare *all* individuals to better manage their classrooms.

In this chapter, we address two basic aspects of classroom management. The first focuses on problem prevention through the use of good management. The second introduces procedures that have been found useful as responses to inappropriate learner behaviors.

DIMENSIONS OF CLASSROOM MANAGEMENT

Many prospective teachers have questions about how to respond when problems occur. The most important aspect of classroom management and discipline, however, is the prevention of problems before they happen. For example, Kounin (1970) found that although successful and unsuccessful classroom managers responded to inappropriate learner behavior in similar ways, there were important differences in how they organized and managed their classrooms.

Successful classroom management requires an understanding of the unique nature of the classroom and the role of the teacher. The classroom is a complex environment. It includes many people who vary greatly in their abilities, backgrounds, interests, maturity levels, and motivations. These individuals are placed in close proximity for significant blocks of time. Events that take place in this type of an environment can be highly unpredictable.

Our role as teachers is to take this mixture of individuals, provide them with appropriate materials, capture their interest, organize the space, and use the time so that learning occurs in ways that leave class members feeling positive about the instructional experience. While we are trying to deal imaginatively with academic content, we must be prepared to respond to unanticipated and spontaneous events in a constructive manner. We face daunting and diverse responsibilities when we are working with our learners, but there are things that we can do to make instruction flow more smoothly and reduce the number of potentially disruptive learner behaviors.

Researchers have suggested that smoothly functioning classrooms result when teachers take deliberate actions to plan a management strategy very early in the school year, or even before school starts (Emmer, Evertson, & Anderson, 1980; Evertson, 1989). In making this connection, Carolyn Evertson (1989) commented, "Solving managerial and organizational problems at the beginning of the year is essential in laying the groundwork for quality learning opportunities for students" (p. 90). Teachers who follow this practice develop clear ideas about how they expect their classrooms to operate, and then communicate those ideas to their learners.

Space Management

Classroom management begins with the organization and management of the classroom space. Architects and psychologists have long emphasized the impact of space on human behavior. In fact, they have coined the special term *behavioral setting* to explain this relationship. A behavioral setting is a space that influences the behavior of the individuals within that space. Consider a church or cathedral, for example. These environments seem to inspire awe in people and to communicate that quiet, respectful behaviors are required within them. In thinking about our own classroom environment, we need to consider what we can do to communicate our behavioral expectations to our learners.

In thinking about this issue, consider your reactions to different environments. How do you feel in crowded spaces where others invade your space? What is your

Good classroom managers take action to ensure that learners understand basic rules.

reaction to clutter or unappealing places? What happens when you are in uncomfortable places where it is too hot or too cold? How are your motivation and learning affected by these variables? Individuals typically find that they are distracted, irritable, anxious, fatigued, and angry when confronted with these conditions. These are not the feelings that we want to engender in our learners.

In planning the classroom for instruction and the prevention of problems, we need to consider the attractiveness of the space, the degree of crowding of our learners, the comfort of our learners, the arrangement of materials and desks, and the location and availability of instructional materials.

Wall Space

An important aspect of providing a stimulating and attractive environment is the use of wall space. Constructive use of wall space enhances the quality of the instructional environment. Parts of the walls can be devoted to motivational displays to stimulate interest in topics that are being studied. Spots can be reserved to display learners' work. (This is particularly important in elementary schools.) Other areas can be used to display schedules, important announcements, and classroom rules. Adding a little color to the wall and keeping it free of unnecessary clutter goes a long way in providing a pleasant classroom environment. It also helps to occasionally change the displays on the walls.

Floor Space

Developing a floor plan of the classroom is useful in addressing the issues of density and convenience. Seating must be arranged so that learners do not feel overcrowded and so that they can see and hear the teacher and see important educational centers such as chalkboards and overhead projector screens.

The nature of the instructional activities that are to be conducted in the space should have a major impact on decisions about the most appropriate organization of classroom floor space. Some types of activities feature whole-group instruction. Others require us to work with small groups of learners. Still others require learners to be scattered throughout the room at different learning or activity centers.

Whole-group instruction requires a physical arrangement that permits all learners to maintain good eye contact with the teacher. Desks must be arranged to provide for this need. Occasionally, we will want to check on an individual learner's work or understanding during whole-group instruction. To facilitate easy movement throughout the classroom, desks need to be arranged to allow for aisles or spaces that permit us to move quickly to meet personally with learners who might be experiencing problems.

In planning floor arrangements for small-group discussion, learning spaces need to be arranged so we can continue to monitor the whole class while working with one small group. If possible, seating spaces for the small group we are working with should be located at some distance from other learners. This diminishes the temptation for small-group members to talk to others in the class. It also helps reduce the general noise level, something that makes it easier for all learners to stay at their assigned tasks.

Learning centers need to be placed in areas of the classroom that are easily accessible to all learners and yet are not distracting to those individuals who are not working at the centers. When centers feature films, filmstrips, or some other projected media, they should be placed out of the direct sight lines of learners who are not working at the centers, because such media can be very distracting to others.

Traffic Patterns

In planning the physical organization of classrooms, traffic patterns must be considered. To start with, we need to identify those parts of the room that are heavily used. These would include such areas as doorways, places where learners' personal belongings and class materials are stored, book storage areas, and the vicinity of the teacher's desk. Spaces around these frequently visited parts of the classroom need to be kept obstruction-free. Desks should be arranged so that people going to and from these areas of the classroom can do so without disturbing other learners.

Teacher's Desk

Many teachers do not give much thought to the placement of their desk; however, where it is placed can have management consequences. In many classrooms, the teacher's desk is located at the front and center of the room. This setup is a custom dictated by tradition rather than sound management. A better choice is an unobtrusive place near the back of the room.

Locating the desk near the rear of the classroom has several advantages. One advantage is that it encourages us to stand up and move around the classroom. This movement, in turn, often leads to more careful monitoring of learners' work. Teachers who circulate through the classroom and avoid sitting behind a desk are perceived by learners as "warmer" (Smith, 1987). A second advantage is that this placement does not allow us to get in the habit of teaching from behind our desk. Teaching while sitting at the teacher's desk does not convey to learners that we are interested in and enthusiastic about what we are doing. A third advantage is that it is normally easier to monitor learners' on-task behavior from the rear of the classroom. Members of our class won't know when we are observing them. A feeling among learners that the teacher might be looking helps minimize problem behaviors. Finally, a desk at the rear of the classroom makes it easier to have individual learner conferences at the desk without attracting the attention of everyone in the room. This helps keep the maximum number of learners on task rather than observing the interaction between the teacher and learner.

Equipment Storage

We use a lot of specialized equipment when we teach. Many schools have items such as computers, projectors (e.g., 16 mm, slide, opaque, or overhead), video- and audiotape recorders, television monitors, and phonographs. Some of these items are kept in individual classrooms. Storage space for this equipment needs to be both secure and accessible. Maintaining equipment in good operating order is a major headache for school officials. The possibilities for misuse or malicious damage decrease when equipment is stored in a way that permits access only by authorized people. When possible, it is wise to store equipment in cabinets or other areas that can be locked.

Time Management

Time management is one of the most important and one of the most difficult of our managerial tasks as teachers. We have a very limited amount of time to accomplish important educational goals. In addition, it is important that the time be used so that learners do not become bored because of wasted time or overwhelmed and frustrated because there is inadequate time. Researchers have found that in many classrooms, a high percentage of time is spent on noninstructional tasks (Smyth, 1987). Not surprisingly, they have also determined that learners in classes where teachers spend more time on instruction learn more (Berliner, 1984).

Time management involves handling routine tasks in a quick and efficient manner, taking action to ensure that members of our class get to work promptly, presenting necessary information in a clear and concise manner, and keeping learners engaged in learning throughout the lesson.

Transitions

Management of shifts from one part of a lesson to another is important. Many beginning teachers forget about transitions. They spend a good deal of time planning lessons and give little thought to what to do between lessons. Transitions occur when there is a shift from one activity to another, and they offer the potential for much class time to be lost.

To avoid wasting time, careful plans need to be made for transition points. When materials are to be distributed or work returned during the transition points, it is useful to organize the material in advance. When this is done, things can be distributed to the learners quickly and efficiently. Sometimes transitions require learners to move from one part of an instructional area to another or from one room to another. Giving clear directions on how to make these changes and establishing a time frame within which the changes need to be made can save valuable time.

Beginning Class

Some teachers take too much time getting their classes started. Lessons that begin promptly engage learners' attention, eliminate potential off-task behavior that can lead to problems, and maximize instructional time. This means that tasks such as taking attendance and other routine administrative duties need to be performed quickly.

It often is useful to establish a signal system that informs class members that it is time for learning. Some teachers move to a special place in the front of the class and look out over the learners. Others use a particular command such as "all eyes up here." At the beginning of the school year, we can explain to our learners the specific signal system we want to use.

A lesson should not be started until all learners are paying attention. When we teach, we have to be careful not to strain our voices. This kind of strain can leave us hoarse and uncomfortable if we have to sustain a volume level loud enough to be heard over learners' unauthorized side conversations. Also, when we insist on quiet before we begin, we signal to learners that what we say is important and worth hearing.

Lesson Pacing

How we pace our lessons has important behavior implications for learners. Lessons should move briskly, but not so fast as to be confusing. A certain amount of repetition is necessary to highlight key points. However, excessive repetition leads to boredom. It is a natural human tendency to seek relief from boredom. In classrooms, the search for relief from boredom often results in inappropriate behavior.

To help them decide on an appropriate instructional pace, some teachers select a "reference group" in their class. Members of the reference group include four or five learners who represent a cross section of class members. We watch members of the reference group to determine their reactions to what we are doing. Based on our observations of these class members, we can speed up, slow down, or maintain the present instructional pace.

Part of planning for pacing requires us to anticipate that some learners will finish assignments sooner than others. Follow-up activities need to be designed for early finishers so that they can immediately make the transition into another productive activity. These follow-up activities we choose should not be "more of the same." If this happens, bright learners may feel that they are being punished for finishing their work quickly. On the other hand, these follow-up experiences cannot be so enticing that learners race through the assigned task just to gain more time for working on them.

Providing Assistance

Often while learners are working on assignments, many of them will seek our help at the same time. A teacher with 25 to 30 learners can be frustrated when trying to help all of those looking for assistance. Frederic H. Jones (1979) has suggested some guidelines for responding to this problem. In his research, he found that the average teacher spends much more time working with individual learners than is necessary. To decrease the total time spent with each person and, hence, increase the opportunities to help more individuals seeking assistance, the following procedure is recommended for use with each learner:

- First, the teacher should build confidence by finding something the learner has done correctly and then praising the good work.
- Second, the teacher should provide a direct suggestion about what the learner should do next. (But the teacher should not do the work for the learner.)
- After completing the first two steps, the teacher should move on quickly to the next learner. The teacher may check back in a short while to make sure the learner is still on task. However, care needs to be taken that the teacher does not get trapped helping just one learner or creating a sense of dependency so that specific learners depend on the teacher to do most of the work and thinking for them.

Jones (1979) has pointed out that this process will enable the teacher to help a large number of learners in a relatively short time period. He has recommended that, on average, no more than 20 seconds at a time be spent with a single learner.

Establishing Routines and Procedures

A basic principle of classroom management is that routines and procedures need to be developed to handle recurring and predictable events. This helps simplify the demands on our time so we can devote our attention to the exceptions or the unplanned and unpredictable events. During a typical day, we experience hundreds of personal contacts with learners. Unless systems for managing these contacts are developed, our emotional reserves will be drained, and the likelihood of making management mistakes will increase. Routines and procedures are often developed for such things as:

- what learners are to do as soon as they enter the classroom
- what learners should do when they have a personal problem to discuss with the teacher
- what procedures are to be used in passing out and collecting materials
- when and where pencils are to be sharpened

- how daily attendance is to be taken
- what learners are to do when they need to leave the room

Once procedures and routines have been planned, those involving learner behaviors need to be explained to class members. With younger learners, this information sometimes is taught as a formal lesson. With more mature, secondary school students, a brief explanation of expectations and procedures may suffice.

RESPONDING TO LEARNER MISBEHAVIOR: CONTEXTS FOR EFFECTIVE PRACTICE

Even in classrooms where lessons are exciting and teachers are good managers, learners occasionally misbehave. Dealing with inappropriate behavior involves more than a bag of tricks to be used in response to a specific incident. The effectiveness of a given response begins with the attitudes and the expectations of the teacher.

Some questions that you might ask yourself are the following:

- What do you expect of students? Do you believe they are interested in learning?
- How do you see your role as a teacher? Do you believe it is wise to "lay down the law"?
- How do you think teachers establish good discipline in the classroom?
- What is your image of the ideal classroom?
- What is your image of young people today?
- What is the appropriate relationship between teachers and learners?
- Are you comfortable sharing power with members of your class?

Answers to these questions can reveal your underlying attitude toward learners and your philosophy of teaching and learning. Your philosophy and attitude will have a strong influence on how you view classroom management and how you will respond when problems arise. Therefore, the images you have of what it takes to be a successful teacher and classroom manager need to be uncovered so that they can be investigated and dealt with in productive ways.

Some people feel that the mere use of the term *management* suggests a metaphor that leads to the creation of an inappropriate classroom context (Bullough, 1994). Management is seen as reflecting top-down control with a primary focus on maintaining adult authority and learner obedience. The teacher sets the rules and establishes learning tasks independent of learner input or concerns. It is the role of the teacher to manage and control; it is the role of the learner to submit and obey.

Others recommend that the management metaphor be replaced with one of *negotiation* (McLaughlin, 1994). Negotiation implies a context in which the wants and needs of all interested parties are considered. This suggests that learners are to be treated with dignity and that they are given some power in deciding what happens in the classroom. The classroom is viewed as a community where cooperative learning, shared decision making, and group problem solving are the defining characteristics.

BOX 3-1	***Establishing Rules and Procedures***

Researchers have found that effective teachers are especially good at establishing rules and procedures (Doyle, 1986). Effective teachers not only establish rules and procedures, they systematically teach them to learners. The rules and procedures need to be written in clear, explicit language so that learners know when they are in compliance. Furthermore, the rules and procedures need to be written and developed as they are needed. It is best to establish the rules with the class; however, there are a few that you may feel are absolutely necessary in your classroom. Take some time to reflect on the rules and procedures you believe you will need as a teacher. The chart supplied will help you in that task.

	Rules and procedures related to classroom conduct	Rules and procedures related to academic work
Rules and procedures that need to be communicated at the beginning of the year		
Rules and procedures that may be established later		

Negotiation as a metaphor is consistent with the *constructivist approach* to learning. This approach holds that learning occurs as individuals process information and construct their own meanings. Control forced on an individual from external sources, such as the teacher, does not provide conditions optimal for learning. What we are looking for are ways to help learners develop internal and personal commitments to desirable patterns of behavior. Some of the most important things young people take away from their years in school relate to experiences that have led to noncoercive self-discipline and self-control.

Negotiation does not mean that there is no control in the classroom and that all power is shifted to learners. Negotiation does not mean abdicating responsibility; it means taking the needs of others into account. As teachers, we are still in charge of the classroom, and we deserve respect from learners in our role as leader. How we exercise our leadership is critical to the success of negotiation as a management technique. What constitutes appropriate leadership will vary depending on individual circumstances. There will be times, for example, when serious disruptions require us to exercise unilateral power.

The case for negotiation as a technique is buttressed by a major purpose of classroom discipline (and of education, in general): teaching learners how to exercise self-control and responsibility. Individuals with a wealth of knowledge but no self-control are unlikely to become productive individuals contributing to the good of humankind. Learning self-control and the acceptance of responsibility is enhanced when individuals are treated with dignity and are given responsibility. As they experience the consequences of their actions, they learn that "I cause my own outcomes. I have the power to choose alternative behaviors" (McLaughlin, 1994).

Several elements are involved in classrooms featuring negotiation. First, the degree to which individuals have self-control and a sense of responsibility is related to how they perceive reality. Those who believe that their environment is warm, trusting, and positive are more likely to exercise self-control than those who believe their environment is cold, indifferent, and negative. Opening many aspects of the classroom to negotiation and looking at the classroom as a place where the needs, concerns, and interests of the learners are taken into account goes a long way toward creating this type of a classroom climate.

Second, when we give young people opportunities to make choices, we help them to develop self-control and responsibility. Making decisions from among alternatives and living with the consequences are important aspects of maturing. Opportunities to choose provide learners with the feeling that they can exercise some personal control over their lives. People who have a sense that their personal actions and decisions count tend to act in more responsible, controlled ways than individuals who lack these feelings.

Third, learners with positive self-concepts are more likely to develop patterns of self-control and personal responsibility than those with negative self-concepts. Self-concepts derive from interactions with others. Since teachers exercise some control over classroom interactions, they are in a position to influence the nature of the self-concept developed by each learner. A success-oriented classroom in which every effort is made to help each person experience some feelings of achievement encourages the development of positive self-concepts among the learners.

Finally, learners who feel that they "belong" are likely to develop good self-control and a sense of personal responsibility. Pride in group membership is important to many young people. Providing learners with responsibility and being open to their concerns and interests can help them feel a sense of ownership and pride in being a part of the classroom.

In summary, creating a context within which good discipline can take place requires much more than just implementing a bag of tricks. It requires us to rethink our view of the "proper" role of the teacher and what it means to teach. In particular, we are challenged to think about how teacher power is defined and used. The following section outlines several different types of power and how they might be used in the classroom.

Discipline and Teachers' Use of Power

When learners misbehave, we have to do something to remedy the situation. The nature of teacher power and how it is used can influence general patterns of classroom behavior. Here are several types of power we can use (French & Raven, 1959):

- expert power
- referent power
- legitimate power
- reward power
- coercive power

Expert Power

Expert power is power that comes to a person as a result of possessing specialized knowledge. In general, people who are acknowledged experts in a given area exercise considerable influence over others. Their opinions are respected because they are thought to know a great deal about their specialties. This type of power is earned rather than demanded.

Referent Power

Referent power is power that results from a warm, positive relationship. Individuals are willing to give another some power when they perceive that the other person is trustworthy and is concerned about them. People accept advice they receive from those whom they like and respect. If we are to enjoy referent power as teachers, we must be seen by learners as respected, trustworthy, and ethical people who genuinely are concerned about our learners. As is the case with expert power, referent power cannot be demanded. It must be earned through actions that demonstrate trust, caring, and concern for others.

Legitimate Power

Legitimate power derives from the particular position a person holds. For example, city mayors can wield certain powers because of the office they hold. As teachers, we have some legitimate power because of the authority delegated by school administrators and the school board. For example, we have the power to make certain decisions about how to teach and how to deal with the behavior of class members.

Problems sometimes result because not all learners accept that teachers have legitimate power. This can cause difficulties for teachers who mistakenly assume that all learners accept their legitimate power. They don't. Teachers who think they can effectively manage classrooms simply by relying on their legitimate power are asking for trouble. On the other hand, teachers who build their authority in the classroom around expert and referent power—powers that have to be earned—will find that their legitimate authority is increased.

Reward Power

Reward power comes to individuals as a result of their ability to provide something that another person sees as desirable. As teachers, we are in a position to provide benefits to learners in the form of praise, grades, and privileges, so we do have some reward power. However, our reward powers are limited. We have a relatively small number of rewards available that can be dispensed to learners. Further, what we view as rewards are not always seen as desirable by all of our learners. Some learners who do not care what grades they receive (and there are such people in the schools) will not be influenced by teachers who offer good grades in exchange for good performance.

The power to give rewards comes with the position of being the teacher and is not a type of power that is earned. It is an effective type of power as long as there are rewards to give that learners value. This type of authority may vanish quickly when the rewards are exhausted or not desired. As with legitimate power, when a teacher establishes expert and referent power as a base, rewards such as grades and praise become more powerful.

Coercive Power

Coercive power is power that people wield because of their authority to administer punishment. As teachers, we are in a position to administer punishment and therefore have coercive power. Teachers who rely heavily on coercive power often do not have classroom environments that learners perceive as warm, caring, and positive. When coercive power is applied, many learners fail to see compelling reasons to adopt behavior patterns favored by their teachers. In an individual situation, when application of coercive power suppresses one undesirable behavior, another undesirable behavior often springs up to replace the first. Again, coercive authority is of little use when the ability to punish is removed or the prospect of being caught is perceived to be slight.

Expert power and referent power are the two types of power that are most important for us as we strive to develop positive working relationships with our learners. These two types of power are also most consistent with the metaphor of negotiation in classroom management. Young people are usually willing to accept leadership from teachers they perceive to be experts and who are ethical, warm individuals.

The desirability of being seen as an expert suggests the need for us to be well grounded in the subjects we teach. A solid grasp of content can give us the credibility needed to establish our expert power. At the same time, we need to establish positive classroom climates. When learners sense that we care about them personally and truly support them, we accrue valuable referent power. When expert and referent types of authority are present, classroom control problems are greatly diminished.

In summary, the way we attempt to establish and use authority and power in the classroom will have a significant impact on our success in controlling the classroom and disciplining learners. Negotiation as a metaphor encourages us to establish an environment where learner needs are addressed and where there is

Getting Tough

John Robbins is nearing the end of his first year of teaching seventh grade history at Ride Middle School. The school is in a suburban area just outside a major midwestern city. John took the teaching job in this school because of the location. He was sure that the parents would be supportive of education and the students would be motivated. He expected fewer discipline problems here than he might encounter in a more "difficult" setting. However, this has not turned out to be the case. In fact, he is wondering if he is up to returning in the fall.

John started his first year upbeat and optimistic. He knew he loved history and was sure that he could convey his enthusiasm to students by sharing the interesting anecdotes and insights he had obtained as a history major in college. He "just knew" he would relate well to students because he was much nearer their age than most teachers and he could talk their language. He had had some difficulties in his student teaching, but he ascribed these problems to being in the classroom of another teacher and not having the freedom to do what he knew would be best.

John started the year by telling his students that he wanted to make things enjoyable for them. He was sure that if the class was fun and if he was friendly and open to the students, they would be motivated to work and cooperate with him. After a month, however, he realized that the class was getting out of control. The students didn't want to listen. They were just interested in playing around. He became angry and decided that it was time to clamp down. Perhaps, he thought, a teacher really *shouldn't* smile until Christmas.

In an effort to regain control, John decided to get tough. He laid down the law to his students and established strict rules and punishments. Although this seemed to stop some undesirable behaviors, it also resulted in students becoming increasingly negative. More and more of them seemed to take every opportunity to test the limits of his rules. He found that being engaged in a constant test of wills with his students wasn't much fun.

As the year draws to a close, John is feeling that he has accomplished very little. Many of his students now are openly expressing a dislike of history and are asking why it is important to learn something about a bunch of dead guys. John wonders if things are this bad in other schools. Maybe not. Perhaps he should try to get a job in a high school. Certainly other schools must have students with more mature attitudes who appreciate the value of learning something about history.

Do you think the problems would be easier at another grade? Do you think the problems are with John or with the students? Specifically, what does John perceive the problem to be? What do you think his students perceive the problem to be? What might have been the sources of the feelings of each?

What mistakes do you think John might have made? What suggestions would you give him? Do you worry about things like this happening to you? What do you think you could do about it? How do you respond to the suggestion of not smiling until Christmas and being tough from the first day of school? What are the alternatives?

shared decision making. Expert and referent power are consistent with the concept of negotiation. They establish a context within which our actions can be effective.

Some Basic Principles of Effective Discipline

Regardless of the number of preventive actions we take, we sometimes have to deal with learner behavior problems. This is simply a part of being a teacher. Young people are human beings who lack experience, and they sometimes make wrong choices. There are some basic principles that we should keep in mind when responding to incidents of misbehavior. Understanding the following principles increases the possibility that our responses will be effective:

- Preserve the dignity of the learner.
- Private correction is preferable to public correction.
- The causes of misbehavior must be addressed, not simply the misbehavior itself.
- Distinctions must be made between minor and major misbehavior problems.
- Learners must be helped to understand that they have chosen to misbehave and, therefore, have chosen to experience the consequences.
- Responses to misbehavior must be consistent and fair.

Preserving Learners' Dignity

When correcting misbehavior, we need to be careful that our comments do not diminish learners' self-worth. Such responses have the potential to lead to more discipline problems (Jones & Jones, 1986). Teacher behaviors that assault learners' dignity often lead to power conflicts. Frustrated learners may feel that their only recourse is to respond with assaults on the dignity of the teacher. Older learners report that one of the reasons they misbehave is that they feel they have been "put down" by their teachers.

Private Correction versus Public Correction

One way we can diminish the likelihood that learners will feel that their self-worth has been attacked is to correct a misbehaving learner in a place where our comments cannot be heard by others. The verbal reprimand might take place outside of the classroom, for example. Private correction takes pressure off misbehaving young people. On the other hand, public reprimands may make them feel pressed to take action in order to "save face" in front of their peers. Private correction also promotes better, more personal contact between teachers and learners. Learners know that we are committing our full and undivided attention to the situation under discussion.

Addressing the Causes, Not Just the Behavior

Teachers who are good classroom disciplinarians take a long-term perspective on learners' behavior problems. Their responses are geared not simply to stopping misbehavior when it occurs, but rather they seek to change conditions so that problem behaviors will not recur. They seek underlying causes of improper behavior and try to remove conditions that reinforce unacceptable patterns (Brophy, 1983).

Serious and persistent misbehavior is often a learner's way of asking for help. It attracts our attention and prompts us to act. Given this sequence, learners occasionally will behave in ways they know are unacceptable simply to attract our attention to a serious problem. We need to recognize that some misbehaving young people are desperately seeking supportive, adult assistance.

Distinguishing between Major and Minor Problems

Many incidents that happen in schools are a result of learners' immaturity rather than serious attempts to challenge authority. We need to be sensitive to the distinction between these minor behavioral lapses and those that represent more serious challenges to our ability to function as an instructional leader. This means we must avoid overreactions that can build learner resentment and lead to more serious misbehavior episodes.

Learners Choose to Misbehave and to Experience the Consequences

In teaching young people to be responsible, it is important to convey to them that unpleasant consequences of misbehavior result from their own irresponsible behavioral choices, not from arbitrary and vindictive actions that we, as teachers, have decided to take. We must help learners see the relationship between inappropriate behaviors and resultant consequences. To accomplish this, learners need to understand clearly what behaviors are unacceptable and what specific consequences will follow if they engage in these behaviors. The purpose is to help young people recognize that by choosing irresponsible behaviors, they are also choosing the consequences.

Consistent and Fair Responses

The principle of consistent and fair responses implies that we need to respond to all incidents of misbehavior. If some episodes are ignored, we signal to learners that there is nothing really wrong with this kind of behavior. When this happens, something that begins as a minor problem often escalates into a major one.

Consistency provides at least two key benefits. First, it communicates to learners that we are serious about discouraging a certain pattern of behavior. Second, it suggests to learners that we are fair. This perception is strengthened when we react similarly to a specified type of misbehavior regardless of which person in the class is involved.

RESPONDING TO MISBEHAVIOR: A RANGE OF ALTERNATIVE RESPONSES

Newcomers to our profession often experience difficulty in knowing how to respond to misbehavior. One way of addressing this situation is by developing a plan that identifies a range of actions that might be taken in response to problems.

This range of actions should begin with appropriately mild responses to minor problems that increase in severity when it is necessary to address more serious ones. This kind of planning allows us to consider alternatives in an unhurried way. Following the plan provides some assurance that we are maintaining consistent and fair patterns of responses when difficulties arise with different learners at different times.

Plans must developed to fit individual circumstances. The subsections that follow list teacher responses in order of their severity. In this scheme, the teacher chooses options from the first several categories when minor problems arise and from categories farther down the list when more serious problems occur.

Category 1: Responses Supporting Self-Control

One of our purposes in teaching is to help our learners exert personal control over their behavior. If we are successful in doing this, a learner may be able to self-correct an unacceptable behavior to an acceptable alternative. Our actions in this category are relatively unobtrusive. They are most appropriate for minor behavior problems.

Reinforcing Productive Behavior

One of the most important things we can do to help learners develop self-control is to reinforce desirable patterns of behavior. This can be done by rewarding individuals and members of an entire class when they have behaved well.

Rewards can take many forms. Verbal praise works well, and there may be special activities that class members particularly enjoy that function well as rewards. The specific rewards we use should vary with the interests of our learners. To be functional, a reward must be something that learners like. Simply because a reward appeals to us does not mean it will necessarily interest members of our class.

Using Nonverbal Signals to Indicate Disapproval

To the extent possible, minor episodes of misbehavior need to be handled so that the flow of the lesson is not interrupted. Nonverbal responses allow us to indicate to a learner that an inappropriate behavior has been noted. Such responses tell learners that they are being given time to correct their behavior and, thereby, to avoid more serious consequences. Nonverbal signals include direct eye contact, hand signals, and facial expressions. These are useful tools in managing learner behavior in the classroom (Grubaugh, 1989).

Using Proximity Control

A minor behavior problem will often disappear when the teacher moves to the area of the classroom where it is occurring because many learners are less inclined to misbehave when the teacher is nearby. When a problem arises during a large-group lesson, often we can eliminate it simply by walking quietly to the part of the room where it is occurring. Often this can be done without interrupting the flow of the lesson.

Proximity control; that is, moving close to individual learners, helps prevent discipline problems and also allows the teacher to monitor learner progress carefully.

Using a Learner's Name in the Context of a Lesson

Using a learner's name during a lesson informs the learner that his or her inappropriate behavior has been noted. It works something like this: If we notice that John's attention is drifting during a discussion of explorers, we can say something like, "Now, if John were a member of the crew sailing for the New World, he would have to—." The use of a learner's name will often result in a quick cessation of the inappropriate behavior.

Redirecting Learner Attention

Redirecting learner attention is especially useful for those of us who work with very young children, but also is sometimes effective with older learners. The idea is to watch class members carefully and take action to redirect misbehaving learners to a more productive pattern of behavior. A few brief words from us to lead the learner back to the assigned task often are all that is required.

Encouraging Learners to Take Personal Action

Encouraging learners to take personal action when they are tempted to misbehave is implemented more frequently in elementary schools than in secondary schools.

The children are taught to take some specific action when they feel compelled to act inappropriately. This approach is designed to give them time to reflect about what they are considering doing. It provides them with a chance to reestablish their self-control.

Sometimes young learners are taught to put their heads on the desk, clench their fists, or count to 10 when they sense themselves to be on the verge of misbehaving. These actions give the learners opportunities to relax and unwind before they do something that they might regret (Brophy, 1983).

In other classrooms, learners are urged to move to another part of the room and talk softly to themselves about the problem they are facing and possible responses they might make. This procedure works best when we have taken time to teach learners the process of coping with problems by thinking about them aloud (Camp & Bash, 1981).

Category 2: Providing Situational Assistance

Responses in this category require more direct teacher intervention than those in category one. When teacher actions associated with category one have not been effective, then category two options should be considered. These actions are a little more direct and intrusive. In using them, we are taking assertive actions to help learners exercise self-control and responsibility. Our focus is on preserving the dignity of the learners and in dealing with the problems in a relatively private manner.

Taking Time for a Quiet Word

To implement taking time out for a quiet word, we move toward the misbehaving learner. We quietly remind this person of the kind of behavior that is expected. Once we have delivered this message, we quickly resume teaching the lesson.

Providing a Rule Reminder

Providing a rule reminder represents a slight escalation from taking time for a quiet word. When a behavior problem occurs, we stop the lesson and speak to the misbehaving learner or learners in a voice loud enough for the whole class to hear. This is an example of a rule-reminder statement: "Bill's group, what does our list of class rules say about not talking when someone is asking a question?"

Removing the Learner from the Situation

To implement removal of a misbehaving learner, we arrange for the offending learner to move. We might require this person go to a different seat nearby or to another part of the room. Instructions related to this movement are brief, direct, and nonconfrontational: "Mary, take your material and go to the empty table. Continue working there." We might also remove the offender to a time-out area. When implemented, this strategy should be carried out quickly and quietly without a display of anger. Arguments can be avoided by simply stating, "Go to the time-out seat. We will talk later."

Responding with Clarity and Firmness

If some of the previous techniques have failed to squelch inappropriate behavior, more intrusive actions are required. Sometimes it is necessary to address a learner by name, using a clear, direct, authoritative, no-nonsense tone of voice. In implementing this approach, we make eye contact with the learner we are addressing, and our demeanor takes on an I-mean-business character as we specify the behavior that must stop and what must replace it.

Arranging Conferences with Misbehaving Learners

A next step often is an individual conference with the offending learner. During the conference, we explain exactly what must be done to correct the behavior problem. Threats are kept to a minimum. Typically, we identify the problem, share our feelings about it, and ask the learner what might be done to solve it.

Some conferences conclude with the preparation of a "behavior contract" that specifies what the learner will do. Behavior contracts often mention some good things that will result if the contract terms are met. Frequently there also are references to consequences that will follow if the unacceptable pattern of behavior continues.

Asking Parents for Help

Beginning teachers sometimes are nervous about talking to parents. They shouldn't be. Parents often are the best allies we teachers have. Nearly all of them are concerned about the progress and behavior of their children. Parents may be unaware that their child is misbehaving in school. Often a call to a parent to explain what is going on will result in an excellent cooperative plan to solve the problem.

Involving parents does not always lead to the desired result, however. The success of involving them in situations related to misbehavior in school depends on many variables. The age level of the learner is a factor, as is the kind of relationship the learner has with his or her parents. The nature of our approach when contacting a parent is also important. In general, we should emphasize our interest in working together to solve the problem rather than assigning blame for inappropriate behaviors.

Category 3: Implementing Consequences

After responses in categories one and two have been tried with no success, or if the misbehavior is very serious, then learners need to experience the consequences of their actions. Consequences are most effective when they are used infrequently and are appropriate to the nature of the offense.

Losing a Privilege

Loss of a privilege functions as an effective punishment for some young people. The success of this approach rests on learners having some privileges available to them. Depending on age levels, these privileges might vary from a classroom job (such as taking care of erasers) to promises of seats in favored sections at athletic events to opportunities to go on out-of-town field trips. To be effective, learners must genuinely value the privilege that is taken away. If they do not, then our action is unlikely to influence their patterns of behavior.

Loss of a privilege works better if the privilege is not taken away permanently. The possibility that a valued privilege might be restored in exchange for a modification of behavior sometimes acts as a potent motivator for young people.

Providing for In-Class Isolation

In some elementary classrooms, teachers designate a certain part of the classroom as an area where misbehaving learners are sent. Often these areas are located in places where it is hard for offending learners to interact with others and observe what other class members are doing.

Sometimes people who have been sent to these isolated areas of the classroom are allowed to continue working on assignments. At other times, they are asked to reflect on the nature of their misbehavior and their ideas for change. Occasionally, learners are told to go to these areas and simply sit quietly. Many younger children find the resultant boredom to be an undesirable consequence.

Removing the Learner

If serious misbehavior persists, it may be necessary to remove a learner from the classroom. When this happens, the learner is often sent to the office of the principal or a counselor. Initially, the objective is not for the principal or counselor to work with the individual; rather, the idea is to send the learner to an area supervised by another professional. Learners are never sent to unsupervised areas such as hallways. If an accident occurred and a learner were injured in such an unsupervised area, we, as the responsible teacher, might be liable for negligence.

Making Up Wasted Time

When we feel that a learner's misbehavior has resulted in class time not being used effectively, we can require the offending individual to make up the wasted time. Depending on the grade level, the learner may be kept in the room during recess or may spend extra time in class either before or after school. It is important that this punishment not be converted into a reward. For example, some learners enjoy chatting informally with teachers. If such activity goes on when wasted time is being made up, this approach to changing an inappropriate behavior pattern may fail.

It is not always possible to insist that misbehaving learners make up wasted time. In some schools, many learners ride buses to and from school. If they are kept after school, they have no way to get home. Many of us who teach also are generally reluctant to keep high school students who have part-time jobs after school.

Category 4: Involving Others

Involving others is a category of last-resort options. When other measures have failed, we must actively involve parents or other educational professionals and arrange a conference to deal with the situation. Those persons included might be administrators, counselors, and personnel from agencies outside the school system.

Involving Parents

There should be initial contact with parents to apprise them of the problem and seek their help in solving it before a formal conference is scheduled. If a conference proves necessary, we must prepare for it carefully. This often involves bringing evidence to the conference, including anecdotal records that document specific examples of problem behaviors and dates when they occurred. The best conferences feature a sharing of information and a communal effort to work out a proposed solution. We need to be particularly careful during this kind of a conference to avoid putting parents in a position of feeling that their own adequacy is being questioned.

Arranging Conferences with Other Professionals

Sometimes it is wise to bring together a group of professionals to discuss a learner's unacceptable behavior patterns. Principals, counselors, psychologists, social workers, and others who might attend need to be introduced ahead of time to documentation regarding exactly what the learner has been doing. It is our responsibility as the teacher to prepare this material in advance of the meeting.

A teacher meets with administrators, counselors, and other teachers to discuss possible ways of dealing with a learner who has become a severe discipline problem.

Meetings of this kind often result in the development of a specific action plan. For example, such a group might decide to place the learner in another class, temporarily suspend the learner from school, or assign the learner to a special counselor. The plan typically is put in place under the authority of the school principal. Usually, there are provisions requiring periodic reporting of results to either the school principal or someone whom he or she has designated to watch over the situation.

Building an action plan along the lines suggested in these four categories will help you deal with many of the behavior problems you will encounter in the classrooms. The vast majority of these problems can be corrected using actions chosen from categories one, two, and three. A well-thought-out plan consisting of systematically escalating responses will be of great value as you work to develop a positive and safe classroom environment for your learners.

• Key Ideas in Summary

- Conveying information and managing learners are among the most important responsibilities of teachers. Teaching and managing are closely connected. Good teaching can prevent control problems, and good management establishes an environment for productive teaching.

- Classroom management is concerned with decisions teachers make regarding the organization of time, space, and materials. This organization is designed to facilitate smooth and efficient instruction. Good management produces an environment that reduces the likelihood of discipline problems. It is a product of careful teacher planning.

- Effective classroom teachers make good use of time. They strive to reduce periods when no productive learning activities are occurring. They plan carefully for how to use their time efficiently when beginning each class period, for helping learners to make a smooth transition from one activity to another, and for working individually with learners who need special assistance.

- It is important for teachers to develop routines for handling recurring classroom events. Teachers who have mastered procedures for dealing with regular occurrences are better able to handle unexpected behavioral problems in ways that respond to problems and that are minimally disruptive to the instructional program.

- The goal of disciplinary procedures in the classroom is to teach learners responsibility and self-control. Methods used should be consistent with this aim.

- Effective classroom managers solve most discipline problems themselves. Only occasionally do they require assistance from principals and other school officials. They seek long-term solutions to behavioral problems, and they look for remedies directed at the underlying causes of unacceptable patterns of behavior.

- Several principles are related to appropriate teacher responses to misbehavior in the classroom. Teachers need to respect learners, deal with problems quietly and unobtrusively, distinguish between minor and major problems, and help learners grasp the connection between unacceptable behaviors and unpleasant consequences that come their way as a result.

- Several basic types of teacher power and authority have been identified. These include expert power, referent power, legitimate power, reward power, and coercive power.
- Teacher responses to misbehaviors range across a number of alternatives. These vary from actions designed to allow the teachers to reassert their self-control to those requiring recommendations of groups of professionals with specialized skills.

• Review and Discussion Questions

1. How serious is the problem of classroom management and discipline?
2. What is the relationship between good classroom management and effective teaching?
3. How does the organization of space influence your behavior?
4. What are some specific problems that are likely to arise as the result of poor time management?
5. What are some procedures and routines you would use for recurring and predictable events?
6. What did you learn about your attitude and philosophy of discipline as a result of reading the chapter?
7. What is your response to the idea of negotiation as a metaphor for dealing with discipline?
8. How do you think a teacher can establish the types of power and authority that are associated with what you would call a good classroom?
9. Which of the basic principles of effective discipline are especially important to you?
10. Which of the alternative responses are most comfortable for you? Why?

• Ideas for Field Experiences, Projects, and Enrichment

1. Observe in a classroom and pay special attention to how time is used in the classroom. How much time is spent on tasks other than instruction? What suggestions might you have about making the use of time more efficient?
2. Interview some teachers and ask them about the types of discipline problems that they find occur most frequently. Consider which of the alternative responses you might use in responding to the common problems identified by the teachers.
3. Interview a principal or school district official. Ask about common difficulties experienced by new teachers in the areas of classroom management and discipline.
4. Interview some school learners about their reactions to discipline problems in the schools. What do they see as the major causes of discipline problems? How can you use an understanding of those causes to plan for the classroom?
5. Begin to develop your plan for discipline by thinking about the rules you will need in the classroom, the ways you will organize the classroom, and the types of responses you will use when confronting misbehavior. Share your ideas with your course instructor and ask for comments.

• References

Berliner, D. C. (1984). The half-full glass: A review of research on teaching. In P. L. Hosford (Ed.), *Using what we know about teaching* (pp. 51–77). Alexandria, VA: Association for Supervision and Curriculum Development.

Brophy, J. (1983). Classroom organization and management. *The Elementary School Journal, 83*(4), 265–285.

Bullough, R. J., Jr. (1994). Digging at the roots: Discipline, management, and metaphor. *Action in Teacher Education, 16*(1), 1–10.

Camp, B., & Bash, M. (1981). *Think aloud: Increasing social and cognitive skills: A problem solving program for children (small group program)*. Champaign, IL: Research Press.

Doyle, W. (1986). Classroom organization and management. In M. C. Wittrock (Ed.), *Handbook of research on teaching* (3rd ed., pp. 392–431). New York: Macmillan.

Emmer, E. T., Evertson, C. M., & Anderson, L. (1980). Effective classroom management at the beginning of the school year. *Elementary School Journal, 80*(5), 219–231.

Evertson, C. M. (1989). Improving elementary classroom management: A school-based training program for beginning the year. *Journal of Educational Research, 83*(2), 82–90.

French, J. R. P., & Raven, B. H. (1959). The bases of social power. In D. Cartwright (Ed.), *Studies in social power* (pp. 118–149). Ann Arbor, MI: University of Michigan Press.

Grubaugh, S. (1989). Nonverbal language techniques for better classroom management and discipline. *High School Journal, 73*(1), 34–40.

Jones, F. H. (1979). The gentle art of classroom discipline. *National Elementary Principal, 58*(4), 26–32.

Jones, V. F., &, Jones, L. S. (1986). *Comprehensive classroom management: Creating positive learning environments* (2nd ed.). Boston: Allyn and Bacon.

Kounin, J. (1970). *Discipline and good management in the classroom*. New York: Holt, Rinehart and Winston.

McLaughlin, H. J. (1994). From negation to negotiation: Moving away from the management metaphor. *Action in Teacher Education, 16*(1), 75–84.

Savage, T. V. (1991). *Discipline for self-control*. Englewood Cliffs, NJ: Prentice Hall.

Smith, H. A. (1987). Nonverbal communication. In M. J. Dunkin (Ed.), *The international encyclopedia of teaching and teacher education* (pp. 466–476). New York: Pergamon Press.

Smyth, W. J. (1987). Time. In M. J. Dunkin (Ed.), *The international encyclopedia of teaching and teacher education* (pp. 372–380). New York: Pergamon Press.

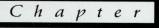

4

The Curriculum

OBJECTIVES

- Point out some basic characteristics of curricula that reflect a needs-of-learners orientation.
- Summarize several advantages and disadvantages of planning curricula that are consistent with a needs-of-learners orientation.
- Describe characteristics of an academic-subject-matter orientation to curriculum planning.
- Point out some advantages and disadvantages of academic-subject-centered curricula.
- Explain features of curricula that are organized according to a broad-fields approach.
- Describe characteristics of a needs-of-society orientation to curriculum planning.
- Point out some advantages and disadvantages of using a needs-of-society orientation as a basis for curriculum planning.
- Describe typical content patterns in elementary and secondary schools.

The term *curriculum* comes from a Latin word that refers to a track for running. Over the years, the term has come to mean a running sequence of learning experiences. In a modern school setting, the curriculum reflects decisions that have been made relating to the selection and organization of content and learning experiences. The nature of these decisions varies from place to place. Even within individual buildings, not all teachers agree about the characteristics of a good school program.

A school's curriculum acts as a kind of screen or filter. Because possible information that might be taught far exceeds the time available for us to teach it, there is a need for a mechanism to establish priorities. That is what a curriculum does — it reflects decisions about the goals of education and the kinds of content and learning experiences that should be provided to help our learners achieve them. Because different people have different values, their educational priorities differ. Larry Cuban (1993), a leading historian of school practices, has pointed out that debates about what should be included in curricula "fire passions, grab headlines, and lead off the evening news" (p. 183).

Some people in our profession are strongly committed to a learner-centered approach that emphasizes learners' individual needs more than subject-matter content. Those who subscribe to this position see personal development as the most important obligation of the school.

Others are convinced that schools should be devoted to helping young people move smoothly into the workplace. They believe that we educators should carefully analyze the needs of society and develop instructional programs that will prepare our learners to meet them. Many supporters of this view are concerned that learner-centered programs may not provide young people with useful employment skills.

Still others reject both learner-centered and needs-of-society approaches. They fear that learner-centered programs lack intellectual rigor. They also like to point out that the needs of society change frequently and hence do not provide dependable guidelines for planning and organizing school learning experiences. Many in our profession who reject these two approaches argue that school programs should be built around the traditional academic disciplines (English, history, mathematics, etc.).

These three basic views are widely represented in our schools today. Partisans of each position are sincere in believing their view to be the best or the most responsible. Differences in priorities reflected in these positions underscore the difficulties that policymakers face when they make decisions about what must be taught. Whatever approaches they take are likely to be applauded by some people and attacked by others.

CURRICULA BASED ON NEEDS OF LEARNERS

An early proponent of focusing on the needs of individual learners was eighteenth-century philosopher Jean-Jacques Rousseau. As he studied the world, Rousseau concluded that human civilization was corrupt. He rejected the idea that learners should be educated to meet the needs of society. In his view, this would result in an irresponsible transmission of corrupt social values from generation to generation.

This teacher examines a curriculum guide supplied by a commercial publisher of textbooks.

Rousseau believed that children were born good, and whatever evil might come to characterize them later in life was imposed by society's negative influences. To remedy this situation, Rousseau believed that the school should protect children from society and furthermore should let the children's naturally good instincts unfold with a minimum of disruption.

Rousseau was convinced that people pass through four distinct growth phases on the way to maturity. From birth to age 5, perceptual skills and muscle coordination develop. At this stage, Rousseau recommended that educators protect children from social restraints and allow them to experience directly the consequences of their own actions.

During the next stage, from ages 8 through 12, Rousseau recommended that there be no formal education. The child should simply be allowed to do what comes naturally. Rousseau felt that personal experience alone was a sufficient teacher for young people in this age group.

Rousseau believed that education should become a formal enterprise during the next chronological stage. During the years from ages 12 to 15, children should be exposed to teachers who would make learning opportunities available to them. Instruction should not be heavy-handed or prescriptive. Teachers should function primarily as motivators, and their roles should be to stimulate learners' curiosity to the extent that they would want to study such subjects as astronomy, geography, and agriculture.

Rousseau saw the final stage of development occurring between the ages of 15 and 20. During this time, he believed that individuals developed refined human-relations skills, an appreciation of beauty, and a sense of personal and religious values. Young people in this age group should be encouraged, but certainly not forced, to study such subjects as religion and ethics.

The needs-of-learners orientation to curriculum has influenced the development of educational programs for many years. For example, many curricular innovations directed at "humanizing" school programs are linear descendants of the beliefs of Rousseau. Perhaps the best-known American to be associated with learner-centered education was the eminent American educational philosopher John Dewey. Dewey believed that the curriculum should be constructed out of the actual experience and curiosity of the child. However, Dewey did not reject inclusion of traditional subject matter; he believed this academic content, when included, should be organized in such a way that it related to learners' life experiences.

Advantages of Curricula Based on Learners' Needs

Probably the most important strength of needs-of-learners programs is that they place concern for individual learners at the heart of the planning process. Such programs remind us of our responsibilities to serve young people and provide experiences that will help them to live rich and fulfilling lives.

Learning experiences associated with this orientation have the potential to break down artificial barriers among subject areas. When the interests of young people become the basis for planning and organizing courses, then we are able to draw specific information from a wide selection of academic specialties. This approach frees knowledge from its artificial compartmentalization into the traditional disciplines. It can also support our efforts to develop highly motivating learning environments.

Disadvantages of Curricula Based on Learners' Needs

Critics of curricula based on learners' needs often focus on the issue of efficiency. They point out that our efforts to diagnose and respond to special needs of each individual are not cost-effective; nor is it practical for us to create unique programs designed to meet the special needs of each learner. Some specific kinds of content, these people argue, should be mastered by all learners, regardless of their levels of initial interest.

There is some concern, too, that learners may be poor judges of their own real needs and will opt for academic experiences that are shallow. The net result of their poor decisions may be graduates who are ill-equipped for the demands of living in a complex, technological society.

CURRICULA BASED ON ACADEMIC SUBJECT MATTER

Throughout history, one of the most common ways to organize the curriculum has been to divide it along the lines of academic subjects. Even in Roman times, educational programs were separated into subjects based on the assumption that there were disciplines (or bodies of knowledge) that grouped together elements of content that were related in some natural way. Learning was thought to be easier when young people were introduced to knowledge that had been organized into academic subjects such as mathematics or music.

Many people who organize school curricula around academic subjects believe that scholars in individual disciplines have developed reliable, responsible, and precise ways of knowing about the world. They contend that there is merit in insisting that our learners master certain kinds of information. It is alleged that mastery of this content will enable young people to gain control of their own destinies. Indeed, some bodies of knowledge are considered so important that they are absolutely critical for everyone. Subjects that have frequently been denoted as essential for all of our learners include English, history, science, and mathematics. Usually, courses dealing with these major subject areas are mandated by state law.

Exactly *which* subjects are musts for our learners has been the subject of considerable debate. Perhaps not surprisingly, scholars in each subject have found compelling reasons for placing a very heavy emphasis on their own specializations. (Mathematicians bemoan the public's lack of mathematical literacy, geographers decry the public's lack of geographic literacy, economists despair over the public's lack of economic literacy, and on and on.) Conflicts among supporters of different academic subjects have become familiar events in state capitals throughout the nation, as legislators have called on expert witnesses to help them define the essential elements of a "basic education."

Some people have maintained that our emphasis should not be on having learners master factual content associated with each subject, but instead on introducing learners to the organizational features of each discipline. Initial interest in the "structure of the disciplines" (the organization of the individual academic subjects and how professionals in these disciplines ask and answer questions) developed after the former Soviet Union launched the earth satellite *Sputnik* in 1957.

Supporters of the structure-of-the-disciplines emphasis believed that many school practices featured too much attention on isolated facts. They favored instead new programs that would help young people to recognize basic principles associated with each major subject area. The idea was to develop learners' thinking abilities and engage them in learning activities that, to the extent possible, paralleled problem-solving procedures used by professional academic scholars in each subject area. There was great interest in this approach through the 1960s and into the early 1970s. An underlying theme was that learners who became thoroughly familiar with the structures of the academic disciplines during their school years would enter college ready to do more advanced work.

Beginning in the 1970s, concerns about the Vietnam War, treatment of minorities at home, and other social issues eroded support for a strong structure-of-the-disciplines emphasis. Mandates for academic programs emphasizing equity and fairness dominated much of the educational debate in the 1970s.

In the 1980s, there was renewed interest in programs with a traditional academic subject focus, but the reform reports of the 1980s tended to promote school programs that sought to familiarize learners with the *findings* of academic specialists, not with the structures of their disciplines. Concerns about the nation's relative intellectual and economic competitiveness prompted critics to call for school programs that would produce graduates who were well-grounded in academics, particularly in content associated with mathematics and the sciences.

During the middle and late 1980s and continuing into the middle 1990s, some critics of school practices expressed increasing concern about whether teachers had adequate preparation in the academic subjects they were teaching. In response to these concerns, many teacher preparation programs have extended the length of their programs. Others, while continuing to offer traditional four-year teacher certification schedules, have increased content requirements in the fields students have been preparing to teach.

Advantages of Curricula Organized Around Academic Subject Matter

Individual subjects tend to organize content that contains many common elements. For example, mathematics courses of all kinds have much more common content than would be found in a course that contained content blended from English and French. The common focus of each academic discipline is thought to make learning easier, as exposure to information in a single discipline introduces our learners to content that is limited in scope and logically related.

As the most traditional form of organizing school programs, this pattern enjoys a certain respectability because of its long familiarity to parents and other patrons of the school. School programs organized in this way provide an aura of stability and continuity that many people find attractive. Teachers, for example, may appreciate the security of knowing that they will be teaching familiar subjects. Administrators generally feel confident in explaining this kind of organizational pattern to parents.

The vast majority of school textbooks are organized on the assumption that they will be used in programs based on traditional academic subjects. For example, there are separate books for classes in mathematics, English, and biology. Textbooks that represent a fusion of content from several academic disciplines are less common. Since the textbook continues to be a widely used instructional resource, it acts as an influence to support an academic-subject-matter orientation throughout the school program.

Today, there is great interest in holding schools and teachers accountable for their performance. Often learners' scores on standardized tests of achievement are used by people who are interested in making comparisons of the relative excellence of individual schools. Though testing specialists often decry this practice, pointing

School programs built around traditional academic disciplines are familiar to parents. This familiarity often makes them less controversial than programs constructed around other approaches.

out that many variables other than the quality of the instructional program can affect test scores, the political reality is that these scores are scrutinized with great interest by the general public. For the most part, standardized tests are organized around traditional academic subjects. Hence, school curricula that reflect an academic-subject-matter organizational pattern may deliver information to learners in ways similar to how it appears on standardized tests.

Disadvantages of Curricula Organized Around Academic Subject Matter

Even though individual academic subjects have a certain internal consistency, it is by no means clear that the world is organized into history, mathematics, English, biology, and other separate subjects. Our learners do not encounter a reality that is neatly sliced and filed into individual disciplines. Since reality is not divided into individual subject areas, some critics of the academic-subject-matter orientation suggest that the school curriculum should be more interdisciplinary in character. That is, individual courses should be organized in a way that allows content to be drawn from many sources.

Other critics argue that dividing school programs into packages associated with academic disciplines inhibits transfer and integration of knowledge. For

Is Relevance Irrelevant?

Sondra McPhee put down the report from the National Center for Educational Statistics. She nodded her head in agreement with its finding that eighth graders believed their social studies classes to have much less relevance for their future lives than their classes in English, mathematics, and science. As a second-year grade 8 U.S. history teacher, Sondra's own observations squared perfectly with this conclusion. She had frequently told anyone who would listen, "My kids just don't seem to care. I think I'm simply boring them to death."

The national report convinced Sondra that her problem wasn't unique and something needed to be done. She spent weeks reading everything she could find about motivation, eighth graders, junior high school social studies, and, most particularly, ideas for inspiring the Hispanic and African-American young people who accounted for about 70 percent of her learners. Late one Saturday afternoon, after several nonproductive hours in the library, she stumbled onto some information about oral history lessons. She dug into the material with increasing enthusiasm. This is *it*, she said to herself.

A few weeks later, she went to visit her principal, Viola Gutierrez. She told Dr. Gutierrez that she had some ideas for changing the grade 8 social studies program, explaining that she wanted to orient the course around the use of oral history techniques. She wanted her Hispanic students to interview their parents and relatives about experiences that they and their ancestors had had during the bloody Mexican revolution of the early twentieth century. She wanted her African-American students to gather information on such issues as patterns of living in the days before the civil rights movement. She pointed out to Dr. Gutierrez that her students would see the topics as relevant, and researchers had found oral history lessons to be highly motivating.

Dr. Gutierrez, a cautious administrator, was noncommittal, but told Sondra that she would think about her ideas. Three weeks later, Sondra found a note in her box from Dr. Gutierrez, asking her to come in during her planning period to talk about the oral history proposal.

Dr. Gutierrez expressed appreciation to Sondra for her willingness to innovate and for her professionalism in searching out pertinent research literature to support her case. Then she went on to say that she was going to deny permission for the oral history project. She proceeded to explain her reasons. *(continues on p. 83)*

instance, some of our learners may produce flawless prose in their English classes but in other classes turn in papers with many mistakes, assuming the attitude: This is history. We aren't *supposed* to write perfect papers here. That's for English. Here we learn names and dates.

Some learners complain that the learning experiences they encounter in the traditional academic subjects are irrelevant. For example, a student studying algebra might ask, "Why should I study this stuff? What good is it?" Although content from algebra certainly does have some important links to real life, many learners fail to make the connection between the content of the course and the demands of life beyond the school.

First of all, Dr. Gutierrez pointed out, the course text didn't emphasize the Mexican Revolution, nor did it deal much with the lives of African-Americans in the years before 1960. She went on to remind Sondra that the state tested all eighth graders at the end of the school year, and test items tended to be drawn from content covered in the adopted textbook.

Dr. Gutierrez also emphasized that very few parents had experienced an oral history approach when they were in school, and many of them might be skeptical of the technique. It was her experience that most parents seemed to prefer textbook-based reading assignments accompanied by traditional homework. If an oral history project was started, some influential parents might view the oral history project as an attempt to "water down" the history program.

Finally, Dr. Gutierrez pointed out that the administrators at the district's high school continued to be concerned about the lack of subject-matter preparation junior high school graduates had when they entered grade 9. She indicated that the school simply couldn't take a chance that an oral history program would make students appear to be even less prepared for high school than they currently were.

What does Sondra view as one of the most important problems she faces as a teacher? Does her sense of priorities tell us anything about her values? In light of her view of her problems in the classroom, what does Sondra see as appropriate and professional responses to them? What do we learn about the kinds of information Sondra believes relevant to a decision about her proposal to introduce oral history into her instructional program? How do others mentioned in this discussion weigh the relative importance of the information Sondra values?

What does Dr. Gutierrez view as the primary responsibilities of teachers in her building? How do her perceptions differ from Sondra's? What forces in her professional life might have acted to shape her world view? We do not get direct evidence here of parents' feelings. We get only Dr. Gutierrez's opinions regarding what these feelings might be. Is Dr. Gutierrez accurately reporting how parents feel, or is she consciously or unconsciously biasing her reports of their feelings because of her own personal attitudes?

What do you think Sondra should do now? Are there others she should involve? Are there ways to bridge differences in perceptions of the various "players" in this situation?

Broad-Fields Curriculum

An approach that seeks to respond to certain criticisms of curricula that have been organized around academic subjects is the *broad-fields curriculum*. In this scheme, two or more traditional subjects are combined into a broad area. These areas sometimes center on large themes such as industrialism or evolution. We can use these themes to prepare lessons that draw on knowledge from several subject areas. This approach has been promoted as a means of breaking down barriers that separate knowledge into individual academic disciplines. It is assumed that learners who are exposed to broad-fields programs will develop the ability to transfer what they have learned to new situations.

This approach is not without its problems. One major difficulty is that few of us who teach possess a breadth of knowledge in multiple academic disciplines. This can be a barrier as we seek to identify and utilize relevant content from a wide variety of sources. It can also lead to trivialized treatment of important subject matter (Harrison, 1990). In addition, few college and university courses that prepare teachers are organized according to a broad-fields approach. Hence, not many of us teaching in the schools have a high level of comfort with broad-fields programs as a result of our having personally encountered content organized in this way.

CURRICULA BASED ON THE NEEDS OF SOCIETY

According to W. H. Schubert, "Part of the reason for the existence of schools is that they fulfill social needs. Societies ostensibly establish schools to help further their goals and promote their values in successive generations" (1986, p. 217). Curricula developed from this perspective may be one of several basic types. Among them are curricula organized according to a problems approach and those designed to promote citizenship development.

The *problems approach* has been favored by educators who believe that schools should provide experiences designed to help our learners develop skills and insights relevant to solving pressing social problems. Supporters contend that the schools are institutions charged with ensuring social survival. They maintain that to accomplish this objective, young people should be introduced during their school years to problems that challenge our social order. Such exposure is designed to produce future citizens who will be willing to confront problems and work for their solution.

Proponents of *citizenship development* point out that adult members of our society need certain basic skills in order to make a contribution. Programs consistent with this emphasis place a high priority on teaching what will be useful to learners in their adult years. Vocational education of all kinds is assigned a high priority. Some partisans of this view are suspicious of school experiences that do not have a clear relationship to what our young people will be encountering as working adults.

The citizenship-development approach has appealed to many pragmatically oriented Americans. Frequently, attacks on so-called frills in school programs are reflections of the concerns of people who want our schools to concentrate more heavily on providing learning experiences more clearly relevant to the future careers and vocational needs of learners.

Advantages of Curricula Organized Around the Needs of Society

Content for school programs associated with this perspective is drawn from a variety of academic subjects. This arrangement helps break down the idea that knowledge must be compartmentalized into artificial categories labeled history, English, mathematics, physics, or something else. Needs-of-society curricula help our young people integrate knowledge from a variety of sources as they use it to make sense of the world as it really is.

Supporters also point to the motivational advantages of organizing programs around reality. For example, if a class we are teaching is oriented toward a career in which some of our learners are interested, they are likely to have a personal desire to learn the material. A learner might find it much easier to master mathematics in the context of studying to become a pilot than by plodding through a traditional mathematics textbook page by page.

There is also an important motivational appeal that often accompanies a focus on important social problems. Our learners can see the relevance of a topic such as consumer rights more easily than one such as decision making in ancient Sparta. Social problems will likely have been discussed in learners' homes. Many of our learners prefer to study issues of concern to their parents, friends, and others in the community beyond the school.

Disadvantages of Curricula Organized Around the Needs of Society

A major problem of the needs-of-society emphasis is the difficulty we face in identifying just which needs to address in school programs. There is a danger that these

The belief that students should develop leadership skills as part of the school experience is consistent with the needs-of-society orientation.

will be identified in haste and the programs we develop will be excessively narrow in scope and nonsubstantive in content.

The rapidity with which needs change also poses difficulties. Some problems pass away; new problems emerge. Over time, technical changes alter job requirements tremendously. When we view needs too narrowly, there is a danger that our instruction will provide learners with information that will be obsolete by the time they leave school. Poorly conceived programs may also produce school graduates who lack the flexibility needed to adapt easily to changing conditions.

Some critics of programs organized around needs of society contend that they encourage our young people to make career choices too early in their school years. Learners who express a personal interest based on a whim or enthusiasm of the moment may find themselves tracked into a set of courses relevant for only a limited number of career options. It may prove difficult for them to switch to another preparation sequence when their interests change.

Needs-of-society programs that focus heavily on social problems sometimes draw criticism from parents and other community members. They may fear that this kind of instruction will impose what they believe to be inappropriate values or perspectives. These concerns have made school authorities in some places hesitant to organize school programs around a social-problems emphasis.

BOX 4-1

Relative Attractiveness of Different Teaching Assignments

Assume you are a newly certified teacher who is faced with the task of deciding which of two job offers to accept. Salaries and general working conditions are about the same in each place, and in both positions you will be expected to teach five classes a day at the high school level. Your assignments for each district would be as follows:

School District One	**School District Two**
American history	Technology and society
American history	Technology and society
World history	(Planning period)
(Planning period)	Militarism
World history	Militarism
World geography	Dynamics of leadership

How would you feel about accepting a position in either of these districts given these prospective teaching assignments?

What Do You Think?

1. In general, would you prefer district one or district two?
2. For which teaching assignments do you have the better college or university preparation? Why do you think so?
3. In which situation do you think you would experience the most difficulty in locating appropriate instructional materials? Why?
4. How do you think learners would react to the courses in the two districts? Why do you think so?

BASIC PATTERNS IN ELEMENTARY AND SECONDARY SCHOOLS

Although there are some place-to-place differences, much uniformity can be found among the basic programs offered in most of the nation's elementary, middle, junior high, and senior high schools. Guidelines governing general categories of information to be taught are often included in state regulations governing education.

Elementary school programs nearly always include instruction in these areas:

- reading and language arts
- mathematics
- social studies
- science
- health
- physical education
- fine arts

It is very common in elementary schools for reading instruction to occur at the beginning of the day. Reading is considered to be a critically important subject, and many educators believe that pupils should be exposed to its instruction when they are well rested and ready to learn.

The amount of time devoted to each subject area in elementary schools varies from place to place. In some parts of the country, there are strict state regulations mandating that minimum amounts of time be devoted each day to certain high-priority areas of the curriculum. In other areas, no such guidelines exist, and time-allocation decisions are left to local districts, principals, and individual teachers. Because proficiency in reading is a key to academic success in so many other areas, nearly all elementary school teachers devote a great deal of time to reading instruction. Recent unfavorable comparisons of U.S. learners' proficiency in mathematics and science as compared to learners in other countries have tended to prompt increased emphases on these subjects in elementary school programs (Smith et al., 1994). Increasingly, too, elementary schools are providing basic instruction in computers.

Middle school and junior high school programs tend to feature many of the same subjects taught in elementary schools. Particularly in grades 7 and 8, options for students with different interests and abilities are available. Several mathematics options may be available, for example; some students may take algebra, others may choose a less rigorous course, and still others may enroll in a more challenging class. Unlike the situation that prevails in most elementary schools, at the junior high school level, students are allowed to take some elective courses.

The programs at the senior high school level are largely driven by state and local high school graduation requirements. These requirements vary somewhat from place to place, but patterns tend to converge around a set that prescribes a minimum number of years or semesters of high school instruction in English/language arts, mathematics, science, and physical education. In many places, there are now requirements that students achieve certain levels of computer literacy. However, large numbers of electives are also available to high school students.

Many reform reports that were issued in the 1980s recommended more work to be required for high school graduation in certain so-called basic subjects, including English, mathematics, social studies, and science. For example, the National Commission on Excellence in Education, in its report *A Nation at Risk: The Imperative for Educational Reform* (1983), called for changes in high school graduation requirements that would require all students to complete a minimum of four years of English, three years of science, three years of social studies, and three years of mathematics. By the late 1980s, there was evidence that these recommendations were having an influence. Whereas only 12.7 percent of all high school graduates in 1982 had taken the number of courses in English, science, social studies, and mathematics recommended by the Commission on Excellence in Education, by 1992 this figure had increased to 46.8 percent (Smith et al., 1994, p. 74).

These figures suggest that more students are taking more of the designated basic courses. What they do not reveal is the nature of the content that these learners are encountering in the courses. At best, displays of curricular programs provide a sketchy outline of what goes on in schools. The real school program continues to be shaped by the actions of teachers as they work with learners in individual classrooms.

THE HIDDEN CURRICULUM

Our schools teach learners more than the topics introduced in the formal, written curriculum. They are also greatly influenced by their exposure to what experts have variously described as the "implicit" or "hidden" curriculum. The hidden curriculum includes all of those things in the school setting that send our learners messages regarding what they ought to be doing and even how they should be thinking. Gail McCutcheon notes that "the hidden curriculum can be thought of as having two characteristics: (1) it is not intended, and (2) it is transmitted through the everyday, normal goings-on in schools" (1988, p. 191).

Curriculum researcher Decker Walker (1990) has pointed out other features of the hidden curriculum. These include (1) teachers' general expectations about how learners should control their emotions in class, (2) what learners should do when there is a need to move from one area of the classroom to another, and (3) how learners should act when they wish to participate in a discussion.

Our actions as teachers help shape the hidden curriculum in our own classrooms. We send signals to learners about what we consider important. If we are unconscious of our hidden-curriculum actions, we may not realize that we are sending unintended messages to members of our class. For example, suppose we are teaching social studies at the high school level. Frequently, we make a point of telling our students that they should read articles on the front page of the newspaper every day because good citizens keep up on current events. If our students see us during morning, lunch, or after-school breaks reading only the sports section, however, they may well conclude that we are insincere. We may *say* the hard news on the front page is important, but we really only pay attention to sports. The "lesson" these students take away from this experience is the kind of thing young people learn from their exposure to the hidden curriculum. In the case of this social studies example, this kind of learning has little to do with either the formal, pre-scribed curriculum or with the teacher's academic intentions.

Some authorities who have studied the hidden curriculum fear that it some-times sends messages to learners that are inconsistent with the values of their own cultural or social group. For example, curriculum experts Michael Apple and Lan-don Beyer (1988) note that the hidden curriculum in many schools emphasizes def-erence to authority and an attitude that competence in school subjects will result in high status and lucrative jobs for graduates. Many learners find these perspec-tives inconsistent with the attitudes of their parents, families, and friends, and hence they may reject the entire school program as irrelevant.

Nearly all authorities agree that the hidden curriculum influences learners' atti-tudes toward the school program. There is a consensus that we should develop a sensitivity to any messages that learners may be getting from our school programs as well as the general school environment. What learners take away from exposure to the hidden curriculum can importantly influence their attitudes toward us as teachers and toward the entire school program.

• Key Ideas in Summary

- The term *curriculum* refers to the selection and organization of content and learning experiences. Because different people use different criteria in making decisions about selection and organization of content, there are important place-to-place variations in elementary and secondary school curricula.
- Curricula that reflect a needs-of-learners orientation are developed as a result of program planners' perceptions of learners' needs and interests. Jean-Jacques Rousseau was an early proponent of this perspective. In this approach, learners are placed at the center of the planning process. These curricula are alleged to motivate learners and avoid unnecessary fragmentation of content. Critics argue that it is impractical to prepare separate academic experiences for each learner's needs and interests. They are also concerned about whether learners are the best judges of their own and society's needs.
- The academic-subject-matter approach to curriculum development divides con-tent into individual disciplines such as mathematics, history, and English. This approach is based on the assumption that material contained within an individ-ual discipline shares certain similarities. These commonalities, it is alleged, make it easier for learners to master the material. Critics of the approach point out that the real world is not divided into separate academic disciplines, and they also note that division of content into packages associated with separate sub-jects fragments learning and makes it difficult for young people to transfer information to situations beyond the setting in which it was learned.
- There have been two general approaches to preparing programs using an acade-mic-subject-matter orientation. The most common of these has featured the development of learning experiences designed to familiarize learners with the findings of subject matter specialists. A second approach has favored familiar-

izing learners with the "structure" of the disciplines. Programs designed in this way seek to introduce young people to the processes that professionals in the disciplines use as they study data and arrive at conclusions.

- Broad-fields curricula attempt to respond to some criticisms that have been made of programs organized around traditional academic disciplines. Broad-fields approaches combine two or more traditional subjects into a single broad area or theme. This theme is used as a basis for planning, and programs are developed that draw content from several disciplines. Broad-fields curricula are promoted on the basis of their capacity for helping learners break down boundaries between and among individual subjects. Problems with the approach include (1) a lack of instructional materials of an interdisciplinary nature and (2) difficulty in finding individual teachers who have enough depth of knowledge in a variety of disciplines that they can draw materials responsibly from a wide selection of content areas.

- Curricula developed according to a needs-of-society orientation are designed to produce learners capable of maintaining and extending broad social goals. These curricula sort into two basic types: some programs focus on content designed to help learners recognize and respond to important problems, and others center on citizenship development. Many of the latter emphasize providing young people with the kinds of skills they will need to make a living. Supporters of these programs suggest that they promote learners' levels of interest because the content is highly relevant to their own lives. Critics suggest that identification of so-called problems may bring teachers into unproductive conflicts with parents and other community members who have different perspectives on these issues. These critics also maintain that vocationally oriented programs may not be responsive to rapid changes in the job market, and school programs may be providing learners with training experiences that will not match up well with the real needs of the employment market they will enter when they leave school.

- Even though there are important place-to-place differences, certain common patterns are found in many elementary and secondary schools. Large numbers of elementary schools require learners to be exposed to instruction focusing on reading and language arts, mathematics, social studies, science, health, and physical education. Increasingly, elementary pupils are also being introduced to the use of computers. In secondary schools (particularly in senior high schools), learners have a number of electives from which to choose. However, they are usually still obligated to take a certain number of courses in such areas as English, social studies, mathematics, science, and physical education. At the secondary level, too, there is an increasing tendency to require students to take at least one computer course.

• Review and Discussion Questions

1. To what does the term *curriculum* refer?
2. What are some characteristics of the needs-of-learners orientation?

3. What are some characteristics of the academic-subject-matter orientation?
4. What are some features of a broad-fields curriculum?
5. What are some characteristics of a needs-of-society orientation?
6. Think about some characteristics of the school programs you experienced during your elementary and secondary school years. Can you identify some aspects of these programs that reflected a needs-of-learners orientation?
7. Some people argue that the entire school program should reflect an academic-subject-matter orientation. What are some strengths and weaknesses of this idea? Today's learners represent a very diverse group. Are there some learners who would profit more than others from such a program? Are there some learners who would be hurt? What is your own position regarding this suggestion?
8. Certain critics argue that our schools are doing a poor job of preparing young people for work in an increasingly technologically complex society. How do you react to this view? If you accept the validity of this contention, what specific changes would you make in the present grades K–12 school program?
9. Supporters of the needs-of-learners orientation point out that learners tend to be motivated by school programs based on this point of view. By implication, are they suggesting that programs developed from the perspectives of the academic-subject-matter orientation and needs-of-society orientation are less motivating? If you agree with these people, what do you think might be done to make school programs based on these orientations more interesting to learners?
10. Some of the reform proposals of the 1980s recommended that students should take more courses in English, mathematics, science, and social studies as requirements for graduation. Does requiring students to take more courses ensure that they will necessarily know more about these subject areas? Why or why not?

• Ideas for Field Experiences, Projects, and Enrichment

1. With the assistance of a school principal or your course instructor, locate in your library a list of subjects taught at two or more grade levels within a given school. From titles and descriptions of these subjects, decide whether they are based on a needs-of-learners orientation, an academic-subject-matter orientation, a needs-of-society orientation, or whether they reflect a combination of two or even all three of these perspectives. Prepare a written report that summarizes your findings.
2. Write a position paper focusing on one of these topics:
   • School programs need to reflect more of a needs-of-learners orientation
   • School programs need to reflect more of an academic-subject-matter orientation
   • School programs need to reflect more of a needs-of-society orientation
3. Examine two or more reform proposals that appeared during the 1980s. (Ask your instructor for suggestions.) Note at least three recommendations for changes in school curricula made in each proposal. Then interview a school principal or a school district curriculum director about changes in local programs made in the last decade. Determine whether any of these changes were in correlation with those suggested in the national reform proposals. Share your findings with members of the class.
4. Interview several teachers within a single building who teach a subject or grade level that interests you. Ask them about state, district, or school requirements for learners who take this subject or who are enrolled at this grade level. Also ask whether these requirements are well suited to learners' needs. Finally, ask these teachers what specific

changes in requirements for students they would recommend. Prepare an oral report of your findings to share with members of your class.

5. Join together with three or four others in your class to prepare a report on one of these topics:
   - What should a "good" elementary school program look like today?
   - What should a "good" middle school or junior high school program look like today?
   - What should a "good" senior high school program look like today?

Present your conclusions in the form of a symposium and then use them as the basis for a short article. Consider sending it to the features editor of your local newspaper.

• References

Apple, M. W., & Beyer, L. E. (1988). Social evaluation. In L. E. Beyer & M. W. Apple (Eds.), *The curriculum: Problems, politics, and possibilities* (pp. 33–49). Albany, NY: State University of New York Press.

Cuban, L. (1993). The lure of curriculum reform and its pitiful history. *Phi Delta Kappan, 75*(2), 182–185.

Harrison, C. J. (1990). Concepts, operational definitions, and case studies in instruction. *Education, 110*, 502–505.

McCutcheon, G. (1988). Curriculum and the work of teachers. In L. E. Beyer & M. W. Apple (Eds.), *The curriculum: Problems, politics, and possibilities* (pp. 191–203). Albany, NY: State University of New York Press.

National Commission on Excellence in Education. (1983). *A nation at risk: The imperative for educational reform*. Washington, DC: U.S. Department of Education.

Schubert, W. H. (1986). *Curriculum: Perspective, paradigm, and possibility*. New York: Macmillan.

Smith, T. M., Rogers, G. T., Alsalam, N., Perie, M., Mahoney, R. P., & Martin, V. (Eds.). (1994). *The condition of education 1994*. Washington, DC: U.S. Department of Education.

Walker, D. F. (1990). *Fundamentals of curriculum*. Orlando, FL: Harcourt Brace Jovanovich.

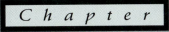

Chapter

5

School Organization and Employees

OBJECTIVES

- Point out basic patterns of school district organization.
- Recognize that the organizational patterns of school districts vary with the size of the learner enrollment.
- Identify some of the kinds of professionals who work in school districts.
- Describe some basic organizational patterns of individual schools.
- Identify responsibilities of different categories of employees who work in individual school buildings.
- Suggest several categories of nonteaching professionals who work in individual school buildings.

Education is big business. In one recent year, expenditures to support the nation's public schools totaled $285 billion (Snyder, 1994). A recent survey determined that there were 4.6 million school employees (Snyder, 1994). In the year of the survey, about 1 American in 50 was a full-time public school employee.

School employees comprise many categories. According to the survey (Snyder, 1994), classroom teachers make up only slightly more than half of the total number (53 percent in 1994). Support staff, including personnel attached to administrative offices, transportation people, food-service personnel, plant-and-maintenance employees, health professionals, and assorted other categories account for about 30 percent of all school employees. Instructional staff other than teachers (classroom aides, instructional media specialists, guidance counselors, and psychological personnel) represent about 12 percent of the total school employment force. The final category, principals and district administrators, account for between 4 and 5 percent of the total.

Leaders of school districts have had to develop sophisticated organizational plans to manage the educational enterprise. Larger school districts have more complex organizational schemes than smaller ones. Similarly, individual schools with many learners also have more intricate organizations than those enrolling fewer learners.

The kinds of contacts teachers have with individuals who play various roles within school districts and buildings vary with district and school enrollment size. For example, teachers in a small elementary school are apt to have frequent (often daily) conversations with the school principal, whereas in a large high school, weeks may go by without a teacher having occasion to speak to the principal. Indeed, in the latter situation, the principal may never step into the teacher's classroom during an entire school year. In large schools, the principal's administrative subordinates often are responsible for handling routine matters with teachers.

There are many employees of school districts with whom individual teachers have infrequent personal contact. For example, much of the custodial work in some districts is done at night after teachers have left for the day. Individual teachers and school nurses (especially in large buildings) rarely have occasion to meet during the working day. Central administrative office support personnel (for example, people assigned to manage the district's transportation system) spend little time in the district's schools. Hence, teachers are not apt to meet many of these individuals.

HOW SCHOOL DISTRICTS ARE ORGANIZED

There are more than 15,000 school districts in the United States (Snyder, 1994). These vary from small operations in isolated rural areas to districts encompassing the densely populated core areas of the nation's major cities. The kind of management scheme needed to oversee the operation of a given district depends, in large measure, on the number of learners enrolled in the district's schools.

Even districts that enroll roughly equivalent numbers of learners reflect some differences in their administrative organizational schemes. These variations result from unique local conditions, special requirements imposed by state education authorities, and long-standing traditions. An example of an organizational scheme for a school district is provided in Figure 5-1.

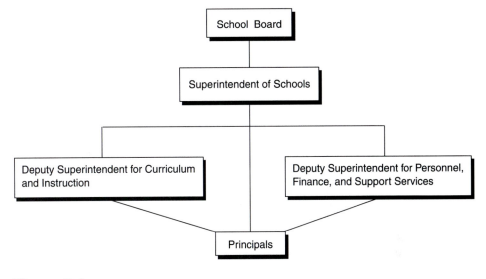

Figure 5-1

Example of the basic administrative organization of a school district

The School Board

The school board is the basic policymaking body of a school district. In some districts, it may be known by other names such as board of education, board of trustees, or school council. School boards represent a link between the local school district and the state department of education. Because the state department of education implements mandates of the state legislature, local school boards are also indirectly linked to the legislature. The state legislature, in fact, exercises ultimate control over local school districts. In most states, the legislature has the right to create, modify, eliminate, and otherwise affect the operation of local school districts.

School boards vary in size, usually containing from five to nine members. Members are elected in most districts; in a few, they are appointed. Members of elected school boards are supposed to reflect general community sentiment regarding the schools. In reality, though, school board members are often well-established community members who reflect mainstream and somewhat conservative thinking. People who agree to serve on school boards often do so as a matter of public service. In many parts of the country, school board members receive no compensation, but they are paid for their work in some places.

The school board's primary responsibility is to establish basic policy for the district. Part of its role is to oversee implementation of state requirements. The school board adopts the budget and reacts to recommendations regarding personnel and curriculum that it receives from the district superintendent and his or her staff.

School board members are among the unheralded heroes of American education. They put in long hours on school-related work. They receive telephone calls late into the night from school patrons who have grievances to air. Their decisions are watched closely by the local media, and sometimes their actions draw negative comments on the editorial pages of local newspapers. Letters to the editor and editorials often question the motives of school board members (and sometimes even their integrity). Angry taxpayers freely let school board members know their displeasure when tax rates have to be hiked to fund school budgets. In short, school board members find themselves torn between the competing perspectives of dozens of contending interest groups, each of which is certain that it holds the key to a policy decision that will improve the schools.

Given the pressures they face, it is a wonder that people want to fill vacancies on school boards. But they do, and in many communities, school board service confers an important status on board members. Schools everywhere are beneficiaries of the willingness of these good people to serve.

Many citizens in local communities believe that school board members are intimately involved in the day-to-day operations of the school, but this generally is not the case. The board directs the superintendent to oversee the running of the school. Its own task is to frame policy and hold the superintendent responsible for implementing it. In some districts, board members do try to involve themselves in operational decisions (see this chapter's Critical Incident). This invariably leads to conflict between the board and the superintendent, which sometimes results in a change of superintendents. Neither the school board nor the superintendent can discharge responsibilities appropriate to each function unless there is trust and confidence on both sides.

These school board members are reviewing the agenda before their meeting begins.

Most school board meetings are open to the public. State laws vary from place to place regarding the kinds of circumstances that allow boards to meet in private (usually called "executive") sessions. Often, boards have the right to do so when they are considering sensitive personnel matters.

At one time, many school boards scheduled their meetings during the day, but this practice is dying out. Increasingly, school boards meet at night to allow members of the community with daytime jobs to attend. It is common practice for school boards to set aside some time after the formal agenda has been completed for members of the public to speak briefly about issues of concern to them. When the board is considering a controversial policy issue (e.g., whether to implement a busing program to establish a racial balance in the district's schools), board meetings are very well attended.

In summary, the school board acts as the district's major policymaking body. It functions as a political entity that allows members of the public to make their influence on school policy decisions felt. At the same time, it represents the broader interests of the state legislature and the state department of education.

The Superintendent of Schools

The superintendent is the chief executive officer (CEO) of a school district. A school district superintendency is a challenging position, particularly in a large school district. In such a setting, executive responsibilities of the superintendent parallel those of top corporate administrators.

Often the superintendent is hired by the school board, but some are chosen in other ways (e.g., some superintendents are publicly elected officials). The superintendent usually attends all school board sessions except for those where his or her own performance is being evaluated. The superintendent, who may argue against a certain course of action when it is being considered by the school board, is obligated to support and implement all school board policies once they have been adopted.

The superintendent exercises some control over the school district's work force because it is the superintendent in most places who officially recommends candidates for employment to the school board. All other employees of the school district are directly or indirectly accountable to the superintendent. Even though specific responsibilities may be delegated to others, ultimately the superintendent is held accountable for their performance.

The superintendent is responsible for all aspects of the school program. For example, he or she monitors all academic programs and arranges for periodic status reports to the school board. The superintendent oversees the maintenance of all school buildings and equipment and approves expenditures of funds within the general guidelines authorized by the school board.

The superintendent works closely with administrative subordinates to ensure smooth functioning of the entire district operation. One of the superintendent's most important jobs is overseeing the preparation of the annual budget, which must be submitted to the school board for review and approval. Budget proposals always attract a great deal of scrutiny from board members and from the public at large.

Critical Incident

A Visit from the School Board

Woong Kim teaches second grade in a suburban district outside of a major West Coast city. He is in his second year of teaching. Woong is particularly interested in teaching reading. As an undergraduate, he was influenced by several of his professors who believed in a whole-language approach to reading instruction. This method builds on learners' natural patterns of oral language, and Woong has found it to be effective in working with his own pupils. Members of his class are a diverse group representing many ethnic groups, some of whom do not speak English at home. Large numbers of families in the area have incomes below the official poverty level.

Loretta Robinson, a newly elected member of the local school board, recently sent a letter to all of the district's elementary school teachers. In the letter, she pointed to some research studies that strongly support the use of a phonics approach to reading. Ms. Robinson went on to note that standardized reading test scores of children in the district are well below national averages, and recommended that teachers adopt the phonics approach to teaching reading. Ms. Robinson indicated that she would be contacting selected teachers in the district later in the year regarding what they were doing to improve their reading programs.

Woong recalled that the university professors who favored the whole-language approach had not had many good things to say about phonics-based reading instruction. Many of them had cited research supporting whole-language instruction that seemed to say quite different things from those studies mentioned in Ms. Robinson's letter.

To get another point of view, Woong checked with his grade-level leader and principal. Both of them said that district policy prescribes no specific method of reading instruction. Teachers are assumed to be professionals who are expected to make instructional decisions

The superintendent, as the chief public relations officer of the school district, must defend school policies in many public forums. Superintendents are often called upon to speak before civic groups and other citizens' organizations. They tend to be individuals who are comfortable with many different kinds of people. Because public relations is such an important part of the job, many superintendents have exemplary writing and speaking skills.

The Deputy Superintendents

In medium- and large-sized school districts, the superintendent has several subordinate administrators to whom responsibilities for specific managerial tasks are delegated. These people have titles such as deputy superintendent, associate superintendent, or assistant superintendent. The administrative scheme illustrated in Figure 5-1 provides for two deputy superintendents: the deputy superintendent for curriculum and instruction and the deputy superintendent for personnel, finance, and support services.

Each of these deputies is responsible for a major component of the district's operation. As the title suggests, the deputy superintendent for curriculum and instruction has responsibility for managing the district's academic programs. This

that are appropriate for the children in their own classrooms. The principal also pointed out that the superintendent has an excellent working relationship with most members of the school board and that it is very unusual for a school board member to make a direct appeal to teachers regarding a specific instructional approach.

After thinking about the situation, Woong initially decided to keep using the whole-language approach. But yesterday something happened that has made him uneasy. He received a letter from the president of the school board announcing that the entire board will spend a day visiting his school. Although it is not clear which board members will visit which classrooms, Woong is worried that Ms. Robinson may visit his. He is afraid she might notice that he is not using a phonics approach, and is wondering whether she might make negative comments about his teaching that could hurt his career.

Specifically, what does Woong see as the problem? What past experiences have conditioned his views? In what ways might they differ from experiences of others who may become involved? How might these experiences have led these people to develop opinions about the whole-language approach that differ from Woong's? What negatives might there be for a school board member in deciding to complain about Woong's approach? What positives? What do you think the most probable result will be?

Is there someone specific he should talk to? What might happen if Ms. Robinson asks him about his commitment to phonics-based instruction and he gives her an honest response? Will honesty hurt his career? Is Ms. Robinson justified in questioning a teacher's instructional approach? How might other school board members react to her actions?

Are there pressures on teachers to conform to wishes of people in positions of authority? Who exerts these pressures? Have you ever been in a situation where you have felt yourself forced to adopt a position that runs contrary to your true feelings? How did you react? Do you think these kinds of pressures interfere with efforts to introduce changes into school programs? Can people who are "change agents" long survive in public education? Why or why not?

person oversees a number of other administrators. Three key subordinates include the executive director of elementary education (responsible for programs in grades pre-kindergarten through 6), the executive director of secondary education (responsible for programs in grades 7 through 12), and the executive director of student support services.

The executive director of elementary education and the executive director of secondary education supervise a number of people who have specialized responsibilities for maintaining and enhancing the quality of the instructional program. Many of these people are specialists in teaching specific academic subjects. The executive director of student support services oversees leaders of the district's psychological services, counseling, and guidance programs; its special education programs; its health service operations; its school-attendance monitoring function; and its federal programs. Figure 5-2 illustrates an example of an organizational plan for that part of a district's operation falling under the jurisdiction of the deputy superintendent for curriculum and instruction.

Note that Figure 5-2 does not provide a separate leadership structure for junior high schools or middle schools. These schools are administered by personnel charged with responsibilities for either elementary education or secondary education.

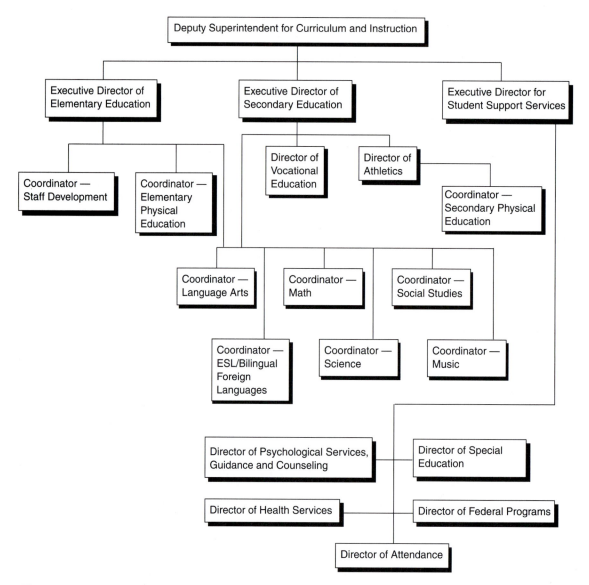

Figure 5-2

Example of the administrative jurisdiction of a deputy superintendent for curriculum and instruction

Even the terms *elementary education* and *secondary education* are not interpreted in the same ways in all places. For example, in some areas, elementary education is often thought of as embracing grades K through 6, whereas in other places, grades K through 8 comprise the elementary program. Similarly, in some districts, secondary education is often interpreted to mean grades 7 through 12, but other districts consider it to be grades 6 through 12, 9 through 12, or some other set of grades. (Grades 10, 11, and 12 are almost always included within the secondary education designation.)

The pattern becomes even more confusing in districts that identify separate organizational structures for junior high schools and middle schools. The term *middle school* has been particularly difficult to pin down in terms of the grade levels it embraces. Where middle schools exist, they ordinarily include grades 6 and 7 (Lounsbury & Vars, 1978; Armstrong & Savage, 1993). Beyond these two grades, middle school grade configurations vary tremendously from place to place. For example, some middle schools have grades 5, 6, and 7; some have grades 5, 6, 7, and 8; some have grades 6, 7, 8; some have grades 6, 7, 8, 9; and some have still other arrangements.

The deputy superintendent for personnel, finance, and support services has a wide range of responsibilities. This person may be assisted by subordinate administrators, each of whom has responsibilities for one of these areas: personnel, finance, and support services. An example of an organizational plan for the part of a district's operations that is the responsibility of the deputy superintendent for personnel, finance, and support services is provided in Figure 5-3.

The executive director for personnel is responsible for screening candidates and making hiring recommendations. These decisions often involve cooperation with other district administrators. For example, it may be necessary to get the concurrence of the principal in the building to which a prospective new employee is to be

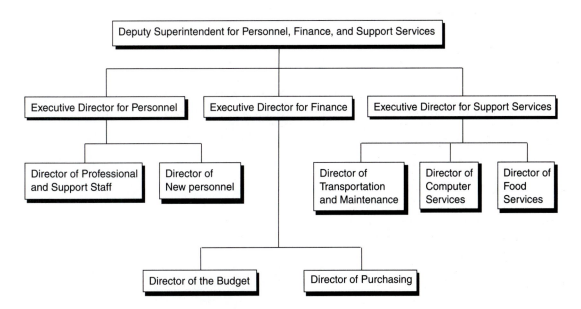

Figure 5-3

Example of the administrative jurisdiction of a deputy superintendent for personnel, finance, and support

assigned. The executive director of personnel's office also often monitors all records of existing faculty and staff members, keeps track of where each person is on the salary scale, monitors employee benefits programs, and takes charge of many other duties having to do with employee relations.

The executive director for finance, as the title implies, has broad authority in areas related to budgeting and purchasing. Often, this office is responsible for drafting initial versions of the proposed annual budget. This administrator is responsible for overseeing expenditures to ensure that they are in line with what has been authorized. School purchases of all kinds are often executed and monitored by personnel attached to the executive director for finance.

The executive director for support services oversees a variety of important functions. For example, this office will often manage all transportation and maintenance operations. Food services provided by the schools frequently come under the jurisdiction of this executive director as well. Other support services, including printing and computer services, may also be managed by the executive director for support services and this person's subordinates.

Other Central Office Professional Personnel

Some school districts, particularly large ones, have many professionals with specialized skills who are headquartered in the district's central administrative offices. (A number of these people are referenced on the charts in Figures 5-2 and 5-3.) Typically, they have responsibilities that are either districtwide in scope or that serve at least some of the district's schools.

Figure 5-2 identifies a number of "coordinators." These are individuals responsible for instruction in the area under their jurisdiction. Some districts use different

Many school districts have bus routes that extend great distances. They own large numbers of buses and employ many drivers. Managing school transportation services is an important responsibility of a central school district administrative office.

terms to describe these individuals; for example, they may called consultants, directors, or district program chairs. Often, these positions are held by former teachers who proved to be exemplary performers in the classroom and have gone on to do advanced study in their specializations and in curriculum. Some states and districts require coordinators to hold special kinds of certificates.

Many school districts have several people attached to an office who are responsible for overseeing guidance and counseling activities throughout the district. For example, there may be one or more professional psychologists attached to this office, as well as other people with advanced training in specialized areas related to the counseling and guidance function.

Many districts employ psychometrists. *Psychometrists* are people who have had advanced training in the construction and administration of sophisticated tests that are designed to measure mental abilities of various kinds. These individuals frequently have advanced degrees and, in many places, must qualify for a special certificate.

There may also be some special kinds of teachers attached to the central administrative offices. These include specialists in such areas as reading who work with teachers and learners in several of the district's schools. Additionally, there may be homebound teachers who are assigned to work with learners in the district who are unable to attend regular school classes. Many teachers in these specialty areas have advanced academic training in their fields.

Some districts have research and evaluation specialists who are charged with monitoring innovations and overseeing the administration of standardized testing programs. Many of these people tend to hold advanced degrees, and some districts require them to hold special certificates as well.

These are just some examples of the kinds of professionals who often work out of a district's central administrative offices. Today's school districts employ large numbers of people besides school principals and regular classroom teachers.

HOW INDIVIDUAL SCHOOLS ARE ORGANIZED

Administrative organizational schemes for schools are varied, although some features are quite common. Most school-to-school differences result because of variations in enrollment. Elementary schools tend to have organizational patterns that distinguish them from secondary schools, which draw learners from several "feeder" elementary schools. This means that, typically, an elementary school enrolls fewer learners than a secondary school. Hence, in most cases, administrative organizational schemes in elementary schools are somewhat less complex than those in secondary schools.

Organization of Elementary Schools

Building Administrators

The school principal is the chief executive officer of an elementary school, responsible for all aspects of the school's operation. The principal oversees the academic program and ensures that it is in compliance with state and local regulations. The welfare of individual pupils is another important responsibility of the principal. Except in the very largest of elementary schools, principals often know the names of a great number of pupils in every grade.

As a rule, parents of elementary school children take an active interest in the operation of the school. The principal is charged with winning parental support for school programs and encouraging active parental participation in parent-teacher groups and other school activities.

Principals are also responsible for the performance of each teacher in their building. Teachers look to the principal for guidance and support. The principal is expected to provide leadership in assisting teachers who may be experiencing difficulty in the classroom. Scholars Sharon Feiman-Nemser and Robert E. Floden (1986), after an extensive review of research studies focusing on teachers' attitudes toward principals, found the following common feelings:

- Teachers do not want the principal to interfere with their daily instructional decisions.
- Teachers expect the principal to act as a buffer between themselves and their critics.
- Teachers expect the principal to take the lead in establishing and maintaining a disciplined learning environment.
- Teachers cooperate best with a principal who is perceived to be properly discharging the legitimate professional role of the principal.
- The most important lever a principal has to achieve high academic standards in his or her school is the good will of the teachers in the building.

Principals also oversee the work of other professional and staff employees. Depending on the size of the school, other employees might include assistant principals, counselors, individual subject specialists (e.g., in reading), special education teachers, nurses, and custodians. Because of their broad-ranging responsibilities, most principals are issued contracts that call for them to be on the job more days during the year than are classroom teachers. Often, principals are expected to be in their buildings for at least 11 months of the year.

Larger elementary schools have one or more assistant principals. They oversee certain aspects of the school program as directed by the principal. Assistant principals' contracts also typically require them to work a longer school year than do classroom teachers.

An example of an administrative organizational plan for a medium-sized elementary school (approximately 450 pupils) is provided in Figure 5-4.

Grade-Level Leaders

Larger elementary schools often have teachers who are assigned to play special leadership roles as grade-level leaders. Grade-level leaders are found in schools where two (and often three or more) classes exist at each grade level. Teachers who fill these positions represent the concerns of all teachers at their grade level in meetings with the principal. They work with all teachers at their grade level to plan and coordinate learning experiences for children. They sometimes take the

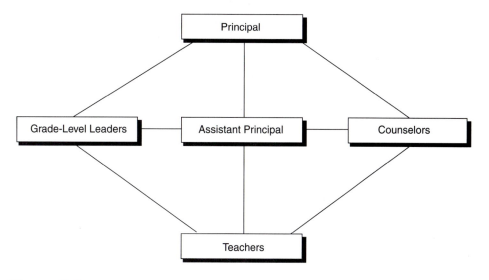

Figure 5-4

Example of the administrative organization of a medium-sized elementary school

lead in introducing new techniques and in modeling their use in the classroom. Often, they are responsible for ordering materials for all teachers at their grade level. Grade-level leaders usually are selected on the basis of their years of successful teaching, interpersonal relations skills, and advanced academic training.

Specialty Teachers

Elementary schools often include a few teachers who have received some type of specialized training. Among them are teachers who are specialists in working with learners who have emotional or physical handicaps. There may be one or more reading specialists assigned to a single building, and/or there may be several teachers with training in working with gifted and talented learners. Some schools have teachers who have been hired to work with other categories of learners for whom special educational support money is available, for example, children of migrant workers.

Other Professional Employees

Several categories of nonteaching professional employees often are employed in elementary schools.* For example, a school nurse may be in attendance for at least part of the school day. This person's responsibility is to deal with minor health problems and to oversee the management of learners' health records.

---

* It should be noted that some principals teach classes. Other nonteaching employees also may have some teaching responsibilities. In general, the term *nonteaching employee* is meant to suggest that the major responsibility of the individual involves something other than classroom teaching.

Reading specialists often are part of the professional staff serving learners in the school. This reading specialist works in an elementary school.

A school may have one or more counselors. Counselors typically are professionals who have taught several years and then gone on to complete advanced course work leading to special counseling certification. Their role is to help learners work through personal and academic problems. They frequently also have responsibilities for administering standardized tests. Counselors often are issued contracts that require them to work two or three weeks longer each school year than do regular classroom teachers.

A title such as "learning resource specialist" increasingly is being used to describe professionals who formerly were known as librarians. The change in title reflects the broadening range of these employees' responsibilities. In addition to managing all aspects of the school library (including teaching classes in library skills), they are often responsible for managing instructional support equipment such as VCRs, film projectors, tape recorders, audiocassette players, television sets, and computers. Many of them have special training in instructional technology as well as in library science. Because of the need to process books, inventory equipment, and take care of other job-related matters, some learning resource specialists work a longer school year than do regular classroom teachers.

Other Employees

Elementary schools have employees who perform many other important functions. One or more secretaries may work in the principal's office. In larger schools, there may also be secretaries assigned to work with the assistant principals and counselors. There may be a supply room clerk who takes charge of ordering and distributing materials. Sometimes this person also is in charge of managing and maintaining duplicating equipment.

Paraprofessionals are people who, although lacking formal professional training as teachers, are hired to assist teachers in various ways. They may work with individual learners who experience problems, help teachers prepare instructional materials, monitor learners when they take tests, and do other things to support the work of classroom teachers.

Many elementary schools prepare lunches for pupils. A kitchen staff headed by a chief cook is responsible for this activity. Additionally, virtually every school has a custodial staff that is responsible for cleaning the building and taking care of routine maintenance tasks. In small schools, there may be only one custodian; larger schools employ several.

Box 5-1 addresses the problem of a lack of public understanding of the diverse roles that nonteaching employees play in the schools.

Organization of Secondary Schools

Building Administrators

Secondary schools vary greatly in size. The complexity of the administrative arrangement tends to increase as school enrollment increases. An example of an administrative arrangement for a high school enrolling between 1,500 and 2,000 students is provided in Figure 5-5.

The principal of a large high school has a demanding job, supervising a huge teaching and support staff. In a school with 2,000 students, for example, there may be more than 75 teachers. The principal must manage a large budget as well. This administrator also has a challenging public relations role. A principal of a large high school must deal effectively with parents and other citizens who have different views about what a good school should provide. This requires the principal to be visible in the local community, which means attendance at all major school events as well as participation in service and other community organizations. Finally, the

---

**BOX
5-1**

Are There Too Many School Administrators?

Schools are often accused of being top-heavy with administrators. This point of view is reflected in the following comments from a recent editorial in a local newspaper:

> Only slightly over half of our school employees are teachers. These teachers complain that they are overburdened with paperwork requests from building administrators. Is it possible that we have too many "chiefs" in our schools and that they generate paperwork requests simply to justify their own existence? Wouldn't it be better to halve the number of administrators, hire more teachers, and decrease class size? We think so.

What Do You Think?

1. Why do you think that people often suppose there are too many administrators in schools?
2. Based on what you know, is this an accurate perception?
3. If you were to write a letter to the editor in response to this editorial, what would you say?

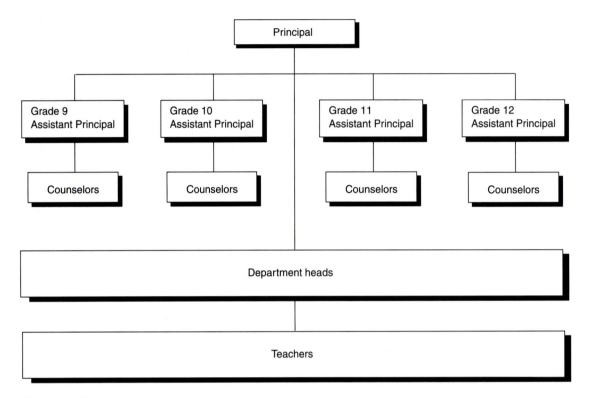

Figure 5-5
Example of an administrative organizational plan for a high school

principal must exercise leadership over the school program and ensure that all federal, state, and local requirements are met.

In most secondary schools, the principal has one or more assistants. In the example provided in Figure 5-5, the principal has four assistant principals, one to work with each class (grade 9, grade 10, grade 11, and grade 12). Individual assistant principals are responsible for instruction, guidance, scheduling, and other functions as they relate to students at their assigned grade level. This arrangement is only one of several that are commonly found in secondary schools.

An alternate scheme followed in many high schools assigns responsibilities for one or more functions to each assistant principal. Each assistant works with students and teachers in all grades, but only in a limited number of areas of responsibility. For example, there may be an assistant principal for scheduling and discipline; an assistant principal for curriculum; an assistant principal for budget, computing, maintenance, and food services; and an assistant principal for guidance and student services. Whatever the administrative arrangement, however, the principal and the assistant principals typically work a much longer school year than do teachers.

In addition to the principal and the assistant principals, a large high school may have other administrators. For example, there may be a head counselor. This person is responsible for assigning responsibilities to members of the counseling staff. There may also be an athletic director. As the title implies, this person oversees budgets and personnel associated with interschool and intramural athletics. Another sort of director found in many secondary schools is the finance director, who oversees a small staff of people who monitor the school budget and manage accounts for student organizations.

There may be a vocational programs director, who monitors mandated federal and state programs designed to prepare high school graduates for specific kinds of jobs. This individual manages the required paperwork and often makes contacts with employers in the local community who cooperate in school-based training programs of various kinds.

The head custodian is an important administrator in large secondary schools. This person supervises a considerable staff of people who clean the building and take care of routine maintenance. Classroom teachers may never encounter some members of the head custodian's staff. In many large buildings, there is a night shift that comes on duty after teachers and students leave for the day.

There often is a head dietitian, who is responsible for planning lunch menus and overseeing a large kitchen and cafeteria staff. The school lunch program is a large and complex activity, and the head dietitian must handle a great deal of paperwork as well as direct the activities of food-service employees.

In large schools, there may also be a head resource specialist. This person oversees the work of school library personnel as well as the staff responsible for maintaining media equipment. Identifying learning resource needs, ordering, and processing new material and equipment also fall under this person's jurisdiction.

Department Heads

Department heads are teachers who lead the individual academic departments in a secondary school. They report either directly to the school principal or indirectly to the school principal through one of the assistant principals. Department heads often are relieved of one instructional period a day to allow them time to take care of departmental business. Their employment contracts often require them to work two or more weeks longer than do other teachers.

Department heads are experienced, respected teachers. Their duties include such activities as informing members of their departments about important administrative policies, working with teachers new to their staffs, passing on concerns of department members to the principal, making recommendations for assigning department members to individual courses, allocating the materials' budget among department members, arranging for textbook distribution, and representing the department at district-level curriculum meetings.

Specialty Teachers

As is the case with elementary schools, secondary schools also include some teachers who have received specialized training. Because the average secondary school is larger than the average elementary school, frequently a secondary school will employ more specialty teachers than will an elementary school. Groups served by these individuals are emotionally disturbed learners and learners with physical disabilities, gifted and talented students, learners with reading problems, and learners in a variety of other special programs.

Other Professionals

Most secondary schools have several counselors who have had advanced course work in guidance and counseling. Many of them have advanced academic degrees. In most places, they hold special counseling certificates, although this pattern varies somewhat from state to state and from place to place within some states. Many counselors handle both academic and personal counseling. In very large schools, some counselors may have specific responsibilities. For example, there may be a counselor who works only with college and university placement issues. Another may be concerned only with vocational counseling and aptitude testing. Another may work exclusively with managing the standardized testing program.

There may also be several school nurses in a large secondary school. These individuals are responsible for maintaining health records and dealing with minor health-related situations that arise during the school day.

There likely are a number of learning resource specialists within a large secondary school. Some of them work full-time in the library. Others may be assigned to work exclusively with specialized instructional support equipment.

Other Staff Members

Secondary schools often have large secretarial staffs. There may even be a head secretary, who is charged with overseeing the work of all other secretaries in the building. Individual secretaries may be assigned to the principal, the assistant principals, the counselors, the finance office, and the main-office reception area. There may be one secretary who is assigned to do nothing but handle incoming telephone calls. Telephones ring constantly at larger secondary schools, and answering them and directing the call to the appropriate party is a time-consuming activity.

Custodial staffs in large high schools are extensive. This also tends to be true for kitchen staffs. Not all kitchen-staff employees work a full eight-hour day, however. Some come in for only a few hours during the middle of the day.

There may be one or two supply room clerks. These people are responsible for maintaining an inventory of paper, pens, pencils, and other items. Teachers contact these clerks when they need supplies. Because of the nature of their responsibilities, supply room clerks are individuals with whom teachers come into frequent contact.

Paraprofessionals are less common in secondary schools than in elementary schools. In the secondary schools that employ them, they function much as they do in elementary schools; that is, they are assigned to help individual teachers and they do many different kinds of things in discharging this responsibility.

• Key Ideas in Summary

- School districts have developed sophisticated organizational plans for managing their activities. In general, administrative schemes are more complex in larger school districts than in smaller ones. Similarly, school buildings enrolling larger numbers of learners tend to feature administrative organizations that are more complex than those serving smaller numbers of learners.

- The specific categories of school personnel with whom teachers are likely to have frequent daily contact vary from place to place. In part, these variations are related to the numbers of learners attending the school. For example, a teacher in a small elementary school may well interact with the principal every day, whereas in a large high school, several days may pass without the teacher even seeing the principal.

- The school board (sometimes known by names such as board of education, board of trustees, or school council) is the basic policymaking body of a school district. It represents a link between the local district and the state department of education. In most places, school board members are elected. The school board hires and monitors the work of the district's superintendent.

- The superintendent is the chief executive officer of a school district, responsible for all aspects of the district's day-to-day operations. Among other responsibilities, the superintendent is the ultimate supervisor of all employees, is responsible for ensuring that academic programs are in compliance with federal and state regulations, is charged with preparing budget proposals for the school board, and is the top professional public-relations spokesperson for the district. Depending on the size of the district, the superintendent may be assisted by one or more deputies, associates, or assistants.

- Principals are the chief executive officers of individual schools, responsible for all aspects of their school's operation. Among other things, they oversee the academic program, monitor learners' progress, check on teachers' performances, manage budgets, and work to maintain good public relations with parents and other citizens. In larger buildings, they are aided by assistant principals.

- In some elementary schools, the principal and assistant principals may be assisted by grade-level leaders. These teachers represent the interests of other teachers at the grade level they teach in interactions with the principals and, sometimes, in meetings with central office personnel. Other professionals in larger elementary schools include school nurses, counselors, and learning resource specialists. There often are other support personnel, including secretaries, food-service workers, and paraprofessionals.

- Administrative arrangements in secondary schools vary somewhat from those in elementary schools. Secondary schools typically enroll more students and, in general, have more elaborate administrative management schemes than do elementary schools. In addition to the principal and assistant principals, administrators in a medium-to-large-sized high school might include a head counselor, an athletic director, a finance director, a vocational programs director, a head custodian, a head dietitian, and a head learning resource specialist.

- Department heads in secondary schools lead the departments with which they are affiliated. They inform department members of important policy decisions. Also, they meet frequently with the principal or an assistant principal and, hence, function as an important conduit between the school administrative office and teachers in the departments they represent. Often, department heads represent the school in districtwide meetings of subject-area specialists. They typically work a slightly longer academic year than do other teachers, and they often have one nonteaching period a day reserved for their departmental administrative responsibilities.

• There are many support personnel in secondary schools. Among these are food-service workers, custodians, secretaries, clerks, and paraprofessionals.

• Review and Discussion Questions

1. In general, secondary schools have more complex administrative organizations than do elementary schools. Why is this true?
2. What are the functions of school boards?
3. What are some of the basic responsibilities of the superintendent?
4. Describe some of the duties of grade-level leaders in an elementary school.
5. In addition to the principal and his or her assistants, a number of other administrators are often found in larger secondary schools. Who are these people and what do they do?
6. Who are some of the professionals who might be assigned to a specific school building for purposes other than teaching regular classes?
7. Should the superintendent try to sell the local community on innovative new programs, or should he or she attempt to read the local community and provide programs that do not need to be sold? Why or why not?
8. Individuals who have studied school board members agree that serving on the school board is a taxing, demanding responsibility. Yet few districts have any difficulty finding candidates to run for vacancies. How can this be explained?
9. Many elementary schools have grade-level leaders and many secondary schools have department heads. Do you think that a grade-level leader is likely to have more influence on a beginning elementary teacher than a department head is likely to have on a beginning secondary-school teacher? Why do you think so?
10. Some critics argue that principals in large high schools are so consumed by basic management issues that they cannot adequately monitor the quality of instruction being delivered in their classrooms. Do you agree or disagree with this position? Why?

• Ideas for Field Experiences, Projects, and Enrichment

1. Set up an interview with a principal of a school at the level you would like to teach. During your interview, ask the principal to identify all of the categories of nonteaching personnel who work in the school. Ask what these people's specific responsibilities are. Take notes. When you return to class, share your findings with others. As a class, identify some common patterns observed by individuals who visited elementary schools and those who visited secondary schools.
2. Attend a local school board meeting. What kinds of topics were on the agenda? How was time allocated among topics to be covered? What kinds of people were invited to speak at the meeting? What sorts of controversial issues were discussed? What role did the superintendent play in the meeting? Were citizens invited to speak on any topics of interest (including those not on the agenda)? If possible, ask a school official how a given issue gets added to a meeting's agenda. Prepare a short written report that summarizes your findings.

•

3. Invite a superintendent to visit your class. Ask this person to describe a typical week on the job. Specifically, ask about what percentage of time is devoted to (a) curriculum and instructional matters, (b) personnel matters, (c) budgetary matters, and (d) public-relations matters. What does the superintendent do to ensure that policies are being carried out in the individual buildings? How do administrators in the buildings communicate their concerns to the superintendent? What kinds of contact, if any, does the superintendent have with beginning teachers? (Devise other questions designed to provide class members with insights about the superintendent's role.)

4. If you are planning to teach elementary school, interview one or more grade-level leaders. If you are planning to teach secondary school, interview one or more department heads. Ask these people what their general responsibilities are, whether they are released from any teaching obligations as a result of their appointment to the position of grade-level leader or department head, and to whom they report. If you are a future elementary teacher, get together with three or four others in the class who also interviewed grade-level leaders. If you are a future secondary teacher, get together with three or four others from the class who also interviewed department heads. In your groups, try to write a formal job description for either a grade-level leader or a department head. Share your work with the course instructor and ask for comments.

5. Select a school district either where you might like to teach or that is convenient to your college or university. Call the district's central administrative offices and ask whether any charts or descriptive materials are available that show the district's basic administrative organizational material. (Many districts have this kind of information on hand.) Look at the organizational scheme of the district you select. How is it similar and how does it differ from the examples of organizational plans displayed in this chapter? How do you explain any differences?

• References

Armstrong, D. G., & Savage, T. V. (1993). *Secondary education: An introduction* (2nd ed.). New York: Macmillan.

Feiman-Nemser, S., & Floden, R. E. (1986). The cultures of teaching. In M. C. Wittrock (Ed.), *Handbook of research on teaching* (3rd ed., pp. 505–526). New York: Macmillan.

Lounsbury, J. H., & Vars, G. E. (1978). *Curriculum for the middle years*. New York: Harper and Row.

Snyder, T. D. (Project Ed.). (1994). *Digest of education statistics, 1994*. Washington, DC: National Center for Education Statistics.

Contexts for Teaching

CHAPTERS

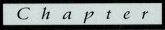

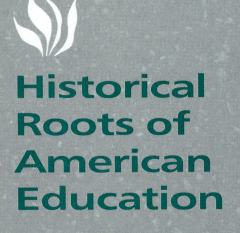

6

Historical Roots of American Education

OBJECTIVES

- Point out that written history is influenced by the perspectives of the historian.
- Describe criticisms that American education has not always developed in ways that served to advantage *all* learners.
- Cite examples of some practices in today's schools derived from European precedents.
- Identify patterns of American education as they developed in the colonial period and years of the early Republic.
- Summarize key 19th century developments that helped shape today's American education.
- Identify basic principles that provided a rationale for the comprehensive high school.
- Describe some contributions of Horace Mann and John Dewey to American education.
- Cite some key issues in the development of twentieth century American education.

What is given to us as "history" is more than a simple recitation of past events. It is a presentation and analysis that is heavily influenced by the historian's beliefs, biases, and values. In the case of the history of American education, many writers have followed a tradition of presuming that today's educational system, although not perfect, is better than it has ever been. This assumption has supported historical writing that has "depicted past developments in education, especially public education, as continuous progress, beneficial to all" (Gordon & Szreter, 1989, p. 8). This kind of educational history reflects many of the biases of the majority of Americans who are white and of European descent. It acknowledges both the general "goodness" of the basic organization of education in this country and the legitimacy of the majority political power that has developed and maintained many long-standing school practices.

Few deny that the schools do reflect traditions that largely trace back to European practices; however, some educational historians today wonder whether our schools have always developed in ways that have well-served *all* learners. Contemporary historical scholarship increasingly questions whether schools have adequately responded to special needs of young people from ethnic and cultural minorities.

Analysis of this issue is tricky. It is not that American educators for many years have failed to embrace the idea of serving all the children. Rather, it is a question of how their practices have actually affected young people from different groups. The key here seems to be the congruence between priorities and values learners bring with them from home and those that are reflected by teachers and in the school curriculum. Children from the majority white culture often have found the world of the school to be a simple extension of the values and priorities prized in their own families. Young people from ethnic and cultural minorities, on the other hand, have sometimes found a jarring discontinuity between expectations of parents and families and expectations of the school.

Even though schools today are much more sensitive to this problem than they were in the past, many learners from ethnic and cultural minorities do not do as well at school as their white majority age-mates. Increasingly, educators are coming to understand that "no child should have to go through the painful dilemma of choosing between family and school and of what inevitably becomes a choice between belonging and succeeding" (Nieto, 1992, p. xxv). For example, efforts are under way to examine curricular materials to weed out negative stereotypes that can undermine the sense of self-worth for learners from certain groups. Think about how native American youngsters must have felt not many years ago when the only textbook references to them mentioned "savages" who were introduced as obstacles to European development and progress.

Many educational historians today take pains to point out that this kind of sensitivity to ethnic and cultural differences is new. Throughout the nineteenth century and well into the twentieth, individuals responsible for schools and school programs largely supported the idea that the majority white European-based culture was the "true" American culture; it was the task of all learners to conform to its perspectives. There was little tolerance or respect for minority culture. "Good" schools were not designed to respond to cultural differences. They were supposed to root them out and turn children from minority groups into "real" Americans (Coleman, 1993). As an example of this point of view, consider this statement from the 1888 annual report for a special residential school for native Americans in which the school's superintendent lamented the negative influences on the school's children when, occasionally, they had to be allowed to leave to go home to visit their families: "Children leaving even the best training schools for their homes, like the swine, return to their wallowing filth and barbarism" (Annual Report of the Commissioner of Indian Affairs, 1888). Given such attitudes, it is not surprising that the idea that school programs should be responsive to ethnic and cultural differences was rarely discussed.

The point of all this is that some learners, particularly those from ethnic and cultural minorities, have not always been well served by our schools. In part, problems have had to do with a lack of sensitivity to cultural differences. Schools *could* have modified some practices to accommodate cultural and ethnic differences years before this became a concern. There were existing educational models among native American groups that could have been adapted in public schools that enrolled some native American learners. There were also educational legacies from Africa, Asia, and the Hispanic world that might have been considered. It is not that such examples were not known, but rather that for many years, educational leaders considered them irrelevant.

American education developed under the assumption that "proper" and "correct" education derived from European practices. The sections of this chapter that follow are not intended to suggest that this was the only course that could have been taken or even that it was the most appropriate. But the reality is that the structure of today's educational enterprise is basically rooted in traditions from Europe. The absence of information about educational models from other areas does not denigrate their importance. It simply reflects an educational history that for many years failed to recognize the legitimacy of perspectives of non-European groups.

The continued growth of ethnic and cultural minorities in our schools and our increasing sensitivity to the need to develop the educational potential of each child are encouraging more attention to the obligation to develop school programs that are responsive to the needs of all. These reforms are being inserted into an American school system that historically did not hold responding to cultural diversity as a high priority. The difficulties that accompany these change efforts can be better understood in the context of historical developments that have acted to shape the American system.

LEGACIES FROM EUROPE

Some things we encounter are so routine that we can hardly imagine a world in which they were absent. For example, we almost never consciously think about a red light at an intersection being a warning to stop or a green light as conferring permission to proceed. Why red, and why green? There is no reason that blue and brown could not have been the colors we used to control the flow of traffic. Only long-standing tradition reinforces our nearly universal acceptance of red and green as our stop and go signals.

Commonplace assumptions about the realities that guide our lives are shaped by culture. Some of the things we do appear bizarre to individuals brought up in other traditions. We most frequently appreciate this point when we find ourselves cut off temporarily from our own cultural group and surrounded by people who have different assumptions about how life should be lived.

Not many years ago, one of the authors found himself alone in a small community on the east coast of Korea. He witnessed women shopping in the village carefully examining live snakes in cages before purchasing one or two to take home to prepare for the evening meal. Next to the live-snake store, there was a shop selling decorative lacquer-ware. In the center of the room, a large roast pig rested atop a table. The pig's mouth was propped open to accommodate a large quantity of paper currency that had been stuffed between its teeth. To American eyes, housewives calmly purchasing live snakes for supper and a knickknack shop featuring a roast pig with a mouthful of money might seem unusual. To the residents of this small village, these events were just an unremarkable part of their everyday lives.

Many practices in our schools are so familiar that we can hardly imagine alternative ways of doing things. We sometimes fail to recognize that many of our assumptions about schools and schooling reflect long-standing cultural choices. For example, chances are you've never worried excessively about any of the following characteristics of American education:

- the idea that content should be organized under major categories or headings
- the idea that knowledge should be divided among individual subjects
- the idea that teaching should occur in a setting that brings young people together in groups for instructional purposes
- the idea that schools should be organized into a sequence of grades
- the idea that as many people as possible should be educated
- the idea that individual differences should be considered by teachers in planning instruction
- the idea that schools should help learners develop rational thinking processes
- the idea that teachers should have some kind of specialized training
- the idea that schooling should be a preparation for responsible citizenship
- the idea that schooling should provide young people with some understandings and skills needed in the adult workplace

Where did these ideas come from? For the most part, they evolved over the centuries from educational practices in Europe. The thinkers of ancient Greece, for example, developed the idea that knowledge could be organized into categories and that logical, rational thinking processes were important. Our concern with education for citizenship likewise has roots in the concern of the ancient Athenians for producing adult citizens who could participate in democratic decision making.

The ancient Romans were very concerned that young people receive a practical education that would provide them with "useful" knowledge. This perspective is one that many present-day Americans share. The Romans, too, had debates on the question of whether harsh punishment for students was needed or whether gentler, more sensitive approaches made sense. Americans today also debate this issue.

Important work on the development of knowledge into individual subject areas occurred during the Middle Ages. The tradition of churches taking responsibility for secular education also traces to this period. American parochial schools continue this legacy.

Our concern for universal education is a continuation of a trend that became pronounced during the Reformation. Many church leaders during this period believed that the Bible was the repository of all wisdom; hence, it was desirable for as many people as possible to learn to read so they would have access to its truths. Somewhat later during the Renaissance, a growing emphasis on the worth and the importance of the individual evolved. It is from this perspective that our schools' concern for meeting individual differences developed.

In the seventeenth century, the work of Francis Bacon and others established the idea that truth could be challenged and modified through observation and careful weighing of evidence. This provided the foundation for the modern scientific method, something that continues to be enormously important in our schools. Another great influence on the development of education in Europe and, later, in the United States, was John Amos Comenius. Among his many contributions were the idea of organizing learning into sequential, graded schools and of viewing education as something that should prepare people for happy lives.

The famous eighteenth century educator Johann Heinrich Pestalozzi suggested that education could be an agent to improve society. This was a revolutionary idea at the time; today it has become an article of faith among many Americans. No matter what intractable social problem is garnering headlines at a given moment, one predictable response to the problem is that more education is needed. Pestalozzi would have agreed. Pestalozzi also introduced the idea that teachers should be provided with special kinds of training.

The nineteenth century witnessed a wave of interest in education throughout Europe that resulted in widespread establishment of mandatory public school systems by the end of the century. The importance of educating young learners was recognized by Friedrich Froebel, who is regarded as the "father of the kindergarten." The idea of preparing systematic formal lesson plans was introduced by another nineteenth century educator, Johann Herbart. His scheme looks remarkably similar to many lesson planning formats used by teachers today. The nineteenth century also witnessed a tremendous growth of interest in the importance of the psychology of learning.

As you read material in the sections that follow, bear in mind that many assumptions that came to be reflected in American schools developed from practices that first appeared in Europe. European settlers of North America brought these perspectives with them. Because the population of today's schools is becoming more culturally diverse, the appropriateness of these European-based models is increasingly being debated. Should there be changes in our schools to better meet the needs of more diverse learners? Or can most existing practices be modified? These are questions you as future educators will be asked to consider.

Why Study in High School?

"Dammit, our system's just not right!" Eric Blanton slammed down the grade book he had been carrying and slumped into one of the old vinyl-covered chairs in the Ryerson High School faculty lounge.

From across the room, Suyanna Muyami, the head of the English department looked up. "OK, Eric, what is it today — taxes, our corrupt politicians, or one of the kids?"

"Oh, I'll be all right, but I've been going round and round again with Roy Flynn. The kid is so bright, but he's just doing nothing, absolutely nothing. He gives things a nice once-over-lightly before the tests and manages to get grades just high enough to squeak by. He'll graduate, but just barely. What really gets to me is that he could be a contender for top academic honors if he would just care."

"If school doesn't turn him on, what does?" asked Suyanna. "Is it the usual love affair with a car?"

"That's exactly it," replied Eric. "He's working 20 and more hours a week to keep it in gasoline."

"And I suppose you've been trying to point out the error of his ways, the tragedy of wasting his God-given talent — all the usual arguments we trot out. Right?"

"Well, yes," responded Eric. "And it makes me mad that he's got all this talent and that he's just tossing it away. Just a few minutes ago I sat him down and tried to have a heart-to-heart with him about his future. The kid's sharp. He has an answer for every argument. What makes me mad is that we've set up a system in this country that encourages insightful kids like Eric to see high school as play time."

"What do you mean?" Suyanna asked.

"Well, I gave him the usual pitch about not preparing himself for college and that his grades are going to make it difficult for him to be admitted to many four-year colleges and universities. He had an answer for that one all figured out. He knows that any community college in the state will take him, no questions asked, once he finishes high school. He says he'll dig into the academics, get grades, and transfer to a good four-year school. And, you know, the system will allow him to do just that."

Suyanna followed Eric's thoughts with interest. "What do you conclude from all this?"

"I conclude," Eric replied, "that we have a system that sends bad signals to some of our brightest kids. They should be studying hard in high school. But why should they? The way things are now, it almost makes sense for these kids to see high school as goof-off time. I mean, we've arranged things so they can always get their academic act together later on."

"Fine, but what's the answer?" questioned Suyanna. "Should we get rid of our community colleges? Just a hint, Eric — that's not going to happen. So, what's your next move with Roy?"

What does Eric see as the problem here? What alternatives does he see? What assumptions does he have about what high school students should value? How does he respond to this situation in light of these assumptions? Are there other responses that might have made sense? Which alternatives might you recommend, and why? How would your suggestions "connect" to what Roy Flynn believes is important in life?

Can you think of examples of incentives in our system that encourage learners to behave in ways you think are inappropriate? What historical situations might have led to the adoption of policies and practices that resulted in these incentives? Did these incentives come into being as a result of conscious acts, or were they unintended side effects of policies and procedures developed for other purposes?

Friedrich Froebel is remembered as the "father of the kindergarten." This early kindergarten is an example of many that were established as a result of his work.

DEVELOPMENT OF AMERICAN EDUCATION

A study of the history of American education reveals that at different times, people have had vastly different expectations of what educators should emphasize. Varying expectations have led to quite different views regarding characteristics of a good school. Differing patterns of educational development over time have resulted in diverse answers to these key questions:

- What is the most important purpose of education?
- Who is to be educated?
- What are learners expected to take away from their educational experiences?
- How are learners to be educated?

As you read about the development of American education, think about how these questions might have been addressed at different periods in our history. An understanding of changing perspectives on these issues will help you better understand positions in today's debates about educational policies and practices.

Colonial Period to 1800

The New England Colonies

Some familiarity with conditions in sixteenth- and seventeenth-century England will help you understand the nature of American education as it developed in New England during the colonial period. In England at that time, there was little room for open discussion of alternatives to the established church, the Church of England. Because it was the official church of the English government, people who espoused religious views in opposition to those of the Church of England were considered by governmental officials to be disloyal not only to the church, but also to the state. In effect, the Church of England was seen as an extension of the legal authority of the government. Consequently, religious dissidents were dealt with harshly. The official view was that such people might represent a subversive threat to the power of the crown.

Views of the Puritans   Political problems in England for groups such as the Puritans, who wanted to reform the policies of the Church of England, led them to develop an interest in emigrating to the New World. Equally important was their fear of remaining in England and exposing their children to what they considered to be the religious errors of the Church of England. The intransigent Puritans had definite ideas about what religious beliefs and practices should be and by no means were a tolerant people. (Witness, for example, their persecution of the nonconforming Roger Williams.) Once they left England, those Puritans who settled in New England sought to establish a church and government different from those in England. Their belief that their own church and government were more consistent with the Bible's teachings had important educational implications.

The Puritans saw the Bible as the source of all wisdom. As a result, they placed a high priority on developing an educational system that would enable large numbers of people to read "God's Holy Word." The Bible, as the Puritans interpreted it, outlined a specific type of preferred government for both church and state. This contrasted importantly with practices in England, where authority in the Church of England was highly centralized and few decisions were left to the discretion of members of individual churches. The Puritans, however, believed that the Bible promoted a different organizational structure. In their view, power should be exercised by local church congregations, and the Puritans' churches in Massachusetts reflected this pattern. Such beliefs also helped establish the more general principle of local control over civil as well as religious affairs. It was out of this context that the tradition of local control of education evolved.

New England School Legislation   Concern for education in Massachusetts was demonstrated early in our history in the Massachusetts School Law of 1642. This law charged local magistrates with the responsibility of ensuring that parents would not neglect the education of their children. Although the law itself did not provide for the establishment of schools, it did require that children attend schools. It represented the first attempt in America to make school attendance compulsory. Reflecting the local-control tradition, this law placed responsibility for enforcement at the local rather than the state level.

The law of 1642 was extended by the famous "Old Deluder Satan Act" of 1647. The name was derived from wording in the act that promoted education as a buffer against Satan's wiles. The law required every town of 50 or more families to hire a teacher of reading or writing. The teacher was to be paid by either the community or parents of the learners. This act represented an early legislative attempt to establish the principle of public responsibility for education.

During the seventeenth century, concern for publicly supported education referred only to the very basic education of young children; few learners attended secondary schools. However, small numbers of secondary schools did come into being during the seventeenth century. One of the most famous of them was the Boston Latin Grammar School, founded in 1635. This school had a specific purpose: preparation of boys for Harvard. The curriculum consisted of difficult academic subjects including Latin, Greek, and theology.

The Middle Colonies

Most Puritan settlers of New England came from an area in eastern England known as East Anglia where opposition to the Church of England was strongest. Many of these Puritan settlers came to the New World during the period 1629–1641 (Fischer, 1989). People who settled the middle colonies of New York, New Jersey, Delaware, and Pennsylvania, however, came from different places than the Puritans and were also a more diverse group. Some of these settlers were descendants of the Dutch and Swedes who originally occupied parts of New York. Many English Quakers came to the New World during the 50 years between 1675 and 1725, and a majority of them settled in Pennsylvania. These immigrants came mostly from the northern Midlands of England and Wales, an area completely different from the East Anglian homeland of many of the Puritans. Western and frontier areas of the middle colonies were largely settled by people originally from the north of England, Scotland, and Ireland during a period extending approximately from 1717 to 1775 (Fischer, 1989).

Not surprisingly, given the mixed origins of the population, patterns of schooling in the middle colonies were varied. For example, merchants in New York sponsored private schools that emphasized commercial subjects thought necessary for young people who would play future roles in business and trade. In contrast, the Pennsylvania Quakers maintained schools that were open to all children. These Quaker schools were notable for their willingness to recognize the educational needs and rights of African-Americans, native Americans, and other groups that usually were not encouraged (and often not allowed) to go to school.

The Franklin Academy   Benjamin Franklin was among the first to give American education a practical orientation. In his 1749 work *Proposals Relating to the Youth of Pennsylvania,* Franklin proposed a new kind of school, oriented to the "real" world, that would be free of all religious ties. Two years later, he established the Franklin Academy, an institution that was nonsectarian and offered such practical subjects as mathematics, astronomy, navigation, and bookkeeping.

By the end of the Revolutionary War, the Franklin Academy had replaced the Boston Latin Grammar School as the most important secondary school in America. Students at the Franklin Academy were able to make some choices about their course of study, thus setting the pattern of elective courses common in high schools today.

For all its strengths, relatively few learners attended the Franklin Academy. It was a private school, and tuition was beyond the means of most families. However, the establishment of the Franklin Academy directed a great deal of attention to the importance of secondary education. This interest was reflected in the subsequent establishment of many other private academies.

Contributions of the Academies   The private academies popularized the idea that secondary education had something important to offer, and they laid the foundation for public support of secondary schools. Collectively, the academies helped establish the following important precedents for American education:

- American education would have a strong orientation toward the practical rather than the purely intellectual or theoretical.
- American education would be nonsectarian.
- American education would feature diverse course offerings.

The Southern Colonies

A revolution in England in the late 1640s resulted in victory for the side supporting Parliament and the Puritans against the king and the established Church of England. King Charles I was executed and for a dozen years, England existed as a Puritan-controlled commonwealth, governed for much of this time by Oliver Cromwell as Lord Protector. This was an especially dangerous period for large landowners, members of the nobility, and others who had supported King Charles and wanted the monarchy restored (something that was finally achieved in 1660 when Charles II assumed the throne).

Because of dangers in England, many supporters of the king's cause migrated to the New World, often settling in the southern colonies of Maryland, Virginia, North Carolina, South Carolina, and Georgia. Large numbers of these settlers came from the southeastern part of England, an area different from both the East Anglian homeland of the Puritans and the northern Midland, northern English, Scottish, and Irish homelands of most of those who settled the middle colonies (Fischer, 1989).

Settlement in the southern colonies was distributed along rivers. There were few towns, and families tended to be separated by considerable distances. Under these conditions, it was difficult to gather sufficient numbers of children in one place to establish schools. Wealthy families hired tutors for their children. People in these colonies continued to identify very strongly with upper-class English values, and they often sent their sons to England to be educated in English schools. Education in these colonies was generally restricted to children of wealthy landowners; little schooling was available for those from less affluent families.

Education from 1800 to the Civil War

During the first 20 years of the nineteenth century, few educational innovations were introduced. American society was consumed with challenges such as settling the nation and providing workers for the nation's growing industries. There was more interest in getting young people into the work force than in providing them with opportunities for extensive education. Schooling beyond rudimentary elementary instruction was generally available only to children of families who were able to pay for this privilege and who did not need the income that a young person could generate. Proposals for an educational system that was universal and free were only just beginning to be discussed.

The Birth of the High School

In the early nineteenth century, only a few students attended secondary schools. The most popular secondary school continued to be the academy, which responded well to an American educational bias in favor of preparing learners for practical problem solving and work rather than for a life of scholarship. Many new academies came into being during the first half of the nineteenth century. By 1850, when the number of academies reached its peak, over six thousand were in operation (Barry, 1961).

Although the academies were highly regarded, they had an important drawback. Overwhelmingly, they were private tuition-charging institutions. This limited their learner population, as only young people from families that were relatively well off could attend. Gradually, people became convinced that larger numbers of young people than were being accommodated by the private academies could profit from secondary-level education. This recognition led to support for a new institution, the public high school.

The first public high school, the Boston English Classical School, was established in 1821. The school's courses closely paralleled the practical curriculum of most academies. The idea of public high schools did not catch on quickly, however. In 1860, there were only 40 in the entire country (Barry, 1961). It was not until 1900 that the number of public high schools surpassed the number of academies that had existed in 1850 (Barry, 1961).

The Contributions of Horace Mann

During the 1820s, Horace Mann began to make his views known. Mann, elected to the Massachusetts legislature in 1827, was an eloquent speaker who took up the cause of the *common school*, one for the average American. Mann's mission was to convince taxpayers that it was in their own interest to support the establishment of a system of public education. He pointed out that public schools would turn out educated young people whose skills would ultimately result in improved living standards for all. In Mann's view, the school was a springboard for opportunity. It was an institution capable of equalizing differences among people from different social classes.

Horace Mann helped convince American taxpayers that is was in their best interests to support public schools.

Mann's arguments were persuasive. In 1837, Massachusetts established a State Board of Education. Horace Mann gave up his career in politics to become its first secretary. In time, Mann's views attracted the attention of people throughout the entire country.

In addition to his interest in encouraging people to get behind the idea of publicly supported schools, Mann also recognized the importance of improving teachers' qualifications. In response to this concern, the nation's first *normal school* (an institution specifically designed to train people to teach) was established in 1839. In the beginning, these normal schools provided only one or two years of formal education for those wishing to become teachers. Their importance is the precedent they set for formalizing the education of future teachers.

Prompted by Mann's work, public schools began to be established throughout the country. By 1860, 50.6 percent of the nation's children were enrolled in public school programs (U.S. Department of Commerce, 1975). A majority of states had formalized the development of free school systems, including elementary schools, secondary schools, and public universities. In 1867, a National Department of Education was established as part of the federal government. By the late 1860s, many of the basic patterns of American education were in place. That these patterns continue is a tribute to the vision, patience, and political skills of Horace Mann.

Certifying Teachers:
An Innovation That Was Slow to Take Root

Horace Mann was a strong believer in normal schools, institutions specifically designed to prepare teachers. The first normal school was established in 1839. Even though many people supported the logic of providing special training for teachers and certifying them before they were allowed to work, these innovations were slow to be adopted. Stringent certification requirements did not become universal until the 1930s and 1940s.

All states had normal schools by the year 1900, but few required teachers to be graduates of these institutions. The state with the strictest regulations regarding teachers' entry into the profession was Massachusetts, which required them to have a high school diploma and two years of formal teacher training. Every other state had less stringent requirements.

As late as 1921, only four states required prospective teachers to have completed formal training programs. In that year, there were 14 states where people could qualify for a teaching credential with no more training than four years of high school. Some of these 14 states required teachers to have only an eighth grade education. In 1921, there were 31 states with *no* official academic requirements for awarding a teaching credential (Bowen, 1981).

Education from the Civil War to 1900

The post–Civil War years were characterized by unparalleled industrial growth. Technological innovations reduced the need for unskilled labor. The resulting demand for workers who had knowledge that was of value in the workplace intensified interest in the vocational preparation function of education.

Serving Immigrants and Financing Secondary Schools

Huge numbers of immigrants entered the United States during this period. These people needed both useful work skills and an orientation to the values of their new country. These needs placed new demands on educators, and there was a great increase in the number of schools. The schools these young people attended were eager to "Americanize" newcomers, and many immigrant learners were exposed to school programs that made light of or even fun of their native cultures and languages. There can be no doubt that American public schools exacted a psychological toll on many of the immigrant children who came into the country during this period.

In the realm of school financing, the famous Kalamazoo case (*Stuart* v. *School District No. 1 of the Village of Kalamazoo*, 30 Mich. 69 [1874]) resulted in a ruling that the state legislature had the right to pass laws levying taxes for the support of *both* elementary and secondary schools. This ruling established a legal precedent for public funding of secondary schools. As a result, there was a dramatic increase in the total number of schools and in the total number of learners who were enrolled as districts began to build many more secondary schools. Because of a widespread desire to provide older learners with "useful" educational experiences, many secondary schools broadened their curricula to include more practical, work-related subjects.

Influences of Professional Organizations

Organizational activity among teachers increased during this period. Prior to 1900, organizations that were the forerunners of today's American Federation of Teachers and National Education Association were established (see Chapter 10 for some more detailed information). Reports of such groups as the NEA's Committee of Ten and the Committee on College Entrance Requirements began to influence public school curricula. In the last decade of the nineteenth century, these groups acknowledged that schools should provide some services to learners with varied academic and career goals, but nevertheless suggested that preparation for college and university study was the primary purpose of high schools. This orientation represented a temporary reversal of a century-long trend to view secondary education as a provider of more practical kinds of learning experiences.

Twentieth-Century Education to World War II

During the first two decades of the twentieth century, the conflict between those who viewed the high school as an institution to serve college-bound learners and those who viewed it as an institution to prepare young people for the workplace

Interiors of many schools in the late 19th century were very plain. Note the total absence of decoration in this classroom.

was resolved by a compromise. This compromise was a new conception of the high school as a "comprehensive" institution. The comprehensive high school was seen as an institution that would include curricula directed at providing both academic and work-oriented instruction. Debate about how much weight should be given to each of these emphases continues even today.

Toward the end of the nineteenth century, there was a recognition that many of the increasing number of learners who were entering high schools were having difficulty doing the required work. Some individuals who studied this problem concluded that something needed to be done to ease learners' transition from elementary schools to high schools. A new institution that came to be known as the *junior high school* was the proposed solution.

The first junior high school was established in Berkeley, California, in 1909. The Berkeley school district developed a 6-3-3 plan of school organization that, in time, came to be widely copied elsewhere (Popper, 1967). The first six grades comprised the elementary program, the next three grades the junior high school program, and the final three years the senior high school program.

The number of public schools and of learners attending them increased tremendously during the first four decades of the twentieth century. Schooling became almost universal during this period. In 1900, only 50.5 percent of young people in the 5- to 20-year-old age group were in school, but by 1940, 74.8 percent of this age group were enrolled (U.S. Department of Commerce, 1975). Given the tremendous growth in the total U.S. population between 1900 and 1940, these figures indicate that millions more children were served by schools in 1940 than in 1900.

The Work of John Dewey

An individual who had a tremendous influence on education during this period was John Dewey (1859–1952), whose work continues to affect educational thought and practice. Dewey viewed education as a process through which young people are brought to fully participate in society. He saw the primary goal of education as that of promoting growth and development of the individual. Hence, school should not set out to serve the goals of society (e.g., turning out electrical engineers if the society is short of them) at the cost of overlooking the unique needs of individual learners. Schools, Dewey believed, should produce secure human beings who leave school committed to their own continuing self-education.

Dewey believed that every learner actively attempts to explore and understand the environment. Because of this, Dewey argued, learners need intellectual tools that they can use to make sound judgments about those things they encounter. They need to be familiar with thinking processes that can be applied to any unfamiliar situation. Dewey maintained that it was much more important for learners to master systematic thinking processes than to know specific items of information. Thinking processes can be applied universally, but a specific item of information often has little value beyond the context in which it is learned.

The thought process that Dewey felt learners should master was the scientific problem-solving method. He believed familiarity with this method would give young people confidence in their abilities to develop rational responses to dilemmas they would face throughout their lives. Interest in teaching problem-solving techniques and a commitment to responding to individual differences still feature prominently in American schools today.

The Testing Movement

Schools today also continue to be influenced by an early twentieth-century movement that first developed in France. Education in France became compulsory in 1904. At that time, a special commission was established there to identify those young people who might benefit from regular instruction in public schools and those who would be better off in special classes. To help with this identification, in 1905 Alfred Binet and his associates developed a test, called the intelligence quotient (IQ) test, that was designed to predict learners' likelihood of success in regular school classrooms. Soon educators from other countries, including the United States, were seeking information about ways to measure intelligence. It is interesting that a test designed to predict school success was viewed almost immediately as a test of intelligence. The presumption was that the school program had been designed so that the most intelligent would do the best. (Today, this idea is debated. Some people, for example, argue that the "most intelligent" learners resist school rules and procedures and do not do well.)

The testing movement in the United States grew during World War I. The military needed a system that could be used to identify individuals who would be suited to a variety of necessary tasks. Intelligence tests were developed that were believed to provide information that could be used to classify individuals by intelligence. At the time they were initially developed, few people doubted that the scores yielded by these tests represented a highly reliable measure of intelligence.

Some of these early intelligence tests were given to European immigrants. Immigrants from western Europe did better than immigrants from eastern Europe. (This was hardly a surprising development because most tests were developed by western Europeans or Americans trained by western Europeans.) There is some evidence that laws passed by Congress restricting numbers of immigrants from eastern Europe resulted from dissemination of these score differences. This might be one of the first examples of the cultural bias that can be embedded within tests of this sort.

During and after World War I, the testing movement was embraced by educators. It became common for learners to be classified and counseled into certain courses on the basis of their IQ scores. There is evidence the patterns of interaction of some teachers with individual learners were affected by their perception of these learners' intelligence as revealed by IQ scores.

In recent years, the use of intelligence tests, particularly paper-and-pencil group intelligence tests, has been challenged. The issue of cultural bias has been raised by African-Americans, Hispanics, and other minorities. Some people have argued that a factor as broad and diffuse as intelligence cannot possibly be measured by a single test. There have been situations in which perfectly normal young people have been assigned to institutions for the mentally retarded on the basis of a faulty IQ score obtained from a group intelligence test. The debate about intelligence testing continues. Although we are far from a consensus on this issue, it is generally fair to say that educators are becoming increasingly hesitant to predict the educational futures of young people on the basis of a single measure such as an IQ score.

The Cardinal Principles

As special circumstances and needs associated with the wartime situation expanded interest in the testing movement during the World War I years, people also became concerned about education's more general purposes. In particular, the last year of war, 1918, was a landmark one for education. In this year, the National Education Association's Commission on the Reorganization of Secondary Education identified seven specific goals for the public schools. These seven goals came to be known as education's "Cardinal Principles:"

- health
- command of fundamental processes
- worthy home membership
- vocational preparation
- citizenship
- worthy use of leisure time
- ethical character

These principles laid the groundwork for the comprehensive high school. They implied that secondary schools should have a broader purpose than simply preparing learners for colleges and universities. In time, publication of the Cardinal Principles led to an expansion of course offerings in high schools. By no means, however, did all high schools give equal emphasis to each of the many subjects that came to be offered; in many, considerable attention (critics would say too much attention) continued to be given to college and university preparatory courses.

Changes in the schools wrought by both attention to the Cardinal Principles and actions taken by groups looking for a more practical emphasis in the curriculum suggested that ever more people were viewing education as a necessity for all young people. Compulsory attendance laws became common during the first two decades of the twentieth century. Increasingly, learners were being required to stay in school until they turned 16.

In the 1920s and 1930s, the influence of those who wanted schools to respond humanely to the needs and interests of individual learners was strong. The term *progressive education movement* has been applied to the general program of people who sought these goals. Supporters of the progressive education movement drew inspiration from the work of John Dewey. The installation of counseling programs in schools, for example, which developed at an especially rapid rate during the 1930s, represented a logical extension of Dewey's concern for individual development.

American Education after World War II

After World War II, the progressive education movement developed into a loosely knit group of people who supported school practices that came to be known as *life-*

adjustment education. In some of its more extreme forms, life-adjustment education programs seemed to encourage learners to do whatever they pleased. Systematic attention to intellectual rigor or subject matter was avoided. Critics of such programs suggested that learners were being shortchanged by schools that failed to provide needed understandings and skills. These critics attracted many supporters, and by the middle 1950s, support for life-adjustment education had greatly diminished.

Sputnik and Rigor

Rarely can change in education (or, indeed, in other social institutions) be attributed to a single event. But in the fall of 1957, the Soviet Union's launch of the first earth satellite, *Sputnik,* so changed the public's perception of education's role that many subsequent alterations in school curricula can be traced back to this single, seminal event. *Sputnik* shocked the nation by challenging America's presumed technological supremacy. Those people looking for an explanation for why Russia was first with such an accomplishment placed a great deal of blame on public education. Large audiences listened sympathetically to critics who told them that American schools had gone soft and that instruction in subject-matter content compared unfavorably with that provided to learners in other countries. Instruction in the sciences was identified as a particularly weak area of the curriculum.

Reacting to pressures to "do something" about the schools, the federal government passed the National Defense Education Act in 1958. This legislation provided federal funds to improve the quality of education. Large-scale curriculum reform projects were launched, first in mathematics and the sciences and later in the social sciences. Special summer workshops designed to upgrade teachers' skills were held on college campuses across the nation. There was a massive effort to improve the quality of textbooks and other instructional materials. People carried high hopes that this revolution in American school programming could be carried to a successful conclusion.

Cultural Change and Education in the 1960s

Although the curriculum reform movement of the 1960s did result in important changes, the modifications fell well short of the expectations of many who had supported passage of the National Defense Education Act. Teachers who attended summer programs became proficient in the use of new techniques and materials, but only a small minority of all teachers participated in such programs. Others who did not take part found themselves ill at ease with many of the new programs, and a majority of teachers continued doing things much as they had always done them.

Another problem involved the new instructional materials themselves. Many were developed by subject-matter experts who had little experience working with public school learners. Consequently, some of the new materials were written at reading levels that were too difficult for many learners. Further, the issue of motivation was not attended to well. Many young people were simply not interested in some of the new instructional materials.

Probably the changing national culture of the 1960s did more than anything else to subvert those changes being pushed by people who wanted to introduce more "intellectual rigor" into school programs. With growing discontent over official governmental policies toward Vietnam and frustrations of minorities in the nation's large cities, the ground was not fertile for changes that appeared to critics to be an effort to push "establishment" values on the young. Increasingly, young people questioned the relevance of school curricula that seemed to favor esoteric intellectual subjects rather than topics of more immediate personal concern.

Junior High School versus Middle School

After World War II, concerns increased about the junior high school as an institution. Many people had originally hoped that junior high schools would be particularly sensitive to the emotional and developmental needs of early adolescents. Over time, however, a majority of junior high schools came to be organized as academic preparatory institutions for the high schools. Middle schools began to grow tremendously in popularity; today there are more middle schools than there are high schools.

The middle school movement began to attract supporters during the 1960s. This interest continued throughout the 1970s, 1980s, and on into the 1990s. Individual middle schools often have one of several different grade-level organizational patterns. Generally, a middle school has three to five grades, and almost always includes grades 6 and 7 (Lounsbury & Vars, 1978). The National Middle School Association and other supporters of middle schools emphasize programs that are sensitive to the special characteristics of learners in the 11- to 14-year-old age group. Today, middle schools are beginning to displace junior high schools as the dominant school type for learners between their elementary and high school years.

School Reform Efforts Since the 1980s

Beginning in the early 1980s, concerns about the quality of American schools led to a period of intense public scrutiny of school programs. There were concerns about the sophistication of thinking being developed by school programs, the readiness of graduates to assume jobs requiring ever more complex levels of technical proficiency, general reading and writing abilities of learners, patterns of scores on academic achievement tests, and unfavorable achievement comparisons between American learners and those in other nations.

A number of major themes have appeared consistently in recommendations to improve the schools that have been broadly circulated since the early 1980s. There has been a frequent call for school programs to become more rigorous. At the high school level, this recommendation has sometimes taken the form of a proposal to reduce the number of electives and to require all learners to take a common core of content drawn from the academic disciplines.

Recommendations have also addressed the issue of teacher quality. There have been suggestions of various ways to attract brighter, more committed people to teaching and to improve the duration and quality of their preparation (Holmes Group, 1986). There also has been a recognition that quality people will not remain in the profession unless there are accompanying efforts to improve teachers' working conditions (e.g., salaries, empowering teachers to make more decisions about how they discharge their responsibilities, etc.).

The issue of school administrative organization has also been addressed. There have been recommendations to decrease sizes of schools to allow for more personal attention to learners. There have also been suggestions that principals spend more time in their role as instructional leaders than in their role as business managers. Additionally, there have been proposals to lengthen the school year to make it conform more to those in countries where learners are doing better on content achievement tests than are learners in the United States.

In the 1990s, discussion of educational improvement has been stimulated by reports of interested national groups and federal government action as well as by increased local interest in providing parents with more choices regarding how and where their children are educated. National efforts have included work of members of The Education Commission of the States and the National Governors' Association. Their work has focused attention on such issues as kinds of school programming that should be provided for students not going on to colleges and universities, improving the technological literacy of graduates of American schools, and enhancing student learning of traditional academic subjects.

Reform efforts of the 1990s have spawned an interest in many of the issues we introduced in Chapter 1. These include (1) efforts to involve local communities and schools in implementing programs responsive to the Goals 2000 initiative; (2) emphases on various approaches to school choice, including voucher plans, open enrollment plans, magnet schools, and charter schools; (3) increased interest in school-business partnerships; and (4) recognition that it may be necessary to establish full-service schools to respond to the varied needs many learners bring with them to school. A theme running through all of these proposals is that reform needs to be *systemic*. That is, problems are multiple and diverse, and no single one can be solved without careful attention to the entire spectrum of difficulties facing schools and children.

In summary, the past decade has witnessed an unprecedented public interest in education. An increasing number of people have become convinced that in the quality of our schools lies the quality of our nation's future. Spirited discussions about how to maintain and improve school quality seem certain to feature prominently in our national life for the remainder of the century.

• Key Ideas in Summary

- The history of American education, as is the case with all history, reflects values and biases of those who have written it. Since the majority of Americans are white and of European descent, it is not surprising that much educational history fails to question the appropriateness for *all* American children of educational practices rooted in traditions from Europe. In times past, some instruction in American schools failed to provide positive models for learners from minority cultures. Educators today are increasingly sensitive to this issue.
- Among educational practices and assumptions that trace their origins to Europe are (1) the idea that content should be organized under major headings, (2) the practice of dividing knowledge into separate subjects, (3) the tradition

of dividing schools into an ordered sequence of grades, (4) the view that teachers should develop instructional plans that take learners' individual differences into account, (5) the idea that as many people as possible should be educated, (6) the practice of providing special training for teachers, and (7) the vision of schooling as a preparation for effective citizenship.

- In the American colonial period, the New England Puritans were motivated by desires to reform policies of the Church of England and raise their children in an environment free from "religious error." This required a society of people capable of reading the Bible, and hence there was an interest in teaching a larger proportion of the population to read.

- Settlers in the middle colonies came from more diverse backgrounds than early residents of New England. In New York, many early private schools sought to prepare young people for commercial careers. In Pennsylvania, Quakers established schools that were open to all children.

- Settlements in the southern colonies tended to be along major rivers. Because there were few towns and cities, it was difficult for children to be brought together in sufficient numbers to support a school. Wealthy people hired tutors to educate their children, and some young people were sent to England for at least part of their education. Little schooling was available to children from less prosperous families.

- The first high school was established in Boston in 1821. Unlike academies, which were mostly private institutions, most high schools were publicly supported. At first, the growth of high schools proceeded slowly. In 1860, for example, there were only 40 high schools in the entire country.

- Horace Mann championed the common school in the 1820s and 1830s. He believed that it was in the taxpayers' interest to support a strong system of public education. He saw schools as vehicles for equalizing differences among people from different social classes and as engines for the future economic growth of the nation. Mann also supported the development of normal schools, formal institutions dedicated to the preparation of teachers.

- The post–Civil War period witnessed many changes in education. The famous Kalamazoo case established a legal precedent for public support of secondary as well as elementary education. Teachers began to organize in professional organizations. The large number of immigrants entering the country challenged educators to develop programs responsive to their needs and to the needs of American employers. Toward the end of the nineteenth century, there was interest narrowing the focus of the school curriculum in the direction of placing more emphasis on knowledge students would need to succeed in colleges and universities.

- During the first 20 years of the twentieth century, one conflict regarding the purpose of the American high school was resolved - arguments between those seeing high schools as college-preparatory institutions and those regarding them as vocational-preparatory institutions were accommodated in a new view of the high school as a comprehensive institution, one having multiple objectives.

- John Dewey had a significant influence on twentieth-century American education. Dewey believed that education should primarily focus on the development of the individual. He was especially interested in providing learners with the kinds of problem-solving abilities they would need to successfully confront the challenges they would face throughout their lives.

- The testing movement, originating in France and developing rapidly during World War I, led to American schools' extensive use of intelligence testing of learners by the second and third decades of the twentieth century. In recent years, much skepticism has been generated regarding the idea that an IQ represents an accurate measure of something as complex and sophisticated as human intelligence.

- After World War II, there was interest in life-adjustment education. Critics felt that this view of education encouraged learners to do only what pleased them and that school programs lacked needed intellectual substance. By the 1950s, much enthusiasm for life-adjustment education had faded.

- In the late 1950s, following the launch of the earth satellite *Sputnik* and continuing into the very early 1960s, there was a push to place heavier emphasis in schools on challenging academic content. There were particular efforts to strengthen programs in mathematics and the sciences. As public disaffection with the nation's Vietnam policy increased, suspicions began to be directed at leaders of many public institutions, including the schools. In time, these suspicions led to widespread rejection of narrow school programs with strong focuses on traditional academic subjects; increasingly, young people questioned the relevance of such programs.

- Beginning in the 1960s, concerns about junior high schools prompted a great deal of interest in middle schools. This interest continues to the present time. Supporters of middle schools believe that their programs tend to be more responsive than junior high school programs to special needs of learners in the 11- to 14-year-old age group.

- Beginning in the 1980s, a large number of proposals to reform the schools were made. These were prompted by concerns about the intellectual levels of school graduates, unfavorable achievement comparisons between American and foreign learners, and perceived learner deficiencies in such key areas as reading and writing. The important Goals 2000: Educate America Act of 1994 represented an effort to translate many suggestions for education reform into federal policy.

• Review and Discussion Questions

1. What are your views on the issue that American schooling has been set up to benefit individuals of European descent more than to benefit others? What evidence do you have to support your views? Should schools try to develop both a common and shared set of values and an appreciation for values of individual cultural groups that might differ from those common and shared values? Why or why not?

2. Some people allege that certain school programs and instructional materials have demeaned learners from some groups. Do you think this continues to be a problem? What might you do in your own classroom to help each learner develop a positive self-concept?

3. You were introduced in this chapter to a number of commonplace educational practices that were adopted by American educators from European precedents. (Recall such

things as the practice of dividing knowledge into separate subjects, division of schools into grades, and so forth.) Suppose early on we had decided not to do these things. How might our schools be different? Why do you think they might be more effective or less effective than they are today?

4. Why were colonial educational patterns different in New England, the middle colonies, and the southern colonies? Which patterns do you think had the most lasting influence on American education and why?

5. Why do you think Americans were much more quick to agree to support elementary schools with their tax dollars than secondary schools?

6. Why do you think American educators were so quick to use intelligence tests in schools once such tests became available?

7. Today, some critics argue that curricula in our schools should place more emphasis on specific technical skills high school graduates will need when they enter the job market. How do you think John Dewey would have reacted to this proposal? What differences do you see between Dewey's values and those favoring more technical skills training? What do you think about this issue, and how do your views reflect your own thoughts about what is really important?

8. In some parts of the country, a backlash is developing to the Goals 2000 legislation. Critics argue that the federal government should keep its hands off educational policy. Why might they feel this way? What are their concerns and priorities? What are your views regarding the proper role for the federal government in the area of educational policy? What do your views tell you about your personal values?

9. What is implied by the term "systemic reform"? How might you go about involving yourself in systemic reform efforts?

10. What do you personally view as the most pressing problems facing schools today? What are some of your ideas regarding how these problems might be productively approached? Describe some barriers that will need to be overcome if your ideas are to be implemented.

• Ideas for Field Experiences, Projects, and Enrichment

1. In the Middle Ages, many people in charge of teaching the young felt that certain kinds of information had to be kept secret. For example, information about the religious practices of the ancient Greeks and Romans was considered particularly dangerous. Do we face any similar situations in education today? Together with several other people from your class, organize a symposium on the topic, "What Learners Should *Not* Be Taught in School."

2. Many lingering influences from European precedents remain in our schools today. As you look ahead to schools during the first quarter of the twenty-first century, which of these influences will weaken? Which will grow stronger? Who stands to benefit from any changes you foresee? Prepare a chart that summarizes your ideas and share it with your class as you briefly summarize your position.

3. Some people argue that the comprehensive high school has outlived its usefulness. They suggest that it would be better to have separate schools for separate purposes. Organize a debate on this topic: "Has the Comprehensive High School Outlived its Usefulness?"

4. Do some research on minority-group dropouts. Is this situation improving or getting worse? Are there different patterns from one minority group to another? Is there evidence that the inappropriateness of the school curriculum influences minority-group learners to leave school before graduating from high school? Based on your research,

draft a letter that might be sent to editors of newspapers in your state that explains the problem and suggests possible solutions. Ask your instructor to react to your letter.

5. The Goals 2000: Educate America Act of 1994 is a complex piece of legislation. Review its various titles. Then prepare a research paper in which you provide examples of specific things that have been done to implement provisions associated with each title. You may also wish to discuss some criticisms that have been made of some parts of this legislation. Present your paper to the course instructor. You may also wish to make a brief oral summary of your findings to your class.

• References

Barry, T. N. (1961). *Origin and development of the American public high school in the 19th century*. Unpublished doctoral dissertation, Stanford University.

Bowen, J. A. (1981). *A history of Western education: Vol. 3. The modern West, Europe, and the New World*. New York: St. Martin's Press.

Coleman, M. (1993). *American Indian children at school, 1850–1930*. Jackson, MS: University of Mississippi Press.

Commissioner of Indian Affairs. (1888). *Annual report*. Washington, DC: U.S. Government Printing Office.

Fischer, D. H. (1989). *Albion's seed*. New York: Oxford University Press.

Gordon, P., & Szreter, R. (Eds.). (1989). *History of education: The making of a discipline*. London: The Woburn Press.

The Holmes Group. (1986). *Tomorrow's teachers*. East Lansing, MI: Author.

Lounsbury, J. H., & Vars, G. E. (1978). *Curriculum for the middle years*. New York: Harper and Row.

Nieto, S. (1992). *Affirming diversity: The sociopolitical context of multicultural education*. New York: Longman.

Popper, S. H. (1967). *The American middle school*. Waltham, MA: Blaisdell.

Stuart v. School District No. 1 of the Village of Kalamazoo, 30 Mich. 69 (1874).

U.S. Department of Commerce. (1975). *Historical statistics of the United States, colonial times to 1970: Part I*. Washington, DC: Bureau of the Census.

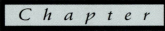

Chapter

7

Practical Influences of Philosophy

OBJECTIVES

- State the importance of philosophy for a teacher.
- Identify practical applications of philosophical ideas to the classroom.
- Define basic categories addressed in philosophy.
- Compare non-Western and Western philosophies.
- Describe different educational philosophic systems.
- Develop a personal philosophy.

What comes to your mind when you hear the term *philosophy*? You may get an image of an arcane subject that deals with issues far removed from the realm of the practical. Some of you may recall unpleasant experiences in undergraduate philosophy courses that required you to confront difficult abstractions. Frustrations in dealing with this kind of content sometimes are behind anxieties many prospective teachers experience when, during a job interview, they are asked, "What is your philosophy of education?"

Philosophy's reputation as a subject that is unconnected to the "real" world is undeserved. Our philosophical positions explain our reactions to what we confront in our daily lives. Philosophy explains our responses to such questions as:

- Are people basically good or bad?
- What is right, and what is wrong?
- How is truth determined?
- What is beauty?
- What is worth knowing?
- How should other people be treated?

All of us have worked out at least informal answers to these questions. In fact, our responses to many of them have become so automatic that we rarely think about them. Our reactions have simply become part of us because of our interaction with the customs and traditions of our culture. We just assume that our ways are a natural or right response to the world about us.

Assumptions we have that reflect philosophical positions greatly influence how we see education. We have adopted ideas about what should be taught, how it should be taught, what is appropriate behavior, and what is a proper relationship with learners. We rarely think about the assumptions we are making or about the implications of what we are doing. Instead, we tend to define educational practices that are consistent with our personal philosophies as those that are normal or right. In times of stability, we may go years without facing challenges to these assumptions. In times of change and uncertainty, however, these "right ways" may well draw attacks on our educational practices. When this happens, stress often results. Few people feel comfortable when confronted with challenges to the rules they have long lived by.

There are several ways that our personal philosophy of education connects with the daily task of teaching. For example, consider decisions about the content to be taught. Researchers find that teachers vary significantly in the amount of time that they allocate to teaching different subjects. Even within a subject, teachers vary widely in the amount of time they designate to certain topics and the time spent teaching ideas and concepts or in drill and practice (Good & Brophy, 1994). This variation is due in part to differing teacher responses to two basic philosophical questions: (1) What knowledge is worth knowing? and (2) Is knowledge fixed or constantly changing?

This variation in content taught from teacher to teacher also prompts another philosophical question — the ethical one — Is it right? What is the ethical obligation of the teacher to present a broad base of information and content to learners?

Teachers' individual assumptions about what constitutes good education often leads to serious discussion when curriculum changes are being considered.

Another way that personal philosophy connects with day-to-day reality is that teachers, by definition, work with learners. How individual teachers interact with learners depends on their general philosophical positions regarding the nature of human beings. Are people basically good or basically evil? Teachers who see people as essentially good work with their learners in ways that differ from those who see people as inherently bad.

Personal philosophies also influence teachers' individual understandings of what conduct is moral or right. This begins with a consideration of what they believe is ethical conduct for teachers and also involves how individual teachers deal with the issues of teaching values and morality.

Still another philosophical factor that influences teaching is the teacher's view regarding what constitutes correct thinking, which relates to rules of inference and consistency. For example, how are conclusions to be defended? Is intuition enough, or must there be some reliance on evidence? If so, what kinds of evidence are appropriate, and how must evidence be organized? It is important to recognize that many teachers make these decisions based on philosophical ideas grounded in the Western tradition.

With an increased diversity of learners in our classrooms — many of whom come from non-Western philosophic traditions — we need to realize that other cultures may place less emphasis on what we define as reason and logic and place more emphasis on tradition and feeling. We have to be sensitive to these differences in perspectives if we hope to build bridges of understanding.

Today, we educators are facing challenges of many kinds. These include proposals to reform education through school choice, voucher plans, national certification of teachers, and through numerous other initiatives. Changes in the linguistic and ethnic makeup of the schools confront us with conditions that differ from what many of us have experienced in the past. Some people on the political fringes of our society go so far as to assert that the schools are an agency of a hostile government that increasingly is driven to undermine individual liberties.

All of these challenges present us with a need to understand diverse philosophical perspectives. Lacking such an understanding, we cannot grasp the positions from which our critics are arguing. Without an appreciation of our own philosophical positions, we are unlikely to respond effectively to serious challenges to what we are doing.

Change and controversy in education require us to have a clear understanding of alternative answers to basic philosophical questions. An understanding of the alternative answers to these questions is more than an abstract intellectual exercise; it is critical to the future of our profession. The decisions that are made now will influence the direction of education, and of the nation, for many decades. These decisions must be made only after thoughtful consideration of the implications of alternative choices. Thus, far from being an abstract subject that is best relegated to an obscure corner of the university, philosophy is a practical subject central to our own actions and survival.

To develop an understanding of different philosophical viewpoints, prospective teachers need to review some of the categories of questions that must be answered as they begin working out their personal philosophies of education. These categories are introduced in the sections that follow.

METAPHYSICS (OR ONTOLOGY)

Metaphysics is concerned with the nature of reality. Metaphysics is defined in the dictionary as beyond the physical or the material. In essence, it deals with questions that go beyond science. Questions in this category cannot be answered by application of the scientific method. This is true because they tend to be speculative and focus on such issues as the nature of cause-and-effect relationships. For example, do cause and effect exist in reality, or are they simply a creation of our mind? Is there a purpose to the universe, or is life basically meaningless? Are humans essentially spiritual beings, or are they creatures who exist in a particular time and space with no meaning beyond self? Is there a set of constant and unchanging principles that guides the operation of things and that, therefore, can be discovered? Is reality a constantly changing entity that is always relative, thus rendering any search for truth fruitless? Obviously, these are not questions that are readily adaptable to experimentation, and their answers cannot be tested against scientific evidence.

Practical Implications

These metaphysical questions may seem remote from the everyday world of the teacher, but they are not. Many serious debates and efforts to change the schools are based on alternative answers to these questions. For example, *theism* is a belief that the universe was created by a God. Meaning in life is found by serving God and learning an established set of unchanging principles that God has given to guide existence. The proper role of education is to help individuals in their search for God and for these unchanging principles. In fact, some theists would contend that there can be no real education that ignores God. Therefore, individuals holding a theistic philosophy are actively seeking to include this philosophical orientation as the basis for education. If this cannot be done in public schools, then theists believe that parents ought to be allowed to send their children to private theistic schools. In an extreme form, there are those who contend that schools without a theistic orientation are basically evil and sending ones' children to such a school amounts to heresy. As a result, there is widespread support for school choice among theists.

Other critics argue that the primary purpose of education is to help learners achieve a well-adjusted or satisfying life. This implies that satisfaction or "happiness" is the answer to a metaphysical question about what the central purpose of life ought to be. Given this orientation, some critics suggest that there is no subject matter worth knowing that is not of clear and pressing interest to the individual learner. Therefore, schools should permit learners to determine what they will study and that, above all, the schools should provide for learners' freedom and individual choice.

Individuals advocating this orientation have made a number of philosophical assumptions about reality. They reject the idea that known principles exist that explain reality and that these should be mastered by all learners. Furthermore, they perceive human beings to be essentially good and trustworthy. Basic to this position is an assumption that if people are given freedom, they will intuitively do what is good.

Many educational issues are divisive because people have arrived at different answers to basic metaphysical questions. Teachers who are familiar with the nature of metaphysical questions — and more particularly with the reality that answers to such questions cannot be tested against scientific evidence — are better prepared to understand the assumptions supporting views about school practices that differ from their own. Teachers with these insights know when an argument is based on metaphysics (and cannot, therefore, be proved with evidence) and when an argument is not (and thus can be challenged or defended with evidence).

EPISTEMOLOGY

A second major category of philosophical theory is *epistemology*. Epistemological questions are concerned with the nature of knowledge. Since educators are interested in the discovery and transmission of knowledge, teachers have a special interest in this category. Answers to epistemological questions provide a rationale for selecting material that is worth teaching. They also suggest how information should be taught.

Two basic epistemological questions are (1) What constitutes knowledge? and (2) Is knowledge fixed or changing? Some people maintain that there is no possibility of obtaining knowledge about ultimate reality. Others counter that it is possible to identify a set of principles that represents "true" knowledge. Still others argue that there are no principles that are true under all sets of conditions, but there is knowledge that is true in certain circumstances. (Stated another way, what these people contend is that knowledge functions in a particular situation, and all we can know is what is "functional.")

In the past, the dominant philosophical orientation to the mind and knowledge was how to help individuals acquire true knowledge of the world external to themselves (Soltis, 1981). However, the shift today is toward viewing knowledge as "cultural" and, therefore, as a human construction. This conception has important implications. It suggests that all knowledge is relative and that there is no right or wrong knowledge.

If knowledge is a cultural construction, then how does one judge which construction is correct? This concern leads to another fundamental epistemological question centering on ways of knowing and the reliability of these ways. How can we be sure that what we claim to know is true? Basically, the issue involves whether we test the truth of knowledge by revelation, authority, intuition, the senses, reason, or experimentation. Today, our culture has a bias favoring the position that knowledge comes from scientific experimentation. Indeed, among some people, this idea is so firmly rooted that they cannot even imagine it being challenged. But even these people sometimes take actions based only on intuition. They do some things just because they "feel" they are right.

Practical Implications

Changes in the way knowledge is perceived have important educational implications. For example, recent changes in teaching theories, such as constructivism (see Chapter 2), are based on philosophical assumptions. In thinking about the constructivist position, we need to consider what it presumes about the nature of knowledge. For example, does the insistence of constructivism that each person constructs his or her own knowledge effectively deny the existence of any universal principles?

How can we as teachers claim to know what is right or appropriate for our young people to learn? In thinking about this issue, we need to recognize that education has a responsibility not only to transmit knowledge, but also to help learners think about and critically test alternative knowledge claims. This implies that a central focus in education ought to be critical and creative thinking. This does not mean that we should not transmit any specific information. Our learners need to start with something before they can construct their own knowledge through the application of sophisticated thinking skills. But we need to be careful that we do not suggest that the specific knowledge we present to learners is taught as a set of fixed truths that are to be accepted and never challenged.

This shift toward the view that knowledge is a cultural construction is a central feature in multicultural programs. James Banks (1994) includes knowledge construction as a key element in multicultural education. He states that it is important for all students to understand that cultural experiences, perspectives, and values influence the knowledge construction of a given culture and that knowledge is dynamic and changing. He advocates making the classroom a forum for debates about different knowledge constructions.

People in many other world cultures place a lower premium on scientific experimentation than do we. Because of differences in views regarding how knowledge is best acquired, we often find it hard to understand the perspectives of people living in unfamiliar cultural settings. When learners lack such understandings, they may conclude that other cultures are strange or even funny. An important objective of the school program is to help learners understand that they see the world through "cultural blinders" of their own. Learners must recognize that there is nothing correct in any absolute sense in the way we think knowledge is best acquired. Our views simply reflect how our culture has decided to view reality (Oliver & Gersham, 1989).

Arguments about the content of the curriculum often grow heated. These debates frequently stem from different philosophical views about the nature of knowledge, and they reflect a diversity of opinion about what should be central to the school instructional program. For example, some people believe the curriculum should feature the so-called classics of Western thought. Others favor a school program dedicated to developing learners' sophisticated thinking skills. Still others support school programs with heavy emphases on preparing learners for the world of work.

Teachers' individual approaches to teaching content say a good deal about their own answers to epistemological questions. Teachers who insist that learners master basic facts and principles, for example, operate on the assumption that there is such a thing as true knowledge. Teachers who are more interested in teaching the processes of learning imply by their actions that there is no ultimate truth and that it is better for young people to master problem-solving skills that can be applied to diverse situations.

Some school subjects feature instructional practices that are derived from differing conclusions regarding the source of knowledge. For example, instruction in the humanities frequently is premised on the assumption that knowledge results at least as much from intuition, feeling, and reason as from scientific experimentation. Critics who do not understand the appropriateness of an approach to truth through any process except scientific experimentation have sometimes labeled the humanities as "soft" subjects; that is, they are soft compared with the "hard" sciences that rely more heavily on scientific experimentation.

The labels hard and soft have nothing to do with the difficulty of the subjects. Rather, they relate to the sources of knowledge deemed appropriate within each discipline. Debates over the worthiness of soft subjects and hard subjects have important curricular implications. For example, if it is decided that only scientifically verifiable knowledge is important, then there will be a much heavier emphasis on the sciences than on the humanities. On the other hand, those advocating the cultural construction of knowledge point out that different fields of inquiry and study have developed different perspectives and forms of knowledge. For example, the perspectives and the criticism of art are very different from that of science.

A truly comprehensive education includes learning experiences derived from different sources of knowledge and ways of knowing. There is merit in helping our young people view the world from different perspectives (Soltis, 1981).

AXIOLOGY

Should teachers stress the acquisition of knowledge or the moral and character development of their learners? Is there a standard of moral behavior that teachers should emphasize? Are there moral or ethical standards that teachers should follow? These questions relate to the area of *axiology*. Axiology focuses on questions about what "ought to be." How should life be lived? What is the highest good? What is moral and immoral? What is beauty? The topics of morality, ethics, and aesthetics fall into this philosophical category.

One important axiological concern focuses on the issue of whether life is worth living. What is the nature of existence? Does life have any meaning? Answers to these questions, particularly as they are developed by learners, are of interest to teachers. For example, the rate of suicide among young people in our society suggests that many of them have concluded that life has no meaning (or at least not a meaning worth living for).

Drug problems in schools can be tied to the issue of the value and worth of life. Many people who use drugs are stating that the highest good amounts to seeking immediate pleasure and living for the moment. In traditional philosophy, such attitudes collectively are referred to as *hedonism*. Even though many learners would be unable to define this term, their actions suggest that hedonism represents their basic philosophy of life. Hedonism is only one perspective that results from a consideration of axiological questions.

Another perspective takes the optimistic view that life is absolutely worth living over the long term and that the highest good involves something other than short-term pleasure. For example, a lot of individuals see the highest good as self-realization or self-perfection. Many star athletes in the schools have this orientation, and social reformers of all kinds who believe in the perfectibility of the human condition also reflect this general position.

Theists find life's purpose through religion. They accept the view that there is an ultimate purpose to life and that every human being has a divine reason for being. They see the highest good being served in the effort to understand God's will and in the attempt to meet God's expectations.

An important axiological question of a different kind concerns the nature of "right" conduct. How should a person behave? What is moral behavior? How does a person know when he or she is doing the right thing? In answering these questions, some argue that there are universal principles or guidelines that can be followed. For example, there are people who cite the Ten Commandments as an example of a universal guide to appropriate behavior. Others reject the idea that there are guidelines that fit every set of circumstances. They contend that "appropriateness" of behavior is situation-specific. An example of this latter point of view occurred during the late 1960s, when some people argued that America's fight against Hitler during World War II was moral but that America's participation in the Vietnam War was not.

Practical Implications

Questions and issues related to axiology have important applications to education. Let us begin with an example. In Chapter 1, there was a discussion of the Goals 2000: Educate America Act. You may recall that one of the central goals of the act is to ensure that by the year 2000, U.S. learners will be first in the world in science and mathematics achievement. By subscribing to this goal, what is it that we as a nation are saying about what we value and about what is important? Is the competition between nations of the world on standardized mathematics tests of such importance that significant resources should be devoted to achieve it? Why are science and mathematics specifically identified? Does this mean that they are the most important subjects? Should we not want to be first in the world in terms of an understanding of democratic processes or in treating all individuals humanely? Attention to these kinds of axiological questions helps us to clarify our thinking and assists us in making important decisions regarding the purposes of education and the use of our scarce resources.

At the classroom level, axiological questions permeate all that we do. Every decision about what to teach, how much time to spend on it, and how to teach it relates to a value decision. Our views about the purposes of education or the highest good have powerful impacts on our decisions. If we believe that the highest good is citizenship and the preservation of the state, then much of what we do will be directed toward helping learners assume that role. If we believe that the highest purpose is preparing individuals for a productive career, then much of what is done will be slanted to providing individuals with skills that will help them achieve success in the world of work.

Another important application of axiology in the classroom is evident in the way we relate to our learners. In establishing relationships with students, we are guided by our sense of ethics. What is my moral responsibility toward those I teach? Should I make an effort to make sure that all of the young people in my classroom have an opportunity for success, or should I devote most of my time to the academically talented who are likely to benefit most from my efforts? Is my discipline plan fair and just, and does it communicate a sense of respect for the dignity of all humans?

All of us have encountered teachers who view their work as nothing more than a job that is to be done as easily and quickly as possible. It might be said of these teachers that they have little sense of any moral responsibilities or of a code of ethics guiding their teaching decisions. We also have witnessed teachers who deal with discipline problems in harsh and uncaring ways. The behavior of these teachers suggests that they do not believe that respecting the dignity of human beings extends to the treatment of the young people in their classrooms.

The content of the curriculum also relates to the area of axiology. As teachers, we often are faced with the need to help learners make value choices. Many

Teachers's patterns of interactions with learners reflect their answers to axiological questions.

polls of public attitudes toward education indicate that the public thinks that the teaching of values and morality is an important responsibility of education. Most indicate that they would like to see more emphasis on this component of education. Recent national attempts to promote "character education" and best-selling books such as William Bennett's *Book of Virtues* are indications of public interest in this domain.

Educators, however, are faced with some difficult questions. What values or virtues should be taught, and how should they be taught? If I choose to try to indoctrinate someone in a given value or virtue, what am I saying about the nature of values and morality? What statement am I making about what I value in terms of individual rights and freedoms? What does this indicate about my values and ethics as a teacher? Questions of axiology do not have easy answers. However, because these issues touch the very essence of what it means to be a teacher, they deserve deep and thoughtful consideration.

LOGIC

The science of exact thought is a subfield of philosophy known as *logic*. Logic deals with the relationships between ideas and with the procedures used to differentiate between valid thinking and fallacious thinking.

There are several reasons why a knowledge of logic is important for teachers. First, logic helps us to communicate more effectively by encouraging a careful, systematic arrangement of thoughts. Second, logic helps us to evaluate the consistency of learners' reasoning. Third, logic helps us assess the reliability of new information we encounter.

There are two basic types of logic, *deductive* logic and *inductive* logic. Deductive logic begins with a general conclusion and then elucidates this conclusion by citing examples and particulars that logically flow from it. Inductive logic begins with particulars. Reasoning focuses on these particulars and leads to a general conclusion that explains them.

Practical Implications

The choice of a deductive or an inductive approach has implications for how we organize and present materials. When a deductive approach is selected, great care must be taken to ensure that learners acquire a solid grasp of the major principle or idea before we move on to illustrate it through the use of examples. Teaching methods such as direct instruction, the use of advance organizers, and the lecture method are basically deductive teaching approaches.

A choice of an inductive approach requires us to locate a large number of examples before instruction can begin. Further, these examples must be selected with great care. It is essential that they accurately represent the larger principle that, it is hoped, learners will come to understand. Inquiry approaches and discovery learning are teaching strategies based on the inductive approach.

There has been much professional discussion about the relative effectiveness of deductive and inductive instruction. Research suggests that neither approach is demonstrably superior to the other. The key issue seems to be how the teacher leads learners through a lesson, regardless of whether it is organized deductively or inductively. Clever teachers who help their learners grasp relationships between ideas and distinguish between valid and invalid arguments find that their learners do well regardless of whether content is sequenced deductively or inductively.

ALTERNATIVE PHILOSOPHICAL TRADITIONS

Most teachers have been reared in cultures that have their bases in Western philosophy. Those of us who come from this kind of background naturally think that our way of viewing the nature of the world and our perceptions of truth and beauty are the "correct" ones. However, there are other cultures that have different world views and, therefore, different understandings. When individuals from these cultures encounter our logic and our values, they may find them bizarre and strange. The meeting of these different philosophical orientations in the classroom can lead to significant conflict and problems. Because our classrooms include significant numbers of students from a variety of cultures, it is important to have some grasp of how these individuals view the world and make sense out of it.

Native American Philosophy

A good place to begin as we compare different philosophies is with that of the first Americans. It is important to remember that there are a variety of groups that are classified under the label *native American*. Therefore, any general description of the native American philosophy runs the risk of distortion for a given group. There are, however, a few general points that can be helpful in understanding the differences between traditional Western philosophy and that of many native Americans.

Western philosophy places high value on scientific experimentation as a source of knowledge. Logic is the preferred method of arriving at truth and knowledge, which is what is generally termed *rational* thought. In addition, progress is considered to be a virtue. Humans are thought to be superior to the rest of nature and are involved in a quest to subdue nature in order to achieve progress.

Native American thought, on the other hand, is generally labeled as *nonrational*. What this means is simply that reason and logic are not considered to be the superior means to arrive at truth and knowledge. Knowledge and wisdom are found in many ways. The brain may be perceived as a tool for memory and action, but not necessarily as the source of truth (Morton, 1988). Truth and knowledge are found in the experiences and the folklore of the elders and may come from the heart. Hence, there is great respect for the elders who are the sources of revelation and wisdom.

The highest value for native Americans is to seek harmony and balance with each other and with nature. This leads to a reverence for the earth and its web of life. Life is viewed as a three-way partnership among humans, animals, and nature. Humans are but one part of the whole, a part of the basic rhythms of the earth, not superior to the other parts (Morton, 1988).

This basic orientation of being but one part of a larger entity affects all aspects of life. Cooperation with others and concern about the group takes precedence over concern for self. Group cohesion and solidarity are among the most highly valued principles. Individual achievements are measured in terms of what the individual contributes to the group. Generosity is considered to be a great virtue. This means generosity with time, advice, caring, and love. Competition is minimized, and self-promotion or self-aggrandizement is discouraged because it is counter to group cohesion and solidarity.

A lack of understanding of these basic differences in cultural philosophies can lead to difficulties between non–native American teachers and native American learners. For example, one of the authors once worked with a school district that had many native American students. Teachers and administrators were often very frustrated when learners would miss school for events such as the birth of a baby to someone in the group. School officials considered these events as simply excuses to miss school. The native American community, however, saw the birth of new members of their group as opportunities to draw people together and reinforce their solidarity.

African Philosophy

The dangers of making sweeping generalizations about native American philosophy are even more true when we consider African philosophy. Africa is much larger than North America, and it is home to incredibly diverse groups of people. Even so, there are some common threads running through the perspectives of many African groups. For example, many African cultures reflect a philosophy that is grounded in nonrational thought. Feelings and personal relationships are viewed as important components in finding knowledge and wisdom (Nieto, 1992). Thus, emotions and expressions of feelings are an important part of life. Art and music are important means of expression and seeking knowledge.

Because of the importance of the communal culture and personal relationships, working cooperatively with others rather than independently may be the preferred mode for learners from this philosophy (Banks, 1994). In essence, the relationships with others are at least as important as success in completing the task. Emotions and feelings cannot be excluded from learning in favor of some cold, analytical process.

As teachers, we need to remember that elements of these deeply rooted philosophical views added to the historical experiences of African-Americans have a powerful impact on the perspectives and attitudes of African-American students (Nieto, 1992). These traditions suggest the importance of group work and of framing lessons that touch on the emotional aspects of education and knowledge. Expressive activities often have a powerful impact on the learning of adherents to this philosophical tradition.

Asian Philosophy

Many traditions of Asian philosophy are rooted in Confucianism, Hinduism, and Buddhism. There are significant differences within as well as between these traditions. As with native American and African philosophies, however, there are some broad generalizations that can be made.

Nearly all of the Asian traditions emphasize the importance of learning. One of the basic tenets of Buddhism is that all of life is suffering and suffering can be ended by overcoming ignorance. Zen Buddhism emphasizes personal enlightenment rather than prescribing a specific doctrine or a study of scripture. The enlightened individual is seen as the ideal (McDermott, 1994). One of the branches of Confucianism emphasizes that human nature is basically good and can be nurtured through study and self-cultivation (Kennedy, 1994). Hinduism identifies knowledge as one of three paths to religious realization (O'Flaherty, 1994).

In Asian philosophy, there is an emphasis on meditation as one of the methods of arriving at truth. Chinese philosophy holds that meditation is a direct and intuitive way to penetrate the nature of the universe (Kennedy, 1994). Therefore, there is an emphasis on keeping quiet as one seeks knowledge, a perspective that is not very consistent with most American classrooms.

Another outlook that may appear different to Americans arguing over science or revelation is an acceptance of the idea that there is no conflict between modern science and philosophy. Asian philosophy points out that Buddha applied the experimental approach to the question of ultimate truth (McDermott, 1994). Young people in our classrooms who come out of this philosophical tradition often have a high regard for learning. The cultivation of the mind is an important component of seeking truth and meaning.

Another common characteristic that runs through much of Asian philosophy is an emphasis on moral codes and correct conduct. Morality is one of the major categories defining the eightfold path of Buddhism. Honesty, compassion, goodness, love, propriety, and integrity are some of the moral virtues emphasized in the moral code.

Because of the emphasis of Asian philosophy on correct conduct and propriety, we need to be aware of the influence our behavior can have on learners. Sarcasm or a mild rebuke that may have little obvious impact on a learner raised in a Western philosophical tradition can be the source of considerable anxiety and embarrassment for a young person grounded in Asian philosophy.

Unlike learners from some of the other philosophical traditions, feelings and emotions tend to be tightly controlled in Asian learners in order to preserve propriety and proper social relationships. This can be frustrating for teachers who rely heavily on nonverbal cues from their learners to assess the impact their teaching is having.

In summary, the majority of us who teach are well grounded in the philosophical traditions of Western philosophy. We tend to consider perspectives associated with this tradition as the natural way to view the world. We grow as professionals as we come to understand that there are different interpretations of reality, knowledge, and morality. Many young people in our classrooms come from cultures grounded in philosophical systems that vary in significant ways from Western philosophy. The more we know about these alternative world views, the better equipped we are to teach *all* of the young people we serve.

EDUCATIONAL APPLICATIONS OF PHILOSOPHICAL IDEAS

As individuals have considered answers to the basic philosophical questions and their applications to education, they have developed systems of philosophy. These are called *systems* of philosophy because there is some logic or consistency in the way they address important questions. Philosophical systems help us clarify our own beliefs about what the goals of education ought to be, what individuals should be taught, and what methods should be used to teach them. They also help us to construct our personal philosophy.

No single philosophical system has been "proved" to be true. For one person, a given philosophical system may appear to be based on solid assumptions and sound arguments, whereas someone else may view it as weak and poorly reasoned. As you read the next section, you need to consider the assumptions and arguments of each system and consider which ones you perceive as strong and which ones you believe to be weak. This exercise will be valuable as you consider educational programs and educational changes. Most arguments and disagreements about education and educational policy are rooted in philosophical disagreements.

Progressivism

Progressivism, as applied to education, has its roots in the work of John Dewey (1902, 1910, 1916, 1938) and in the spirit of progress that characterized the close of the nineteenth century and the beginning years of the twentieth. Progressivism

Comparing Philosophies

It is helpful to understand how different philosophies respond to basic philosophical issues. Fill in the chart provided to help you clarify the differences.

	Metaphysical Views	Epistemological Views	Axiological Views
Native American Philosophy			
African Philosophy			
Asian Philosophy			
My Personal Philosophy			
Other Philosophies You May Wish to Add			

What are some implications of each of these differences for you as a teacher?

---

emphasizes change as the essence of reality. It views knowledge as something tentative that may explain present reality adequately but has no claim to being true forever. Reality is seen as undergoing continuous change.

Progressives consider an educated person to be someone who has the insights needed to adapt to change. They believe that schools should teach learners how to solve problems and inquire about their natural and social environments. Since there are no unchanging truths that must be taught, knowledge that is of value is that which can help people think about and respond to problems associated with their need to adjust to change.

Progressives view human beings as basically good. They believe that people who are free to choose generally will select a course of action that is best for them. Applied to schools, this perspective suggests that learners be given some choices regarding what and how they will study. Some principles of education that are consistent with progressivism include the following:

- Direct experience with the environment is the best stimulus for learning.
- Reliance on authoritarian textbooks and methods of teaching are inappropriate for the education of free people.

John Dewey, one of the giants of American educational thought, developed much of the intellectual foundation for progressivism.

- Teachers should be instructional managers who establish the learning environment, ask stimulating questions, and guide learners' interests in productive directions.
- Individuals need to learn how to inquire about their environment.
- Schools should not be isolated from the social world outside of the school.

Dewey did not object to the introduction of new content to learners; however, he believed that the content should be presented so that the interest of the learner was stimulated through an interaction with the environment. Dewey recommended that subject matter be organized in ways that would take advantage of learners' interests. By using personal interests as a point of reference, teachers could impart valuable problem-solving skills to learners.

Some of the later progressives went far beyond Dewey's ideas to suggest that the entire scholastic program should consist only of what the learners wanted to study. When putting this theory to practice in some of their classrooms, the learners pursued activities of doubtful significance. For example, a class might study native Americans by building a paper teepee in the room and eating the foods the early native Americans were supposed to have eaten. In some of these programs, there was an assumption that the "experience was the thing."

The more irresponsible applications of progressive principles led some critics to allege that the entire progressive education movement was anti-intellectual. Although Dewey and other leading progressives clearly acknowledged the importance of sound academic content, the entire progressive movement was tainted by critics' concerns about what was going on in some experience-is-the-thing classrooms. Consequently, since the end of World War II, there has been an increasing reluctance among educators to identify themselves publicly as progressives.

Essentialism

Essentialism began as an organized tradition in education in the 1930s. It owes much to the work of William C. Bagley (1941). Essentialism began as a reaction against some of the more extreme variants of progressivism.

Essentialism is based on several important propositions. First, the school program should not be diluted by any trivial and nonessential courses. Second, the academic rigor of American education is threatened by many of the perspectives of the progressives. Third, schools should not lose sight of their fundamental purpose — the provision of sound practical and intellectual training.

Essentialists hold that there is a core of knowledge and skills that should be taught to all learners. This common core includes those subjects that are essential for preparing a person to function as a productive adult in society. For example, the basic subjects of reading, writing, and arithmetic should form the core of content taught at the elementary level. At the secondary level, science, mathematics, English, and history should be among the core requirements. Essentialists perceive serious knowledge as residing primarily in the sciences and the technical fields. Vocational subjects are favored because they meet the important criterion of practicality and usefulness.

In this perspective, the arts and humanities are fine for personal pleasure, but are generally not considered to be among those essentials that are needed for a learner to become a useful adult. Many essentialists view these subjects as frills and, when budgets are tight, suggest that they should be the first courses cut. Essentialists argue that the schools should not waste time dealing with topics that are of little practical utility.

Essentialists believe that the primary role of the teacher is to impart information to learners. For their part, learners are expected to learn and retain this factual information. Teacher-centered techniques such as the lecture are favored, as are any new technologies that are thought to be capable of transmitting new information quickly and efficiently.

Essentialists tend to believe that people are not basically good and that individuals who are left to their own devices will not develop the habits and knowledge necessary for them to become good people. Therefore, the authority of the teacher, hard work, and discipline are important values for the essentialist. Because essentialists believe that character development is important and that teachers instruct by example, they are convinced that the character and habits of the teacher must be above reproach.

Essentialism reflects the hard-work and can-do spirit of Americans. These perspectives can be traced to the earliest days of our country. Recall, for example, that Benjamin Franklin was interested in making the school a "more practical" place. Current trends suggest that the essentialist position continues to be a potent force in American education.

Perennialism

Perennialism views truth as unchanging, or perennial. Perennialists such as Mortimer Adler (1982), Arthur Bestor (1955), and Robert Hutchins (1936) contended that education should focus on the search for and dissemination of these unchanging principles. Although perennialists grant that changing times bring some surface-level alterations in the problems that people face, they believe that the real substance of our lives remains unchanged over generations. Furthermore, they believe that the experiences of human beings through the centuries have established which truths are worth knowing.

Perennialists believe that Western society lost its way several centuries ago. They decry what they see as a trend to rely too much on experimental science and technology and thus ignore enduring truths. They argue that the growing status of scientific experimentation has led to a denial of the power and importance of human reason.

Perennialists favor schools that develop the intellect of all learners and prepare them for life. This preparation is best accomplished when individuals have mastered the truths discovered through the centuries. Such wisdom is seen as important regardless of the career or vocation an individual ultimately chooses to follow.

Because the perennialist views knowledge as consisting of unified and unchanging principles, the emphasis of essentialism on separate subjects and on the learning and retention of so-called practical information is soundly condemned. The separate subjects that the perennialist might support are those that are broadly defined as the classical liberal arts. The perennialist points out that what the essentialist considers essential is constantly changing. Therefore, a school program focused on the essentials runs the risk of teaching learners information that, in time, will have little relevance for their lives.

Perennialists are particularly vocal in their opposition to vocational training in the schools. They believe that vocational education represents a sellout of the true educational purposes of the school to the narrow interests of business and government. This concern is directed not only at public schools, but at colleges and universities as well.

Perennialists believe that higher education has developed entirely inappropriate emphases on developing students' research skills and on preparing them for future careers. In the eyes of perennialists, courses with these emphases divert students away from a "genuine education" that would emphasize a mastery of lasting truth. If they could, perennialists would ban all research and practical training from colleges and universities and turn these responsibilities over to technical institutes.

The perennialist shares with the essentialist the idea that the primary goal of education is to develop the intellect. In the perennialist view, however, learners should pursue truth for its own sake, not because it happens to be useful for some vocation. This pursuit of truth can best be accomplished through the study of the great literary works of civilization. Perennialists are especially attracted to courses in the humanities and literature. These classics are believed to be important because they deal with universal issues and themes that are as contemporary today as when they were written.

One branch of perennialism is relevant to some current debate about school curricula. Supporters of this variant of perennialism contend that universal truths flow from God. Therefore, they see education as distorted and incomplete unless theology and religious instruction accompany the study of other topics. The protests of some religious groups about schools and schooling are manifestations of this branch of perennialism.

Existentialism

Existentialism, a philosophical position of relatively recent origin, is difficult to characterize in general terms. Many individuals associated with the existentialist position reject the view that existentialism is an all-embracing philosophy with widely agreed-upon tenets. However, one theme that runs through most descriptions of existentialism is that people come into this world facing only one ultimate constraint— the inevitability of their own death — and in all other areas they should have freedom to make choices and identify their own reasons for existing. Existentialism suggests that individuals do not fit into any grand design of God or nature. There is no logic in the events of the world. People are viewed as being born into a world devoid of any universal meanings. It is within each individual to define truth, beauty, and right and wrong. Education should challenge people to create personal meanings of their own design (Morris, 1966).

It is fair to say that existentialism has influenced education less than the other basic philosophies. In part, this may be true because schools, as institutions designed to provide at least some common experiences to learners, promote goals that are inconsistent with the existentialists' commitment to personal freedom. Learner-designed programs and other courses that seek to maximize personal choice are examples of school-based offerings that have been influenced by the existential perspective.

A good illustration of existentialism applied to education is the Summerhill program established by A. S. Neill (1960). The ideas of Summerhill have been applied in a number of private schools in the United States. These programs are organized around the assumption that children have a natural tendency to want to mature, to be competent, and to be like older children and adults. There is no fixed curriculum; activities of learning are organized around the questions and the requests of the learners. If learners request instruction in what might be termed the traditional subjects, then instruction is given in those subjects. Generally, the program includes lots of options with an emphasis on field trips and experiential learning. The intent is to help young people explore the world and to seek their own meaning and understanding, not to impose upon them the meanings of others. Learner freedom in this quest is viewed as a critical ingredient.

Participatory governance is another key characteristic of an existentialist application. Learners participate in a democratic form of governance whereby all students and staff are allowed a vote and a voice in the operation of the school. The traditional view that adults know what is best for students is rejected.

Reconstructionism

Similar to the perennialists, *reconstructionists* believe that society has lost its way. A classic work laying out the basic position of reconstructionism is George Counts's 1932 work, *Dare the Schools Build a New Social Order?*

Whereas perennialists seek answers from the past, reconstructionists propose to build a whole new social order. They believe the aim of the school should be to serve as an important catalyst in the effort to improve the human condition through reform. For reconstructionists, the legitimate goal of education is to promote a critical appraisal of all elements of society. As a result of schooling, individuals should be in control of their own destinies and capable of promoting social reform.

Reconstructionists favor curricula that emphasize the importance of creating a world of economic abundance, equality, fairness, and democratic decision making. They see this social reconstruction as necessary for the survival of humankind. The school program should focus on the ills of society and awaken individuals' consciousness about social problems. Learners should be taught to critically analyze all aspects of life and to question rather than accept the pronouncements of those who hold political power. The reconstructionist curriculum draws heavily on insights from the behavioral sciences, which reconstructionists believe can be used as the basis for creating a society where individuals can attain their fullest potentials.

Teachers have a direct and important role to play in the education program of the reconstructionists. Their role is not to transmit knowledge, but instead to raise issues and direct learners to relevant resources. There is an emphasis on active participation by the learners. Ideally, the classroom reflects the values of equality and social justice. Teachers seek to create a classroom environment that mirrors the kind of just society that the reconstructionists seek.

BUILDING A PERSONAL PHILOSOPHY OF EDUCATION

We began this chapter by pointing out that applicants for teaching positions are often asked what their philosophy of education is. Now we want to ask you a question of our own: Why is the question of a philosophy of education an important one?

Before you respond, take some time to consider what books like this one and the education courses that use them are for. The ultimate goal is to improve education through the preparation of teachers. This is attempted by introducing thinking and research about educational practices in the hope that this information will later be applied in school classrooms. However, all information presented in books and in courses passes through what might be called the personal filter of each enrolled student.

What's the Problem?

For his first two years as a teacher, Roberto Lopez taught sixth graders in an inner-city school. This year, he moved to another sixth grade position in an affluent suburban school district in the same county. Roberto has continued to use the same general approach to teaching that served him well during his first two years in the profession. He has been pleased by comments he has received from parents in the new school district. Many of them have told him their children have become quite excited about what is going on at school.

Roberto is convinced that young people need to be actively involved in their own education and that they are most interested in learning when they have a voice in deciding what to study. To make this happen, he works hard to build his program around the questions and interests of the learners in his class. He helps them identify pressing problems that people are facing in the real world. Then he assists them to learn what they need to know to understand the problems and think about possible solutions. All of this has resulted in lessons that integrate content from many subject areas.

For example, the class considered some of the problems created when political decisions are influenced by large corporations. The class did some investigating and had some debates on the role of government and of citizens. They examined how past civilizations made decisions. They looked at some of the values inherent in some business practices that seemed to consider human beings as pieces of a machine that could be discarded when no longer needed. Members of the class drew on content from science as they looked at negative environmental side effects of practices of some irresponsible corporations. Language arts lessons related to this topic involved class members in writing letters supporting their points of view to state and federal regulatory officials. Members of the class got very involved in this learning activity, and they were particularly pleased when they received thoughtful responses to some of their letters from government officials.

Because of the positive reactions of his learners, Roberto — until today — would have responded with an enthusiastic Great! if anyone had asked him how things were going.

Your personal filter includes those beliefs, attitudes, and values you have acquired from your unique life experiences. It influences your visions about the purposes of education, the nature of those you will teach, the content you will select, the kinds of conduct you will be willing to accept, the types of interpretations you will make of the behaviors of others, and the personal view you will have regarding your sense of morality and ethics as a teacher.

Your personal filter basically is your philosophy of education. Because it is so important, we want you to think about your personal philosophy. It will have a tremendous impact on what you learn about being a teacher and on your behavior once you join our profession. It is because your personal perspectives are so important that employers ask the what-is-your-philosophy-of-education question. They want to know how your beliefs correspond with the goals and purposes of the school district and the community.

However, after this afternoon's conference with the school principal, he is angry and confused. The principal, Ms. Fifer, visited Roberto's classroom for an observation and asked him to stop by for a debriefing at the end of the day.

Ms. Fifer told him that although she was pleased with his teaching skills and the ease with which he related to the young people in his class, she was very concerned about what he was teaching. She pointed out that he was straying too far from the prescribed curriculum. Ms. Fifer emphasized that the adopted curriculum included certain key knowledge that young people need to master. If they do not learn this information, they will not do well on the state tests. Should this happen, parents will become angry.

Ms. Fifer went on to point out that sixth graders are too young and immature to deal with the problems they were discussing in any meaningful manner. She said the discussions she observed in Roberto's class were simply a sharing of ignorance. To be able to handle this kind of an activity, young people first must develop an adequate understanding of basic information. She pointed out that lessons based on the adopted textbooks would help learners build the needed information base and would ensure that when these learners became older, they would be able to engage in productive consideration of difficult issues. She concluded by suggesting that Roberto's instruction bordered on the unethical in that he was denying his young people access to content in the textbooks that had been carefully selected by experts. If he continued his present instructional program, members of his class would be denied the foundation of information that would help them in later years of education and in their life.

Roberto left this meeting very confused. He thought he was doing an excellent job. Now, Ms. Fifer has essentially told him that he is being irresponsible and, possibly, is even on the verge of harming his learners. Roberto finds this difficult to accept. He has seen the enthusiasm of the students, and he believes that helping young people learn how to make our society better is one of the most important outcomes of education. He's not sure what he should do next.

What do you think is the root of the problem between Roberto and his principal? What philosophical orientation does Roberto seem to have? Explain some differences in fundamental values between Roberto and Ms. Fifer. How would you characterize the philosophical orientation of Ms. Fifer? What do you see as the strong points in each of their arguments? What do you think ought to be done now? What does this situation suggest to you as you think about your future as a teacher?

The culture in which you were reared, your socioeconomic background, the experiences you have had in your schools, and a wide array of other factors have helped to shape your personal philosophy. It is probable that you have never paused to bring many of your fundamental convictions to a state of conscious reflection. We urge you to do so. This kind of personal philosophic assessment will facilitate your development as a teacher.

As you think about your own philosophy, review some of the questions raised in this chapter. Re-examine the different philosophical systems, and identify those positions and ideas that you think are strong or reasonable and those you think are weak and not so reasonable. How sound are your arguments for the positions you agree with? What merit can you find in those positions with which you disagree? What points do they make that you consider valid? You may find that there is no one system that you agree with totally. You may find that there are elements of different systems that make sense to you. If so, you have what is termed an *eclectic philosophy*, one that includes different elements of different philosophical systems.

Once you have identified the basic elements of your personal philosophy, you need to think about their implications. What does your philosophy mean in terms of the content that you think is important? How will it affect how you interact and treat learners? How does it relate to the methods that you will select for use with the learners you will teach? Think about these questions as you go about the business of identifying your personal philosophy of education.

• Key Ideas in Summary

- Most of us operate on a set of assumptions about what is right that is the product of our culture and our past experiences. We need to make these assumptions and ideals explicit so that we can investigate and clarify them.

- Most of the debates and disagreements about the direction education should take and about how it should be reformed are basically disagreements over philosophical issues.

- *Metaphysics* deals with the nature of reality. Answers to metaphysical questions have implications for the identification of educational goals, the selection of appropriate content, and the formation of attitudes regarding the general nature of learners.

- *Epistemology* is concerned with the nature of knowledge. It has relevance for such educational issues as determining the types of knowledge to be taught and deciding on the reliability of alternative ways of learning content.

- *Axiology* deals with the nature of values. It has implications for teachers in identifying what is believed to be important, in deciding on a code of ethics for how they relate to learners, and in defining the contents of moral or character education.

- *Logic* centers on the clarity of thought and on the relationships between ideas. It provides people with a process they can use to make clear distinctions between valid and fallacious thinking. For this reason, educators should be concerned that learners develop a solid grounding in logical thinking.

- Most teachers have been reared in the Western philosophical tradition. There are other philosophical traditions that view the nature of reality, knowledge, and values very differently than Western philosophy. Understanding the basics of other philosophical systems can serve to open our own thinking to new ways of viewing the world as well as helping us understand learners and avoid conflicts.

- Several systematic philosophies have developed that help guide educational thought. Those philosophies of education include *progressivism, essentialism, perennialism, existentialism,* and *reconstructionism.* None of these philosophical systems has been proved to be true. They need to be evaluated based on the soundness of their assumptions and arguments.

- Clarifying one's personal philosophy is an important step in becoming a teacher in times of change. There are many and varied proposals about what education ought to be and how teachers ought to teach. A sound personal philosophy will help teachers sort through these proposals and make decisions.

• Review and Discussion Questions

1. What are some examples of ways that philosophy influences teacher decisions?
2. Why is it that school personnel officials so often ask prospective teachers about their personal philosophy of education?
3. What are some arguments that have been made in support of the view that an understanding of knowledge construction should be a key element in multicultural programs in the schools?
4. What are some examples of ways that an unexamined personal filter or personal philosophy might hinder a person learning to be a teacher?
5. What philosophy of education seems to have the most current support?
6. What contemporary issues in education are related to axiological questions?
7. What do you think should be included in a code of ethics or morality for teachers?
8. What would be some instructional emphases that you would expect from a school that is strongly committed to perennialism?
9. How would the curriculum of a school organized around social reconstructionism differ from that of a school organized around essentialism?
10. What evidence can be seen of the influence of Dewey and progressivism in the schools?

• Ideas for Field Experiences, Projects, and Enrichment

1. Review some of the changes in education and some of the proposals for reform that were mentioned in Chapters 1 and 2. What are the philosophical underpinnings of these changes?
2. Sketch out the elements of your personal philosophy. What do they imply in terms of the kind of school and the kind of classroom where you would be most comfortable? Define a list of questions you might ask or things you might observe when looking for a school that would be consistent with your philosophy.
3. Review either state curriculum guidelines or a local school district curriculum. See if you can identify elements of the different philosophical systems in the guidelines.
4. Observe in a classroom and pay close attention to what is emphasized and how the class is conducted. What elements of different philosophies can you note?
5. Interview a school personnel officer. Ask what patterns people who are responsible for hiring new teachers are looking for when they listen to how candidates respond to the what-is-your-philosophy-of-education question. Ask this person whether he or she believes all districts are looking for the same kinds of answers or whether expectations will vary from school district to school district.

• References

Adler, M. (1982). *The Paideia proposal.* New York: Macmillan.

Bagley, W. (1941). The case for essentialism in education. *National Education Association Journal, 30*(7), 202–220.

Banks, J. (1994). *Multiethnic education* (3rd ed.). Boston: Allyn and Bacon.

Bestor, A. (1955). *The restoration of learning.* New York: Knopf.

Counts, G. (1932). *Dare the schools build a new social order?* New York: John Day.

Dewey, J. (1902). *The child and the curriculum.* Chicago: University of Chicago Press.

Dewey, J. (1916). *Democracy and education.* New York: Macmillan.

Dewey, J. (1938). *Experience and education.* New York: Macmillan.

Dewey, J. (1910). *How we think.* Boston: D. C. Heath.

Good, T., & Brophy, J. (1994). *Looking in classrooms* (6th ed.). New York: HarperCollins.

Hutchins, R. (1936). *The higher learning in America.* New Haven: Yale University Press.

Kennedy, T. (1994). Chinese philosophy. *Encarta.* Bellevue, WA: Microsoft. (CD-ROM)

McDermott, J. (1994). Buddhism. *Encarta.* Bellevue, WA: Microsoft. (CD-ROM)

Morris, V. (1966). *Existentialism in education.* New York: Harper and Row.

Morton, E. (1988). *To touch the wind: An introduction to native American philosophy and beliefs.* Dubuque, IA: Kendall/Hunt.

Neill, A. (1960). *Summerhill: A radical approach to child rearing.* New York: Hart.

Nieto, S. (1992). *Affirming diversity.* New York: Longman.

O'Flaherty, W. (1994). Hinduism. *Encarta.* Bellevue, WA: Microsoft. (CD-ROM)

Oliver, D. , & Gersham, K. (1989). *Education, modernity, and fractured meaning.* Albany: State University of New York Press.

Soltis, J. (1981). Education and the concept of knowledge. In J. Soltis (Ed.), *Philosophy and education: Eightieth yearbook of the National Society for the Study of Education.* Chicago: University of Chicago Press.

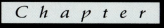

How Groups Affect Schools and Learners

OBJECTIVES

- Explain how values reflected in schools and school programs might not always "fit" all learners comfortably.

- Describe functionalist, economic class conflict, and status group perspectives on schooling.

- Point out roles schools are expected to play as institutions.

- Explain potential conflicts between teachers' in-school and out-of-school roles.

- Cite ways in which groups to which individual learners belong can influence how they behave in school.

- Point out possible sources of conflict for learners that can be caused by differences between expectations of teachers and school officials and expectations of their parents and guardians, their religious groups, and their friends.

Schools are not value-free places. What we teach, how we teach it, and what we expect learners to do represent social choices. These choices are invisible to some of our learners because what we do is consistent with expectations of their parents, relatives, and friends. For others in our classrooms, however, the initial encounter with a public school is a jarring introduction to an unfamiliar world. This is true for many children of immigrant parents whose families may know little about expected patterns of behavior for children in American schools. It is also often true for young people from ethnic, racial, and linguistic minorities who find themselves called upon to behave in unfamiliar ways when they come to school.

Today, we are more sensitive than we used to be to the possibility that groups to which learners belong can affect their adjustment to school. In the nineteenth century, for example, educators often took a highly negative and condescending view toward learners from minority cultures. Parents of native American learners were widely criticized for allowing their children to "run wild." Many educators believed that these youngsters needed to experience the "benefits" of a highly controlled public school environment if there was to be any hope of turning them into model United States citizens (Coleman, 1993).

Similarly, nineteenth century immigrants from Ireland and Eastern Europe initially encountered public schooling that was insensitive to their cultural perspectives (Scruggs, 1979). African American culture was so little valued in the nineteenth century that those few African Americans who were allowed to go to school had to embrace a dominant world view that openly dismissed their worth. This was hardly a set of circumstances designed to help these young people emerge from their educational experiences with an enhanced sense of self-worth (Nieto, 1992).

Teachers must work sensitively with learners from many cultural and ethnic groups.

Although conditions have improved greatly since the nineteenth century, it is still true today that prevailing school practices are perceived in different ways by young people from various groups. Their views reflect a combination of reactions to the prescribed curriculum, to perspectives of families and friends, and to general views of their cultural and ethnic groups. These social factors suggest the importance of considering questions such as these:

- Whose interests do schools serve?
- What functions are fulfilled by schools?
- What roles do teachers play?
- How do families, ethnic groups, and other groups affect learners' reactions to school programs?

In this chapter, we introduce material that will shed light on some of these important issues.

THREE VIEWS OF SCHOOL PROGRAMS

Scholars who have studied how learners are affected by schools have worked from several perspectives. Among these are (1) the functionalist view, (2) the economic class conflict view, and (3) the status group conflict view.

The Functionalist View

Functionalists see society as sharing a common set of values. Over time, these values have led to the development of institutions such as schools, families, governmental units, and religious bodies. Each of these institutions has a specialized responsibility or function. Performance of these functions helps keep our society going. Functionalists believe society is worth maintaining in its present form. This is true because they believe that people in our society share more common values than values that might lead to conflict and discord. This harmonious social order deserves to be preserved and passed from generation to generation.

In our society, schools now are expected to discharge responsibilities that once were taken care of by families. This is particularly true in the area of preparing our young people for the world of work. Today, most work is performed away from the home. Skills needed by employers have become so specialized that parents are no longer able to train their children for their future vocational roles. One result is that the role of families has increasingly become limited to providing for children's emotional and psychological needs. Preparation for economic life has largely been turned over to specialists in the schools.

Talcott Parsons (1959), a leading American functionalist, saw the school as the social agency that had the basic responsibility for providing our society with trained workers. Functionalists assume that all learners have the ability to profit from programs offered by the school. Those who get the best jobs are learners who, by virtue of their individual abilities and effort, take full advantage of what the schools have to offer. There is an assumption that economic rewards will be distributed on the basis of individual merit and that the school provides equal opportunities for all (Dougherty & Hammack, 1990).

The functionalist view is popular. It suggests that schools, by training people for occupations needed by our society as a whole, provide the necessary conditions for economic growth. This economic growth, in turn, is thought to yield benefits that will improve the lives of everyone. Functionalists believe that the potential of schools to stimulate economic growth establishes a rationale for spending tax dollars to expand educational services. This expansion is thought to benefit disadvantaged as well as advantaged groups.

Functionalists believe an important task of educators is to establish school programs that will provide learners with information they will need as adults. Once this is done, all learners will derive maximum benefits from their school experiences. Critics of this view argue that functionalists fail to adequately consider differences among groups of learners who attend our schools. They contend that school programs are not designed to serve interests of all learners equally well.

The Economic Class Conflict View

Supporters of the *economic class conflict* view reject functionalism's premise that there is broad agreement as to what the "common values" of our society are. They see our society as a battleground where contesting groups strive for supremacy. They perceive schools as places where contending interest groups compete for educational advantages. The "winners" succeed in having important educational resources dedicated to programs to serve their children. In general, it is believed that economically powerful groups win most competitions. Hence, young people from economically impoverished groups do not receive the educational advantages that are routinely provided to children from more affluent families.

Historically, the economic class conflict position traces its origins to the work of Karl Marx and Friedrich Engels. Marx and Engels argued that the defining feature of a society was the conflict between a capitalist class that controlled the means of production and a working class that was forced to serve the capitalists.

As applied to education today, the economic class conflict position has led to two somewhat different interpretations of what goes on in school. According to the *class reproduction* view, school programs have expanded primarily because of capitalists' desires to serve the needs of their own class. People who believe this to be true cite efforts to infuse computer technology, advanced mathematics, and similar specialized content into the school programs as evidence of an intent to create school programs to meet the needs of future managers and owners. Similarly, attempts to upgrade vocational programs are seen as efforts of the managerial and ownership class to ensure a steady supply of trained workers.

Another variant of the economic class conflict position is the *class conflict* view. Its supporters argue that educational change has not come about because of capitalists' desires to make school programs serve their own interests. Rather, changes have occurred because economically disadvantaged groups have expressed their unhappiness with existing school programs. Their actions, it is argued, have led to many changes in what schools do. In particular, they have been successful in promoting the adoption of better learning opportunities for minorities and females.

Critics of the economic class conflict position suggest that its supporters place too much emphasis on the economic standing of groups as an explanation for changes in school programs. They point out that many Americans have little personal sense of membership in a particular economic class. For example, recent national elections have witnessed large numbers of people with modest incomes identifying with the same Republican candidates who have been strongly supported by large business interests. Further, there is evidence that many learners who come from working-class families manage to acquire the education necessary to move into managerial and executive positions. Even though social mobility is not guaranteed by access to schooling, it happens much more often than might be predicted if schools were really controlled by wealthy and influential people who sought only to promote their own narrow economic class interests.

The Status Group Conflict View

The economic class conflict position suggests that social status and power are a function of economics. The *status group conflict* position, largely based on the philosophy of the German sociologist Max Weber, proposes that change results from conflicts among groups that compete for reasons that go beyond narrow economic interests. According to this view, the economic condition of people alone is too narrow a basis for determining individual or group status. Status is awarded to influential leaders in social organizations, governmental units, religious bodies, and in other groups. These groups that award status to certain of their members are designed to serve the interest of people who work for or are affiliated with them. In doing this, they often come into conflict with other groups. It is conflict between these diverse status groups that is thought to explain why educational changes occur.

Supporters of the status group conflict position suggest that today's school programs have resulted from efforts of specific groups to advance their own interests. For example, organization of school knowledge into separate subject areas and the division of the school day into time periods have been interpreted as a reflection of industrial managers' desires to familiarize learners with the working environment of an industrial culture (with its departmentalized functions and careful attention to time schedules) (Khumar, 1989). Physical education programs have been supported by military leaders who are interested in having a supply of people in good physical condition ready for military service. Student government and other groups that require learners to work on committees to solve problems have been viewed as schemes to familiarize young people with the roles of government officials and to prepare some of them for future employment in government service.

Critics of the status group conflict position contend that its adherents overemphasize conflict as the primary determinant of what goes on in our schools. They acknowledge that there are differences between groups that frequently lead to disputes. They accept, too, that these conflicts sometimes influence school programs.

However, these critics continue to point to the existence of important shared national values that cut across individual groups. These shared values as well as between-group conflicts influence what goes on in our schools.

People committed to functionalism, economic class conflict, and status group conflict look at efforts to change school programs in very different ways. For functionalists, disagreements about present school programs are seen as arguments within a basically warm and harmonious family whose members are trying to define a common ground that all can support. Changes are adopted when it is believed they will be helpful to our entire society. Functionalists ask two basic questions: (1) Is this change consistent with broadly held values? and (2) Is it designed to benefit all?

People who are committed to either of the two conflict positions take a different view. They look for potential "winners" and "losers" when proposals to change school programs are put forward. They do not see discussions of change as part of an effort to achieve a societywide benefit. Instead, such proposals are considered to be part of a recurring pattern of conflict between groups — a pattern that almost always results in individual decisions that benefit some groups more than others. A major objective of conflict position supporters is to expose to public view the likely consequences of a proposed school policy or program change for members of individual groups. They see debates about potential changes focusing on this question: Will this change benefit groups that deserve to benefit?

The functionalist position and the conflict positions often lead people to quite different conclusions about what schools are doing and what schools should do.

BOX 8-1

Who Benefits from an Advanced Calculus Course?

A reader recently made these comments in a letter to the editor of a local newspaper.

> Our school board has done it again. Now we are to be "gifted" with a high school curriculum that features a spanking new *advanced* calculus course. We already have a regular calculus course that, according to my information, serves a grand total of 10 percent of the school population. The new advanced course will be taken just by a select few who do well in the regular calculus course.
>
> Why are we committing scarce school district funds to a program that will benefit a tiny fraction of our students? I think I know the answer, and I don't like it. The well-heeled families who have a lot of political stroke around here want their kids to have an extra edge when they head off to the engineering program in the prestigious private colleges and universities. As for the rest of our kids — a vast majority, I might add — well, too bad. The district won't have money this year to take care of their needs.

What Do You Think?

1. Are these comments most consistent with the functionalist view or with one of the conflict views?
2. What values are reflected in the statements of this writer?
3. What arguments might you make if you wished to challenge the position taken in this letter to the editor? What arguments might you make if you wanted to support this point of view?

For example, a functionalist might view a high school curriculum featuring many electives as a positive indicator of a program that is responsive to varying interests and needs of students. But someone committed to one of the conflict positions might see the same curriculum as a clever scheme of powerful interest groups to direct learners from noninfluential groups into courses that fail to prepare them for well-paid, high-status jobs.

ROLES OF SCHOOLS

As important social institutions, schools play many roles. Among them are responsibilities associated with:

- transmission of the general culture
- dissemination of academic knowledge
- preparation for the world of work
- promotion of social and group relationships
- encouragement of social change

Transmission of the General Culture

Our schools transmit certain values, beliefs, and norms to learners. These perspectives are those with broad support in our society. But this does not mean that all individuals and groups subscribe to every value, belief, and norm that is explicitly or implicitly included in school programs. Disagreements about the extent of the school's responsibilities for shaping learners' attitudes sometimes lead to acrimonious debates about the proper limits of educators' socialization responsibilities.

Part of the difficulty results because the school is only one of several influences on learners' values. Families also greatly influence young people's patterns of behavior and thinking. This is especially true of younger children, but families continue to exercise some influence over older learners as well. Social organizations, churches, friends, and other groups also influence the perspectives of young people.

As an example of how cultural context influences people's beliefs, consider the findings of prominent Indian educational sociologist Krishna Khumar (1989), who compared representations of children in texts used in India and Canada. Khumar found that many more children were featured in the Canadian than in the Indian texts. Further, the children in the Canadian texts were portrayed as engaged in more creative and imaginative activities than those in the Indian texts. Khumar attributed the infrequent use of children as characters and their relative passivity in the Indian texts as a reflection of the cultural context of India. He pointed out that because death rates among children are extremely high in India, not much "personhood" is attached to them. Consequently, relatively little thought is given to the special characteristics of children. On the other hand, in Canada, where survival rates of children are much higher, children are seen as people of consequence; hence, they play much more dominant and active parts in stories featured in Canadian school books.

Most of us in education today realize that we need to respond to differences in learners who come to us from different family backgrounds. At the same time, we sense an obligation to transmit some common perspectives to all the young people we serve. Some school activities that we undertake to socialize our learners tend to be more controversial than others. One that has not engendered much objection is the idea that we in the schools have a special responsibility to prepare young people for the world of work (Goslin, 1990). Few families and other groups in our society have the needed expertise to discharge this responsibility.

The kinds of socialization programs that sometimes prompt hostile parental reactions are those that relate to personal behavior, for example, sex education. Critics of instruction that deals with these kinds of personal issues often argue that this kind of teaching should be left to family members or to religious bodies.

Dissemination of Knowledge

As educators, we have an obligation to transmit specialized knowledge, particularly academic knowledge, to learners. The quantity and sophistication of information needed by young people today goes beyond what most parents know. Experts in the schools are expected to draw on their specialized information and pass it along to their learners.

The vast quantity of knowledge and time limitations prevent us from teaching "everything." The adopted curriculum functions as a screen or filter that identifies the limited amount of information that we teach in our school programs. Because the curriculum is a general repository of what we present to youngsters in our classrooms, its contents sometimes are attacked by certain groups because of their concerns about the adequacy of the information we may be providing to learners.

Some ways of selecting and organizing content have persisted for so many years that we sometimes find it difficult to imagine alternative ways to do this. For many years, the settlement and development of the United States has been described in terms of a wave of migration from the Atlantic Coast to the Pacific Coast. Some parents and educators who note that in just a few years Hispanics will become our most numerous minority group, wonder about this traditional east-to-west presentation of United States history. They point out that this organizational scheme has made it difficult for us to include much information about Hispanic contributions to the development our country. This is true because the Hispanic population, generally, has occupied the country from south-to-north rather than from east-to-west. It may be that more history curricula in the future will present settlement of the United States from both an east-to-west and a south-to-north perspective.

Occasionally, some of our learning materials include information that includes an unintended "lesson" that implies members of certain groups are less worthy than members of other groups. Krishna Khumar (1989) describes a widely used school story in India about a wealthy merchant who listens to the complaints of a poor worker who concludes his life is worthless. The wealthy merchant offers to buy one of the poor worker's eyes for a small price. The worker rejects the initial offer but continues to negotiate with the rich merchant, who gradually increases his offer to the princely sum of 100,000 rupees. At this point, the poor worker realizes that he does have value and thanks the merchant for providing him with this insight.

There are several messages in this story that some groups might find objectionable. It seems to imply that wealth, wisdom, and virtue go together. It also suggests that the poor should follow the ideas of the rich. The subtext of the tale might be summarized as Don't rock the boat, but appreciate what you have, even if you're poor.

Preparation for the World of Work

The economic existence of every society depends on the availability of people to perform the kind of work that needs to be done. The various jobs that are required in a society vary greatly in terms of knowledge and skills needed. One of the functions of the school is to prepare young people for these diverse job roles. In a sense, the school functions as a sorting agency for future employers. As learners progress through their educational programs, they develop varying levels of expertise that help them qualify for some positions and eliminate them as serious candidates for positions that require different kinds of abilities and talents.

Some occupational roles carry with them more prestige and, often, higher financial rewards than others. School programs that help our young people prepare for these valued occupational roles usually are academically rigorous. For example, learners who want to pursue careers in engineering often enroll in challenging mathematics courses. In theory, the difficulty of some of these courses ensures that competent people will enter engineering curricula. It also ensures that the number of potential engineers will not be too large and that many individuals who are attracted to engineering early in their school years will switch to other career paths.

Controversy sometimes accompanies our decisions to advise individual learners to pursue courses of study that seem related to preparation for particular careers. For example, there may be suspicions that we are directing certain kinds of learners (perhaps those from economically impoverished households or from certain cultural and ethnic groups) away from courses of study needed by people interested in entering high-prestige occupations. Today, educators everywhere are working hard to ensure parents and other patrons of our schools that decisions to recommend particular courses to individual pupils and students do not reflect unprofessional biases against certain categories of learners.

Promotion of Social and Group Relationships

Schools foster the development of our learners' social and group skills. This occurs both by design and as a side effect of the special environment of the school setting. Recurring activities such as pep assemblies and athletic contests are among regularly scheduled events that encourage the development of a common group identity among all learners in a given school.

One function of the school is to help learners participate successfully as members of groups.

When learners identify strongly with their schools, they have more positive attitudes toward teachers, classmates, and the entire educational enterprise. This kind of group identity stands as a proxy for what many of the young people we work with will be encouraged to do as adult employees of businesses and government agencies and as members of religious groups and other organizations.

Most schools, especially secondary schools, have official clubs and organizations. Young people who participate in these groups gain experience in working with others and, to some extent, in competing with people in other groups (for meeting space, financial resources, and so forth). Other organizations that are not formally sponsored by the school sometimes arrange to use school facilities when classes are not in session. These include scouting groups, church youth groups, and junior branches of fraternal organizations. Many learners who are in these groups derive benefits from their membership in the same way that they and others profit from participation in school-sponsored organizations.

Schools are places where our learners acquire socially appropriate patterns of interpersonal relations. School classes enroll learners from varied backgrounds. They provide opportunities for learners to meet people who may be very different from themselves. Male and female relationships begin to flourish in schools as young people mature. Some school functions such as dances are specifically designed to support socially acceptable ways of developing these friendships.

Learners are taught many things in school that are not part of the formal program. (For more information about this *hidden curriculum*, see Chapter 4.) Much of what young people take away from their experiences in school comes to them from their membership in clubs, organizations, and other kinds of out-of-class activities.

Identify at least six things that you "learned in school" outside of the formal classroom that have proved useful to you later in your life.

1. _____

2. _____

3. _____

4. _____

5. _____

6. _____

Encouragement of Social Change

Many people see the schools as social improvement agencies. This is particularly true at times when the public is concerned about serious social problems (Goslin, 1990). Faith in "better education" as a curative agent is widespread. Few politicians miss opportunities to make clear their intentions to reduce the crime rate, defeat alcoholism, diminish the use of illegal drugs, or combat promiscuity and unwed motherhood through the institution of "sound educational programs."

The view that schools can function as powerful social reform agents appeals to some educators. Others question it. Critics of this position point out that schools are part of the larger society that has produced the very problems they are charged with "fixing." For this reason, they doubt that changes in school programs will do much unless there are also changes in our society as a whole.

When policymakers ask us as educators to take on a task such as reducing illegal drug use, there is a good chance that even our best efforts will fail. Poverty, a lack of belief in a secure economic future, absence of strong families, a dearth of good role models outside the school, and many other variables may lead a given individual to turn to illegal drugs. The scope of the problem simply may be beyond what we can address in the schools. This is not to say we should not cooperate with other groups to work on the problem. However, to suggest that educators alone have the capacity to solve it is to ignore reality.

Despite concerns that have been raised about the appropriateness of asking schools to solve intractable social problems, the belief that education is a potent reform agent has wide support. It is probable that political leaders will continue to look at the schools as important institutional players in efforts to "improve" society.

LEARNERS' PERCEPTIONS AND ROLES

Even though our learners share many common school experiences, they do not all perceive them in the same way. Educational sociologists sometimes find it useful to develop classifications of learners based on their reactions to school programs (Bernstein, 1977). These are four categories that are sometimes used (see Figure 8-1):

- high adapters
- estranged learners
- irrelevant perceivers
- alienated learners

High adapters are learners who believe that the content of the school program is important and who experience success in their classes. They see a good fit between the agenda of the school and their personal hopes and aspirations (and probably with those of their families, friends, and social, religious, and ethnic groups). These learners tend to support what we do as teachers. They rarely challenge what goes on at school.

Estranged learners are also convinced of the importance of the school program. However, for intellectual, social, or other reasons, they do not do well in our classes. They often develop negative self-concepts and worry that their lack of success in school will permanently tag them as "losers." These young people often become increasingly disenchanted with school as the years go by. Many of them drop out before graduating from high school.

Irrelevant perceivers have the capacity to succeed in school. However, they do not consider school work to be important. Often they have personal priorities that they view as having little connection to what we ask them to do in the school classroom. One of the authors once had a young man in his class who was the son of a local wrecking yard owner. By the time he began high school, this boy had been working for his father for years. He was already earning good money, and he was looking forward to working full-time once he finished high school. In general, this young man thought we teachers were rather a sorry lot who had strange interests and who did not make enough money to be taken seriously. He did just enough work in school to pass his courses and qualify for a diploma.

Figure 8-1

Four categories of learner reactions to the school program

	Tend to cope with class work successfully	Tend to have great difficulty with class work
Tend to believe school work is important	High adapters	Estranged learners
Tend to believe school work is not important	Irrelevant perceivers	Alienated learners

Alienated learners do not see the school program as personally important. They have not experienced success on those occasions when they have seriously tried to do the work. Often these young people have little good to say about those of us who teach them or about the school in general. They frequently feel trapped in a situation that requires them to do things they do not believe are important under conditions that will not allow them to succeed. Many of these young people drop out of school before they graduate. Those who stay often experience problems. Their frustrations sometimes lead them to become behavior problems in our classes.

In part, differences among our learners who are high adapters, estranged, irrelevant perceivers, or alienated stem from social influences that have helped shape their view of the world. Our learners are called upon to play many roles, and some of these may conflict with others. Difficulties in school may arise when there are conflicts between roles we expect learners to play as members of the school community and roles that are expected of them as members of families, specific cultural or ethnic groups, or religious and social organizations.

Learners as Members of Schools

Schools impose certain behavioral expectations on learners. Many of these are unwritten norms. One of the most basic of these is our expectation that learners will accept our direction as their teacher. Even though we do encourage young people to raise questions about certain things as we teach them, for the most part, we assume they will accept the validity of the content we are providing.

We expect learners to follow rules regarding such things as when and how they will move from place to place, where they will sit in classrooms, what they must do to complete assigned tasks, when they may eat, when they may leave the classroom, and when they may converse freely with others. Learners who adapt easily to the school environment cope easily with the many regulations that govern their behavior. Others find this difficult to do.

Learners as Members of Families

Learners often take on as their own those views that are prevalent among members of their immediate families. For example, young people whose parents are working people with strong commitments to organized labor often will espouse a commitment to labor unions. Views of families are not in every case passed on intact to members of the younger generation, but as a rule this is quite common. As a result, when values or positions introduced at school conflict with those of learners' families, students in our classes may become less interested in what is introduced at school. Someone from a home where the union movement is held in high esteem may find it hard to accept conclusions included in a textbook written by an author with a strong anti-union perspective.

We need to be careful when we introduce value-laden content. We do need to teach such information, but we must take care to identify conclusions as consis-

Is Dancing Devilish?

Gilberto Figueroa, a first-year fourth grade teacher, slumped wearily into the faculty lounge couch. "This," he announced to the two or three old hands who had gathered around the coffee pot, "has been *some* day."

"What's up, Gil?" The speaker was Latisha Carter, the school's long-time middle grades team leader.

"Sit down, Latisha. This is going to take a while."

Latisha took a seat on the couch, settled her coffee cup on the table, and looked up. "OK, Gil, let's have it."

"You remember when I told you about the folk dancing we did last summer in my physical education methods class? Well, it hit me a couple of nights ago that I could tie some folk dancing to some of the things we're doing in social studies. They're always after us to break down barriers between subjects, and this seemed a natural."

"Anyway," Gilberto continued, "I did some additional checking, found some music, and relearned the steps of four dances from four different countries. I took the kids to the gym this morning. I explained what we were going to do and taught them the steps. I thought everything was going splendidly until I noticed I was getting a lot of frowns from Louis."

"What was that all about?" Latisha asked.

"At first, I just didn't know," Gilberto replied. "I didn't let it bother me and kept on teaching. Then, I put some music on and let the kids try the steps. It was at *that* point all hell broke loose. Louis jumped up on a bench, started shaking his fist at everyone else, and began shouting, 'You're all going to hell!' Some of the other kids were really scared. In fact, Nellie and Joe spent some time with the counselor after lunch. And that's not the end of it."

"What else happened?" Latisha asked.

"About two o'clock I got a message from the office to call Louis's mother. He'd gone home for lunch and told her what he had done. I figured maybe she was calling to apologize for his behavior. Was I ever off base on that idea! I called her after school, and she proceeded to read me the riot act for subjecting her child to immoral activities. She lectured me for 20 minutes on the scriptural basis for the idea that dancing is the 'devil's work.' She's coming to see me tomorrow. I think I'm in for it. Got any ideas?"

What is Gilberto really worried about? Is it the impending confrontation with Louis's mother? Or, is he worried about where Louis's mother may go next? Or, is something else of greater concern? What alternatives might be open to Gilberto? Has he thought these through? What do we learn about Gilberto's values? How might these differ from those of Louis's mother? If there is a difference in these values, is Gilberto obligated to change his instructional program? Why or why not?

Are there others from whom Gilberto should seek advice? What do you think he should say to Louis's mother? Is there anything he could have done to avoid this situation? What are some specific alternatives open to him now? What are some advantages and disadvantages of each of them? How would you respond if you were confronted with this situation?

tent with a given point of view, not as unalloyed truth. When we take care to do this, learners understand that a variety of views, including those they hold personally, are acceptable.

Learners as Members of Ethnic and Cultural Groups

The world views of individual learners are partially conditioned by their ethnic and cultural groups. These ethnic and cultural perspectives can affect their receptivity to what we do at school. To illustrate the point, let's think about a young native American girl who is taking a junior-level English course in high school. The teacher has asked the class to read some of Mark Twain's books. Recently, they have been reading *Roughing It*, a novel based on Twain's travels and experiences in the Far West. In this novel, Twain describes native Americans as "prideless beggars" (Twain, 1872/1985, p. 167).

It is doubtful that this girl sees herself, her family, and other native Americans as prideless beggars. If the teacher does not take care to instruct members of this class that the phrase represents an isolated statement by one author (who, elsewhere, deals much more fairly with native Americans) made at a specific time and in a particular historical context, the girl may conclude that whatever else is taught in the course is irrelevant. The conclusion that native Americans are prideless beggars does not square with her view of reality. It would make sense, too, for the teacher to introduce other materials that provide a more positive view of native Americans and other groups of people who were not always treated sensitively by authors who wrote at a time when cultural diversity was less prized than it is today.

Many young people acquire some of their values because of their association with special groups and organizations.

Learners as Members of Religious and Social Organizations

Many of our school learners are active in various religious and social organizations. These groups often have strong commitments that are shared by their members. Sometimes these perspectives conflict with what learners encounter in school. For example, school counselors and teachers may encourage females to work hard to master mathematics because a good background in this subject is needed for many high-paying jobs. Some religious groups view women's roles in a very restricted way. They may object strongly to anything we do at school that promotes the idea that women should prepare for employment options that will take them away from their traditional duties as homemakers.

Learners who are members of groups whose views are at odds with what is being taught at school may find themselves torn between a desire to please their teachers and a desire to please their religious leaders. These kinds of conflicts are common. We have to recognize that many of our young people are under pressure to do things that may be at odds with what we believe to be in their long-term "best" interest.

• Key Ideas in Summary

* What is done in schools is a reflection of a particular set of values. Whereas many learners come from homes that share the same values orientation as the school, this is not always the case. As a result, some learners find themselves in an unfamiliar social situation when they first come to school. Inconsistencies between the perspectives of the home and the school sometimes cause problems for learners who find themselves caught between conflicting sets of behavioral expectations.

* People who subscribe to the *functionalist* position believe that our society is strongly committed to a common set of values. These values ought to be reflected in school programs. Functionalists believe that when this is true, there is an excellent chance that all learners will commit to these values. It is assumed that school programs that are developed in response to common values will allow all learners in the school to take advantage of the benefits of schooling.

* Supporters of the *economic class conflict* position disagree that our society features a large set of commonly held values. They argue that different kinds of people are committed to different values and that these differences lead to conflict. In particular, they see conflict between capitalists, who control most of the wealth and the means of production, and workers, who must do the bidding of the capitalists. According to the economic class conflict position, school reforms result from one or the other of two reasons. Some proponents of this view believe changes result from an interest in keeping our economic system going in a form that will maximize capitalist control and supply adequate numbers of workers to serve as employees. Others believe that school reforms

come about because of challenges brought by working-class people who do not want school programs that promote the idea that present economic arrangements will go on forever.

- Individuals who are committed to the *status group conflict* position also believe that there is more conflict than consensus in our society. They believe conflict involves more groups than simply capitalists and workers. They draw much of their inspiration from the work of Max Weber, who pointed out that change often results in conflicts between many status groups. Status groups include social organizations, economic organizations, religious organizations, governmental organizations, ethnic and cultural organizations, and other groups. These groups try to maximize the benefits of their members. In doing so, they often come into conflict with members of other groups. Educational change comes about as a result of these conflicts. More specifically, changes are made in directions favored by conflict winners.

- As institutions, schools play many roles. Among them are their roles as (1) transmitters of the general culture, (2) disseminators of academic knowledge, (3) preparers of learners for the world of work, (4) promoters of social and group relationships, and (5) encouragers of social change.

- Not all learners react in the same way to the school program. *High adapters* believe content of the school program to be important, and they generally experience success in their classes. *Estranged learners* believe content of the school program is important, but they often develop poor self-images because they experience little success in their classes. *Irrelevant perceivers* are learners who doubt the importance of the school program. They have the ability to succeed, but they commit only marginally to their studies, and often their performance levels fall short of their real abilities. *Alienated learners* neither believe in the importance of the school program nor do well in their classes. Many of them drop out of school before completing high school.

- Young people play many roles in addition to their roles as learners in school. For example, they are also family members, members of ethnic and cultural groups, and members of religious and social organizations. Perspectives of these groups may be at odds with some views to which learners are exposed at school. When this happens, learners may experience psychological pressures as they are torn between competing allegiances to people at home and in organizations and to teachers and the school.

• Review and Discussion Questions

1. Why is it that some learners do not adapt as well as others to the expectations of teachers and the schools?
2. What are some characteristics of the functionalist position?
3. What are some similarities and differences between the economic class conflict position and the status group conflict position?
4. In what ways do schools transmit the general culture and disseminate academic knowledge?

5. What are some things schools do to make learners more comfortable in group and social settings?
6. What kinds of roles do teachers play in schools?
7. What are some potential conflicts teachers face between their in-school professional roles and their roles as members of families and out-of-school groups and organizations?
8. Why is it that many parents assume the worst when they get a call from the school about their child, and how might schools do more to change this expectation of bad news?
9. How can learners' roles as family members, ethnic and cultural group members, and religious and social organization members place pressures on them at school?
10. What are some things teachers can do to help learners deal with potential conflicts between values reflected in their classes at school and values prized by out-of-school groups to which learners belong?

• Ideas for Field Experiences, Projects, and Enrichment

1. Invite a member of a local school district's central administrative staff to talk to your class about how the district responds to concerns that may be raised by parents or other school patrons about certain aspects of the curriculum. What kinds of concerns have been voiced? Have groups been satisfied with the district's responses? Are new teachers provided with guidelines for handling complaints from community groups?
2. Interview several teachers about the different roles they play both in and out of school. Ask about problems they face in managing their time. How do they resolve pressures they may face? Prepare a short report to share with others in your class.
3. Are our school programs designed to maximize the development of all learners, or are they designed to benefit a select few? Prepare a position paper in which you support one of these two positions. Ask your instructor to comment on what you have written.
4. Ask five or six secondary students whether they have ever been told anything at school that conflicts with what they have been told at home. How did they feel when this happened? What did they do? What did their teacher do? Prepare a short written summary of your interview and share it with others in your class.
5. Alienated learners often reject what schools have to offer, and they usually do not do well in their classes. Along with several other fellow class members, do some reading on the subject of learner alienation. What are some things the experts see as leading to this condition? What can teachers and other educators do to help these young people? Present your findings to your class in the form of a symposium.

• References

Bernstein, B. B. (1977). *Class codes and control* (Vol. 3, 2nd ed.). London: Routledge and Kegan Paul.

Coleman, M. (1993). *American Indian children at school, 1850–1930*. Jackson: University of Mississippi Press.

Dougherty, K. J., & Hammack, F. M. (1990). *Education and society: A reader*. San Diego: Harcourt Brace Jovanovich.

Goslin, D. A. (1990). The functions of the school in modern society. In K. J. Dougherty & F. M. Hammack (Eds.), *Education and society: A reader* (pp. 29–38). San Diego: Harcourt Brace Jovanovich.

Khumar, K. (1989). *Social character of learning*. New Delhi, India: Sage Publications India.

Nieto, S. (1992). *Affirming diversity: The sociopolitical context of multicultural education*. New York: Longman.

Parsons, T. (1959). School class as a social system: Some of its functions in American society. *Harvard Educational Review, 49*, 297–318.

Scruggs, O. M. (1979). The education of the Afro-American: An historic view. In K. Hall & A. Young (Eds.), *Education and the Black experience* (pp. 9–24). Palo Alto, CA: R & E Research Associates.

Twain, M. *Roughing it* (1985). New York: Penguin Books. (Original work published 1872)

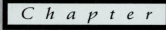

Chapter

9

Technology's Growing Importance

OBJECTIVES

- Explain why the federal government has established improvement of our technological capacity as a national priority.

- Describe some implications for educators of the present emphasis on effective utilization of new technologies.

- Point out some key differences between earlier innovations and the electronic innovations that are making news today.

- Cite some examples of information on the Internet that might be useful to teachers.

- Describe differences between kinds of information that can be accessed using Gopher and by using a browser on the World Wide Web.

- Name some of the major commercial on-line services and suggest ways they can be used by teachers in preparing lessons and in getting assistance from others in the profession.

- Point out some things today's instructional and managerial software can do that are useful to educators.

- Explain the basics of CD-ROM technology and describe how it can be used to support instruction.

- Describe some educational applications of electronic bulletin boards.

- Suggest some potential benefits of interactive distance learning systems for learners in isolated areas.

Increasing our technological capacity has been adopted as an important national goal. In 1995, President Clinton pointed out that an investment in technology makes sense for three key reasons:

- Technology is the engine of economic growth.
- Scientific knowledge is the key to the future.
- Responsible government advances science and technology.

Improved technological capacity will build important communication links. Sharing information through new technology has the potential not only to promote economic growth but to make societies more stable. Speaking to this issue, Vice President Gore (1995a) made these comments:

> Communication is the beginning of community. Whether it is through language, art, custom or political philosophy, people and nations identify themselves through communication of experience and values. A global information network will create new communities and strengthen existing ones by enriching the ways in which we do and can communicate.

Schools are expected to play an important part in the technological revolution. In particular, schools have been designated as one of the key players in the effort to develop an advanced National Information Infrastructure, more popularly known as the *information superhighway*. The information superhighway will be a seamless web of communications networks, computers, and data bases. It will make huge quantities of information available to users everywhere. A consortium called the National Information Infrastructure, formed in 1993, has been working on the development of the information superhighway. Its members include academic institutions, government laboratories and agencies, and major private sector firms in the telecommunications and computer industries. As a matter of national policy, the federal government has challenged the telecommunications industry "to connect every classroom, library, clinic, and hospital to the information superhighway by the year 2000" (Gore, 1995b).

The emphasis on technology requires educators to develop programs that will do more than simply expose learners to technologies. Increasingly, there is an expectation that graduates will be able users of technology who are prepared to enter a world of work confident in their abilities to utilize sophisticated electronic tools of all kinds.

Pressures on schools to incorporate state-of-the-art technology pose problems, however. The rapidity of technological change requires frequent upgrading of equipment. Not all schools have the financial capacity to stay technologically current. An emphasis on technology has the potential to sharpen differences between programs offered in wealthy and impoverished school districts. Further, many teachers in the schools today have had little experience using new technologies. Some are not eager to embrace them. Younger teachers often are more familiar with newer electronic innovations than their older colleagues, and many school districts look to their younger, less experienced teachers for leadership as technological changes are implemented. For those of you who are going into the profession, this represents an excellent opportunity to share expertise with more senior

Today's employees increasingly are being expected to have sophisticated understandings of computers and other electronic technologies.

people in your buildings. There is every indication that the emphasis on technology is going to accelerate in the years ahead. Newcomers to the teaching profession who are well versed in the use of advanced technologies will be prime candidates for leadership.

TODAY'S TECHNOLOGICAL INNOVATIONS

The World Wide Web of the Internet, major on-line services, sophisticated new personal computer software, CD-ROM, electronic bulletin boards, and interactive distance learning systems are among technological innovations that are influencing school programs. Looked at in one way, these innovations are simply a continuation of a long-standing tradition of incorporating new technologies into instructional programs. There is, however, an important feature of the newer electronic innovations that makes them different from older technologies.

Earlier innovations featured improvements of a mechanical rather than an electronic nature. Such innovations as high-speed book presses and self-threading film projectors, for example, featured hundreds of moving parts. Although it is possible to design mechanical parts that move at high speeds, there are practical limits to how fast purely mechanical devices can operate. Friction caused by moving parts results in wear. Thus, in mechanical devices, there is a tendency for functional problems to increase as the speed of operation increases.

Electronic innovations have fewer upper-limit restrictions on their speed of operation. This is true because they do not depend on moving mechanical parts.

Instead, they rely on electronic impulses that can flow through circuits at incredibly high speeds. The absence of moving mechanical parts has the added advantage of reducing the types of breakdowns that occur in equipment in which physical movement of parts produces friction and, in time, wear.

Today's electronic innovations have been made possible because of discoveries in microelectronics. Microelectronics is concerned with the production of extremely small electronic devices, particularly switches and circuits. Thousands of circuits can be embedded on small chips about the size of the smallest fingernail on an adult's hand. These chips, called microprocessors, are now manufactured by the millions. Once a production line is started, it is relatively inexpensive to produce many additional copies of a similar circuit. As a result, many of today's electronic devices are small and inexpensive.

EXAMPLES OF TECHNOLOGIES THAT AFFECT TEACHERS AND SCHOOLS

With the national commitment to make access to the information superhighway available to schools everywhere, educators throughout the nation are making increased use of technology to support instruction. However, there are enormous place-to-place differences in both the sophistication of technologies that are available and the intensity of their use. A number of these electronic innovations depend on the availability of personal computers. These are now common features in schools, although there are great differences in the number of computers and the modernity of computers in individual schools.

This section introduces some technologies that are increasingly influencing the nation's instructional programs. Among these are:

- the Internet
- major on-line services
- instructional and managerial software
- CD-ROM
- electronic bulletin board systems
- interactive distance learning systems

The Internet

The Internet is a collection or linkage of computer networks throughout the world. People who can access it can retrieve information on a vast number of topics. There are also means available that allow users to send out information electronically to others who have electronic links to the Internet. The shunting of information around the globe via the Internet is what people are talking about when they speak of the communication benefits of the information superhighway. In the United States and elsewhere, efforts are under way to make access to the Internet easier and to ensure that electronic circuits do not become clogged as more and more users establish Internet connections.

**BOX
9-1**

Will Technology Undermine Our Sense of Community?

The following comments appeared in a letter to the editor of a local newspaper.

We hear all the time about the wonderful things technology is going to do for us. It's time we paused to reflect on this issue. Whether we all will be better off because of changes being brought about by technology is debatable.

Consider, for example, the home computers and the Internet. These technologies allow more and more people to do much of their work at home. They provide a technological reinforcement for a "fortress" mentality that has developed in this country over the past decade that has witnessed people seeking personal and psychological security behind guarded gates of cloistered residential communities. Before the proliferation of home computers and development of the Internet, these people at least had to leave these protected enclaves during the work day. Presumably, the drive to work brought them into some kind of contact, however minimal, with environments and people much different from themselves.

Advances in technology are taking away the opportunity for even limited contacts with different kinds of people. In the absence of such experiences, how can we expect people to develop an appreciation of differences? Commitment to active social and civic participation is already at a low ebb. Won't the kind of isolation technology encourages make this situation even worse in the future? Do we really want a world where people avoid person-to-person contacts and are satisfied by an exchange of electronic impulses over the Internet?

What Do You Think?

1. Is there a tendency for us to presume that technological change always represents an improvement?
2. Do individual technological changes affect different people in different ways? For example, are some young people likely to be advantaged by an increased emphasis on the use of computers in schools, whereas others may become more disadvantaged?
3. What are some general reactions you have to this letter to the editor? If you were asked to write a letter to the same editor commenting on the position taken by this writer, what would you say?

The Internet is accessed with a modem-equipped computer and a telephone line. There are a number of Internet service providers. Some of these providers are specialty firms that do nothing but sell access to the Internet to users for a monthly fee. Others are services that are included with membership in such on-line services as America Online, CompuServe, and Prodigy. Schools that make Internet access available must make access arrangements with an Internet service provider before teachers and learners can use the system.

One of the problems in using the Internet is navigating through the tremendous thicket of information to find something specific. In response to the need to impose some order on the process of searching out information, a number of special tools have been developed. One of these is called *Gopher.*

Gopher

Gopher is a system that organizes Internet information into categories. It is a layered system that allows the user to begin with a very large category of interest and proceed to narrow the focus until the desired specific information is obtained. In a sense, Gopher can be thought of as a system for indexing information in the Internet.

Gopher is an extremely useful tool for educators. There is an incredible amount of information available on the Internet that can be quickly accessed using this system. Entire magazines are available for perusal. All kinds of federal government information can be retrieved. Many school districts and even individual schools put up information on the Internet related to special types of programs. Gopher provides an excellent way for teachers to gather information quickly about a wide variety of topics.

Good as Gopher is, the system does have limitations. It is capable only of gathering information that takes the form of text files. Whereas much information on the Internet is in prose form, the Internet includes many other forms as well, such as photographs, paintings, and graphics of all types. There are also motion pictures and even sound clips. None of these can be accessed using Gopher. To remedy these limitations, a system called the World Wide Web has been developed. The World Wide Web provides true multimedia access to resources on the Internet.

The World Wide Web

The World Wide Web is a fairly new innovation. It resulted from work at the European Particle Physics Laboratory in Switzerland, and the first prototype became available as recently as 1990 (Turlington, 1995). Developers wanted to establish a system that would allow easy and dependable information sharing among physicists throughout the world. The World Wide Web allows for transmission and reception of any kind of a text, graphics, or video document. Further, the World Wide Web allows users to quickly locate other documents in the Internet that treat content that bears some relationship to the content of the document they have on their computer screen. The World Wide Web's ability to link together documents allows for huge and efficient searches of the Internet.

To get to the World Wide Web, a user needs a personal computer, a modem, an Internet connection, and a Web browser. A *Web browser* is a program that is designed to read the electronic language of the World Wide Web. It allows users to access individual *Web sites*. These are electronic addresses where specific kinds of information are available. Individual sites may include text, graphics, sound, or a combination of all three. On a good monitor, the clarity of color photographs and graphics is as a good as on a commercial movie screen. A number of Web browsers are available. These include Netscape, Cello, Quarterdeck Mosaic, Mosaic in a Box, NCSA Mosaic, and ElNet. The most widely used of these is Netscape (Pearlstein, 1995). Members of such electronic on-line services as America Online and Prodigy have access to built-in browsers they can use to locate specific information on the Web.

World Wide Web addresses are called Uniform Resource Locators, or URLs. When a given URL is requested using a Web browser such as Netscape, information on the *home page* of the Web site appears on the screen. The home page typically provides some details regarding the organization or group that has provided the information; lists of available local print documents, photos, and sound bites that can be accessed at the site (research project results, position statements from political candidates, full text of speeches, photographs of tropical fish, brief musical samples from forthcoming recordings, and menu items from a Chinese restaurant are examples of the kinds of information that may be available on a given home page); and links to other documents dealing with similar topics located elsewhere on the World Wide Web.

For educators, the Web is an incredibly rich resource. Not only can a wide array of information be accessed, but specific items can be downloaded, saved, and printed. The Web has the potential to bring resources from throughout the world into classrooms in even the most isolated areas of the United States. Many schools throughout the country have recognized the potential of the Web as a means of disseminating information about some of the good things they are doing and are developing their own home pages. An example of what a school-based home page looks like is provided in Figure 9-1.

Notice that a number of categories of information are available. By clicking on any one of these, additional information is provided. For example, information about the city of Edinburg (a community near the southern extreme of Texas) is

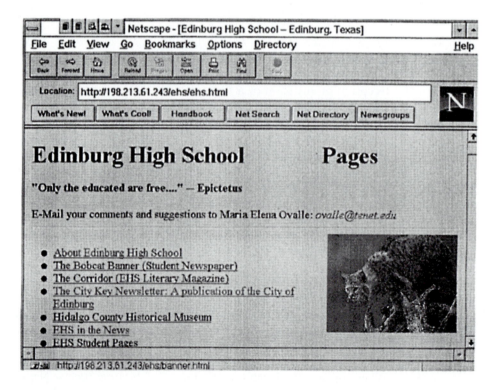

Figure 9-1

An example of an Internet home page for a high school

provided under the heading "The City Key Newsletter: A publication of the City of Edinburg." Other categories include information of interest to students, teachers, and staff members. Note, too, the invitation to communicate directly with someone at the high school using electronic mail. Increasing numbers of URL sites are encouraging this type of exchange. As more schools develop World Wide Web home pages, there will be wonderful opportunities for educators throughout the country to exchange ideas on common issues of concern.

Perhaps one of the greatest benefits of the World Wide Web for teachers is the accessibility it affords to all kinds of information. Are you interested in what is going on in the executive branch of government? Use the World Wide Web to find the "White House Home Page" (The URL is http://www2.whitehouse.gov/WH/Welcome.html). In 1995, this interesting page provided access to a huge quantity of information ranging from White House press releases to historical information about the White House to photographs of the first family to recorded "meowed" greetings from the first cat, Socks. Here are a few other World Web Sites you might find of interest. This list is not comprehensive — just a sampler of what is available.

- For Shakespeare materials, try the "Complete Works of William Shakespeare." The URL is http://the-tech.mit.edu/Shakespeare/simple-works.html
- For information from the Library of Congress, go to "The Library of Congress World Wide Web Home Page." The URL is http://lcweb.loc.gov/homepage/lchp.html
- For information on investing, try the "Security APL Quote Server" page. The URL is http://www.secapl.com/cgi-bin/qs
- For a tour of the solar system that features images, sound files, data from spacecraft, and other interesting information, try "The Nine Planets" home page. The URL is http://seds.lpl.arizona.edu/nineplanets/nineplanets/intro.html
- For a list of Internet school sites in the United States, go to the "Hotlist of K–12 Internet School Sites — USA." The URL is http://www.sendit.nodak.edu/k12/
- For information about holdings, events, items for sale, and other details regarding all the museums that collectively comprise the Smithsonian Institution, go to the "Smithsonian Institution Home Page." The URL is http://www.si.edu
- For information about admissions requirements, programs, views of campuses, costs, and other issues associated with colleges and universities, go to the home page titled "Directory of WWW.*.EDU Servers." The URL is http://www.zurich.ibm.com/wwwedudirectory.html
- For a report of a trip to Antarctica that features text, a day-by-day diary, audio recordings, and wonderful photographs, go to "A Tourist Expedition to Antarctica." The URL is http://http2.sils.umich.edu/Antarctica/Story.html
- For information on work of Columbia University's Institute for Learning Technologies to advance the role computers play in schools, go to "LiveText." The URL is http://www.ilt.columbia.edu/k12/livetext/index.html
- For a fascinating "encyclopedia" with entries developed by kids, go to the "Kidopedia" home page. The URL is http://rdz.stjohns.edu/kidopedia

The preceding list of sites represents a fraction of what is now available on the Web. New ones are being added almost daily. Good books are available that provide URL addresses for hundreds of interesting Web sites. Two excellent resources of this kind are:

- *New Riders' Official World Wide Web Yellow Pages.* (updated annually). Indianapolis, IN: New Riders Publishing.
- Turlington, S. R. *Walking the World Wide Web: Your Personal Guide to the Best of the Web.* Chapel Hill, NC: Ventana Press, 1995.

Major On-line Services

Commercial on-line services represent excellent opportunities for teachers and other educators to join in the revolution in electronic communication technology. These services cater to novices and, in their desire to appeal to as many potential customers as possible, they have gone to great lengths to make it easy for people to communicate with one another and to locate information of all kinds quickly and simply.

On-line services require users to have a personal computer with a modem attached and a phone line. The same phone line can be used to handle both regular telephone calls and transmission of data between the user and the on-line service to which he or she subscribes. All of the on-line services provide free software that enables new customers to join their system in a matter of minutes. Typically, these firms charge a flat monthly fee that authorizes a member to access the system with no additional charges for a given number of hours. Additional time is charged at a per-hour rate. At the time of this writing, basic fees average around $10.00 per month with additional hours billed somewhere between $2.00 and $3.00 per hour. So many attractive options are available on these systems that some users find they must monitor themselves carefully to avoid unexpectedly large bills at the end of the month.

Millions of subscribers are now members of on-line services. Subscribers include many schools as well as thousands of individual teachers who have personal memberships for computers they use at home. The largest of these companies are America Online, CompuServe, Prodigy, Delphi Internet, and GEnie. For information about joining any of these on-line services, call one of the listed 800 numbers:

- America Online: 800 827-6364
- CompuServe: 800 848-8199
- Prodigy: 800 776-3449
- Delphi Internet: 800 695-4005
- GEnie: 800 638-9636

On-line services provide ready access to a huge array of information sources. They include newspapers, magazines, travel information, sports information, information from the major television networks and press agencies, information on real estate, information on investments, and information on numerous specialty areas — notably education. These services generally also have embedded Web browsers so members can access all of the information on the World Wide Web. All of them allow users to send and receive electronic mail. This e-mail capability allows members to actively participate in discussions and to communicate with anyone else who has an e-mail address.

Increasingly, the on-line services are attempting to develop areas of particular interest to members in specific professions. Teachers have been identified as one of the priority target groups. As an example of what is now available, let's look at what America Online offers in its "Teachers' Information Area." This part of America Online includes a "Teachers' Forum" where different educational issues are discussed each week with opportunities provided for members to type in their own comments and participate in the dialogue. It also includes "The Newsstand," an area that features articles from leading journals in education.

Another interesting area is "The Idea Exchange." This functions as a kind of electronic bulletin board where teachers can exchange ideas on a number of topics. "Teachers' University" features teachers teaching other teachers how to use specific kinds of instructional techniques. The area titled "Lesson Plan Libraries" includes a huge assortment of lesson plans and other practical ideas for planning instruction. Other areas focus on writing grants, on exchanging ideas about how technology can be used to improve instruction, on upcoming conventions and conferences in education, and on exchanging multimedia resources of all types to improve education.

One of the big pluses for the on-line services is the opportunity they provide for building a sense of community among teachers and educators. Much of what a teacher does happens in isolation within the classroom. The on-line services afford teachers an opportunity to share concerns with professionals throughout the country. This engenders a positive teachers-helping-teachers situation — something that can provide practical solutions to problems as well as some needed moral support from others who have experienced and overcome similar difficulties.

Instructional and Managerial Software

Personal computers have become common in the schools. Because of this, software vendors have dramatically increased the quantity and quality of programs designed to be used in schools. This situation represents a great improvement over circumstances prevailing a decade ago, when many educational programs represented little more than conversions of dull workbook activities to a computer-based format. Vendors have also recognized that computers in many schools are not up-to-date models, and thus much software is available that will work even on somewhat dated computer hardware.

Much early school-related software was directed at teaching learners computer programming skills. Today, this is a minor emphasis. Instructional software increasingly is oriented to teaching academic content associated with the individual school subjects. For example, software is available that focuses on developing learners' writing skills, increasing their sophisticated analytical thinking processes through exposure to data associated with simulation activities, and helping them develop mechanical drawing proficiency. The best of the new instructional programs require students to confront content and work actively with it to develop a "product" (a chart, written response, formal presentation, or something else that will indicate that higher-level thinking processes have been engaged).

Do School Programs Featuring Up-to-date Technologies Help Everyone?

Nine people serve as members of the Site Management Council of Fernlawn Senior High School. The local school district, following a national trend, six years ago established Site Management Councils at each school. These groups have authority over many issues pertaining to establishment of discipline policies, approval of curriculum change, oversight of extracurricular and cocurricular activities, and other concerns having to do with the overall managerial policies of the schools. The Fernlawn Site Management Council consists of two administrators, two teachers, and five community members.

Rich Lawson is a history teacher at Fernlawn. he has had an enduring interest in computers and technology and believes that social studies teachers should make more use of up-to-date technologies in their programs. Last fall, Rich spotted a request-for-proposal announcement from the state department of education. The announcement called for proposals for projects that would directly involve students in nontechnical subject areas in the information superhighway. As much as $75,000 per year for five years would be awarded to those receiving grants.

Rich and some other social studies teachers spent weeks putting together a proposal. They submitted it just before the November 10th deadline. Just last week, they received word from the state capital that they had been awarded $62,000 a year for five years. Their proposal called for the money to be used to buy multimedia computers, high-speed printers, Web browsing software, and access time to the Internet. Provision was also included to train all social studies teachers in the department to use the equipment and, more specifically, to take maximum advantage of resources available on the World Wide Web. Students in their classes were to be trained to use this equipment and would be required to prepare at least half of their assigned papers using sources exclusively drawn from the World Wide Web.

Paulette Johnson, principal at Fernlawn, was pleased to learn that Rich's proposal had been funded. She pointed out that district policy required him to secure final approval from the Fernlawn Site Management Council before the new program could be implemented. The Site Management Council met last night. Rich Lawson concluded his presentation with these comments.

> I just want to say that this represents a great opportunity for our students. Everything we read tells us how our young people need to be really comfortable with technology. We now will have the resources that will allow our students to work directly with the information superhighway — something that such people as Al Gore have been advocating for a long, long time. Few other high schools are in a position to give their students this kind of an opportunity. Our graduates are going to have experiences that will put them ahead of most others in the state.
>
> Finally, I would point out, this is going to occur at almost no cost to the school. The needed equipment and training will be paid for from our grant. This change is an academic win for our students, and it is a public relations win for our school. I hope you will agree with me that this represents a wonderful opportunity for Fernlawn High School.

Excellent software is now available to assist teachers and administrators with many of their managerial tasks. For example, there are programs that teachers can use to record attendance, create and print individual lesson plans, and record and average grades. School administrators often use software to generate master sched-

After he concluded his comments, Rich sat down expecting a quick vote of support for the project. The chairperson of the group thanked Rich for his comments and then recognized Gracine Tyson, one of the parent members of the council, who had raised her hand seeking the floor.

I am somewhat reluctant to say what I must say, and I want to begin by expressing my great appreciation to Mr. Lawson for his good intentions. However, I have some very serious reservations about this project.

Many of the students in our school come from homes where money is in very short supply. There certainly is not enough to buy home computers. Now I recognize that Mr. Lawson's program proposes to use computers here at the school. But, if I am understanding the terms of the grant, students are to do at least 50 percent of their research using Internet resources. This feature is going to advantage students who have access to computers at home as well as Internet access at school. Students who must depend only on the computers at school are going to be at a tremendous disadvantage.

Instead of spending time preparing teachers for a program that depends on expensive technologies that will increase the competitive advantage of our more affluent students, I feel we should emphasize the importance of using library resources, textbooks, and other learning materials that are truly as available to our students from impoverished backgrounds as to our students from more economically blessed homes.

A general discussion ensued. At the end of the meeting, the chairperson suggested that each member of the council solicit reactions to Rich Lawson's proposal from other interested parties. A final vote on the matter would be taken at the next meeting.

The next day, Rich Lawson, in a highly agitated state, dropped in to visit again with Principal Johnson:

It just doesn't add up. We work our tails off putting together a proposal to do something good for kids, and somebody accuses us of trying to do something that will make some of our students relatively worse off than they would be without the program. Aren't these people listening to what people in government and industry are telling us about the need to get with it technologically? I'm really disgusted that a sincere effort to do something positive may just go down the drain.

What does Rich Lawson see as important priorities for the school? How does he support his conclusions? How does he believe the quality of the overall program at Fernlawn High School will be judged? What might have led him to this position? Is there evidence that he has considered other positions? To what extent is his image of himself as a competent professional at stake in this situation?

What does Gracine Tyson see as important priorities for the school? How does she respond to Rich's proposal in light of these priorities? What are her assumptions regarding the likely impact of the proposed new program on different groups of students? What kinds of prior experiences might have led her to adopt these views? Did any of these experiences result from conscious school policies, or were they unintended side effects of policies that were put forward with generally good intentions?

In considering the perspectives represented by Rich Lawson and Gracine Tyson, what comments might you make to each? Is compromise likely? If not, what "histories" might lie behind the views of both Rich and Gracine?

ules, keep track of budgets, maintain addresses of learners and parents, and produce memoranda and informal notices for faculty and staff members. Counselors, school nurses, and other school personnel also are finding software that allows them to perform some aspects of their duties more effectively.

Many firms publish good education-related software. Some of the following companies are among the leaders in this field:

Aquarius
P.O. Box 128
Indian Rocks, FL 33535

Broderbund Software
345 Fourth Street
San Francisco, CA 94107

Educational Activities
1937 Grand Avenue
Baldwin, NY 11510

Grolier Electronic Publishing
Sherman Turnpike
Danbury, CT 06816

Learning Arts
P.O. Box 179
Wichita, KS 67201

MicroEd
P.O. Box 24750
Edina, MN 55424

Milliken
1100 Research Boulevard
St. Louis, MO 63132

Scholastic Incorporated
P.O. Box 7502
Jefferson City, MO 65102

SVE
1345 Diversey Parkway
Chicago, IL 60614

Tom Snyder Productions
90 Sherman Street
Cambridge, MA 02140

Unicorn Software
2950 E. Flamingo Road
Las Vegas, NV 89121

CD-ROM

Compact disk read-only memory, or CD-ROM, is a technology that has revolutionized management of computer, audio, and visual information. In CD-ROM, infor-

This student is using computer software to complete an English assignment.

mation is stored in digital form on a small disk (4.75 inches in diameter). Information is recorded on the disk by a light beam that burns tiny pits on the surface. It is read by a device connected to a computer that interprets reflections of a laser light that bounces off the disk and converts this information into computer language.

For educators, there are two important advantages of CD-ROM technology. First, information can take many forms, including audio, graphics, printed text, and video. Second, each disk has an enormous storage capacity. A single CD-ROM "disk is capable of storing the equivalent of 1,200 floppy disks, 250 large reference books, 2,400 full screen photos, or 550 MB [megabytes] of storage" (Phillipo, 1989, p. 40). To take full advantage of CD-ROM technology, it is necessary to have a computer equipped with both a CD-ROM drive and good speakers.

Learners can access information contained on a CD-ROM disk in many ways. They can browse through pages of an electronic encyclopedia in much the same way they would use a printed version in the school library. They can use key words or phrases to locate specific information. They can easily transfer prose and graphics from the CD-ROM disk to a floppy disk or a computer's hard disk. Using word-processing and desktop publishing programs, this information can be incorporated into term papers and other learner-produced materials with ease.

CD-ROM technology affords many opportunities for teachers to prepare customized instructional materials. Conceivably, an entire series of textbooks could be produced in CD-ROM format. Assuming that copyright releases were obtained, teachers would have little difficulty in preparing different configurations of this material for different learners in their classrooms.

There are marvelous commercially prepared CD-ROMS that enjoy large markets among educators. The quantity of material on a single CD-ROM disk is enormous. In a conversation among themselves, the authors of this text concluded that they could have written nearly every paper they produced in their high school days using information contained on *Encarta*, a particularly fine CD-ROM encyclopedia produced by Microsoft Corporation. One advantage of CD-ROM titles is their wide availability. Many bookstores, for example, will have such titles as Broderbund's *Where in the World is Carmen Sandiego?* (an outstanding game for teaching important geographic skills), Pro One Software's *Holidays Clip Art, Vols. I and II* (contains excellent visuals for elementary teachers wanting to make displays related to individual holidays), Microsoft's *Art Gallery* (magnificent color reproductions of paintings from the world's leading galleries), and Compact Publishing's *Time Almanac 1990's* (an excellent overview of events that have shaped recent history).

Some firms that market CD-ROMs designed for use by teachers and schools are listed here:

Broderbund Software, Inc.
17 Paul Drive
San Rafael, CA 94903

Compact Publishing, Inc.
P.O. Box 40310
Washington, DC 20016

Encyclopedia Britannica Educational Corp.
Britannica Centre, 310 S. Michigan Avenue
Chicago, IL 60604

Grolier Electronic Encyclopedia
Sherman Turnpike
Danbury, CT 06816

Microsoft Corp.
Box 97017
Redmond, WA 98073

PC SIG Inc.
1030 Duane Avenue, Suite D
Sunnyvale, CA 94086

Pro One Software
P.O. Box 16317
Las Cruces, NM 88004

Tri-Star Publishing Company
475 Virginia Drive
Ft. Washington, PA 19034

Xiphias
8758 Venice Boulevard
Los Angeles, CA 90034

Electronic Bulletin Board Systems

Electronic bulletin board systems allow for exchanges of messages between personal computer users. The computers with modems are tied electronically to the "bulletin boards" via telephone lines. More and more schools are providing teachers with modems and phone lines that permit them to access electronic bulletin board systems with their computers. These systems allow for school-to-school communications as well as for exchanges of personal information, sharing of lesson plans and units, and communications about tests. In some places, these systems can be used by teachers to order instructional materials. Learners can use them to search data bases for information needed to complete assignments. Periodicals serving the interests of people interested in multiple uses of personal computers, such as *Computer Shopper*, often publish lists of electronic bulletin boards and the phone numbers needed to access them.

There are many possibilities for instructional use of electronic bulletin boards. Some teachers of foreign languages are encouraging their students to write letters in the target foreign language to learners in a country where the language is spoken. For example, Spanish teachers may have their learners post letters on an electronic bulletin board that is accessible to young people in Mexico or elsewhere in Spanish-speaking Latin America.

At the elementary school level, pupils in many schools regularly use classroom computers to tap into the National Geographic Society's Kids' Net to share information about classroom science experiments. This system allows for a nationwide sharing of data gathered about a common problem, such as acid rain.

Learners in one West Virginia school have used their computers to develop pen pal friendships with students in a Moscow school. Another group in Massachusetts has been writing descriptions of New England for the benefit of a Saskatchewan class in western Canada. Efforts to date suggest that electronic bulletin boards offer excellent opportunities for linking learners with information and people located at great distances from the school.

Interactive Distance Learning Systems

Distance learning has been around for years. The term refers to a system of instruction whereby learners are located at a considerable distance from the place where the instruction is delivered. Correspondence courses are an example of distance learning. For many years, educators in Australia have used the radio to broadcast lessons to learners in that country's remote outback. Televised instruction is another example of distance learning.

Throughout much of its history, distance learning has been a noninteractive, one-way phenomenon. That is, the teacher presented information to learners at remote sites, but there was no way for the teacher and the learners to interact as the lesson was being taught. Modern electronic technology has made this kind of interactive communication possible.

Of particular interest are systems that allow for two-way visual and sound communication between learners and a teacher who is located at a site that might

This teacher is using interactive video technology to communicate with learners who are located many miles distant from the teacher's location.

be quite remote from where the learners are situated. Better systems also feature dedicated facsimile lines that allow for materials to be quickly shunted back and forth between teacher and learners using a fax machine. Some interactive video systems use satellite technology to carry visual and sound information. This tends to be an expensive option. In the past several years, there has been interest in the use of compressed video transmission schemes. These systems allow signals to be sent over regular telephone lines. Because the bandwidth of signals that can be accommodated by telephone lines is more restricted than what can be handled when satellites are used, the movements on the television screens are somewhat jerky, but not to the point that they interfere seriously with the usability of the system.

Even compressed video transmission of signals can be expensive. Phone line charges can be extremely high when signals are sent for long periods of time over great distances. Professionals who are interested in this technology are working hard with utility regulatory authorities to establish special education tariffs that, in time, may bring down the costs of using compressed video transmission.

Interactive distance learning technologies have the potential to provide specialized instruction to isolated communities. For example, small towns may not have enough students in their high schools to warrant offering a course such as advanced calculus. Using interactive distance learning, an advanced calculus teacher in one location might provide classes to students scattered throughout many rural locations in the state. Such an approach has been tried successfully in New Hampshire and in other locations.

The isolation of learners in remote locations has long concerned educators. Interactive systems can meet the academic needs of these learners and, at the same time, diminish any sense of psychological separateness they might feel from their peers in larger population centers. The technology now exists for young people in even the most remote areas of the country to feel that they can participate as active, contributing members of a class (even though other members may be hundreds of miles away).

ELECTRONIC INNOVATIONS: SOME IMPLICATIONS

Predicting the future is always hazardous. Unforeseen circumstances often shape events in unanticipated ways. Yet the temptation remains to look carefully at emerging patterns and suggest what kind of future they may portend. The following changes may be among those resulting from an increased use of electronic technologies by professional educators:

- Teachers will increasingly serve as information guides for their learners, showing them how to access information sources outside of the school.
- More learning will occur outside of the classroom.
- Schools will communicate more effectively with the communities they serve.
- Teachers will sense more identity with the national community of educators.

Teachers as Information Guides

Information sources that are becoming available to teachers through computers linked to data sources via telephone lines are almost limitless in their scope. Those of us who teach in the future may need to spend a good deal of our time becoming familiar with the contents of various sources and with procedures for accessing information. An important part of our instructional role will be to direct learners quickly to electronic information sources containing material needed to complete assignments.

Learning Outside the Classroom

The traditional classroom made sense as an educational innovation when learning resources had to be physically located at the same place as the learners. The classroom was an efficient way to serve a large number of learners by gathering them together at one place that featured expensive learning materials and a trained teacher.

Today, computers and phone lines allow individuals to tap into information sources that may be hundreds or even thousands of miles away. Potentially, learning can take place wherever access to a computer and a phone line is available. Hence, it may be that learners in the future will do much more of their academic work in their own computer-equipped homes than is presently the case. When students work with information in the comfort of their own homes, they may develop important lifelong learning habits. To make this happen, we will need to engage in very careful planning. Clarity of expression will be more important than it has ever been. This is true because many of our learners may not have the continuous personal access to us that young people enjoy who are with us in the same classroom.

Staying in Touch with Parents and School Patrons

In the future, schools may be able to maintain almost continuous lines of communication with parents and other school constituents. Information about upcoming events, scheduling of classes, absences, and other matters can easily be sent to home computers over phone lines, even using today's technology. In the future, electronic systems may allow reactions to proposed school policies to be transmitted back to those of us who work at the school. This kind of electronic dialogue has the potential to generate considerable interest in problems facing schools and to develop a broad base of support for their programs.

Establishing Ties with the National Community of Teachers

Teaching has sometimes been described as a lonely profession. Many teachers are in situations where they work alone with their learners with very little adult contact during the day. There is little opportunity for sharing concerns and hopes, successes and failures with colleagues at work. The colleagues, too, are busy in their classrooms working with their own young people. The electronic revolution we are now experiencing affords the possibility of opening unprecedented lines of communication among the national community of classroom teachers.

Teachers today who belong to various on-line services or who have access to electronic mail through other means are able to communicate during the evening and on weekends with teachers throughout the country (and, to a more limited extent, throughout the world). Anyone who has looked in on one of the teacher-focused discussion groups sponsored by a commercial on-line service will be impressed by the amount of sharing and support that is occurring. Building this kind of community of interest can help us as individual teachers recognize that we are not alone. Thousands of other professionals share our concerns and cherish our successes.

• Key Ideas in Summary

- The federal government is strongly committed to improving the nation's technological capacity. In part, this policy is driven by a conviction that application of sophisticated technologies is essential to continued economic growth. As part of the emphasis on technology, our nation's leaders have challenged the telecommunications industry to connect all classrooms in the country to the information superhighway by the year 2000.

- Responding to the desire to improve the nation's technological capacity poses challenges for schools. Sophisticated equipment is expensive, and it must be replaced frequently if it is to be kept current. Further, relatively few teachers are well trained in some of the newer electronic technologies. All of this presents a particular opportunity for newcomers to the profession who become technologically proficient. They may be called upon to share their expertise with more experienced teachers and administrators.

- The technological innovations that are drawing attention today largely are based more on electronic circuitry than on moving mechanical parts. This feature makes wear and tear less of a problem in electronic systems because there are few mechanical parts that move and create friction. Because electrons move incredibly fast through circuits, many of these new innovations work at astonishing speeds.

- The *Internet* is a collection of computer networks throughout the world. People who use it can retrieve information on a vast number of subjects. The shunting of information around the globe via the Internet is what people refer to when they describe the *information superhighway*. The Internet is accessed with a computer equipped with a modem and a telephone line that is used to connect with one of a number of providers of Internet connection services.

- A problem with using the Internet is navigating through the tremendous volume of available information. One tool that has been designed to help users do this is called *Gopher*. Gopher, which is basically an indexing system, organizes Internet information into categories. Gopher users see information as text files. They can read these on their own computers, or they can save them on their own disks for later use. Gopher can be used to locate all kinds of information of potential interest to educators.

- There are many other types of information available on the Internet besides prose text. These include audio recordings, film clips, paintings, and photographs. Several years ago, a system called the World Wide Web was developed that allows for retrieval of information regardless of its format. To access information from the Web, users use a *Web browser* such as Netscape, Quarterdeck Mosaic, or NCSA Mosaic. Most of the on-line services such as America Online, CompuServe, and Prodigy also provide members with a useful Web browser as part of their membership. The Web is an incredibly rich resource for educators. Teachers who use it can locate text, audio, and graphic information; can save it; and can use it later with their own students. It has the potential to bring all kinds of instructional resources to learners even in the most isolated areas.

- Major on-line services make it easy for people to join the revolution in electronic communication. Among the larger on-line services are America Online, CompuServe, Prodigy, Delphi Internet, and GEnie. On-line services provide electronic access to newspapers, magazines, travel bureaus, major television networks, national and international press agencies, governmental agencies of all kinds, and almost every other imaginable information source. They also provide access to the World Wide Web, and they give users access to electronic mail. This latter feature allows members to send and receive messages to anyone with an electronic mail address. The electronic mail capability is particularly useful as a means for teachers to communicate with educators throughout the country. Indeed, some of the on-line services have taken pains to organize discussion groups that feature teachers helping teachers.

- Personal computers have become common in the schools. In response to their growing presence, software vendors have increasingly focused on producing materials for the growing education market. Today, sophisticated programs are available for teaching rigorous academic content. Administrators also find useful programs for handling school budgets, planning teaching schedules, and handling other challenging managerial chores.

- CD-ROM technology allows for extremely compact storage of huge quantities of audio and visual information. A single CD-ROM may store as much information as 1,200 floppy disks. Outstanding CD-ROM disks are available now that include entire encyclopedias, collections of paintings, synopses of long historical periods, and other kinds of audio, video, and prose text content.

- Electronic bulletin systems allow for exchanges of messages between personal computer users. Computers with modems are tied electronically to the bulletin boards by telephone lines. All sorts of instructional uses are possible that take advantage of electronic bulletin systems. For example, some foreign language teachers use them to connect their learners electronically with native speakers of the target language.

- Interactive distance learning systems deliver instruction to learners who are at different physical locations from their teacher. These systems allow for learners and the teachers to communicate with one another. Increasingly, these systems use both visual and audio technologies. This allows parties at both ends (the teacher at one location and the students at another) to see and hear one another. Various means are being used to transmit the signal, and efforts are under way to reduce the costs of such systems. Interactive distance learning systems offer a way to provide instruction on sophisticated topics to learners who live in isolated areas.

- Electronic communication technologies have the potential to build a greater sense of community among the nation's teachers. This is true because these technologies make electronic communications between people in distant locations possible. They also provide learners with access to learning resources of extraordinary depth and richness. Learners in isolated areas need no longer be educationally disadvantaged because of their distance from good libraries; information resources can be brought to them electronically. The electronic revolution also opens up the possibility of more frequent communication with parents and other patrons of the school.

• Review and Discussion Questions

1. Why are leading government officials so interested in taking steps to improve our nation's technological capacity?
2. What are some challenges that must be overcome as schools attempt to keep their programs technologically up-to-date?
3. How do today's electronic innovations differ from some technological innovations that affected teachers, learners, and schools in previous times?
4. What is the Internet, and what kinds of equipment are required to access it?
5. How would you describe differences between types of information that can be retrieved using Gopher and using a World Wide Web browser?
6. Many teachers today belong to one of the major on-line services. Why might such a membership make sense for a beginning teacher? Describe some specific kinds of help a teacher might get.
7. Use of CD-ROMs in the schools has grown tremendously in recent years. Does it make sense for schools to invest in multimedia computers that have CD-ROM drives and speakers? What advantages might these units have over computers that can use only conventional software?
8. How might you use electronic bulletin boards in your own classroom? Does this technology have more applications for some subject areas than others? Explain.
9. Interactive distance learning systems have the capability of distributing the instructional services of a single teacher over a broad area. Does this technology pose a potential threat to teachers' employment? That is, will a small number of "super teachers" be hired whose instruction will be beamed to vast audiences of young people at individual school sites, thus eliminating the need for many local teachers? Explain your answer.
10. Some people argue that the new electronic technologies will build a stronger sense of community among the nation's teachers. Why do they assume this will be true? Do you agree or disagree?

• Ideas for Field Experiences, Projects, and Enrichment

1. Conduct a survey in a local school to find out which of the following are being used:
   • Gopher
   • Web browsers and the World Wide Web
   • electronic mail
   • CD-ROM
   • computer software
   • electronic bulletin boards
   • interactive distance learning

   Share information you find with others in your class. Look over all of the information that has been collected. Did your group find some of these technologies being used more widely than others? Did you find some schools to be more technologically up-to-date than others? What might explain these differences?
2. Do some research on three or more of the major on-line services. Select from America Online, CompuServe, Prodigy, Delphi Internet, and GEnie. What are some specific features of each that might be of particular interest to teachers? If possible, interview some teachers who are members of one of these services. Ask them how they use the service. Share your findings with others in your class.

3. Read five or six articles in magazines such as *Electronic Learning, T.H.E. Journal*, and *Educational Technology* that focus on imaginative uses of electronic technology. Share your findings with your class and comment on possibilities for spreading these uses to other schools.
4. Invite a school administrator in charge of curriculum and instruction to visit your class. Ask this person to comment on the kinds of problems that arise when teachers are asked to work with unfamiliar technologies.
5. Join with a few other class members to form a research team. As a group, review professional journals for information about new electronic technologies and their potential effects on education. (You may wish to consult the *Education Index* for article and journal titles.) Present your findings in the form of a symposium on this topic: "A School with State-of-the-Art Technology — What Might It Be Like?"

• References

Clinton, W. J. (1995, March 31). To the Congress of the United States. Washington, DC: The White House, Office of the Press Secretary. (Press release)

Gore, A. (1995a, February 28). Remarks by Vice President Al Gore to G-7 ministers meeting on the global information initiative (Brussels, Belgium). Washington, DC: The White House, Office of the Vice President. (Press release)

Gore, A. (1995b, March 7). Vice President, Secretary Riley kick off administration's technology learning challenge program. Washington, DC: The White House, Office of the Vice President. (Press release)

Pearlstein, J. (1995). Where to find multimedia on the World Wide Web. *Multimedia World, 2*(7), 86–90.

Phillipo, J. (1989). CD-ROM: A new research and study skills tool for the classroom. *Electronic Learning, 8*(8), 40–41.

Turlington, S. R. (1995). *Walking the World Wide Web: Your personal guide to the best of the Web.* Chapel Hill, NC: Ventana Press.

Section Three

Today's Diverse Learners

CHAPTERS

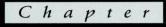

Chapter

10

Meet Today's Learners

OBJECTIVES

- Point out that attitudes and values of large numbers of American children and youth are not greatly different from those of adults, but that there is great diversity represented within the total population of young people.

- Identify some categories of learners present in elementary and secondary school classrooms.

- Describe some implications for our practice as teachers that result from our having a wide variety of young people in our classes.

- Recognize signs that may indicate a member of our class has been abused or neglected.

- Cite examples of age- and development-related characteristics of young people that we might expect to see at different grade levels.

- Point out some teacher characteristics that seem to associate with learner success at different grade levels.

What are children and young people like today? People have different responses to that question. Consider the possibilities in these two scenarios.

Scenario one

Drug abuse is rampant among young people today. Use of such drugs as alcohol, marijuana, amphetamines, LSD, and cocaine is up dramatically from levels of 15 years ago.

Disinterest in school among young people is reflected in their eagerness to accept part-time employment. Too many students in high school are working an excessive number of hours at the same time they are trying to go to school. A higher percentage of today's high school students work 20 hours a week than did students who were in high school 20 years ago.

The kinds of institutions that are important to adults are little prized by young people. For example, organized religion and public schools are not held in high esteem. On the other hand, they place great faith in what they see on television.

Young people tend to reject traditional role models. Parents and teachers are not particularly highly regarded. Heroes of young people tend to be musicians and actors and actresses. Occupational roles that young people consider to be important for a "good society" deviate markedly from those chosen by adults. Young people place little stock in the importance of school teachers and scientists as opposed to the importance they assign to rock musicians.

Scenario two

Educators and others continue to be concerned about drug use in our society. On a positive note, there is evidence that the number of children and young people who report using alcohol, marijuana, amphetamines, LSD, and cocaine at school is going down.

Many young people in high school have part-time jobs. However, the number of students who work 20 or more hours a week has gone down over the past 20 years.

Institutions viewed as important by children and young people are not greatly different from those prized by adults. For example, they hold organized religion and public schools in high esteem, and they don't regard television very highly.

Children and young people, when asked to identify role models who are important to them, identify parents and teachers as people they particularly admire. They tend to rate rock musicians low. When asked to comment on the importance of various groups to maintaining a "good society," young people rate school teachers and scientists high and rock musicians low.

Which one of these scenarios seems most credible to you? If you chose scenario one, you would have made a choice that doubtless many members of the general public would make. This view of young people is consistent with much of what we see on television and read in the newspapers. The emphasis on "problems" of young people helps focus proper attention on issues that deserve public attention, but it can also generate a distorted view of the characteristics of typical American children and young people.

In truth, the picture of children and young people provided in scenario two is more consistent with the best evidence we now have about characteristics of our society's younger members. The information regarding drug use and employment comes from data gathered by the National Center of Educational Statistics, a part of the United States Department of Education (Smith et al., 1994). This organization is charged with gathering information about a variety of educational issues using the best scientific techniques available. The information about the attitudes of young people regarding high-status individuals and groups comes from an interesting survey of the nation's 10- to 17-year-olds that was recently sponsored by Junior Achievement, Inc. (Van Scotter, 1994).

Although the attitudes of young people on many key issues do not seem to deviate markedly from perspectives of many adults, we need to keep in mind that the data represent averages of a huge group. Within the enormous population of young people in the schools, now numbering around 43 million, many different perspectives are represented. This is a particularly critical point for those of us who work in the public schools.

Our workplace is unique in that it tends to bring together a cross-section of our entire national population. Whatever attitudes and perspectives are out there among the general population are sure to be represented in our classrooms. This diversity adds spice (and sometimes great difficulty) to the lives of those of us who have chosen careers in the schools.

SOME CHARACTERISTICS OF TODAY'S LEARNERS

The diversity of learners always impresses visitors who have not been in a school for a long time. Today, we educators are challenged to recognize and respond to common characteristics of young people. At the same time, we have to adjust instruction to meet unique needs of individual learners.

Families of Learners

Television programs used to promote an image of a "typical" American family as consisting of a father who is employed, a mother who stays in the family's well-appointed suburban home, and two well-scrubbed children who romp endlessly with the family's shaggy dog. This image, in all its dimensions, never was typical and certainly does not represent today's norm. Most young people in the schools are either children of two parents living together who both work, or they are children of single parents. Of children in this latter group, many live with a single female with no male present (Smith et al., 1994).

Current family and employment patterns indicate that large numbers of children in the schools spend many hours with babysitters and at daycare centers. The kind of generation-to-generation communication that went on in traditional families happens less frequently today. As a result, we in the schools often provide social and personal information to learners that, in years gone by, was passed on by parents. Increasingly, the dividing line separating responsibilities of the home and the school is blurring.

Poverty and Children

Poverty continues to be a depressing national problem. This condition is particularly widespread among the young. Rates of poverty vary greatly from ethnic group to ethnic group. Particularly at risk are minority children living with a female with no male present in the home. In the early 1990s, 45.4 percent of all white children, 81.8 percent of all African-American children, and 43.8 percent of all Hispanic children living in these kinds of households were living in poverty (Smith et al., 1994). The percentage of Americans under age 18 living in poverty has generally increased over the past 25 years.

For many reasons, children from economically deprived homes often do not do well in school. Too many of these learners are assigned to special education classes because of cognitive and developmental deficiencies. Many of these problems result from the mothers' inability to pay for quality prenatal care (Reed & Sautter, 1990). Also, poor children often do not receive adequate diets, which may affect their performance in school.

Even though we are living in the computer age, few computers are found in economically impoverished homes. Many poor families cannot even afford newspaper and magazine subscriptions. Poor children are not nearly so likely to observe their parents reading as are children from more affluent homes. When reading is not modeled by adults at home, it is common for learners to place much less value on acquiring good reading skills. This can begin a cycle of failure, because poorly developed reading proficiencies in the early grades almost always lead to poor academic performance in later school years.

Present trends suggest that teachers will be dealing with at least as many learners from economically impoverished backgrounds in the future as they do now. Helping these learners succeed requires careful planning of instructional programs that respond to the special needs of these young people. A failure to attend to these children's special circumstances will place many of them in a situation where failure is a certainty.

Minority-Group Children

Minority-group children are becoming a larger proportion of the total school population. By the early 1990s, they accounted for over 30 percent of all young people in school. About 17 percent of the nation's school children are African-American. More than 12 percent are Hispanic. About 4 percent are of Asian or Pacific Islander descent. Remaining minorities include native Americans, Alaska natives, and others (Snyder, 1994). Nationally, Asians and Hispanics are the fastest growing minority groups in the schools. Specific racial makeup of schools varies greatly from region to region and even from school district to school district within individual states.

Minority-group students, with the exception of some learners of Asian heritage, often have not adapted well to school programs. For example, scores of African-American and Hispanic learners on standardized tests typically are below those of white children. There is evidence that differences in performance between

Today's schools encourage learners from varied backgrounds to work together.

white, African-American, and Hispanic learners are now narrowing (Smith et al., 1994). This may suggest that educators are beginning to do a better job of responding to the learning needs of these minority-group learners.

"Crack Babies" as School Learners

Crack is a crystallized, smokable derivative of cocaine. It is a drug that started to become widely available only in the mid-1980s. Since that time, its use has skyrocketed. A report issued in 1990 estimated that one million pregnant women were using the drug (Rist, 1990).

Before they are born, so-called crack babies suffer developmental damage that affects their central nervous system. This occurs because crack cocaine use results in a diminished supply of oxygen to the placenta's blood vessels. In addition to harming the central nervous system, a pregnant mother's crack cocaine use can also cause physical malformations in the developing child.

How many of these crack children are there? Figures vary widely. A conservative estimate places the annual number of crack babies born each year at between 30,000 and 50,000. This figure represents between 1 and 2 percent of all babies born in the United States each year (Rist, 1990).

Crack-cocaine children began to be old enough to start school only in the late 1980s. When these young people first entered school, there was great concern about how they would cope with complex educational environments featuring many simultaneous stimuli. What we have learned is that there is great variability among children who were prenatally exposed to crack. Severity of effects of this exposure seems to depend on how frequently their mothers used the drug, how large the doses were that their mothers ingested, the stage of fetal development at the time their mothers took the drug, and the particular genetic characteristics of each fetus (Barone, 1994).

As a result of these differences, we are coming to appreciate that no single educational response is going to be effective with all crack children. Whereas, in general, it is fair to say that many of these young people may experience difficulty in doing school work, some early results suggest that they are performing within the normal range on tests of individual intelligence (Cohen & Taharally, 1992).

Very Young Children in the Schools

Today, increasing numbers of mothers have full-time jobs outside the home, and others are either seeking such positions or are involved in education and training activities that occupy much of their time during the day. A side effect of these out-of-the-home activities has been an increasing interest in enrolling young children in educational programs. Because of the expense and uneven quality of private day-care operations, public schools have been under pressure to expand programs available to 3- and 4-year-old children.

Growth of these programs has been striking. In 1970, for example, only about 13 percent of 3-year-olds and 28.7 percent of 4-year-olds were in formal educational programs. By the early 1990s, these figures had increased dramatically. In 1992, for example, 28.7 percent of 3-year-olds and 52.1 percent of 4-year olds were enrolled in school programs (Smith et al., 1994).

Expansion of school programs for young learners has prompted much debate. On the pro side, supporters have cited some research evidence suggesting that early childhood programs can help young children to develop positive self-images and the ability to work productively and harmoniously with others. On the con side, critics have argued that expansion of early childhood programs imposes obligations on schools that properly should be discharged in the home by parents. Forces supporting expansion of school programs seem to be carrying the day, as economic pressures that encourage mothers of young children to work are heavy. The years ahead probably will witness an even greater expansion of school programs for very young learners.

Learners with Disabilities

In the past, learners with disabilities were often kept away from other children in the schools. This practice was justified by the claim that such learners needed special training that was unavailable to them in the "regular" classroom. Since the mid-1970s, however, this situation has changed. The Education for All Handicapped Children Act (Public Law 94-142) of 1975 (renamed in 1990 the Individuals with Disabilities Education Act) required schools, to the extent possible, to teach learners with disabilities in traditional classrooms.

In part, this federal legislation was the result of concerns that past practices of isolating learners with disabilities were tending to stigmatize them as being less than real learners. Now, during a typical day, teachers may work with learners with a wide variety of disabilities.

Programs for the disabled are directed at learners who comprise between 11 and 12 percent of the total school population (Smith et al., 1994). By far the largest group of learners in this category, representing 45 percent of the total, are young people classified as "learning disabled." Other major groups within this total and the percentages they represent (Smith et al., 1994) are:

- learners with speech impairments, 20%
- learners with some degree of mental retardation, 11%
- learners suffering from severe emotional disturbance, 8%

Abused and Neglected Children

Problems of abused and neglected children have attracted public interest for years. For more than a quarter of a century, every state in the country has had laws requiring that those with authority over children, including teachers, report any injury that appears to be nonaccidental (McEvoy, 1990). Because of these concerns, there has been a trend for reported incidents of child abuse to increase in number (McEvoy, 1990).

A child with disabilities learns piano at summer camp.

Suspected abuse is handled in most communities by Child Protective Services (CPS) (Haase & Kempe, 1991). This organization usually operates within a state or county agency, which might be known as the Department of Social Services, Department of Human Resources, Department of Social Welfare, Department of Public Welfare, or by some other similar name.

There are four general categories of abuse that teachers need to be aware of. It is important to be alert to the indicators of each. The following list draws from information contained in an *American Teacher* article ("How to Identify," 1989/1990):

1. *Physical abuse:*   Signs of physical abuse may include bruises, welts, burns, bite marks, and other unusual marks on the body. Another indicator is if the learner is having what seem to be too many accidental injuries at home. The following are some behavioral indicators of physical abuse:
   • Learner is hard to get along with and may frequently be in trouble
   • Learner is unusually shy, or too eager to please
   • Learner is frequently late or absent, or comes to school too early and seems reluctant to go home
   • Learner shies away from physical contact with adults
   • Learner seems frightened of parents
   • Learner may seek affection from any adult
2. *Neglect:*   Learners who have been neglected at home may come to school dirty. They may often be without their lunch money. These young people sometimes seem to be more tired than others in the class. They may need glasses and dental care. Their clothing may be unkempt, or they may wear clothes that are inappropriate given prevailing weather conditions. Some of these young people may beg food from their classmates.
3. *Emotional abuse:*   Often, emotional abuse is reflected in extreme or excessive behavior patterns. Emotionally abused young people may be too compliant and passive; on the other hand, they may be very aggressive. Other behavioral indicators of possible emotional abuse would be behavior that is either too adult-like or too immature, given the learner's age, and if the learner is behind in physical, emotional, and intellectual development.
4. *Sexual abuse:*   One indicator of this condition is that a learner's underclothing is torn, stained, or bloody. Or, the learner may experience pain or itching in the genital area. Other behavioral indicators of sexual abuse include the following:
   • learner is very withdrawn, or learner engages in fantasy-like or baby-like behavior
   • learner has poor relationships with other children
   • learner engages in delinquent acts or runs away from home
   • learner says he or she has been sexually assaulted

Many groups in our society are interested in doing something about abused and neglected children. They recognize that teachers can play an important part by recognizing potential abuse and reporting it to authorities. The two groups listed here will, upon request, send information on how to spot abuse. Write them at these addresses:

The National Center on Child Abuse and Neglect
P.O. Box 1182
Washington, DC 20013

National Committee for the Prevention of Child Abuse
332 S. Michigan Avenue, Suite 1250
Chicago, IL 60604-4357

Performance at School and Learners' Attitudes

Particular personal and situational backgrounds of some young people make it less likely they will succeed at school than their age-mates. Experts have identified a number of *risk factors* that are typical of many learners who do not perform well at school, which include (Ogle, Alsalam, & Rogers, 1991):

- living with only one parent
- having parents who failed to complete high school
- household income below $15,000 per year
- limited English proficiency
- having a brother or sister who left school before high school graduation
- spending more than three hours a day home alone

In addition to these risk factors, how learners react to our classes may be affected by the importance they attach to the content we are teaching. There tend to be widespread differences in the views of young people about the perceived importance of individual school subjects. See Table 10-1 for details.

PATTERNS OF CHILDREN'S DEVELOPMENT

Ideas about how children develop influence ideas about how they should be educated. Teachers must base their procedures on up-to-date knowledge about human development, not on outdated views. Some perspectives that were very much in vogue at one time seem bizarre to us today.

One early view had it that children were mindless creatures who were incapable of feeling or knowing anything. Interesting ideas about education flowed logically from this idea. For example, any plans to spend money on early childhood education were not well received because formal education for very young children was seen as pointless. Adults' roles were limited to meeting children's physical needs and to keeping them out of mischief.

Another historical view held children to be essentially miniature adults. Aside from their small size, children were seen as having adult characteristics, lacking only knowledge and experience. If these could be provided, it was assumed that children would be able to discharge adult roles at a very early age. Learning materials designed for use by adults were considered to be perfectly appropriate for children as well. If children failed to learn, this failure was simply attributed to their laziness. The tradition of punishing children for failing to learn comes out of this view of childhood.

Table 10-1

Percentages of children aged 10–17 who described individual school subjects as providing them with a "great deal" of preparation for life

Subject	Percentage of Males	Percentage of Females
Math (Arithmetic)	74	73
Science	58	49
English (Language Arts)	50	52
Health	48	52
History or Social Studies	48	49
Physical Education	46	42
Art or Music	22	28

Source: Data are from "National Youth Survey: Attitudes and Expectations Regarding Society, Education, and Adulthood," conducted for Junior Achievement, Inc., by The Gallup Organization, Princeton, NJ, January 1994, p. 29. Copyright 1994 by Junior Achievement. Reprinted with permission.

Still another historical perspective maintained that children came into the world totally lacking any personalities of their own. They were simply animated clay or putty awaiting appropriate "modeling" by adults. There was an assumption that young people, when appropriately guided, would turn into good citizens. In the schools, this view resulted in educational practices that were planned and delivered exclusively by adults. Children's interests were considered to be of little importance (see Box 10-1).

Most of these views from history have not stood up well to the rigors of modern scholarship. Today, we know that each child has unique qualities, and that these qualities affect how individual children react to school. Although teaching might be simpler if young people were just so many "lumps of clay," that is just not how it is. Diversity among learners is the reality.

For example, consider the physical characteristics of young people in a typical junior high school classroom. Differences among such individuals are striking. Some of them are small and immature in appearance. Others may be as large and as physically well developed as the teacher. Some of the boys may even sport mustaches (much to the envy of their smaller, less physically mature classmates). Differences in learners' rates of physical development present problems related not only to their ability to perform physical tasks, but to their psychological development as well.

Characteristics of Preschool and Kindergarten Children

Children of preschool and kindergarten age are extremely active. They have quite good control of their bodies, and they seem to enjoy activity for its own sake. Because of their frequent bursts of activity, these children need regular rest periods.

BOX
10-1

Denying the Importance of the Individual Characteristics of Learners

Children have not always been viewed as we see them today. At some times in the past, they were believed to have no individual identities at all. When young people were perceived in this manner, teachers were expected to mold young people in ways that would reproduce abilities and attitudes of adults. In her novel *The Prime of Miss Jean Brodie*, Muriel Spark (1962) described a teacher who tried to do this and the disastrous results of her approach. You might find this book interesting.

What Do You Think?

1. Did you have teachers who were insensitive to individual differences of learners? How did people in your classes feel about these teachers?
2. In what ways did these teachers' approaches to teaching differ from those of teachers who seemed more sensitive to special needs of individual learners?
3. How effective were these insensitive teachers in transmitting information to learners in their classes?

When rest periods are not provided, the children often become irritable. Emotional outbursts often result when over-tired children in this age group encounter even minor frustrations.

At this age, children's large-muscle coordination is better developed than their small-muscle coordination. As a result, tasks that require small-muscle control can be frustrating. Many children in this group have trouble tying shoestrings, fastening buttons, and managing other fine-motor tasks that older children do easily. Some children in this age group may not yet have fully developed eyes and eye muscles. They may experience difficulty in focusing on small objects and in completing tasks that require good hand-eye coordination.

Boys in this age group tend to be slightly larger in size than girls, but girls are more advanced by almost any other measure that is applied. This is particularly true in the area of fine-motor-skill development. At this age, girls tend to display much better fine-muscle coordination than boys.

Teachers of preschool and kindergarten children must be patient and able to tolerate a lot of activity in the classroom. They must understand that there are certain things children in this age group simply cannot do. They must be prepared to spend time tying shoes, mopping up paint spills, and buttoning coats, and they must do these things with a smile. Children need a lot of affection at this time of their lives.

Characteristics of Primary Grades Children (Grades 1 to 3)

The great need for physical activity that is characteristic of kindergarten children carries through the first year or two of the primary grades. The large muscles still tend to be more fully developed than the small muscles. This large-muscle development gives these children a tremendous confidence in their ability to accomplish certain physical tasks. Many youngsters in this age group develop more confidence in their physical abilities than is warranted. The accident rate among primary grades children is very high.

The early primary grades are difficult for many young people. Many of them still have a high need for activity. This need persists at a time when school programs begin to expect more "in-seat" learning, a clear break from the almost nonstop activity routine of many kindergarten classrooms. When there is too much forced sitting, youngsters in this age group may develop nervous habits such as pencil chewing, fingernail biting, and general fidgeting. These represent attempts of the body to compensate for the lack of physical activity that it needs.

Typically, handwriting is introduced during this period in a child's schooling. Learning how to perform this task can be a trying experience for late-maturing children who may still have very poor control over the small muscles. During this phase, teachers need to be very sensitive in their comments to children regarding their first efforts at cursive writing. If small-muscle development is inadequate, no amount of admonishment will lead to improved writing skills.

The eyes do not fully develop until children are about 8 years old. Hence, many children in the primary grades may experience difficulty when asked to focus on small print or small objects. This situation has important implications for educators. Serious reading instruction ordinarily begins in grade 1. Teachers of these young children need to understand that difficulties experienced by some of their charges may be due to inadequate eye development, and these children may not yet be able to maintain a focus on objects as small as printed words.

When their teachers have been sensitive to their needs, slow-developing children, as their physical development accelerates, generally have little difficulty in catching up to performance levels of learners who have matured earlier. But if insensitive teachers have falsely attributed problems of physically slow-developing learners to laziness, there is a distinct possibility that these children will come to believe they have no potential for success. When learners develop this kind of self-image, it is common for them to stop trying. A pattern of failure established early in their education can follow learners through their remaining years in school.

Primary grades children have a high need for praise and recognition. They want to please the teacher and do well in school. When they get positive recognition from teachers, they tend to blossom. A positive adjustment to school during these years often sets a pattern for success that will persist as they move through the rest of the elementary and secondary school program.

Characteristics of Upper Elementary Children (Grades 4 to 6)

In grades 4 to 6, most girls and a few boys experience a tremendous growth spurt. It is not uncommon for 11-year-old girls to be taller and heavier than 11-year-old boys. Many girls reach puberty during this period and, especially toward the end of this time, they tend to become very interested in boys. On the other hand, many boys, even at the end of this period of their lives, have little interest in girls.

Friendships tend to divide along sex lines; boys tend to associate with boys, and girls tend to associate with girls. There is a good deal of competition between boys and girls. Insults are a common feature of interactions between groups of boys and groups of girls.

Learners' fine-motor control is generally quite good by the time they reach this stage of development. Many of them develop an interest in applying their new abilities to make their fingers do what they're supposed to do by getting involved in crafts, model building, piano playing, and other activities demanding fine-muscle control.

Teachers face a different set of challenges in working with children in grades 4 through 6 than do their colleagues who teach primary grades children. Teachers of children in grades 4 and 5 must pay particular attention to motivation. Additionally, they must develop ways of dealing with children's emerging sense of independence.

Many young people in this age group tend to be perfectionists. Frequently, they set unrealistically high standards for themselves. When they fail to perform up to these standards, they may suffer extreme feelings of guilt. We need to be sensitive to these feelings and devise ways of letting these children know that they are developing in a satisfactory way.

Many teachers of grades 4 to 6 derive great pleasure observing their pupils' growing abilities to behave in sophisticated ways. Interests of many learners broaden tremendously during these years. Some of these young people become voracious readers, some develop a great deal of technical expertise about computers, while others develop a surprising depth of knowledge about a wide range of additional topics. At the same time, these children still retain an engaging air of innocence and trust. They tend to be extremely loyal to teachers they like.

Misbehavior problems faced by teachers of children in this age group tend to be more serious than those faced by primary grades teachers. At this time of life, young people increasingly begin to look to their peer group rather than to adults for guidance regarding what is appropriate behavior. This can prove very frustrating for a teacher. For example, the peer group may have decreed that reading is boring. Given this dictum, the teacher faces a difficult challenge in motivating the class during the reading period. Teachers of children in this age group must become experts in group dynamics and keen observers of individual friendships within their classrooms. Armed with such insights, they can often act to prevent the peer group from taking a negative position on important academic issues.

As is true of teachers working with primary grades children, teachers of children in grades 4 to 6 need a healthy dose of patience. These children often find some school assignments to be frustrating and difficult, and they need positive support from the teacher. Learners in this age group make many mistakes. An understanding teacher allows them the freedom to make mistakes, yet maintains a reasonable and firm set of expectations. In this kind of atmosphere, children can make tremendous personal strides during these years.

Characteristics of Students in Grades 7 to 9

Many educators consider young people in these grades to be difficult to teach. There is evidence that a certain kind of teacher is needed to be successful with this group. Part of the challenge teachers face has to do with these learners' incredible diversity. There are great differences in maturity levels among learners, and even great day-to-day differences in patterns of behavior of a single student. A given 8th-grader may at one moment be the very image of sophistication and at the next moment little different from a 4th-grader. Learners at this time of their lives swing crazily back and forth between adult and very childish behavior. This chapter's Critical Incident presents a situation in which a teacher is confronted with a student's potential risk-taking behavior.

During these years, most girls complete their growth spurt. For boys, growth may not be complete until the end of this age range or even later. Nearly all individuals of both sexes will have attained puberty by the end of this period. Young people in this age group tend to be greatly concerned about the physical and psychological changes they are experiencing. Many wonder whether they are developing properly. Some young people become extremely self-conscious during this time of their lives, sometimes feeling as though their every action is being observed and evaluated. For many young people, their middle school/junior high school years are not a particularly comfortable time.

Rates of physical development vary widely among individuals in grades 7 through 9. Eighth graders are a particularly diverse lot—note the differences in height of the students in this picture.

Should Ms. Stearns Take Advantage of Her Special Knowledge?

Laura Stearns is in her mid-50s. She has been an enthusiastic 8th-grade mathematics teacher at Drake Middle School (formerly Drake Junior High School) for 30 years. She is a high-spirited professional who looks forward to going to work each day. She tells her friends that she "gets pumped up" by her contact with the 13-year-olds who come bouncing and shoving into her classroom each period of the day.

Laura has always taken a sincere personal interest in her students. She feels that her own experience in raising her two children (now both adults, college graduates, and working in other cities) helps her to empathize with what young people go through during the difficult middle school and junior high school years. She is not at all pleased by one problem that has become increasingly serious at her school. With each passing year, more and more of the girls are getting pregnant. Last year, it happened to nearly 15 percent of the 8th-graders.

In her role as sponsor of the pep club, Laura overhears lots of casual student conversations. Students also tend to confide in her. She sometimes has commented to her friends, "Parents of my kids would blush if they knew what their kids tell me about what goes on at home." Recently, Laura has learned that Beth McFarland, one of her outstanding math students, has been getting a lot of attention from a boy who is a junior in high school. Beth talks about the boy constantly and gives other evidence of having developed a very strong emotional attachment to him. Laura suspects that an intimate physical relationship is about to develop. She hopes that it has not yet happened.

Beth comes from a family with strong middle-class values. Both parents are deeply committed to their church. They have friends who are very much like themselves. In Laura's view, neither parent has any idea about what social pressures students encounter in present-day junior high schools. Their view of the world is very much the one that used to be depicted on the old "Brady Bunch" television program.

Laura is quite certain that any talks Beth has had with her parents about sex have been very circumspect. She is positive that Beth's mother would be incredulous at the suggestion that her daughter might be about to engage in an intimate physical relationship with a high school boy.

As a professional educator, Laura Stearns is outraged at the waste of human capital that results when young girls get pregnant and, sometimes, end up quitting school. As a parent, she senses the pain that might come to Beth's parents should she become pregnant. And, as a realist, Laura recognizes that, despite these negative consequences, pregnancy (or even AIDS) looms as a real possibility for Beth unless something is done *now*.

What is Laura's view of the problem? What past experiences might have shaped her attitudes? In what ways might her view of Beth's likely future behavior differ from the view of Beth's parents? What might account for any differences in the way Laura and Beth's parents might see the present situation playing itself out? What should Laura do? Should she talk to Beth's parents? If she does, will they believe her? Will they think her comments an unconscionable intrusion on the family's private business? Should she take it upon herself to provide birth control information to Beth? Should she counsel Beth about the need to avoid a physical relationship? Should she involve the school counseling staff? Should other teachers or administrators be brought into the picture? What kinds of actions can be taken that will resolve the problem and still maintain confidentiality?

Teachers who experience success with these students understand and are sensitive to the psychological changes that these young people are experiencing. They are tolerant of the acting-out behavior and the occasionally loud, emotional outbursts displayed by students in this age group. Teachers of these grades need to be flexible individuals who can deal with wildly varying emotional, intellectual, and behavioral patterns in their classrooms.

Characteristics of Students in Grades 10 to 12

Much has been written about learners in this age group. Parents frequently report great difficulty in communicating with their high school–aged children. Students in this age group often are frustrated as they attempt to come to terms with their world. Several factors contribute to their difficulties.

One important issue for young people at this time of their lives is their search for personal identity (Erikson, 1982). They are trying to find personal selves that are distinct from those of their parents. They ask themselves questions such as, Who am I? Will I be successful? and Will I be accepted? In their attempts to establish their personal identities, young people in this age group often experiment with behaviors that they believe will show the world that they are independent. They seek to become rulers of their environment. At the same time, they desperately look for evidence that others are accepting them as individuals.

A leading learning theorist, David Elkind (1981), has suggested that young people may experience problems as they begin to move into the formal operations (abstract reasoning) stage of their lives. With their newfound ability to think in abstract terms, a number of adolescents concern themselves with abstract notions of self and personal identity. It may be that some adolescents who have developed the ability to view their own identity as an abstract idea are unable to distinguish between what they think about themselves and what others think about them. Elkind (1981) has suggested that this view sometimes takes the form of either an "imaginary audience" or a "personal fable."

Adolescent behavior in response to an imaginary audience results when the adolescents fail to distinguish between their own thoughts about themselves and those held by others. When this happens, they tend to view themselves as perpetually "on stage." They are certain that everybody is carefully scrutinizing their every move. The imaginary audience concept explains much about the behavior of young people in this age group. Shyness, for example, is a logical result of their feeling that any mistake made in public will be noticed and criticized. The slavish attention to fashion trends results from an expectation that deviations from the expected norm will be noticed and commented on negatively.

In explaining the personal fable, Elkind (1981) has noted that adolescents often become disoriented by the many physical and emotional changes they experience. At the same time, many of them find these changes to be utterly fascinating. Some of them believe that their new feelings are so unusual that no one else has ever experienced them (particularly not parents or teachers). They may believe that they are living out a one-of-a-kind personal fable. Sometimes they keep diaries that are written out of a conviction that future generations will be intensely interested in their "unique" feelings and experiences.

As students in this age group have more life experiences, the validity of the imaginary audience and the personal fable is tested against reality. In time, the imaginary audience gives way to the real audience, and the personal fable is adjusted as young people's interactions with others reveal that many of them have experienced similar feelings and have had similar opinions.

High school teachers work with students who are capable of quite abstract thinking, yet these students have characteristics that separate them from college and university students and from older adult learners. They have emotional needs that require teachers' attention. Successful high school teachers strike a balance between their concerns for their students' psychological development and their commitment to provide these students with a respectable grounding in the academic subjects of the curriculum.

• Key Ideas in Summary

- Learners in today's schools make up a very diverse group. Young people in the schools represent a huge cross-section of people. This means that abilities, attitudes, and perspectives characterizing our entire national population are represented in school classrooms.

- Families of typical learners by no means match the traditional family stereotype of an employed father, a mother who stays at home, and two children. Many families are now headed by a single parent, usually a female. Because so many parents and guardians work, many more children today spend much of their out-of-school time in daycare centers or with babysitters.

- Large numbers of children in the school come from families with annual incomes below the federal poverty level. This situation has worsened over the past 25 years. More African-American and Hispanic children come from poor families than do white children. Children from economically impoverished homes often do not perform well in school.

- With each passing year, minority-group children comprise a larger percentage of the total school population. African-Americans currently represent the largest minority group in the schools, but this situation is changing rapidly. Each year, the percentages of minority learners who are Hispanic or Asian increase. The makeup of the minority population of schools varies greatly from state to state and from school district to school district within individual states.

- Children of mothers who used crack cocaine during pregnancy are beginning to enter the schools in large numbers. Crack babies suffer developmental damage that affects the central nervous system. We have learned that there is great variability among children who were prenatally exposed to crack. The degree to which they experience educational problems is associated with such issues as (1) the frequency of crack use by their mothers, (2) the size of crack dosages used by their mothers, (3) their stage of fetal development when crack was used, and (4) individual genetic characteristics of the fetus.

- Over the past quarter century, there has been a great increase in the number of 3- and 4-year-olds enrolled in school programs. In part, this trend has been spurred by the tendency for more mothers to hold down full-time jobs outside the home. Additionally, there have been concerns about the quality and the expense of programs offered by private daycare facilities. Today, about 29 percent of 3-year-olds and 52 percent of 4-year-olds are enrolled in formal school programs.

- Between 11 and 12 percent of learners in the schools are eligible for programs directed toward the disabled. These learners have widely varied characteristics. The largest number of young people receiving these services are classified as learning disabled. Other large groups within this population are the speech-impaired and mentally retarded learners.

- Every state has laws requiring teachers to file reports with the appropriate authorities when they observe injuries to children that appear to be nonaccidental. Episodes of child abuse appear to be on the increase. Among categories of abuse are (1) physical abuse, (2) neglect, (3) emotional abuse, and (4) sexual abuse. Teachers are expected to know and recognize behavioral indicators of possible abuse.

- Children's general characteristics vary enormously as they progress through the school program. For example, preschool and kindergarten children tend to require high levels of physical activity. Learners in grades 1 to 3 still have underdeveloped fine-motor control, and they are often frustrated by tasks requiring them to manipulate small objects and do detailed work with their hands. In grades 4 to 6, girls are often physically larger than boys. For the most part, friendships among learners in these grade levels do not cross sex lines. There are tremendous differences in the physical development of individual learners in grades 7 to 9. These differences sometimes occasion great personal anxieties on the part of these young people. During grades 10 to 12, many students are engaged in a search for personal identity. By this time in their development, many young people are able to deal with quite abstract levels of thinking.

• Review and Discussion Questions

1. What are some popular ideas about what young people consider to be important, and how do these square with studies that have been made of their attitudes? How do you account for any discrepancies between what the general public may think young people are like and what careful studies have revealed about the actual characteristics of young people?

2. Because more and more parents work, many young people today spend a considerable amount of each day in daycare centers. One result of this trend is a reduction in time parents have to teach their children basic information about appropriate patterns of behavior. Should teachers pick up the slack and spend more time in school teaching this kind of content to children? Why or why not?

3. For the past quarter century, there has been an increase in the percentage of Americans under the age of 18 who live in poverty. What are your speculations regarding why this trend has developed? Based on your own understanding of present social trends, do you expect the poverty rate among children and young people to increase or decrease over the next decade? Why do you think so?

4. Schools are under increasing pressure to introduce young people to computers and other up-to-date technologies. Some critics allege that the "computer age" will confer unfair

advantages on children from affluent homes where parents are able to buy computers for home use. Is this a potential problem? Do you think schools should be expected to provide funds for computers that students can use at home? Why or why not?

5. Why might it be a mistake for educational specialists to develop a single instructional approach for teachers to use when working with young people whose mothers used crack cocaine during pregnancy?

6. What are some categories of child abuse, and what are some indicators we can look for that might suggest a child is being abused?

7. What kinds of behavior sometimes result when preschool and kindergarten children are not provided with enough physical activity?

8. Some people argue that because of the changing nature of our society, teachers increasingly are expected to take on much of the nurturing function that formerly was provided by children's parents. To what extent do you believe this is true? Are teachers prepared to do this? If not, what kinds of additional professional training should they receive?

9. Young people who are old enough to attend middle schools or junior high schools sometimes are considered to be difficult to work with. Is this reputation deserved? Are there special skills that you think teachers assigned to work with young people in this age group should have? If so, what are they?

10. Many students, particularly during the first several years of high school, sense that their every move is being watched and commented upon critically. What things might you, as a teacher, do to help individual students appreciate that they really are not under the microscope and that people, in general, are much more tolerant of their attitudes, opinions, and behaviors than the students might suppose?

• Ideas for Field Experiences, Projects, and Enrichment

1. Interview two or more teachers at a grade level you would like to teach (and in your subject area if you are interested in secondary school teaching). Ask them to comment about the family life of learners in their classroom. In particular, seek information about economic status, family values, and the extent to which there is support in the home for what learners are expected to do at school. Share your findings with others in your class as part of a general discussion on the nature of learners in the schools.

2. Review some suggested lessons in a course textbook or a professional journal that are directed toward learners in a grade you would like to teach. Interview a teacher who teaches the learners for whom the lessons are intended. Are the lessons appropriate for the intellectual and maturity levels of these learners? Do they respond well to the interests of these young people? If the teacher would change anything in the lessons to make them more effective, what would he or she make different? Prepare a short report of your interview to share with your instructor.

3. Visit a classroom that includes learners from a cross section of cultural and ethnic groups. Take note of any variations in ways members of different cultural and ethnic groups participate. You might wish to ask the teacher about his or her own observations regarding this issue. Share your findings with others in your class.

4. Crack children have begun to enroll in schools in large numbers within the last decade. Research is still accumulating on the nature of problems some of these young people have and on what kinds of responses should be provided to meet their needs. Read some articles in professional journals that focus on these learners and prepare a short oral report for presentation to your class in which you describe some approaches being tried

in various places to help such students better adjust to the demands of school. Be sure to explain that there are great variations among crack learners and, consequently, that different approaches might be effective with different individuals.

5. Invite a panel of three to five middle school and junior high school teachers to visit your class. Ask them to comment on some special challenges of working with learners in this age group and to suggest aspects of working with these learners that they find to be particularly satisfying.

• References

Barone, D. (1994). Myths about "crack babies." *Educational Leadership, 52*(2), 67–68.

Cohen, S., & Taharally, C. (1992). Getting ready for young children with prenatal drug exposure. *Childhood Education, 69,* 1, 5–9.

Elkind, D. (1981). *Children and adolescents: Interpretive essays on Jean Piaget* (3rd ed.). New York: Oxford University Press.

Erikson, E. H. (1982). *The life cycle completed: A review.* New York: Norton.

Haase, C. C., & Kempe, R. S. (1990). The school and protective services. *Education and Urban Society, 22*(5), 258–269.

How to identify signs of abuse. (1989, December/1990, January). *American Teacher,* p. 12.

McEvoy, A. W. (1990). Child abuse law and school policy. *Education and Urban Society,* pp. 247–257.

Ogle, L. T., Alsalam, N., & Rogers, G. T. (Eds.). (1991). *The condition of education, 1991.* Washington, DC: National Center for Education Statistics.

Reed, S., & Sautter, R. C. (1990). Children of poverty: The status of 12 million young Americans. *Phi Delta Kappan, 71*(6), K1–K12.

Rist, M. C. (1990, July). The shadow children: Preparing for the arrival of crack babies in school. *Research Bulletin.* Bloomington, IN: Phi Delta Kappa Center on Evaluation, Development, and Research.

Smith, T. M, Rogers, G. T., Alsalam, N., Perie, M., Mahoney, R. P., & Martin, V. (Eds.). (1994). *The condition of education, 1994.* Washington, DC: National Center for Education Statistics.

Snyder, T. D. (Project Ed.). (1994). *Digest of education statistics, 1994.* Washington, DC: National Center for Education Statistics.

Van Scotter, R. (1994). What young people think about school and society. *Educational Leadership, 52*(3), 72–78.

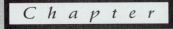

11

Multi-culturalism

OBJECTIVES

- Identify a rationale for paying particular attention to school experiences of minority-group and female learners.

- Recognize the changing demographics of learners and implications for educational practices.

- Point out some patterns of within-school segregation that persist despite attempts to eliminate patterns of within-district segregation.

- Describe how some school programs have used race, ethnicity, or gender as criteria for determining the kinds of educational experiences to be provided for certain categories of learners.

- Recognize the growing discontinuity between demographic characteristics of teachers and demographic characteristics of learners.

- Identify sources of information for materials and programs designed to sensitize teachers to multicultural and gender equity perspectives.

Newcomers to our profession are almost certain to encounter many learners who have ethnic and cultural roots that differ from their own and with which they may have little familiarity. (See Table 11-1.) Our schools have an obligation to serve all who attend, and we must be sensitive to learners' varied backgrounds. The more we are able to accommodate the special perspectives of young people in our classes, the more successful they will be. Successful learners feel good about themselves and their experiences in schools. These positive attitudes, in turn, positively reinforce what we do. They can reduce discipline problems and help us grow in confidence as we see members of our class profiting from our instruction.

The laudable objective of maximizing each learner's potential has implications not only for how members of diverse ethnic and cultural groups are treated, but also for the issue of gender. Today's adult females are as likely to be employed as are adult males. For this reason, "we . . . are no longer willing to accept the hypocritical inequities that this society has traditionally laid on our African-Americans and Native Americans, on our Hispanic and immigrant populations, and on all our poor and minority people, and our women" (Clinchy, 1993, p. 507). Women occupy important positions in government, the arts, medicine, law, and many other areas.

Female learners have not always had the same educational opportunities that have been available to males. Today's school programs recognize that human capital is a precious resource. Talents of females and members of ethnic and cultural minorities deserve to be fully developed. Society stands to benefit from their contributions when females leave school as confident, competent young adults, fully prepared to assume positions of responsibility and leadership.

Today, educators strive to ensure that opportunities in all subject areas are available to male and female learners alike. As this photo shows, some subjects, such as woodworking, were in the past considered to be "male"; others, such as sewing and baking, were considered to be "female."

Table 11-1
Percentages of learners in the public schools from different racial and ethnic groups

Group	Percentage of the Total School Population
White, Non-Hispanic	67.8
African-American, Non-Hispanic	16.2
Hispanic	11.5
Asian/Pacific Islander	3.4
Native American/Alaskan Native	1.0

Source: Data are from *The Condition of Education 1994*, edited by T. M. Smith, T. T. Rogers, N. Alsalam, M. Perle, R. P. Mahoney, and V. Martin, 1994. Washington, DC: U.S. Department of Education, Office of Educational Research and Improvement, National Center for Education Statistics.

A BRIEF HISTORY OF ATTITUDES TOWARD MINORITY-GROUP LEARNERS

Educators have long been aware that large numbers of learners from minority groups have not done well in school. An early explanation for this phenomenon was the "genetic deficit" view (Savage & Armstrong, 1996). People who subscribed to this position believed that minority-group learners lacked the necessary intellectual tools to succeed in school. Individuals who accepted this premise were reluctant to divert school resources to improve instructional programs for children who were perceived as incapable of profiting from them.

By the 1960s, the genetic deficit position had given way to a "cultural deficit" view (Erickson, 1987). Those who subscribed to this argument contended that poor school performance could be blamed on the failure of minority-group children's parents to provide an intellectually stimulating home atmosphere that prepared the learners for the expectations of the school. The cultural deficit view seemed to allow schools a way out when confronted with statistics revealing high dropout rates and other evidence of mediocre levels of school performance on the part of minority-group learners. This position permitted blame for these dismal statistics to be placed on learners' homes rather than on the school.

A more recent explanation for the schools' failure to adequately serve needs of minority-group learners has been the "communication process" position (Erickson, 1987). According to this view, language patterns of minority-group learners are substantially different from those of their teachers and majority-group learners; hence, they are not capable of understanding much of what goes on in the classroom. The communication failure accounts for their poor academic performance. This position has been attacked because it fails to explain why some minority-group learners do extremely well in school.

In recent years, professional educators have been downplaying explanations for difficulties of minority-group learners that seem to shift the blame away from the schools. Increasingly, it is argued that school programs have failed to plan seriously for the success of *all* learners (even though educators' rhetoric has espoused this intent for years). Because of this failure, many minority-group learners and their parents may not believe the schools' claims that they are truly interested in promoting the development of each child. To establish credibility, we need to avoid instructional practices that can undermine the self-confidence of our learners and to prepare lessons that help our young people appreciate the benefits of living in a culture where diversity is seen as a national asset (Savage & Armstrong, 1996).

Today, educators are unwilling to make excuses for poor academic performance. This position is promoted by an "all students can learn" premise that undergirds many education reform programs (Henson, 1995). If the curriculum is centered in truth, it will be pluralistic because human culture is the product of the struggles of all humanity, not the possession of a single racial or ethnic group (Hilliard, 1991/1992).

Even though our diverse society includes people who have many different views on the issue of multicultural education, in general, we remain strongly committed to the idea of multiculturalism. This point was made clearly in a respected recent national poll that revealed that three-fourths of the public think the schools should promote both a common cultural tradition and the diverse cultural traditions of the nation's different population groups (Elam, Rose, & Gallup, 1994).

DESEGREGATION AND ITS INFLUENCES ON LEARNERS

For many years, it was difficult to promote the development of intercultural and interracial sensitivities in the schools because many schools were racially segregated. Then and now, concerns about desegregating schools and promoting more communication between learners from different racial and cultural backgrounds fall into three distinct categories (Simon-McWilliams, 1989):

- concerns about ending legal segregation and following court-ordered plans to achieve integration
- concerns about *within-school* segregation of minority-group learners and females
- concerns about achievement levels of minority-group learners and females

Efforts to End Legal Segregation

The 1954 Supreme Court case *Brown v. Board of Education* established a legal guideline that led to the dismantling of segregated school systems. However, the effort to achieve a school system featuring a cross section of students from a wide variety of ethnic and racial backgrounds has been only moderately successful. A key 1974 Supreme Court decision in the case of *Milliken v. Bradley* held that courts lacked authority to order busing between districts for the purpose of achieving racial balance in the schools. This has meant that busing has been authorized as an option only within the boundaries of individual school districts.

In districts with homogeneous populations, the *Milliken v. Bradley* restriction has made it difficult for school authorities to organize schools that reflect a broad ethnic and racial diversity. For example, the nation's inner cities are becoming increasingly African-American and Hispanic, while the suburbs remain predomi-

Who Cares about an African-American German Teacher?

LaShandra Pierson, who is African-American, teaches German at Milligan High School. Milligan is located in a suburban school district on the edge of one of the nation's major cities. The school has seen a great change in the makeup of its student body in recent years. Today, about 60 percent of the students are white, 25 percent are African-American, 20 percent are Hispanic, and 5 percent are Asian and native American.

This is Ms. Pierson's third year at the school. Her interest in German traces to her family background. Her father, a career army officer, was stationed for many years in Germany. She began speaking the language almost as soon as she began speaking English. As she grew up, she learned to love the language, the literature, the music, and other aspects of the culture of Germany. When asked, she also willingly admits that her warm feelings for Germany stem from her recollections of being able to travel about Germany in her teen years without encountering much evidence of racial prejudice.

The impact of her experiences in Germany influenced her choice of German as a major when she entered an East Coast university. Her commitment to sharing her enthusiasm for the German language and people led her to pursue a program leading to teacher certification. Her undergraduate years went well, as did her student-teaching experience. After graduation, she was offered jobs at several schools and chose Milligan.

At Milligan, her life has not been at all what she expected. First of all, she finds that almost all her students are white. She has no problem with teaching white students, but, as an African-American, she had thought she would have more influence on African-American students. She had hoped they would enroll in her classes, and even if they did not get caught up in her enthusiasm for German, they might at least be influenced to complete high school and go on to college.

nantly white. As a result, a large number of inner-city schools are overwhelmingly African-American, Hispanic, or a combination of both. Similarly, many suburban schools are overwhelmingly white. Despite efforts to achieve integrated schools, "there is evidence that the number of U.S. students attending racially isolated schools is now on the rise" (Bates, 1990, p. 9).

Today, many learners attend schools with others who are much like themselves. This pattern suggests that they have few opportunities to interact with young people from other cultural and ethnic backgrounds. This means that many young people go to schools with student populations that are not representative of the cultural and ethnic makeup of our pluralistic society (Vergon, 1989). Educators continue to be concerned about this situation.

Within-School Segregation

Even in school districts that have managed to create student bodies that embrace a mixture of learners from different cultural and ethic groups, segregation continues

Ms. Pierson has complained to some of her friends that many of the African-American students in the school have been rude and even hostile to her. One angry young man accosted her at a football game and demanded to know why she was "wasting her time" teaching a "white" subject like German.

At the same time, some of the white faculty members have assumed that as an African-American, Ms. Pierson is one of the "resident experts" on all matters related to cultural and ethnic minorities. She has been quizzed about her views on Jesse Jackson, Malcolm X, Martin Luther King, Jr., and a host of other present and past African-American luminaries. As well, she has been assigned to countless district-level committees charged with developing programs to serve the needs of African-American and other minority-group learners.

LaShandra Pierson is disillusioned. She feels that no one cares about her hard-won expertise in German. She senses that the very African-American students she wants to help resent her accomplishments. She suspects many of the administrators and faculty think she is just an "intelligent African-American face" to whom they can delegate troublesome duties associated with minority programming. In short, LaShandra Pierson has found the reality of education to be different from her expectations. She is thinking about changing to a different career.

What were LaShandra Pierson's priorities when she began teaching? What did she imagine the world of the school would be like? What might have contributed to this perspective? What are her priorities as a teacher?

In what ways do some of the world views of LaShandra's students vary from her own? Why might these students have adopted these perspectives? In expressing her concerns to friends, is LaShandra accurately describing the feelings of all of her students? Are there ways that differences in priorities of LaShandra and her students can be bridged? If so, how?

How does LaShandra perceive her appointment to committees and other groups charged with dealing with issues related to minority students? What might have been motivations of administrators who asked her to assume these responsibilities?

Is leaving the profession LaShandra's only real option?

to be a concern. The issue in such places relates not to a legal, physical separation of learners along ethnic or racial lines, but instead a kind of segregation that may result from how learners from different groups are assigned to courses.

Within-school segregation of students along cultural, racial, and even gender lines is particularly serious at the secondary school level. College preparatory courses in many high schools enroll disproportionately high percentages of white students. Remedial courses, on the other hand, frequently have much higher percentages of minority-group students enrolled than these students' numbers within the total school population would warrant.

Male students comprise high percentages of some high school classes. For example, 80 percent of students enrolled in high school physical science classes are male (Simon-McWilliams, 1989). Males are also overrepresented in many special education classes; they are 1.7 times as likely as females to be classified as mentally retarded, trainable mentally retarded, or seriously emotionally disturbed. Minority-group students are 1.6 times as likely as white students to be placed in special education classes (Simon-McWilliams, 1989).

*Perspectives of individuals from different ethnic and cultural backgrounds enrich understand-
ings of all learners.*

There is a relationship between a student's race or ethnic group and his or her
likelihood of being suspended from school. Minority-group students are suspended
from school at nearly twice the rate of their white counterparts. African-American
students are particularly likely to be suspended; their rate of suspension is three
times that of white students (Bates, 1990).

Professionals who are concerned about the issue of within-school segregation
are not satisfied with a simple count of the number of learners from various ethnic
and racial groups who are enrolled in a given school. They want evidence that there
are efforts to serve *all* learners in ways that will maximize their individual development. Further, they argue that learners will not develop multicultural sensitivity
and an acceptance for diversity if individual classes within the school resegregate
the learner population.

Concerns about Achievement Levels

This issue ties closely to concerns about within-school segregation. If academic
standards in classes to which certain groups of learners have been assigned are

BOX 11-1

Is Within-School Segregation a "Natural" Condition?

This is how a teacher described one school's efforts to achieve integration:

I used to think we could really integrate this place, but I'm beginning to have my doubts. I mean, we've done a good job keeping a good racial balance in all of our classes, including the advanced sections. We probably do a better job than most other places when it comes to making sure that we don't assign higher percentages of blacks and Hispanics than whites to our special education programs. In fact, we seem to have done everything we possibly could to make sure that everybody has access to the best academic programs we offer. Yet, we still aren't really integrated.

Take a look in the lunch room. Black kids sit with black kids, Hispanic kids sit with Hispanic kids, white kids sit with white kids. There's even a small bunch of Asian kids who always sit in the far corner. I see the same pattern at football and basketball games. How much integration *really* goes on at this place? These kids are in the same school, but are they really interacting with people from other racial groups?

What Do You Think?

1. If this situation is truly as this teacher describes it, what might have brought it about? The teacher sees this as a "bad" situation. Is it? How might others react to it?
2. Are there limits on how far schools should go to promote contacts between learners from different racial and ethnic groups? If so, what are they?
3. Is there something specific that should be done here, or would the best course be to accept the situation that has been described? Explain your response.

not high, it should be no surprise when these learners fare poorly on achievement tests. Many high school students who aspire to continue their education in a college or university take the Scholastic Achievement Test (SAT). African-American and Hispanic students' scores on these tests have continually lagged behind white students' scores, and females have generally received lower scores than males on the quantitative portion of the SAT. These patterns suggest that the benefits of schooling are not equally accorded to students regardless of their race, ethnicity, or gender.

Generally, more benefits accrue to a learner the longer he or she stays in school. Ideally, there should be no difference in the dropout rates associated with race or ethnicity. This, however, is not the case. For example, in one recent year, percentages of eighth graders who were no longer in school four years after the end of the eighth grade year were 9.4 percent for white learners, 14.5 percent for African-American learners, and 18.3 percent for Hispanic learners (Smith et al., 1994).

As these figures suggest, dropout rates are especially high for Hispanic learners. Since Hispanics are the nation's most rapidly growing minority group, these figures greatly concern educators. Unless we do a better job of preparing Hispanic learners, an ever larger percentage of our population is going to be ill-prepared to contribute to a society that increasingly requires an educated work force.

We mentioned earlier the failure of females to score as high as males on the quantitative sections of the SAT. Although more women than men complete baccalaureate degree programs, relatively few elect to pursue advanced work in mathematics and the sciences. The dearth of females in this group is often explained by the inadequate mathematics background that has been the legacy of their experiences in the public schools.

Some authorities have hinted that public education has not made a serious effort to develop female learners' abilities in mathematics because of a faulty assumption about their aptitude for the content (Chipman & Thomas, 1987). Some research has demonstrated very minor gender-related differences in males and females in terms of their abilities to deal with spatial abstractions. Chipman and Thomas (1987) argue that there has never been any established connection between the kinds of spatial abilities for which there are slight gender differences and the ability to master mathematics; however, a mythology has developed that females are not good at mathematics. Hence, at least in some schools, female students have not been held to the same achievement expectations in mathematics as have been males.

Unless this pattern is broken, females may be disadvantaged in their efforts to break into technical fields. Today, fewer females than males enroll in university programs in mathematics and the sciences (Oakes, 1990). A continuation of this pattern will result in a great underdevelopment of their talents, and it will bar many females from well-paid technical employment. Even though more and more women are entering the work force after they complete their education, there is evidence that they are underrepresented in some technical fields where salaries are high and the demand for trained workers is great (Chipman & Thomas, 1987).

THE NEED FOR ACCURATE INFORMATION

To plan effective school programs, we need accurate information about minority-group learners and the capabilities of male and female learners. Superficial understanding of these issues can lead to school practices that fail because they rest upon faulty assumptions. For example, as noted previously, research has found no basis for the widespread belief that females, as a group, are not good at mathematics. The companion piece of street wisdom about males is that they are not as good at reading and writing as are females. Research has also failed to support this myth.

Assumptions about learners from cultural and ethnic minorities also sometimes prompt irresponsible actions on the part of school officials. For example, some educators fail to recognize the important differences that exist *within* individual groups. For example, values and perspectives of African-Americans in rural areas may have little in common with those of African-Americans in the nation's inner cities. (Additionally, there is by no means a common world view that characterizes all urban African-Americans or a common world view that characterizes all rural African-Americans.)

The nation's Hispanic population is extremely diverse. Some critics charge that there has been a tendency for school authorities to view all Hispanics as linguistically at risk and to treat them as "culturally deficient and linguistically deprived foreigners. This treatment helps to explain their high dropout rate, their underrepresentation in advanced courses, and their low rate of college attendance" (Grant,

1990, p. 27). Grant also points out that only about a quarter of Hispanic students have a native language other than English. Clearly, school programs that presume them to be linguistically deprived foreigners do them an injustice.

Developing school programs that reflect a genuine appreciation for issues associated with multicultural and gender equity requires us to be well-informed. The need for us to develop sensitivity to the special perspectives of groups from which our learners come is growing more important as the nation's school population grows more diverse.

GOALS AND GENERAL SUGGESTIONS FOR TEACHERS

Many individuals and professional groups have been interested in improving school programs in ways that will better serve the needs of ethnic and cultural minorities and females. There is a growing recognition that the nation can ill afford to do anything less than fully develop the talents of all of its young people. The high rate at which minority-group students are dropping out of school is of particular concern. The Quality Education for Minorities Project, in its report *Education That Works: An Action Plan for the Education of Minorities* (Marshall, 1990), pointed out that between 1985 and 2000 there will be a 30 percent increase in the number of jobs open to college graduates and a 35 percent increase in the number of jobs open to nongraduates, but only a 10 percent increase in the number of jobs open to high school graduates. Clearly, young people with less than a high school education are going to find it difficult to secure employment.

At the beginning of this decade, the Quality Education for Minorities Project issued a number of goals (Marshall, 1990). These goals, targeted for accomplishment by the year 2000, are as follows:

- Ensure that minority students start school prepared to learn.
- Ensure that the academic achievement of minority youth is at a level that will enable them, upon graduation from high school, to enter the work force or college fully prepared to be successful and not in need of remediation.
- Significantly increase the participation of minority students in higher education with a special emphasis on the study of mathematics, science, and engineering.
- Strengthen and increase the numbers of teachers of minority students. (This goal refers to the need to provide for better training of all teachers who work with minorities, to ensure that exceptionally able teachers are assigned to work with minority-group learners, and to recruit more teachers who, themselves, are minorities.)
- Strengthen the school-to-work transition so that minority students who do not choose college leave high school prepared with the skills necessary to participate productively in the world of work and with the foundation required to upgrade their skills and advance their careers.
- Provide quality out-of-school experiences and opportunities to supplement the schooling of minority youth and adults.

Numerous recommendations have been made regarding what educators should do to respond to multicultural and equity needs (Banks with Clegg, Jr., 1988; Bates, 1990; Marshall, 1990; Savage & Armstrong, 1996). Several of these suggestions are discussed under the topics that follow.

Commitment to the Idea That All Can Learn

Unless we sincerely believe that young people from ethnic and cultural groups can learn, there is little likelihood their learning performance will improve. Our assumptions about our learners influence our expectations regarding what they can do. If we don't expect much, we are not likely to be surprised when few in our classrooms achieve high levels of academic excellence. Learners of whom little is expected do not learn a great deal. Such a regimen fails to encourage them to stay in school. It certainly will not produce the self-confident, academically able individuals needed to compete in a workplace that demands increasingly sophisticated skills from even entry-level employees.

Modifying Grouping Practices

Grouping practices in many schools have acted to the disadvantage of ethnic and cultural minority students (Bates, 1990; Marshall, 1990). Learners who are shunted into a low-ability group early in their school years tend to fall farther behind their peers with each passing year.

Grouping decisions occur at several levels. Sometimes, ability grouping results in the creation of entire classes of learners who are thought to be in a given category. For example, a high school may have a freshman English class specifically designated for low-ability students. This kind of grouping can undermine learners' confidence in their own abilities. The content is likely to be much less rigorous than that introduced in so-called regular classes, thus impairing students' preparation for more advanced work.

Grouping within classes may also have negative consequences where such grouping is based on the teacher's view that learners' ability level is low and is established in such a way that so-called low-ability groups include disproportionate numbers of learners from cultural and ethnic minorities. In general, within-class groups function more positively when they are not organized with a view to standardizing ability levels of members within each group and when learners in each group constitute a representative racial, cultural, and gender sample of the entire class.

Accommodating Learning Style Differences

Learners vary in terms of the particular instructional styles to which they will respond positively. Research has documented that learners' cultural backgrounds influence their preference for a given instructional style (Grant & Sleeter, 1994). This conclusion suggests a need for us to plan lessons that allow individual learners to approach content in different ways. Some young people profit from opportunities to touch and manipulate objects. Others do just fine when they are asked to read new information. Still others respond well to opportunities to work with photographs, charts, or other graphic representations of data. The tendency for individual learners to change their preferred learning styles as they mature complicates matters for us as teachers (Sternberg, 1994). This implies a need for us to be "prepared to understand and meet the needs of students who come to school with varying learning styles, and with differing beliefs about themselves and what school means to them" (Darling-Hammond, 1993, p. 775).

Becoming Aware of Our Own Perspectives

Because majority-group perspectives are so pervasive, those of us who are white fail to recognize the extent to which our own world views have been conditioned by our membership in the majority. The reality is that all ethnic and cultural groups, including the white majority, have certain established assumptions about "how the world is" and about what constitutes "proper" behavior.

If we have not taken time to think about our own assumptions about reality, we may make the mistake of assuming that everybody shares our basic views. This kind of thinking can create problems for us when we work with learners from ethnic and cultural minorities whose fundamental perspectives may be quite different from ours. For example, if we have not bothered to learn anything about the traditional culture of Thailand, we may be surprised at the negative reaction of a Thai child to a light touch on the head. Our intent may be to convey concern and friendship, but to a child raised in a Thai home, the gesture may be interpreted as an offensive invasion of privacy.

Less Reliance on Standardized Tests

In recent years, the producers of standardized tests have enjoyed boom times. Legislators throughout the nation have clamored for information about the quality of public school programs, and standardized test results have proved irresistibly attractive. They summarize tremendous amounts of information in numerical form, and they allow for easy comparisons among schools. The public also finds numerical ratings easy to understand.

At best, standardized tests provide an extremely limited view of an individual learner's capabilities. Many of these tests probe only very low-level kinds of mental processes; few can assess higher-level thinking skills. Because of the importance of test scores, in some places there are great pressures for teachers to "teach to the test." This has the potential to trivialize the kinds of content we address. It encourages us to deemphasize higher-level thinking skills.

Standardized tests pose particular problems for learners from ethnic and cultural minorities. Critics contend that standardized tests serve to deny opportunities for minority-group learners to continue their education beyond the high school level (Marshall, 1990). The same critics point out that a system that limits the continued academic development of the fastest-growing component of the total school population makes little sense. We need assessment techniques that will foster the maximum development of minority-group learners' talents. Further, assessment techniques should encourage the development of sophisticated thinking abilities, not simply reinforce the recall-level thinking called for on most of today's standardized tests.

New assessment procedures need to take into account background characteristics that are likely to typify many minority-group learners. The vocabulary of assessment instruments needs to be responsive to the learners' environments. As well, opportunities these learners have had outside of school need to be considered. (For example, how many poor inner-city children will have computers at home? How many will have traveled extensively? How many of their families subscribe to a large number of periodicals?) We need assessment techniques that look at these young people's potential for future development, not at what they have failed to learn because of conditions beyond their control.

Avoiding Favoritism in the Classroom

All of us who teach are human. We have better relationships with some people than with others. We enjoy some of our learners more than others. In the classroom, however, professionalism demands that we make an effort to encourage each learner's development. It is particularly important for our learners to believe that they will not be singled out in any kind of a negative way because of their ethnicity, race, or gender.

We need to strive for equity in our relationships with our learners. Episodes of misbehavior must be treated similarly, regardless of who the offender is. Encouragement needs to be meted out to all who perform well. The bottom line is that all of our young people need to feel they will be treated fairly. Our credibility depends on this perception. When our learners believe we are not being fair, their motivation declines and academic performance deteriorates. Usually, too, discipline problems increase.

Providing Good Teachers

In some instances, this concern is related to the issue of grouping. The best teachers may be assigned to high-ability classes that often have small numbers of ethnic and cultural minority-group learners. This means that many learners who greatly need motivating, caring teachers are denied them. We need to encourage outstanding teachers to work with minority-group learners. This step will require a clear break with present trends. One recent study revealed a pattern that typifies the situation in much of the country, showing "that teachers in predominantly minority schools were the least experienced, held the most emergency credentials, and were likely to be teaching out of their fields" (Marshall, 1990, p. 43).

PROMISING INITIATIVES

Success in promoting positive attitudes about various cultures requires a willingness for us to go beyond just studying about these cultures. We also have to teach our learners about them. There is a growing recognition that multicultural perspectives need to be developed across the entire curriculum. Minority-group learners are enrolled in every subject schools offer. It only makes sense for us to take their needs into account when we plan our instructional programs. Some teachers fail to do this because they think they know too little about cultures other than their own. This situation has been described as our educational "system's weakest link in teaching about diverse cultures" (Alexander, 1994, p. 267).

Increasing numbers of teacher preparation programs now include content related to multiculturalism. In fact, the National Council for Accreditation of Teacher Education (NCATE), the national accrediting body for teacher education programs, insists that such training be provided and that future teachers have opportunities for field experiences that bring them into contact with culturally diverse learners. Over time, these preparation programs may provide our schools with more teachers who have the knowledge base necessary to respond effectively to perspectives and needs of young people from varied ethnic and cultural backgrounds.

Problems associated with learners' race, ethnicity, and gender are serious, but there are school programs in operation that are addressing them successfully. We will examine two such programs here.

The Work of James Comer

Beginning in the late 1960s, James Comer and several of his associates from the Yale Child Study Center developed a program that was adopted in two schools in New Haven, Connecticut. Learners in these schools had the lowest scores on standardized achievement tests and the poorest attendance records of all schools in the district. Populations of the two schools were 99 percent African-American, and the vast majority of learners came from families whose incomes fell below the official poverty line. The Comer team installed a program based on well-researched principles of child development and participatory management. Fifteen years after the program began, although the racial and economic makeup of the schools' population was unchanged, standardized test scores of learners were above national averages. These scores were close to the top of all New Haven schools' scores, and attendance records of learners at the two minority schools were outstanding (Comer, 1988).

The plan initially instituted in the two New Haven schools, known now as the "Comer model," has been widely adopted. Perhaps its most important feature is *shared decision making*. Principals in Comer-model schools invite parents, teachers, and school support staff members (particularly those concerned with learners' mental health) to take part in the decision-making process. These individuals constitute a management team that sets school policies. The Comer model places an emphasis on developing solutions to problems rather than on assigning blame when young people fail to learn. These solutions have been supported by an undergirding assumption that all pupils and students in the schools *can* learn. The inclusive management structure and the flexibility to take quick action to respond to problems have been credited with much of the success of Comer-model schools.

James Comer has found shared decision making to be an important ingredient in schools that have successfully served large populations of minority-group students. These parents, teachers, administrators, and school support staff members are considering some changes in the school curriculum.

Features of Schools That Do a Good Job with Language-Minority Learners

Millions of learners speak a language other than English as their first language. They need to know English to succeed in school and to be competitive in the job market. Congress recognized the special needs of these children when it passed the Bilingual Education Act in 1968. This act requires schools to provide initial instruction in a learner's first language until a level of English proficiency is reached that will allow for success in classrooms where only English is used.

The concern for educating these learners was underscored in the 1974 decision of *Lau v. Nichols*, which required local school districts to develop approaches that would ensure that learners with limited English proficiency were not denied a meaningful education. The court argued that simply providing these learners with the same curriculum and texts as native speakers of English would not suffice.

Many programs have been established to help non-native speakers of English succeed. Lucas, Henze, and Donato (1990) reported on characteristics of some schools with successful responses to this need. Their study focused on secondary schools with huge majorities of students who had Spanish as their native language. Contrary to the national pattern, students in these schools scored high on standardized tests, tended not to drop out of school, and had much higher than average high school graduation rates. The researchers found special features in these schools that seemed to account for their success. Specifically, the team (Lucas et al., 1990) identified the following characteristics:

- Value is placed on students' languages and cultures.
- High expectations of language-minority learners are made concrete.
- School leaders make the education of language-minority learners a priority.
- Staff development is explicitly designed to help teachers and other staff serve language-minority students more effectively.
- A variety of courses and programs for language-minority students is offered.

- A counseling program gives special attention to language-minority students.
- Parents of language-minority students are encouraged to become involved in their children's education.
- School staff members share a strong commitment to empower language-minority students through education.

These schools pay particular attention to developing learners' levels of proficiency in *both* English and Spanish. For example, advanced literature classes are available that allow students to study the works of Cervantes and other luminaries of Hispanic literature in the original Spanish. The entire program builds learners' pride in their cultural heritage at the same time that it provides them with the tough intellectual tools needed to qualify for both university entrance and decent jobs in the workplace.

USEFUL INFORMATION SOURCES

Many sources are available for materials that can help educators become more sensitive to issues associated with cultural, ethnic, and gender equity. Professional periodicals regularly publish useful articles with helpful ideas that we can use in our classrooms. Some excellent books are available. A particularly good one has been written by Carl A. Grant and Christine E. Sleeter, *Making Choices for Multicultural Education: Five Approaches to Race, Class, and Gender* (New York: Maxwell Macmillan International, 1994). It contains excellent lesson ideas for teachers.

A useful calendar with references to dates and events of interest to many different ethnic groups is the "Ethnic Cultures of America Calendar." The calendar is published each year and is available from:

Educational Extension Systems
P.O. Box 259
Clarks Summit, PA 18411

The following places are sources of other material that we can use to prepare lessons with a multicultural focus. Write them to ask for materials for classroom teachers and learners. In your letters, suggest grade levels of learners for whom you might be preparing lessons.

The Balch Institute for Ethnic Studies
18 South 7th Street
Philadelphia, PA 19106

Center for Migration Studies
209 Flagg Place
Staten Island, NY 10304

Center for the Study of Ethnic Publications
Kent State University
Kent, OH 44242

Immigration History Research Center
University of Minnesota
Minneapolis, MN 55455

Institute of Texan Cultures
University of Texas
San Antonio, Texas 78294

There are also a number of information sources for materials with a gender equity focus. A good list of materials is available from the Upper Midwest Women's History Center for Teachers. The address is:

The Upper Midwest Women's History Center for Teachers
Central Community Center
6300 Walker Street
St. Louis Park, MN 55416

Other good sources for gender equity information and materials include the following:

Organization for Equal Education of the Sexes, Inc.
P.O. Box 438
Blue Hill, ME 04614

Population Reference Bureau, Inc.
2213 M. Street N.W.
Washington, DC 20037

National Women's History Project
P.O. Box 3716
Santa Rosa, CA 95402

WEAL: Women's Equity Action League
1250 I Street N.W.
Washington, DC 20005

ISIS, Women's International Information and Communication Services
P.O. Box 25711
Philadelphia, PA 19144

• Key Ideas in Summary

- There is a growing demographic discontinuity between the learner population of the schools and teachers. The learner population is becoming increasingly diverse in terms of its cultural and ethnic makeup. At the same time, the teacher population is becoming increasingly white and female. Because of special perspectives of learners from cultural and ethnic minorities, teachers need to develop lessons carefully keyed to respond to needs of the diverse young people in their classrooms.
- An important objective of our educational system is to maximize every child's learning potential. School programs have often failed to serve the best interests

of minority-group and female learners. Because the entire society benefits from the contributions of well-educated citizens, our schools can ill afford not to develop the talents of any learner.

- In the early and middle years of the twentieth century, many learners from ethnic and cultural minorities were viewed as having a genetic deficit that accounted for their low levels of academic achievement. Later, this explanation gave way to a cultural deficit view that attributed poor school performance to a failure of the learner's home environment to support school learning. The genetic deficit and cultural deficit positions are now generally rejected. It is recognized that the failure of many minority-group children to learn is due to the failure of schools to provide programs responsive to their needs.

- The case of *Brown v. Board of Education* (1954) led to the dismantling of segregated school systems. A subsequent decision, *Milliken v. Bradley* (1974), held that courts did not have a right to order busing *across* district lines for the purpose of integrating schools. As a result, schools in many places continue to enroll disproportionately large numbers of learners from certain cultural and ethnic groups because the groups are very heavily represented within the boundaries of their given school district. Many inner-city school districts, for example, have populations that are largely African-American or Hispanic. There are not enough white learners in these districts to supply a high percentage of such learners to any school, even when the district tries to achieve a racial balance.

- There are many concerns today about within-school segregation. Many college preparatory programs in high schools enroll higher percentages of white students than are represented in the overall student body, while learners from ethnic and cultural minorities are overrepresented in special education classes. Segregation by gender has also been observed; for example, the overwhelming majority of learners in high school physical science classes are male.

- Standardized achievement scores of African-American and Hispanic learners have continually lagged behind those of white students. Dropout rates are also higher for African-Americans and Hispanics than for whites. In recent years, the dropout rate for African-American learners has improved; however, the rate for Hispanics has worsened. Since the Hispanic population is the fastest growing of the nation's minorities, the inability of our schools to hold Hispanic learners has become a priority concern of educators.

- In responding to needs of minority-group learners and females, educators must take care to operate on the basis of accurate information. It is particularly important that they do not make some incorrect generalizations on the basis of inaccurate or incomplete information. For example, the idea that females are less capable of learning mathematics than males persists in many places despite contrary evidence. Generalizations regarding Hispanics sometimes hint at their probable difficulty with English because it is not their native language, whereas, in fact, English *is* the first language for about three-quarters of all Hispanic learners. Similarly, not all African-Americans live in the inner city or are economically deprived.

- Recommendations for improving the quality of educational services for ethnic and cultural minority learners include (1) a commitment to the idea that everyone can learn, (2) modification of grouping practices, (3) making certain that teachers are aware of their own perspectives, (4) relying less on standardized tests, (5) ensuring that teachers avoid favoritism in the classroom, and (6) assigning good teachers to work with minority-group learners.

- James Comer and his associates have developed a model for organizing schools to promote greater achievement levels among minority-group learners. Achievement gains by learners in these schools have been impressive. The Comer-model schools feature shared decision making, whereby principals are but part of a management team that also includes parents, teachers, and school support members.

- This nation has a strong commitment to bilingual education, which involves teaching learners in their native language until they become proficient in English. This commitment was evidenced by the passage of the Bilingual Education Act in 1968 and was buttressed by a famous 1974 court case, *Lau v. Nichols*, which, in effect, required schools to provide meaningful programs for learners with first languages other than English.

• Review and Discussion Questions

1. In what ways do ethnic and cultural characteristics of learners in the schools differ?
2. How would you assess the adequacy of the genetic deficit and the cultural deficit positions as explanations for the failure of many minority-group learners to do well in school?
3. What are some reasons that certain schools, despite national progress toward desegregation, still enroll learners who overwhelmingly are members of a single ethnic group?
4. Give some examples that illustrate within-school segregation.
5. What are some characteristics of schools that have high percentages of minority-group learners who score well on tests of academic achievement?
6. What does research say about females' abilities to learn mathematics?
7. What are some problems that have resulted when people have made careless generalizations about *all* members of a particular minority group?
8. Why have people who are concerned about the education of minority-group learners often criticized the schools for relying too much on information from standardized tests?
9. In the case of *Milliken v. Bradley* (1974), the Supreme Court held that courts could not order buses to cross school district lines for the purpose of achieving racial balance in a number of school districts in a given area. What were some consequences of this decision?
10. What are some features of Comer-model schools?

• Ideas for Field Experiences, Projects, and Enrichment

1. If possible, arrange to visit some classes that include a mix of learners from different ethnic and cultural backgrounds. Observe participation patterns. How frequently did learners from minority groups volunteer to answer questions? How often were they called upon? (You may wish to identify other questions that will help you to pinpoint

the degree to which minority-group learners were actively involved in lessons.) Share your findings with others in your class and, as a group, respond to these questions:
- Were minority-group learners as involved in lessons as were majority-group learners?
- What specific patterns did you note?
- What might account for these patterns?

2. Some school districts have helped to provide special training for white teachers to sensitize them to perspectives of learners from ethnic and cultural minorities. Interview some local school administrators about programs that may have been implemented in their schools. Alternatively, consult professional journals for descriptions of such programs. Prepare a short paper for your course instructor in which you describe either one or two local programs, or several programs that have been outlined in journal articles.

3. The chapter listed several sources for materials related to multicultural and gender equity issues. Try to add at least five additional sources to those already provided. You might begin by looking for articles in professional journals. The *Education Index* may suggest articles to consult, and your instructor may have other ideas about where to locate such information. Share your five sources with your instructor. He or she may wish to prepare a composite list of all suggestions that come in from class members.

4. Read about the Comer model and other successful attempts to improve the achievement levels of minority-group learners. Get together with four or five other classmates who have been working on the same task. Organize a symposium to present to your class on the topic "Hope for Learners from Ethnic and Cultural Minorities: Practical Examples from Real Schools."

5. Some have argued that schools, particularly in urban areas and their surrounding suburbs, would benefit if the courts supported busing learners across district lines for the purpose of achieving better racial balance in every school. Others disagree with this approach. Organize a debate on the issue "Resolved: Cross-District Busing to Improve Racial Balance in Schools Will Improve Education."

• References

Alexander, J. (1994). Multicultural literature: Overcoming the hurdles to successful study. *The Clearing House, 67*(5), 266–268.

Banks, J. A., with Clegg, A., Jr. (1988). *Multiethnic education: Theory and practice* (2nd ed.). Boston: Allyn and Bacon.

Bates, P. (1990). Desegregation: Can we get there from here? *Phi Delta Kappan, 72*(1), 8–17.

Brown v. Board of Education, 347 U.S. 483 (1954).

Chipman, S. F., & Thomas, V. G. (1987). The participation of women and minorities in mathematical, scientific, and technical fields. In E. Z. Rothkopf (Ed.), *Review of educational research* (Vol. 14, pp. 387–430). Washington, DC: American Educational Research Association.

Clinchy, E. (1993). Needed: A Clinton crusade for quality and equality. *Educational Leadership, 74*(8), 605–612.

Comer, J. P. (1988). Educating poor minority children. *Scientific American, 259*(5), 42–48.

Darling-Hammond, L. (1993). Reforming the school reform agenda. *Phi Delta Kappan, 74,* 756–761.

Elam, S. M., Rose, L. C., & Gallup, G. M. (1994). The 26th annual Phi Delta Kappa/Gallup poll of the public's attitudes toward the public schools. *Phi Delta Kappan, 76*(1), 41–56.

Erickson, F. (1987). Transformation and school success: The politics and culture of educational achievement. *Anthropology and Education Quarterly, 18*(4), 335–356.

Grant, C. A. (1990). Desegregation, racial attitudes, and intergroup contact: A discussion of change. *Phi Delta Kappan, 72*(1), 25–32.

Grant, C. A., & Sleeter, C. E. (1994). *Making choices for multicultural education: Five approaches to race, class, and gender.* New York: Maxwell Macmillan International.

Henson, K. T. (1995). *Curriculum development for education reform.* New York: HarperCollins.

Hilliard, J. (1991/1992). Why must we pluralize the curriculum? *Educational Leadership, 49*(4), 12–13.

Lau v. Nichols, 414 U.S. 563 (1974).

Lucas, T., Henze, R., & Donato, R. (1990). Promoting the success of Latino language-minority students: An exploratory study of six high schools. *Harvard Educational Review, 60*(3), 315–340.

Marshall, R. C. (Chair). (1990). *Education that works: An action plan for the education of minorities.* Cambridge, MA: Quality Education for Minorities Project, Massachusetts Institute of Technology.

Milliken v. Bradley, 418 U.S. 717 (1974).

Oakes, J. (1990). Opportunities, achievement, and choice: Women and minority students in science and mathematics. In C. B. Cazden (Ed.), *Review of research in education* (Vol. 16, pp. 153–222). Washington, DC: American Educational Research Association.

Savage, T. V., & Armstrong, D. G. (1996). *Effective teaching in elementary social studies* (3rd ed.). New York: Macmillan.

Simon-McWilliams, E. (Ed.). (1989). *Resegregation of public schools: The third generation.* Portland, OR: Network of Regional Desegregation Assistance Centers and Northwest Regional Educational Laboratory.

Smith, T. M., Rogers, T. T., Alsalam, N., Perie, M., Mahoney, R. P., & Martin, V. (Eds.). (1994). *The condition of education 1994.* Washington, DC: National Center for Education Statistics.

Sternberg, R. J. (1994). Allowing for thinking styles. *Educational Leadership, 52*(3), 36–40.

Vergon, C. B. (1989). *School desegregation: The evolution and implementation of a national policy.* Paper presented at the annual meeting of the American Educational Research Association, San Francisco.

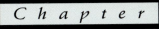

Learners' Rights and Respon- sibilities

OBJECTIVES

- Identify places where decisions originate that affect the legal standing of learners.
- Point out some responsibilities of learners in school.
- Explain how application of the legal doctrine of *in loco parentis* has changed in recent years.
- Describe *due process* and point out conditions under which it is applied.
- Explain limitations of freedom of expression in school settings.
- Describe some principles used in deciding cases involving challenges to curriculum content.
- Explain some standards that are applied in search and seizure situations.
- State conditions where establishing grooming and dress codes might be constitutional.
- Describe implications for teachers of the Family Rights and Privacy Act.

Years ago, professional educators had little need to concern themselves about rights of learners. Schooling was largely regarded as a privilege. In exchange for this privilege, learners were expected to conform unquestioningly to rules and guidelines established by school authorities. Young people who failed to abide by school regulations could be summarily dismissed.

Today this situation is much changed. By and large, young people in the schools enjoy the same constitutional protection as adult citizens. Those of us who teach today have to be aware of the legal rights of our learners to ensure that we avoid doing something that could make us subject to legal action.

Keeping up-to-date on legal guidelines affecting young people in the schools is not easy. Over the past few decades, many courts have considered learners' rights cases. In some instances, decisions have acted to clarify and expand learners' rights. In others, courts have chosen not to do so. In still other cases, decisions have been a confused mix of expanding learners' rights in certain narrowly defined circumstances and keeping them much as they have been traditionally viewed in others. In this chapter, we provide information that illuminates some general trends in legal thinking regarding the appropriateness of various learner, teacher, and administrator actions.

THE RELATIONSHIP BETWEEN LAW AND EDUCATION

The side-by-side existence of two court systems, one state and one federal, contributes to the difficulty in discerning clear patterns among decisions related to learners and schools. Each of these systems has a series of courts with different jurisdictions. Key players at the federal level are the thirteen circuit courts of appeal. Each has jurisdiction over a specific geographic region. Sometimes, a circuit court in one region of the country may rule quite differently on a common issue than a circuit court in another area of the country. Only the United States Supreme Court has jurisdiction over the entire United States. Its decisions are binding on all other courts.

The states also have several levels of courts. The majority of cases involving schools are decided in state courts. Often, state courts are organized around counties. Decisions of these courts may be appealed to the state supreme court. Rulings of a state supreme court are binding on all of the courts in that state.

Because the Constitution of the United States is silent on the issue of education, public schooling has been primarily the responsibility of the individual states. For many years, few challenges to public school practices and policies reached the federal courts. A few issues that were adjudicated quite early by the federal courts concerned such issues as public funding of high schools and setting aside land for school use. An early federal court decision in the area of learners' rights focused on whether school districts could require vaccinations as a condition for entry into school (Zirkel & Richardson, 1988).

Involvement of federal courts in learners' rights issues began to accelerate during the 1960s. Federal courts began to hear more school-related cases as part of a general trend for more concern about protecting citizens' civil rights and about ensuring the national welfare by guaranteeing access to education and training (Valente, 1994). From these beginnings, there has been a tremendous growth in the number of federal cases involving rights of learners in the schools.

Sources of Law Relating to Education

Legal authority with implications for learners, teachers, and schools comes from several sources. These include written constitutions, statute law, administrative law, and court decisional law (Valente, 1994).

Constitutions

Constitutions represent the highest legal standard. A constitution is considered to be the voice of the people, and it represents an expression of principle with which all court decisions are supposed to remain consistent. Constitutional authority supersedes all others. Constitutions are intended to be documents that apply to changing circumstances and are difficult to alter. For this reason, the judges spend considerable time grappling with the intent of written constitutional principles as they apply them to current issues (Valente, 1994).

Statutes

Statutes are enactments by elected legislatures. They are the second highest form of law. As long as these statutes satisfy constitutional requirements, they are binding on all citizens (Valente, 1994). Each state has many statutes dealing with education. This means that each state has a unique set of requirements that govern the operations of its own schools. Legislative bodies periodically produce new statutes and modify old ones. Those related to education often are assembled into something called a *school code*.

Administrative Law

The largest and most detailed mass of law is found in administrative law. This includes the specific rules, directives, procedures, and regulations that must be followed in conducting the day-to-day operations of the schools. Statutes passed by legislative bodies are generally quite broad. These statutes are then turned into administrative directives concerning the specific application of the statute. These administrative procedures and directives have the full force of law as long as they are consistent with the higher levels of law (Valente, 1994).

Court Decisional Law

The courts provide the ultimate check on the actions of school officials. As the courts respond to legal challenges concerning educational issues, they may fashion legal principles not covered in other sources of law. As they seek to interpret and apply constitutional guidelines to specific cases brought to them, they often formulate a legal principle to guide their decision. These principles are then applied to future cases that concern related issues (Valente, 1994). Courts may also rule legislative statutes or administrative law to be unconstitutional.

To avoid preventable legal entanglements as teachers, we need to have some basic knowledge of some of the principles that are embedded in the Constitution of the United States and the constitution of our own state. We also should know something about the school code of our state and have some familiarity with court decisions in areas concerning relationships between teachers and learners.

LEARNERS' RESPONSIBILITIES

Over the past several decades, there has been a general trend in court decisions and in statute law to expand rights of learners. This trend sometimes leads us to downplay the point that, in addition to rights, learners in schools also have important responsibilities.

Attendance

The most fundamental responsibility of the learner is to attend school. It has long been recognized that the state has a compelling interest in the education of all citizens. Therefore, compulsory attendance has been firmly upheld by the courts. However, the courts have also recognized the rights of parents to direct the upbringing of their children. Courts, too, have recognized the relevance to school learners of the First Amendment to the U.S. Constitution, which bars the state from imposing requirements that force individuals to act against their religious beliefs (Valente, 1994).

The courts have decided that the state cannot require that all children must attend a *public* school. In response to this situation, most states have established provisions under which parents may educate their children at home. Attendance at a private or home school is often acceptable if the alternative arrangement provides an education that is "at least equivalent" to what the state requires in its public schools.

There have been many court cases focusing on the issue of what constitutes equivalency. Many of these have involved situations where parents have sought to educate their children at home. In an Illinois case, the state supreme court upheld the rights of parents to teach their daughter at home. In its decision, the court ruled that whereas state law required all children to be educated, it did not specify the place and particular manner of their education. The court further went on to note that the conditions of instruction in the home were consistent with the state's standards for private schools (*People v. Levisen*, 1950).

In a Maine case, a court ruled that the state had the right to impose reasonable standards on parents seeking to educate their children at home. When the parents in this case refused to submit their home schooling plans for approval, their children were declared to be truant when they did not present themselves at the local public school (*State v. McDonough*, 1983). Similarly, a Kansas court found that home schooling that was unplanned or unscheduled and taught by a parent who was not certified did not meet the legal requirements for an "equivalent education" (*In re Sawyer*, 1983). In general, the ability of private and home schools to meet compulsory attendance standards depends on the individual state's laws and on how the courts have chosen to interpret the equivalent education requirement.

Violation of compulsory attendance can lead to criminal charges of child neglect against parents that could even result in their loss of custody of the child. Learners who are habitually truant may be declared delinquent. They can be turned over to a social service agency for supervision or even be placed in a special institution. It is possible in cases of severe truancy for a learner to be declared in contempt of court (Valente, 1994).

Behavior

Learners also have a responsibility to follow reasonable school rules. School officials have the right to establish reasonable rules and regulations in order to ensure a productive and safe educational environment. Learners have the responsibility to comply with those regulations and to submit to the authority of the teacher. For example, the California School Code indicates that every teacher in the public school shall hold each learner accountable for his or her conduct on the way to and from school, on the playgrounds, and during recess. Any certified employee can exercise reasonable physical control over a learner in order to protect property, learner safety, or to maintain conditions conducive to learning. Disrupting school and willfully defying valid authority are grounds for suspension and expulsion from school (California Teachers Association, 1992).

Learners also have a responsibility to refrain from destroying property. The California School Code provides yet another example. Parents or guardians are

This teacher is explaining playground rules to these children. Teachers can be held accountable for learners' conduct in this setting.

liable for damages of up to $7,500. Grades, diplomas, or transcripts may be withheld if a student or his or her parents have not paid for damages to school property (California Teachers Association, 1992).

Learners must refrain from unsafe practices such as hazing and bringing weapons or controlled substances to school. Most states provide for immediate suspension and potential expulsion if a learner brings weapons or controlled substances to school. In addition, harming or threatening physical injury to another person is grounds for suspension and expulsion.

Learners are expected to behave in socially appropriate ways. In one situation, a high school student delivered a speech that was filled with sexual metaphor and innuendo when nominating a friend for a school office. Although the student did not use explicit language, he was informed the next day that he was suspended for three days and that his name had been removed from the list of possible graduation speakers. The student filed suit, claiming that these actions violated First Amendment rights to freedom of speech. The court ruled that rights of the student needed to be balanced against society's interest in teaching young people within the boundaries of socially appropriate behavior. Since the speech was plainly offensive, the actions of the school district were upheld (Zirkel & Richardson, 1988).

Learners do have a responsibility to behave in a responsible manner. They do not have the right to interfere with the establishment of a safe and effective school environment. They must submit to the reasonable rules and regulations of school officials.

LEARNERS' RIGHTS

In Loco Parentis

The traditional legal doctrine governing the relationship of the school and the student was known as *in loco parentis*. According to this doctrine, the school acted "in place of the parent." This meant that the school and its designates (administrators .and teachers) were free to treat young people much as they would be treated by their parents. Common-law precedents relating to the parent-child relationship were extended to the school.

For example, children cannot take their parents to court and demand a hearing on the grounds of a disagreement over some parental directive. Parents are legally defined as having a custodial relationship with their children. Under *in loco parentis*, this same custodial relationship was vested in the school. Buttressed by this legal doctrine, school officials were given substantial authority in establishing rules and in disciplining students.

The application of *in loco parentis* to school actions began to change in the early 1960s, when a number of human and civil rights issues captured public attention. Efforts to extend full constitutional privileges to all racial groups prompted people to become interested in whether constitutional guarantees really apply to everybody or only to "some everybodies." University groups were quick to speak out against institutional practices that seemed to deny students the same constitutional protection they would enjoy if they were not enrolled in institutions of higher learning. Finally, an increasing public suspicion that the government was not being responsive to the general public will concerning the Vietnam War led to a closer scrutiny of all traditional sources of authority. In this context, it was only a matter of time before questions began to be raised regarding the *in loco parentis* relationship between school officials and school learners.

Some critics of *in loco parentis* charged that the doctrine represented an outdated view of the relationship between schools and students. Early schools were different from today's public schools. Many of them were very small and were clearly institutions of the local community. The ability of local leaders to hire and fire teachers ensured a congruence between instructional practices and local values. Given the kind of person likely to be hired as a teacher, parents were not at all reluctant to accept the teacher as a surrogate parent for their children. If the economics had been right, many parents would have enjoyed having their children at home as contributing workmates. But since this was not the case, parents willingly turned them over to the school and the teacher, because they expected the actions of the teacher to be consistent with those they would take as parents.

The situation has changed, however. Parents feel that they have much less control over education and therefore are reluctant to accept all of the actions of school officials as consistent with what they would do as a parent. For example, if a parent requests that the school not use corporal punishment, how can the school justify such punishment on the grounds of *in loco parentis* (Fischer, Schimmel, & Kelly, 1987)? Similarly, would a parent turn his or her child over to the police for possession of a controlled substance?

Clearly the relationship between the teacher and the learner has changed, and so has the application of *in loco parentis*. As teachers, we can no longer assume that parents and others will always assume our actions are in the best interests of learners. We need to be aware that members of our classes now enjoy considerable constitutional protection, and we must develop patterns of interaction that will not leave us open to unwanted legal challenges.

Education as a Privilege or a Right

Schooling was once regarded as a privilege to be enjoyed by those who could live by the rules, not a right that society felt was owed to all young people. Because schooling was not a right, learners were not considered to have any legal recourse when they were removed from school for violating a school rule or regulation. In those days, the absence of formal schooling or a school diploma was not seen as a serious limitation to the economic future of an individual.

The view of schooling as a privilege rather than a right started to unravel when critics began to point out that literacy had become necessary for economic survival in our society. Given the need for an educated population, it was illogical to argue that public school, the best available mechanism for promoting literacy, should be considered as something other than a right to which all citizens were entitled. A tax-supported public education had become so fundamental that people began arguing it should be regarded as a "substantial right."

This important shift in the legal view of education as a right rather than a privilege carried with it important constitutional implications. The U.S. Constitution protects certain rights of citizens. Included in this protection is a requirement that "due process of law" be observed in situations that could result in the loss of a right. In the famous *Tinker v. Des Moines Independent Community School District* (1969), the Supreme Court of the United States indicated that once states establish public schools, learners have a property right in them. The Court further declared that neither learners nor teachers shed their constitutional rights at the schoolhouse door. This decision clearly established that learners have a right to a public education and that they enjoy the constitutional protection of any citizen. These rights cannot be abridged unless specific *due process* procedures are followed.

Due Process

The Fourteenth Amendment to the United States Constitution outlines principles of due process. To be entitled to due process protection, a learner must show that he or she has potentially been deprived of either a "property" or a "liberty" right. In education, the loss of a free public education has been considered a property right, and the subsequent loss of reputation due to expulsion has been considered a liberty right.

Although most people have a general feeling that due process is designed to ensure that people receive fair treatment in an adversarial situation, the specific components of due process are less well known. There are two of these. The first, the *substantive component*, includes the basic set of principles on which due process is based. The second, the *procedural component*, consists of the procedures that must be followed to ensure that due process rights have not been violated.

The Substantive Component

The substantive component of due process can be thought of as including the following principles:

- Individuals are not to be disciplined on the basis of unwritten rules.
- Rules are not to be vague.
- Individuals are entitled to a hearing before an impartial tribunal.
- The identity of witnesses must be revealed.
- Decisions are to be supported by substantial evidence.

In times past, educators sometimes overlooked one or more of these principles. For example, some administrators failed to specify rules out of a fear that a set of written regulations would undermine their flexibility to respond to problem situations. Furthermore, many rules and regulations that were written were couched in such vague terms that people could not easily determine whether or not they were in compliance.

In the days when the courts were not insisting on due process guarantees for school children, there was a general reluctance to release witnesses' names to young people who were charged with violating school rules or regulations. There was a fear that such a disclosure might result in witnesses being intimidated and that, in future cases, people would hesitate to come forward with information.

It is doubtless true that the necessity to protect the due process rights of young people has increased the work of school administrators and has somewhat reduced their flexibility. On the other hand, given the amount of documentation that now must support charges, there probably has been a healthy reduction in the number of miscarriages of justice in cases involving young people and school authorities.

The Procedural Component

The procedural component is concerned with the procedures that must be followed to ensure that principles of due process will be observed. In general, the procedural component of due process includes the following:

- Rules governing learners' behavior must be distributed in writing to learners and their parents at the beginning of the school year.
- Whenever learners have been accused of a rules' infraction that might result in a due process procedure, the charges must be provided in writing to learners and their parents.
- Written notice of the hearing must be given such that there is sufficient time provided for learners and their representatives to prepare a defense. Usually, the hearing must be held within two weeks.
- A fair hearing must include these features:
  - right of the accused to be represented by legal counsel
  - right of the accused to present a defense and introduce evidence
  - right of the accused to face his or her accusers
  - right of the accused to cross-examine witnesses
- The decision of the hearing board is to be based on the evidence presented and must be rendered within a reasonable period of time.
- The accused must be informed of his or her rights to appeal decisions.

A legal precedent for requiring due process to education was the landmark *Goss v. Lopez* (1975) case. School law in Ohio allowed principals to suspend learners for up to 10 days without giving them notice of the reasons for suspension or an opportunity for them to explain their side of the issue. When several individuals were suspended, they challenged this law. The case ultimately was decided by the United States Supreme Court. In its decision, the Court indicated that these learners had sufficient property and liberty rights to require at least minimal due process regardless of the length of the suspension. Those suspended for fewer than 10 days are entitled to (1) oral or written notice of the charges, (2) an explanation of the evidence if the student denies the charges, and (3) an opportunity for the student to present his or her view of the incident (Zirkel & Richardson, 1987). Suspension for longer than 10 days and expulsion both require a more formal and complex due process procedure.

Freedom of Expression

One of the fundamental rights we have as U.S. citizens is that of freedom of expression. A landmark case relating to freedom of expression was the famous *Tinker v. Des Moines Independent Community School District* case cited earlier. In this incident, several learners decided to wear black arm bands to protest United States' involvement in Vietnam. In response, their school district passed a rule that prohibited wearing arm bands.

When some of the learners refused to remove their arm bands, they were suspended from school. The case was finally decided by the United States Supreme Court. In its ruling, the Court struck down the rule banning the wearing of the arm bands on the grounds that wearing the arm bands was a form of free speech. This ruling, however, did not give learners unrestricted free speech rights. If evidence can be presented that shows that exercising the right of free speech will materially and substantially interfere with the work of the school, then a limitation can be imposed.

The decision in the Tinker case prompted much debate in educational circles. Some teachers were confused regarding exactly what authority they retained in the area of controlling learners. A few people saw the Tinker decision as an interference in the school management process that could undermine the smooth functioning of the educational program. Others drew different conclusions from their review of the Tinker case. In their view, the Supreme Court had done little to undermine the real authority of school officials. Instead, these people saw the Court as confining its concern to the processes followed by school officials in exercising their authority. According to educators who viewed the Tinker decision positively, the effect of extending rights enjoyed by adults to school learners provided educators with an opportunity to develop procedures that would enhance public confidence in the schools. Not only would these procedures be constitutional, but they would also blunt the criticism from people who felt that many actions of school authorities were arbitrary and irresponsible.

The freedom of expression issue was also addressed in the *Hazelwood School District v. Kuhlmeier* (1988) decision. In this case, a school principal censored an article in the school paper that dealt with the topic of teenage pregnancy in the school. The students claimed that this was a limitation of their freedom of expression. The Supreme Court ruled that activities such as student publications, theatrical presentations, and other school sponsored activities are a part of the curriculum and carry the implicit endorsement of the school. Therefore, this type of expression was subject to more control than would be expected to be imposed on expression outside of the school. Furthermore, this type of freedom of expression was distinguished from the type of expression in the Tinker case. Whereas expression in the Tinker case was viewed as "political speech," expression in the Hazelwood case was viewed as "educational speech." This latter category, in the Court's view, could be legitimately regulated by school authorities.

Freedom of expression for learners does extend to allowing them to criticize school policies as long as they do it in a nondisruptive manner. However, critical speech that incites violence, calls for a learner strike or a building takeover, or abuses school officials with vulgar and profane language is not protected.

Critical Incident ───────────────────────────────

To Search or Not to Search?

Ms. Shin, a first-year teacher at Upper Madrona Middle School, parked her car in the teachers' lot and began walking toward the office. She noticed a small group of students clustered at the end of one of the hallways. She recognized several of the boys as seventh graders who were in an English class taught by Madeline O'Toole, one of her friends. She had heard Madeline describe the boys as "discipline problems."

As Ms. Shin watched, she observed one of the boys take something out of his backpack and give it to the others in exchange for money. She thought she might be witnessing a drug transaction. She headed quickly over toward the boy with the backpack. What should I do? she wondered. Should I make him open the backpack? Can I legally do that? What are my rights here? What if this kid refuses to cooperate? Do I go ahead and look anyway?

As Ms. Shin approached, the boy noticed her coming and quickly zipped his bag. He started to move away.

"Wait a minute," Ms. Shin called out. "What are you boys doing?"

"Not a thing," one of them replied. "Just talking."

"Come on, you'll have to do better than that," said Ms. Shin. "I saw some stuff come out of that bag and some money change hands."

"Oh, well, we were just swapping some trading cards." The speaker was the boy who had zipped up his bag.

"Could I see them?" asked Ms. Shin.

"Naw, they wouldn't interest you," the boy replied.

What presuppositions does Ms. Shin have about what might be going on when she sees this group of youngsters gathered together in the hall? Are her views based on solid evidence that relates to what is going on here, or does the information she believes she has about these particular individuals color her perceptions?

How do the boys perceive Ms. Shin's line of questioning? Are their perceptions accurate? What prior experiences may have led to the kinds of feelings they may have about this situation?

What should Ms. Shin do next? Does she have a right to demand that the boys allow her to search their belongings? If they refuse, does she have the right to conduct a search? Do you think the courts would consider her actions justified in the event the student or his parents challenged the legality of her actions? Should she just go on and report the behavior to the principal? Should she simply accept their explanation about swapping trading cards and ignore what she saw? What would be the possible consequences if she decided to forget about the incident and it later turned out that these boys had been dealing drugs?

Freedom of Conscience

Controversies in this area have centered around several key issues. Among them have been concerns related to the teaching of certain content, objections to requirements for learner participation in ceremonies involving saluting the flag, and disputes relating to the issue of free exercise of religion.

Objections to the Curriculum

In general, the courts have agreed that learners can be excused from certain parts of the academic program if they have religious or moral objections to what is being studied. Two issues have often been considered in deciding cases of this kind. The first relates to whether the subject being objected to is deemed essential for citizenship. The second issue concerns the degree to which the schools have a right to make and enforce regulations to ensure the efficient and effective operation of schools. Court decisions have tended to focus heavily on the specifics of the situation being litigated.

Several cases have been brought by people who have objected to the teaching of evolution. In Arkansas, the state legislature at one time passed a law forbidding schools in that state to include evolution in the prescribed curriculum. The Supreme Court ruled this law to be unconstitutional on the grounds that it violated the First Amendment clause relating to the establishment of religion (*Epperson v. State of Arkansas*, 1968).

In some places, there have been attempts to force the schools to teach "creationism" or "scientific creationism" along with evolution. These efforts have generally been found to be unconstitutional on the grounds that creationism is a religious belief and that requiring it to be taught would violate the First Amendment's establishment-of-religion clause. On the other hand, at least one court has implied that creationism could be introduced in a social studies class provided it was described simply as a belief held by some people (*McLean v. Arkansas Board of Education*, (1982).

Saluting the Flag

In general, the courts have agreed that learners can refuse to salute the flag because of religious or moral convictions. The courts have decided that a refusal to salute the flag does not constitute a serious threat to the welfare of the state; hence, the state has no compelling interest in ensuring that every learner does salute the flag. In the absence of this compelling interest, the courts have given precedence to the individual moral and religious principles of learners. The courts have also ruled that a learner cannot be required to stand or leave the room while others participate in the flag-salute ceremony (*Lipp v. Morris*, 1978).

Religious Observances

Contrary to some popular opinion, the courts have not required that religion be completely excluded from public schools. It is permissible for learners to study religion in such courses as comparative religion, art, music, and social studies. To be legal, the study of religion must take place in such a way that lessons do not advance or inhibit a particular religion. For example, a school musical group may perform compositions with religious themes so long as the primary purpose is secular, not religious.

During the mid 1990s, the issue of school prayer surfaced as a legislative item. Numerous politicians ran on platforms advocating the return of prayer to schools. Some of those adopting this position appeared to be unfamiliar with the nature of

Federal court decisions have decreed that students cannot be forced to participate in flag-saluting ceremonies.

the kind of prayer the courts had found objectionable. Specifically, what is prohibited are mandatory school prayers given over a loudspeaker or delivered live by teachers or learners in front of the class.

Court decisions regarding prayers that occur in public schools but that take place outside of the classroom have reflected a mixed pattern. In an Iowa case, the court determined that prayer at a graduation ceremony was unconstitutional because the primary purpose of the practice was viewed as being religious (*Graham v. Central Community School District*, 1985). On the other hand, a Michigan court determined that prayer represented only a solemn opening for a graduation ceremony—a practice with a long tradition—and therefore served a purpose that was at least as much secular as it was religious. Hence, this court ruled the prayer to be permissible (*Stein v. Plainwell Community Schools*, 1985). The current trend of court decisions appears to be moving in the direction of prohibiting organized prayers at any official school function.

Search and Seizure

The Fourth Amendment to the U.S. Constitution protects individuals against unreasonable search and seizure. Recent concern about drug abuse and crime in the schools has brought forth numerous challenges to the rights of school officials to conduct searches.

Two general principles govern the right to search: *probable cause* and *reasonable suspicion*. Probable cause means that evidence of wrongdoing is sufficiently convincing to strongly support the view that a party is guilty of illegal behavior. Often, probable cause requires the testimony of a reliable witness. Probable cause normally is required before authorities will issue a search warrant. It is a very strict standard.

Reasonable suspicion is a much less stringent standard, requiring only that there be some reasonable suspicion that someone is guilty of an offense. Typically, this is the standard applied when school authorities decide that a search is warranted. More specifically, school authorities apply two other guidelines: (1) the expectation of privacy and (2) the potential intrusiveness of the search. A search to be conducted in an area in which the individual has little expectation of privacy does not need as much justification as a search in an area in which an individual has a great expectation of privacy. For example, little expectation of privacy is associated with a school desk, which is public property. On the other band, a purse is a personal possession and, logically, a person might have a higher expectation of privacy regarding its contents.

In general, the issue of intrusiveness has to do with the degree to which a search might come into close contact with a person's body. The closer the search comes to the body, the more intrusive it is. The most intrusive search of all is a strip search. Some states prohibit strip searches in school. In California, for example, no school employee is allowed to conduct a search that involves the removal or rearranging of clothing (California Teachers Association, 1992).

When considering whether any kind of search is appropriate, school officials often apply four basic tests. The first concerns the target of the search. The greater the potential danger to the health or safety of learners in the school, the greater is the justification for the search. A gun or a bomb poses an immediate and serious danger; on the other hand, a stolen CD player may offer little immediate threat. Hence, school officials might need a great deal of evidence to establish the likelihood that the object would be found before they would authorize a search.

A second test relates to the quality of the information that has led to consideration of a possible search. The reliability of the people reporting the information must be assessed. Several reliable individuals who divulge similar information provide a more defensible ground for a search than a tip from an anonymous caller.

The third test concerns the nature of the place to be searched. If this is an area where there is a high traditional expectation of privacy, school officials will want very solid information before authorizing a search. However, they might be willing to authorize a search based on less convincing information if the search is to be conducted in an area such as a school locker, where there is little traditional expectation of privacy.

The fourth test focuses on the nature of the proposed search itself. If searches of individuals are to be conducted, authorities will want a great deal of evidence before giving their approval. The age and sex of the person to be searched is also often a consideration.

In summary, case law in the area of search and seizure does not provide absolutely clear guidelines to educators. Because of this uncertainty, as teachers, we probably should not attempt searches on our own initiative. Responsibility for authorizing searches should be left in the hands of those school administrators who are in a position to check their legal position with the school district's legal counsel.

Personal Appearance and Dress Codes

The issue of learner appearance and dress codes has arisen as an important question during the 1990s. Interest in this subject escalated when gang violence in schools became a matter of broad concern. Members of many gangs wear gang colors, insignias, jackets, or caps. In addition, some clothing styles, such as loose-fitting clothes became associated with gang activity because they made it easier for gang members to hide weapons. In response to concerns about gangs, many school officials moved to limit the type of clothing that could be worn to school.

Some people wanted to go even farther and require all learners to wear prescribed uniforms to school. They claimed that this would eliminate any sort of

This dog is sniffing for drugs.

gang identification, would help decrease discipline problems, and would lead to a healthier school environment where the emphasis was on learning. Some parents have agreed and have supported efforts to establish dress codes. Others view such proposals as an unreasonable interference with their and their children's right to choose what they wear to school.

School dress regulations that preserve health, safety, and school discipline have been found to be constitutional (Valente, 1994). Therefore, if a school can demonstrate that wearing certain objects or attire results in violence or disrupts the educational environment, they generally do have the authority to prohibit those items. Similarly, unsanitary clothing or clothing that is vulgar or offensive can be subjected to regulation by school officials.

Guidelines are not so clear on some other, related issues. These include attempts to regulate hair length of males or prohibit the wearing of jeans by females. Challenges to appearance and dress codes generally focus on two issues: (1) whether choice of dress or appearance is a type of symbolic free expression protected by the First Amendment and (2) whether choice of dress involves constitutional "liberty rights."

The United States Supreme Court has yet to rule on learner dress codes or appearance based on either of these claims. Different circuit courts have ruled in different ways. For example, federal appeals courts in the First Circuit, Fourth Circuit, Seventh Circuit, and Eighth Circuit have all declared that an individual's right to establish personal grooming standards is constitutionally protected. On the other hand, courts in the Fifth Circuit, Ninth Circuit, Tenth Circuit, and Eleventh Circuit have declared that no such constitutional protection exists and, thus, courts should not interfere with school officials' attempts to establish grooming standards for learners.

Prohibitions on the wearing of jeans by females have been upheld in Kentucky but overturned in Idaho and New Hampshire. The wearing of tight skirts or skirts over six inches above the knee has been upheld in Arkansas (Valente, 1994). In one case, a principal argued that hair length of male students needed to be regulated for reasons of health and safety. The court rejected this argument, noting that no compelling argument had been made why a similar requirement should not also restrict the length of girls' hair (*Crews v. Cloncs*, 1970).

It is apparent from these conflicting decisions that no clear standards exist for judging the appropriateness of dress and appearance codes. Schools that wish to implement them need to make sure that they are reasonably connected to school needs and are not unduly vague or broad.

Marriage and Pregnancy

Until relatively recent times, schools routinely excluded pregnant learners whether they were married or unmarried. One rationale for these policies was that teenage marriage should be discouraged and that the presence of pregnant learners in school would promote an unhealthy interest in early matrimony. Some people also thought that married girls might be prone to talk with others about the more intimate aspects of the marital relationship, thereby exercising a "morally corrupting" influence over other young people. The moral corruption argument was particularly common when rationales were built in support of excluding unmarried pregnant girls from school.

In recent years, the courts have tended to make decisions designed to protect the rights of all learners to complete an education. There has been a trend to support the idea that school policies denying pregnant learners the privilege of attending school undermine their potential to acquire the knowledge they need to support themselves and their dependent children. Although practices vary, most districts today make provisions for girls who are pregnant to continue their education.

Family Rights and Privacy

Beginning in the 1960s and continuing into the 1990s, there has been a growing concern over potential misuses of all kinds of records, including school records. For example, some people have worried that a learner who had difficulty with a teacher in the early elementary grades might be stigmatized throughout his or her entire school career by records suggesting that the learner was a troublemaker. Concern about possible misuse of records helped ensure passage of the Family Educational Rights and Privacy Act in 1974.

This act required schools to provide parents free access to any records on their children. Furthermore, learners over age 18 and those in postsecondary schools gained the right to view these records themselves. The act also restricted how schools could distribute these records. Before the act was passed, it was customary for many schools to release these records on request to government agencies, law enforcement agencies, and others. Since passage of the Family Educational Rights and Privacy Act, schools have been allowed to release records only after strict guidelines have been followed.

An implication for teachers is that we need to choose our words carefully when we enter information on learner records. Unsubstantiated or derogatory comments that label a learner unfairly can lead to legal action. Comments that reflect negatively on the learner must be supported by facts.

This act also has implications for future teachers as they seek initial teaching positions. Usually, in preparing placement papers for teacher candidates, personnel at the college or university placement center will ask whether individuals wish to have an open or closed file. If an open file is chosen, the candidate retains the right to read everything that goes into it. If a closed file is chosen, the candidate waives the right to see what is placed inside.

People who write recommendations usually are notified by the placement center whether a candidate has opted for an open file or a closed file. Some professors and others who write recommendations hesitate to provide them to undergraduates who have opted for an open file. Furthermore, some school district personnel people tend to look differently at placement files that are open and those that are closed. Rightly or wrongly, some of them feel they get a more honest appraisal of a candidate's strengths and weaknesses in a closed file.

To summarize, learners are individuals with rights guaranteed to any citizen. We need to recognize this reality and make sure no actions we take are viewed as

Do Learners Have Too Many Rights?

During earlier periods in the history of American education, schooling was considered to be a *privilege*. Accordingly, professional educators were free to impose rules and enforce sanctions, including expulsion, without much concern for legal rights of learners.

Over the past few decades, schooling has been redefined as a *right*, and full constitutional protection has been extended to school learners. This has placed limits on the kind of actions school authorities can take. Today, educators cannot do things that infringe upon the constitutionally protected rights of the young people they serve.

Some people think the move to extend full constitutional protection to learners has been a major cause of discipline problems in schools. In their view, teachers and administrators have had their hands tied and are no longer able to respond to problems in a forceful manner.

What Do You Think?

1. Should schooling be redefined as a privilege so that professional educators can move aggressively to respond to problems without having to be so concerned about legal rights of learners?
2. Critics of the trend to extend more rights to learners contend that this has greatly contributed to discipline problems in our schools. How do you react to this assertion? Do you have evidence to support your view?
3. Do you think all of the different groups that collectively make up American society have similar views regarding the issue of extending full constitutional protection to learners? What are some groups that might include a large number of people favoring this trend? What are some others that might include a large number of people opposing it? How might you account for differences in the views of these people?

interfering with learners' legal rights. On the other hand, our learners need to realize that their rights are balanced by the need for educators to establish an orderly and safe educational environment. We do have the right to establish reasonable regulations and rules, and our learners have the responsibility to follow them.

• Key Ideas in Summary

- The existence of two different sets of courts, federal and state (with several levels of courts in each system), results in much confusion concerning the legal principles associated with learners' rights and responsibilities.
- Constitutions are considered to be the highest level of law. Statutes and administrative law cannot establish principles that run contrary to constitutional provisions. Judges interpret the constitution and use it as a guide in determining legal decisions. Their decisions may result in legal principles that are applied in future cases dealing with similar issues.
- Learners have responsibilities as well as rights. The most fundamental responsibility is that of attending school. Other responsibilities include respecting

school authorities, following reasonable school rules and regulations, and behaving in socially appropriate ways. The courts try to balance the rights of a learner with those of the school to establish an orderly and safe educational environment. In short, learners cannot interfere with rights of school officials to operate the school or the rights of other young people to learn.

- Traditionally, the legal doctrine governing relationships between school authorities and learners was *in loco parentis*. In essence, this doctrine implied that the legal relationship between school and learner was much like that existing between parent and child. One implication of this doctrine was that learners did not enjoy the full rights of citizens and could not take school authorities to court to protest decisions. This doctrine began to break down in the 1960s, and today most rights enjoyed by citizens in the general public are extended to school learners.

- Today, due process guarantees apply to learners in the schools. Due process is designed to ensure that people are treated fairly in adversarial situations. The *substantive component* of due process references the basic principles on which due process is based; the *procedural component* outlines procedures to be followed to ensure that due process rights have not been violated.

- A number of First Amendment guarantees have been extended to school learners. A key case in extending Bill of Rights guarantees to learners was *Tinker v. Des Moines Independent Community School District* (1969). In this case, the Supreme Court acted to establish the principle that free speech guarantees should be extended to learners in the schools. However, the issue of free speech in school does not allow learners total freedom. Expression that is considered a part of the curriculum can be controlled.

- A number of issues related to freedom of conscience have come before the courts. Among topics litigated are concerns related to the teaching of certain content, objections to learner participation in flag-saluting ceremonies, and disputes concerning the issue of free exercise of religion. In arriving at decisions, the courts have tended to weigh heavily unique dimensions of the specific situation under consideration.

- In considering the appropriateness of searches of learners and their property in schools, the courts have tended to consider the expectation of privacy and the intrusiveness of the search. In general, the less the expectation of privacy and the more distant the search is from the body of a learner, the more willing courts have been to support the search authority of school officials.

- Dress and grooming regulations that relate to preservation of health, safety, and discipline are constitutional. Of more questionable constitutionality are dress and grooming codes that are not reasonably connected to school needs. Challenges to appearance standards are usually based on the theory that dress and appearance is a form of symbolic speech or it involves a constitutional "liberty right." To date, the Supreme Court has not rendered a definitive decision on a case involving school dress and appearance codes. Different federal circuit courts have ruled in different ways on appearance standards.

- School records are open to inspection by parents as well as by learners over the age of 18. They cannot be released to others without the permission of the parents or guardians. Teachers need to take care to ensure that comments entered on permanent records are done so in a professional manner and do not slander a learner.

• Review and Discussion Questions

1. What is your response to the kinds of responsibilities of learners mentioned in the chapter? Do you agree with those who claim that learners have too many rights and too few responsibilities?
2. Do you think that recent court decisions extending rights to learners have resulted in more instances of learners defying teachers and administrators?
3. In what ways do you think the issues discussed in this chapter will influence your role as a teacher?
4. What are implications of the substantive and the procedural components of due process for teachers?
5. Do you believe that the full force of *in loco parentis* should be restored to teachers? Why or why not?
6. Some people have argued that it makes sense for older students, particularly those in senior high schools, to be granted full rights of citizenship, but that these privileges should not extend to younger learners in elementary schools. The argument for this position is that these younger children lack the kind of maturity and insights people should have before full rights of citizenship, logically, should be extended to them. What are your views on this issue?
7. Parent protests and calls for censorship of certain curriculum content have become increasingly common. What is your view of the proper role of the school in responding to censorship and complaints about the curriculum?
8. What are some arguments that individuals are making about requiring organized prayer in schools? What is your position?
9. Different federal circuit courts have made different rulings on a number of issues related to rights of school learners. How do you explain these differences?
10. How do you feel about requiring all students attending a school to wear uniforms? In particular, would this approach lead to less gang violence? Do you think the courts would find school regulations requiring students to wear an official school uniform to be constitutional?

• Ideas for Field Experiences, Projects, and Enrichment

1. Review copies of professional education journals, such as *Phi Delta Kappan* or *Educational Leadership*. Look for articles and sections dealing with legal issues in education. Identify the legal principles that are being discussed and applied to learners' rights and responsibilities. Share your findings in an oral report to your class.
2. Invite a local school administrator to speak to your class. Ask this person to describe the legal issues relating to the rights and responsibilities of learners that are particularly important for newcomers to the profession to understand. You might also ask this person to provide examples of difficulties some teachers may have encountered over the years because of a failure to understand the nature of rights learners enjoy today.

3. Organize a debate on one of the topics discussed in this chapter. For example, you might debate an area such as requiring uniforms for all learners in a school or protecting learners by censoring certain kinds of curricular content.
4. Obtain a copy or a summary of the education code for your state. Identify state rules in areas such as corporal punishment, expulsion, suspension, and mandatory attendance.
5. Review articles in the news for the past several months that focus on legal issues relating to the rights and responsibilities of learners. Identify any recent trends in the types of cases that are being brought forward or in the direction of court decisions. Write a brief paper that summarizes your findings.

• References

California Teachers Association. (1992). *Guide to school law.* Burlingame, CA: Author.

Crews v. Cloncs, 432 F.2d 1259 (7th Cir. 1970).

Epperson v. Arkansas, 393 U.S. 97 (1968).

Fischer, L., Schimmel, D., & Kelly, C. (1987). *Teachers and the law* (2nd ed.). New York: Longman.

Graham v. Central Community School District, 608 F. Supp. 531 (S.D. Iowa 1985).

Goss v. Lopez, 419 U.S. 565 (1975).

Hazelwood School District v. Kuhlmeier, 484 U.S. 260 (1988).

In re Sawyer, 672 P.2d 1093 (Kan. 1983).

Lipp v. Morris, 579 F.2d 834 (3d Cir. 1978).

McLean v. Arkansas Board of Education, 529 F. Supp. 1255 (E.D. Ark. 1982).

People v. Levisen, 90 N.E.2d 213 (Ill. 1950).

State v. McDonough, 468 A.2d 977 (Me. 1983).

Stein v. Plainwell Community Schools, 610 F. Supp. 43 (W.D. Mich. 1985).

Tinker v. Des Moines Independent Community School District, 393 U.S. 503 (1969).

Valente, W. (1994). *Law in the schools* (3rd ed.). New York: Macmillan.

Zirkel, P., & Richardson, S. (1988). *A digest of Supreme Court decisions affecting education.* Bloomington, IN: Phi Delta Kappa Educational Foundation.

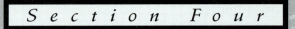

Teachers and Their Work

Effective Teaching

OBJECTIVES

- Identify the role of research in teaching.
- Define the basic features of active teaching.
- Explain the importance of teacher clarity.
- Identify different time decisions teachers make, and explain how each relates to learner achievement.
- Describe how teachers' expectations influence learners' levels of achievement.
- Recognize elements of effective teacher-questioning techniques.
- Describe some procedures that can be used to gather and record data about what goes on in a classroom during an observation session.

Instruction is what we are expected to provide as teachers. It is true that we also manage classrooms, take care of certain administrative responsibilities, and accomplish other tasks. However, instruction more than any other activity defines the role of teaching and clearly sets our work apart from that of other professions.

Teachers have long been judged on their instructional effectiveness. Debates over this issue have sometimes centered on the question of whether there exists a body of research-validated knowledge that adequately defines "effective" teaching. Some people argue that such knowledge does exist and prospective teachers need specific training related to sound instructional methodology. Others maintain that no such specialized training is necessary and that good teaching will automatically follow for teachers who have a good understanding of the subjects they teach. The position of those who argue that teachers can profit from specialized training is strengthened by a growing body of research, which is beginning to pinpoint certain categories of behaviors that have been found to be associated with effective teaching.

Most research on effective teaching has focused on teacher behaviors that are associated with increasing learners' academic attainment. Instruction certainly also has other purposes. For example, learners' psychomotor development, social adjustment, and personal growth are important outcomes of education. Because there is so much present interest in the academic integrity of American schools, we have restricted our discussion of teacher effectiveness to those teacher behaviors that have been found to enhance academic achievement.

Research on teacher effectiveness differs from research in such areas as the physical sciences. It focuses on people who may have different personal backgrounds, motivations, and experiences. Findings of teacher effectiveness research do not categorically assert that a specific procedure will work in a predictable way with every learner. Rather, this body of research seeks to identify principles that can guide us as we make decisions appropriate for our own instructional settings.

Teaching is a decision-making process. Familiarity with research findings related to teaching effectiveness can help us diagnose instructional problems and consider alternative courses of action. Results of teacher effectiveness research we present here are organized under these major headings:

- active teaching
- productive use of class time
- teacher expectations
- teachers' questions

ACTIVE TEACHING

A growing body of research suggests that active teaching is associated with enhanced learner achievement (Good & Brophy, 1994). The term *active teaching* refers to situations when the teacher directly leads the class and plays such roles as:

- presenter of new information
- monitor of learner progress

- planner of opportunities for learners to apply content
- re-teacher of content (to learners who fail to learn the content when it is initially presented)

The active-teaching role is in contrast to the view of the teacher as a general manager or facilitator of instruction who does not get directly involved in leading the class and personally overseeing learning activities. Several important dimensions of active teaching are introduced in subsections that follow.

Program Planning

The Problem of Match

Active teachers play a leadership role in determining their learners' instructional programs (Good & Brophy, 1994). One problem we face is matching instructional programs to the special characteristics of our learners. To accomplish this task, we must make two kinds of decisions.

First, we must consider the difficulty level of the new material in light of our understanding of our learners' capabilities. If selected materials are too difficult, frustration is certain to occur and little learning will take place. If the materials are too easy, boredom and motivation problems may result.

Second, we need to match the program materials to learners' interests. This is not to suggest that we should introduce no content in which learners do not initially display a high level of interest. Rather, our task is to identify interest levels and, when they are found to be low, think about creative ways to generate greater learner interest and enthusiasm. Ideally, we develop plans for lessons that will stimulate learners to want to acquire the new information. Successful planning of this kind requires us to know our learners well. Our strategy for each lesson should be right for the content selected for that lesson (Acheson & Gall, 1992), right for the learners, and right for us (Walker & Chance, 1994/1995).

Task Analysis

As we make judgments about the suitability of content for a given group of learners, we need to engage in task-analysis activities. These require us to look at a proposed body of content that our learners are to master with a view to breaking it into several smaller components or subtasks. To determine whether learners have the needed prerequisite information, we identify what each subtask presumes learners know before they begin work on it. Box 13-1 provides a step-by-step breakdown of task analysis.

Specifying Objectives

After we determine which content is appropriate, we next specify objectives. These identify what learners should be able to do after they have mastered the new content. Often, separate instructional objectives are written for each of the subtasks identified during the task-analysis phase. Learner attainment of these objectives provides evidence we can use to judge whether they have mastered the new material.

Components of Task Analysis

Task analysis consists of two basic parts: (1) identifying the specific information learners will need in order to master some specific content and (2) determining a logical beginning point for instruction.

Suppose you were planning to teach a two- to three-week unit in a subject and at a grade level of your choice. Make a list of specific knowledge and skills your learners will need in order to master this content.

Needed knowledge: _____

Needed skills: _____

Now, prepare a brief description of how you would begin instruction. To make this determination, you first need to find out how much of the needed knowledge and skills your learners already possess. Then you can identify the appropriate starting point.

Lesson Presentation

As active teachers, we need to play a leadership role during all phases of instructional planning and implementation. This is particularly evident when we are actually presenting our lessons.

Stimulating and Maintaining Interest

We need to pay particular heed to what motivates learners during the process of identifying and selecting content. The emphasis on motivation needs to be maintained during actual instruction as our learners become actively engaged in working with new material. During the presentation-of-instruction phase, these three distinct periods of motivation need to be considered:

- motivation at the beginning of the learning sequence
- motivation during the learning sequence
- motivation at the conclusion of the learning sequence

The purpose of initial motivation is to engage learners' interest and to encourage them to want to learn the material. At this stage, we try to build on learners' general curiosity. Introducing something novel, unusual, or puzzling often works well. Learners need to understand how the new material connects to their own lives. What will learning it help them to do or understand? Why should they commit themselves to mastering it? We need to be prepared to answer these kinds of questions during the first phase of motivation.

As instruction goes forward, we continue to introduce novel or unusual material to help sustain interest levels. Learners are motivated by success. When they accomplish parts of a larger instructional task, we praise them for what they have done. This kind of support helps keep interest levels high. In general, motivation is facilitated when we maintain a positive classroom atmosphere that is free from threats and fear. Learners need to know that they have our solid support as they struggle with new content.

*This teacher is using the principle
of novelty to motivate learners.*

Motivation at the conclusion of an instructional sequence is important. We should take particular care to point out to learners how much they have accomplished. A sense of achievement functions as an important motivator. Achievement during one instructional sequence makes it easier for learners to be motivated as they begin the next one.

Sequencing

Over the years, many schemes have been proposed regarding sequencing of instruction. Centuries ago, the ancient Spartans developed a four-part sequence that required the teacher to follow these steps in presenting new material to learners (Posner, 1987):

- introduce material to be learned
- ask learners to think about the material
- repeat the material again and work with learners individually until they have it memorized
- listen to learners as they recite the material from memory

In the nineteenth century, the famous learning theorist Johann Herbart suggested a lesson cycle featuring these steps (Meyer, 1975):

- preparation for learning
- presentation of new information

- association (tying new information to old)
- generalization
- application

In recent years, many school districts have recommended that teachers follow an instructional sequence suggested by Madeline Hunter and Douglas Russell (1977). The Hunter-Russell scheme includes these steps (Hunter & Russell, 1977):

- anticipatory set (focusing learners' attention on the instruction that is about to begin)
- objective and purpose (helping learners understand what they will be able to do as a result of their exposure to the instruction)
- instructional input (conveying information to learners)
- modeling (providing learners with examples or demonstrations of competencies associated with the lesson)
- checking for understanding (evaluating whether learners have the information needed to master the objective)
- guided practice (monitoring learners as they work on tasks calling on them to apply the new information)
- independent practice (assigning learners to work with new content under conditions where they will not have direct teacher assistance available)

There are other sequencing models that have been developed (e.g., Denton, Armstrong, & Savage, 1980; Posner, 1987) that share many common features. Particularly notable is the emphasis that nearly all of them place on the importance of giving learners opportunities to apply new knowledge. Researchers have consistently found improved learning to be associated with instruction that allows learners to engage in application activities (Good & Brophy, 1994).

Lesson Pacing

Good active teaching features a presentation of lessons that moves at a brisk pace and provides for high levels of learner success. We need to maintain a smooth, continuous developmental flow, trying to avoid spending too much time on certain points or matters that are not directly related to the central content. As the lesson develops, we ask questions and take other actions to ensure that members of our class are learning the material.

Within-Lesson Questioning

Active teaching demands the skillful use of questions. Research reveals that questions should be asked at regular intervals and addressed to a large number of class members (Good & Brophy, 1994). Questioning of this type serves two basic purposes. First, it allows us to check on levels of learner understanding. Second, when learners know that we will be asking many people in the class to respond to questions about what they are learning, they stay alert. They realize that they need to pay attention because we might call on them at any time.

Monitoring

Monitoring, a key ingredient of active teaching, occurs continuously throughout a lesson. It is particularly important after we assign our students to practice what they have learned by working on assignments that require them to use the new information. Effective monitoring cannot occur when we sit at our desks. We need to move about the classroom and check on learners' progress.

We must provide feedback both to learners who are performing the task correctly and to those who are experiencing difficulties. Successful performers need to know they are on the right track (Goodlad, 1984) and to hear our supportive comments. Those learners who are having problems or who are not doing the work properly also need to be helped. We need to give them specific details regarding (1) what they are doing wrong and (2) how they can change what they are doing so they will experience success.

When, as a result of careful monitoring, we discover that many learners are not performing at an acceptable level, we need to halt the independent practice activity. At this point, we engage in re-teaching to clear up misunderstandings. Successful re-teaching is tightly focused, dealing with only those points that seem to be causing problems for learners.

Teacher Clarity

Research reveals that instructional practices of effective teachers are characterized by clarity. *Clarity* includes several variables, among which are:

- the teacher's verbal and nonverbal style
- the teacher's lesson-presentation structure
- the teacher's proficiency in providing cogent explanations

Verbal and Nonverbal Style

Several issues come into play when defining a given presentation style. One of these involves *paralanguage*. Paralanguage includes those things that help shape what is conveyed by words that are spoken but that are not the words themselves. Elements of paralanguage include voice intonation, precision of articulation of words, and rate of speaking. Paralanguage, which also includes many of our nonverbal behaviors, has a great influence on how listeners hear and interpret what we say.

We acquire paralanguage as a natural overlay on our language skills as we grow to maturity within our families, friendship groups, and communities. There are important regional and cultural differences. When the paralanguage patterns of a speaker and listener differ, the listener may have difficulty understanding all that is being said.

For example, if we were brought up in a part of the country where speech rates and vowel sounds differ dramatically from those in the area where we are now teaching, we may find that the learners sometimes have difficulty grasping what we say. We have to understand that communication problems sometimes result not from the level of difficulty of the words or message, but from the patterns of speech we use to deliver them.

Nonverbal behaviors sometimes also get in the way of clear communication. This can happen when we send a nonverbal message that is not consistent with our spoken words. For example, suppose we scowled and shook a fist at our class while saying, "I'm really proud of the good work you're doing." Signals here are mixed: the nonverbal behaviors are hostile and threatening, but the verbal behavior is warm and supportive. The resulting message is confusing.

It is not unusual for people to be unaware of many of their nonverbal behaviors. Because these behaviors are important, we need to develop some awareness of our nonverbal patterns. Class observers sometimes can help by providing feedback to us about what we are doing nonverbally to support our verbal instruction.

Lesson-Presentation Structure

Learners profit from an understanding of the general subject matter of new lessons and of how the content is to be organized. One way we can help learners grasp the framework of new lessons is through the use of *advance organizers*. An advance organizer is a label that describes a large and important category of content to be covered. It helps learners to sort out fragmented pieces of information and organize them under certain specified category labels. This simplifies their learning task.

Consider the following example. Suppose a secondary school teacher wanted students to study advertising. One purpose of the unit might be to help class members understand that some advertisers make claims that go beyond the evidence available to support them. The teacher might give these instructions to students: "Look through any five magazines of your choice. By Wednesday, bring me three or four ads that you believe make untrue or unfair claims."

This assignment is going to bring students into contact with a huge volume of information. The task, as assigned, provides few guidelines for them to follow in deciding which ads might be better than others as examples of misleading advertising. The students' task would have been greatly simplified had the teacher provided them with one or two advance organizers.

For example, the teacher might have begun the class with an explanation and a discussion of the term *glittering generality*. The assigned task might then have been stated in this way: "Look through any five magazines of your choice. By Wednesday, bring me three or four ads that contain glittering generalities." This assignment would have provided students with a good sense of direction by clearly communicating to them what needed to be done to complete the task to the teacher's satisfaction.

A widely used type of advance organizer is the lesson objective. To assist learners in understanding what the lesson will emphasize, we often provide a learning objective that indicates what they should know or be able to do when they have completed the lesson. Objectives that are conveyed in verbal form need not be complex. For example, we might say something as simple as, "When we've finished this lesson, you should be able to identify at least four main parts of a short story."

As lessons are being taught, we strive to maintain connected discourse. This means we try to achieve a smooth, point-by-point development of the content that is being introduced. Once started, the lesson is pursued and carried along to its logical conclusion. There are few digressions that take away from its main flow. The effort is to avoid mid-lesson stoppages that could result in confusion and, ultimately, diminished levels of learner achievement.

It is also important for us to take time to provide *internal summaries* as we teach our lessons. These are pause points that allow us and our learners to stop, take stock, and reflect upon what has been learned so far. Internal summaries allow us to clarify any misconceptions. When internal summaries are a regular feature of our teaching, learners tend to pay attention. This is true because they realize we may stop from time to time to ask someone in the class to summarize what has been learned.

Clarity is also enhanced when we use *marker expressions*. These are statements that underline or highlight something that has been said. Marker expressions are employed to communicate the importance of certain kinds of information. Examples include statements such as:

- Write this down.
- Pay close attention to this.
- Listen carefully to this explanation.

The importance of specific content can also be "marked" through changes in vocal intonation or volume.

A final aspect of lesson structuring is the summary provided at the end of a lesson presentation. The summary includes a recapitulation of major ideas that have been covered, drawing together what has been learned in a way that facilitates retention.

Providing Explanations

At various times during a lesson, we may be called on to explain something. Several things can be done to enhance the clarity of our explanations. For example, we need to take particular care in defining potentially confusing terms clearly. Beginners in our profession sometimes assume that learners know more than they really do.

One of the authors remembers a time when a friend who was a high school teacher developed a marvelous presentation to a class on the topic "Recent Political Trends." At the end of the lecture, a student cautiously raised a hand to ask, "What is a trend?" The teacher had not considered the possibility that the word *trend* would not be in the working vocabularies of all of the students.

Our explanations communicate best when they are free from ambiguous, vague, and imprecise terms. Some examples of phrasing we need to avoid include terms of approximation such as *kind of, sort of,* and *about*. Ambiguous designations such as *somehow, somewhere,* and *someone* also often fail the clarity test. Additionally, probability statements such as *frequently, generally,* and *often* do not mean the same thing to all learners.

PRODUCTIVE USE OF CLASS TIME

Researchers have found that learners in classes in which teachers maximize the amount of class time used for instruction perform better than those in classes where less time is spent on instruction (Good & Brophy, 1994). In some classrooms, as much as 50 percent of available time is devoted to nonacademic tasks. This situation deprives learners of much time that they need for working on academic tasks. It can have a strong, negative, long-term influence on achievement.

The time decisions that we make in the classroom involve three basic types of time. These are *allocated time*, *engaged time*, and *academic learning time*.

Allocated Time

Allocated time decisions are those we make concerning how much time is to be devoted to learning specific subjects or materials. Some of these decisions are made in light of state or local regulations. However, many of them fall to us as individual teachers, and researchers have found that those of us in the profession vary greatly in terms of how much time we allocate to given subjects or skills (Berliner, 1984).

Our decisions about how to allocate time result from several considerations. Among them is a tendency to vary the amount of time allocated based on the difficulty of the material and the level of our own interest in it. Researchers have found that we allocate more time to difficult topics and topics in which we, personally, have high levels of interest. These findings suggest a need to provide sufficient time for learners to master content that may not be particularly interesting or exciting to us. Our time allocation decisions need to be based on our learners' needs not our personal preferences.

Engaged Time

Allocated time is the total amount of time set aside for instruction related to a given subject or topic. Engaged time is that part of allocated time when instructional activities related to the subject or topic are occurring; other activities such as distributing materials, responding to learner questions of various kinds, and dealing with classroom management issues detract from the total amount of engaged time. Research reveals that teachers whose classrooms are characterized by high percentages of engaged time produce learners who achieve better than teachers whose classrooms are characterized by lower percentages of engaged time. Maintaining a high percentage of engaged time appears to be a particularly important variable in promoting the academic development of low-ability learners.

Engaged time is time spent on work that clearly relates to the lesson objective. There is no facilitating effect when learners are kept busy on make-work activities that are unrelated to lesson content. However, when assignments are relevant and learners participate actively, they learn more (Finn, 1993).

Academic Learning Time

Academic learning time is that portion of total engaged time when the learner is experiencing a high degree of academic success while working on the assigned task (Berliner, 1984). This definition goes beyond a concern for learners' working on content-related tasks to a concern for their success rates while they are so engaged. Higher rates of academic learning time are associated with increased levels of achievement (Berliner, 1984).

Teachers whose classes are characterized by high percentages of academic learning time monitor learners carefully to ensure that the learners understand the lesson. These teachers frequently ask learners what they are doing, and circulate through their classrooms as learners work on assigned tasks, providing corrective feedback to those students who are experiencing difficulties.

TEACHER EXPECTATIONS

Teacher expectations refer to our attitudes about learners' potentials for academic success. They predispose us to look for different levels of achievement from different people in our classes. These expectations are rarely verbalized; however, they do exert subtle influences on how we interact with different learners. Learners themselves often are affected by their comprehension of what we expect them to be able to do.

Suppose a learner for whom we have low academic expectations volunteers to answer a question and is recognized. If this learner stumbles at the beginning of the response, we may conclude that his or her difficulty results from a lack of knowledge. In response, we may give the learner part of the answer, call on someone else, or even praise the learner just for being willing to volunteer. Such responses communicate our lack of confidence in the learner's ability to respond correctly.

Our actions may be quite different when we perceive the volunteering learner to be academically talented. If such a learner initially experiences difficulty, we may provide cues and continue to work with the person until the correct response, which we believe the learner really knew all the time, is elicited. When we act in this way, we communicate to bright learners that we will hold them to a high standard of performance and work with them until they meet it.

Good and Brophy (1994) point out a number of findings from research studies focusing on teacher expectations. Some of these include:

- Teachers have certain behavioral expectations of learners in their classes.
- Teachers' behaviors toward individual learners vary according to their expectations regarding what the individual learners can do.
- Differences in how they are viewed by teachers result in different learner self-concepts, levels of motivation, and aspirations.
- Teachers who are conscious of the impact of their expectations can monitor and adjust them in ways that can result in enhanced learner performance.

TEACHERS' QUESTIONS

The view that to teach well is to question well has long had historic standing (DeGarmo, 1903). A large body of research supports the idea that effective teachers ask more questions than less effective teachers. In one study, effective junior high school mathematics teachers were found to ask an average of 24 questions during a class period, whereas their less effective counterparts asked an average of only 8.6 questions (Rosenshine & Stevens, 1986).

Interest in questioning encompasses more than the issue of how many questions teachers ask. For example, many researchers have looked into the character and quality of the questions themselves, and schemes have been developed to categorize types of questions. One very simple approach divides questions into two general groups: (1) lower-level questions and (2) higher-level questions. Lower-level questions call on learners to recall specific items of previously introduced information. They do not demand sophisticated thinking. Higher-level questions, on the other hand, require learners to apply, analyze, integrate, create, or synthesize and use relatively complex thinking processes.

When to Use Lower-Level and Higher-Level Questions

Lower-Level Questions

Lower-level questions are appropriate when our purpose is to check learners' understanding of basic information. A productive pattern for this kind of questioning involves a three-part sequence:

1. We ask the question.
2. The learner responds to it.
3. We react to the learner's response.

Research suggests that these questions should be delivered at a brisk pace and that learners should be expected to respond quickly (Good & Brophy, 1994). This allows for a large number of recall questions to be asked in a short period of time. It also provides opportunities for many learners in a class to respond. A fairly fast-paced pattern of questioning keeps learners alert, and gives us opportunities to diagnose and respond to any misunderstandings revealed in answers from a wide cross section of class members.

Higher-Level Questions

If our aim is to stimulate more sophisticated learner thinking, then higher-level questions sometimes are preferred (Ramsey, Gabbard, Clawson, Lee, & Henson, 1990). Redfield and Rousseau's review of research related to questioning (Redfield & Rousseau, 1981) revealed that teachers' use of higher-level questions is associated with better learner achievement. However, more recent summaries of research reveal inconsistent results regarding the effects of higher-level questions on learner achievement (Good & Brophy, 1994).

For example, we now understand that asking higher-level questions, by itself, will not ensure academic success. Learners must have the knowledge base necessary to engage in complex thinking tasks. For a well-prepared high school class, a higher-level question such as, "How would you compare and contrast the late nine-

Does Thinking at School Spell Trouble at Home?

Naomi Belton is in her sixth year of teaching 4th-graders at Lomax Elementary School. During the summers and at night, she has been working on a master's degree in education. At this stage of her career, she is especially interested in improving her classroom instruction. This interest has prompted her to read the teacher-effectiveness literature in great depth, and she has also taken several courses on instructional improvement. From her study, she has decided to use more higher-level questions in her discussions. She understands that, under some conditions, this might prompt people in her class to more serious thinking. She has been quite pleased with the results of this change in her questioning patterns. Her pupils are doing a better job of analyzing sophisticated issues. They have also started to ask more penetrating questions on their own.

This success has come at a price. For the first time, she has had parents complaining to her principal. Only three parents have been involved, but for someone like Naomi, who never had a parent ever complain about her instruction, this development has been something of a shock.

Although specific concerns that individual parents have raised have not been exactly the same, all the complaints have centered around her efforts to turn her learners into more able thinkers. Pupils, it seems, are taking their new-found thinking powers home. They are beginning to challenge statements their parents are making. The principal told Naomi that one parent said, "I'm tired of having a 9-year-old question my judgments. These kids are too young for this sort of thing. I want my child to listen to what I say and do what I tell her to do. Lately, it's just argue, argue, argue."

What does Naomi see as the purpose of her new questioning technique? Is it her intention to make members of her class more difficult for parents to deal with? How might some members of her class be perceiving her changed instructional style? What might they believe the purpose of this kind of teaching to be? In what ways might their views differ from Naomi's?

How legitimate are the concerns of the parents who have complained? Specifically, what are they worried about? What do they believe Naomi's instructional priorities should be? How would Naomi react to their views about the purposes of "good" teaching?

To what extent should Naomi be concerned about the reactions of these parents? Should this situation be viewed as particularly troublesome by the principal? What might the principal recommend? What does this situation tell us about some differences between the values of Naomi and those parents who have complained? What do you think Naomi should do? What do your recommendations tell you about your own values and priorities?

teenth-century foreign policies of France and the United Kingdom?" might produce some insightful responses from learners. On the other hand, if students who were asked this question lacked basic information about the nineteenth-century foreign policies of the two countries, responses probably would reflect more wild guessing than sophisticated thought.

Whether higher-level or lower-level questions are "best" seems to be determined by variables associated with the particular goals we have established for a specific lesson and with variables related to the individual instructional context (Good & Brophy, 1994). The impact of questions of various kinds on learners continues to be an area of interest to educational researchers.

Learner-Initiated Questions

Discussions about the effect of questions sometimes overlook the important category of learner-initiated questions. The questions they ask often reveal a great deal about the effectiveness of what we have taught. They can also be an important information source for regarding some misconceptions they may have. Insights we gain from learner questions can be an invaluable aid to us as we plan lessons that are responsive to their real instructional needs (Heckman, Confer, & Hakim, 1994).

Clarity of Questions

One difficulty we face is wording our questions so that learners clearly understand what we are asking. Many questions that appear deceptively simple on the surface can, upon closer examination, be responded to in many ways. For example, a learner could logically answer the question, "Who was the first President of the United States?" with any of the following responses:

- a man
- a Virginian
- a general
- a person named George Washington

To avoid this situation, we need to word questions in ways that make it unnecessary for learners to guess at the nature of the information we are seeking.

Some research suggests that we should avoid beginning a discussion with a series of questions. Cazden (1986) has argued that it is better for us to provide some general background information before beginning to ask questions. This establishes a context for the questions to follow and results in better learner answers.

One practice that greatly interferes with clarity is asking a large question that contains two, three, or even more questions within it. Learners find this confusing, and they are often puzzled as to where to start their answers. Some of them deal with this dilemma by refusing to answer the question at all. It is much better for questions to be asked one at a time. Shorter questions are preferred (Good & Brophy, 1994). Additionally, the vocabulary we use in our questions should be within the grasp of our learners.

Checking on Learner Responses

Planning for successful questioning requires us to do more than prepare good questions. We must also be prepared to listen to what learners say and to respond appropriately. At one level, this amounts to nothing more than listening to responses to ensure that learners have a basic understanding of the content. If they don't, additional information needs to be presented, and low-level questions must then be asked to confirm whether or not they now understand it.

Our responses will vary based on what is happening in the classroom. For example, we often use probing questions to challenge learners' judgments when they jump to premature conclusions about complex issues. When a discussion featuring many questions has gone on for some time, we often pause to summarize what has been said. When learners are using vague terminology, we step in to ask for clarification. In summary, our reactions should convey to learners that their answers are being listened to carefully. This suggests to learners that their responses to questions are important and should be made thoughtfully.

Wait Time

The interval between the time we ask a question and when a learner responds is called *wait time*. Teachers have been found to wait an astonishingly short period before either answering their own questions, rephrasing their questions, or calling on different learners to respond. Rowe (1986) reported that, on average, teachers wait less than one second for learners to respond.

Abundant research exists that supports a connection between the length of time we wait for responses after asking questions and learner achievement. Achievement levels on tests demanding higher-level thinking have been found to be higher for learners in classes where we teachers wait at least three seconds for responses to questions (Tobin, 1987).

Efforts to increase teacher wait time have produced interesting results. When our average wait time increases, we tend to ask a smaller number of total questions but to increase the number of higher-level questions among those we ask. When we wait longer, we also seem to make greater use of learners' answers in class discussions. Finally, when we change our behavior and increase our wait time, we often change our attitudes about the capabilities of some learners in our classes (Rowe, 1986). This attitude change appears to stem from the fact that when average wait times are longer, some learners who have not previously answered questions become more active participants in discussions, and these increased levels of involvement result in our raising our estimations of these learners' general abilities.

HOMEWORK AND LEARNING

We sometimes rely on homework as a means of checking on what learners have derived from a lesson or series of lessons. Sometimes we assign homework out of a belief that it facilitates achievement. Sometimes it does, and sometimes it doesn't.

Herman Cooper (1989) reviewed many research studies focusing on the relationship between homework and learner achievement. He found that studies generally reported that although homework had a positive influence on achievement, the magnitude of this effect varied greatly depending on learners' ages. Homework was found to have the most impact on the achievement of high school students. Homework's benefit for junior high school students' achievement was only about half as great as that for senior high school students. For elementary learners, homework was found to affect their levels of achievement only marginally.

For junior high school and senior high school students, length of homework assignments appears to have an impact. Academic achievement for junior high school students tends to go up with length of homework assignments until a limit somewhere between one and two hours a night is reached; longer homework assignments were not found to have a facilitating effect on the learning of these students. Senior high school students profit from somewhat longer homework assignments than do junior high school students.

OBSERVING IN THE CLASSROOM

We may want to know whether our patterns of classroom behavior are consistent with those researchers have found to be effective. There are some basic tools we can use to gather this kind of information. These include *event sampling* and *time sampling*.

Event sampling requires the presence of an observer who records information about specific classroom events that might interest us. For example, an observer might be interested in noting what we do to motivate learners. In such a case, the observer would simply write down everything we did during the lesson that related to the general issue of motivation.

In time sampling, the observer records what is happening in the classroom at selected time intervals. For example, an observer could decide to take a sample once every 15 seconds. If we were lecturing at the end of the first 15-second interval, the observer would simply note "1 — lecturing." If the lecture were still going on at the end of the next 15-second interval, the observer would write "2 — lecturing." If we were asking a question at the end of the third 15-second interval, the observer would write "3 — teacher question." This kind of a scheme results in information that provides a general profile of activity during a lesson. It tends to capture the flow of a lesson and provides us with a great deal of information for analysis.

Many different kinds of observational tools can be developed based on event sampling, time sampling, or a combination of the two approaches. Some examples are introduced in the following subsections.

Narrative Approaches

Observers using narrative approaches, sometimes referred to as *scripting* approaches, try to capture information about what is going on in the classroom by rapidly writing down everything that is observed. Since much of what happens in a classroom is verbal, narrative approaches focus heavily on what we and our learners say.

A basic problem with an unstructured narrative approach is that much happens in a classroom so quickly that it is impossible for everything to be recorded.

This classroom observer is using an observational tool to gather information that will be shared later with the teacher. The teacher will use the information to make decisions about changes in procedures.

What is recorded may provide us with just a partial picture of what happened. To avoid this limitation, some observers prefer to use a more narrowly focused version, called *selective verbatim*.

When using a selective verbatim approach, the observer identifies a particular dimension of classroom verbal interaction as a focus. Then the observer records everything said that falls into this targeted category. Targeted categories might include such areas as "teacher questions," "motivational statements," "classroom control statements," and "praise statements." The focus for a selective verbatim approach is limited only by the creativity and interests of the observer.

Suppose an observer were interested in the types of praise statements we made during one of our lessons. During the observation period, the observer would write down everything we said each time a learner was praised. (Sometimes observers make an audio recording of the lesson so they can recheck the accuracy of what they wrote down during the live observation.)

Results of a selective verbatim observation can be organized into a selective verbatim record, which can provide data for a useful analysis. For example, had the focus been praise behavior, an observer may want to consider such questions as:

- Did the teacher use a variety of praise statements?
- How adequate was the quantity of praise statements?
- Were praise statements tied more to academic performance or to other kinds of learner behavior?
- Were more praise statements directed toward individuals or to the class as a whole?

An example of a selective verbatim record is provided in Figure 13-1.

Figure 13-1
Example of a selective verbatim
record

Focus: **Teacher Praise Statements**

Kind of lesson: **Arithmetic—Grade 5**

Time	*Teacher Statements*
9:02	Thank you for sitting down.
9:03	I appreciate that.
9:05	You have really been doing a good job on this unit.
9:09	Good answer.
9:10	Okay, good.
9:13	Good, I like that.
9:13	Right!
9:15	Good.
9:18	Juan, you used a good method for finding the answer.
9:20	I'm glad you all started to work so promptly.

Frequency Counts

Frequency counts focus on the number of occurrences of behaviors of interest. Behavior categories are identified by the observer before the observation begins. Frequency count observations might focus on such categories as:

- the number of teacher praise statements
- the number of high-level teacher questions (demanding sophisticated thinking)
- the number of low-level teacher questions (demanding only simple recall of basic information)
- the number of classroom disruptions
- the number of times individual learners visit learning centers
- the number of times learners made correct (or incorrect) responses to teacher questions

Frequency count systems are easy to use. A simple record is maintained of the number of times each selected focus behavior occurs. Tally marks are often used to indicate each occurrence.

An example of a frequency count system is provided in Figure 13-2. Look at Figure 13-2. Because frequency count systems do not require much writing, it is possible for tallies to be made related to a fairly large number of behaviors. This example yields information that might help an observer to suggest some teacher behaviors that seemed to prompt learner involvement in the lesson.

Figure 13-2

Example of a frequency-count system

Focus: **Teacher Statements and their Relationship to Learner Participation in a Discussion**

Directions: Tally each teacher behavior that has a positive impact on getting learners involved in the discussion. (These are found under the heading "Teacher Facilitating Moves.") Also tally each teacher behavior that has a negative impact on getting learners involved in the discussion. (These are found under the heading "Teacher Inhibiting Moves.") Tally learner responses that are correct and those that are incorrect. Also provide a tally for each time the teacher asks a question and there is no learner response at all. Finally, tally each time a learner initiates a question or a comment. (These are to be made under the heading "Learner Responses.")

Teacher Facilitating Moves
   Asks clear question:
   Asks for learner response (waits more than three seconds):
   Praises learner comment:
   Uses learner comment in lesson:
   Provides positive nonverbal reinforcement:

Teacher Inhibiting Moves
   Asks ambiguous question:
   Asks multiple questions:
   Does not wait for learner response:
   Criticizes learner response:
   Sends negative nonverbal signals:

Learner Responses
   Number of correct learner responses:
   Number of incorrect learner responses:
   Absence of any learner responses to question:
   Number of learner-initiated questions or comments:

Coding Systems

Coding systems require the use of codes or symbols that represent behaviors of interest to the observer. Symbols may vary in their complexity, from a simple system of checks, minuses, and pluses to a complex scheme that assigns numbers to a wide array of individual behaviors. Usually, a record using the codes is made after a pre-established interval of time has passed. For example, the observer might use codes to record behaviors once every 20 seconds.

It is not always necessary for an observer to have the entire coding scheme completely developed before a classroom observation begins. Sometimes new codes can be added during the observation itself as interesting behaviors occur that had not been included in the initial scheme. This ability to add new codes even during the observation gives a great deal of flexibility to observation systems using coding schemes.

For example, suppose an observer began an observation with a very simple coding scheme in mind. It might feature just these two codes:

1 — indicates a learner who is working on the assigned task
2 — indicates a learner who is not working on the assigned task

During the actual observation, the observer might note that some learners were out of their seat, talking, or working on school work other than the assigned task. The observer may decide to add specific codes to indicate these behaviors. (One way to do this would be to designate code *2a* for "out of seat," code *2b* for "talking," and code *2c* for "other school work." Code *2* would be reserved for all additional examples of learners' not working on assigned tasks.) An example of an observation system using coding is provided in Figure 13-3.

Seating-Chart Systems

Observation systems involving the use of seating charts often are appropriate when the focus is on learner behaviors. For example, we might want to know which learners are contributing to a discussion or which ones are staying on task when we assign seat work. A system might be devised that would record information about which learners we worked with during a given class period. Seating chart schemes also work well when we are curious about our location in the classroom during different parts of an instructional period.

In developing a seating-chart system, the observer begins by making a sketch of the classroom that includes the locations of individual learner seats. Once this basic chart has been completed and learners have entered the classroom, the observer may want to record whether individual seats are occupied by males or females. This can be done by writing a small *m* for male or a small *f* for female on each seat represented in the chart.

Next, the observer develops a set of symbols to represent the various aspects of instruction that are to be emphasized. For example, a simple arrow pointing to a seat might indicate a teacher question to a particular learner, and a simple arrow pointing away from the seat might indicate a communication directed from a particular learner to the teacher.

Numerals or letters can be designated to stand for different kinds of things individual learners are observed doing at selected time intervals during the lesson. The location of the teacher at specific places in the room at different times could be indicated by a sequence of circled numbers (*1* indicating the first location, *2* indicating the second, and so forth). Any symbols that work for the observer are acceptable.

Figure 13-4 provides an example of an observational system that features a seating chart. Many interesting questions can be answered by examining data gathered from a seating chart system. Look at the sample information provided in the chart featured in Figure 13-4. Using this information, an observer might be able to answer questions such as:

• How many learners were involved in the discussion?
• Were more males or females called on?

Figure 13-3
Example of a coding system
observation scheme

Focus: Motivational Strategies

Directions: During each five-minute time segment of the lesson, record the letters indicating the motivational strategies used by the teacher. Record letters in the sequence of their occurrence. If new motivational strategies are used that are not on the list, add them and give them a letter.

Motivational Strategy	Record
	5 min.
a. Uses novelty	_____
b. Appeals to curiosity	_____
c. Provides concrete reinforcer	_____
d. Provides dramatic buildup	_____
e. Indicates importance of task	_____
	5 min.
f. Relates to learner needs, interests	_____
g. Provides encouragement	_____
h. Predicts success or enjoyment	_____
I. Warns about testing, grades	_____
j. Threatens punishment for noncompletion	_____
	5 min.
k. _____	_____
l. _____	_____
_____	_____
_____	_____
_____	_____
	5 min.
_____	_____
_____	_____
_____	_____
_____	_____
_____	_____

- Did the teacher have a tendency to call more frequently on learners seated on one side of the room? seated in the front as opposed to the back of the room?
- How many learners who volunteered were not recognized by the teacher? What might be the long-term impact on a learner's willingness to volunteer if he or she were rarely recognized?

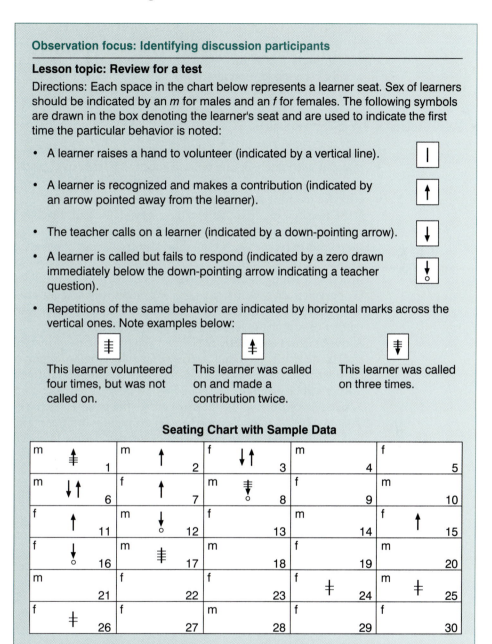

Figure 13-4

Example of a seating-chart observation scheme (with sample data)

These observational techniques have relevance for you who are planning to become teachers. When you use them to make carefully planned observations, you can gain important insights about kinds of teacher behaviors that "work" in the real world of the school classroom.

• Key Ideas in Summary

- Arguments have long raged about the existence of a body of research evidence that can adequately define what is meant by "effective" teaching. Increasingly, though, evidence is indicating that at least some variables associated with effective teaching have been discovered.

- Most research on effective teaching has focused on teacher behaviors associated with increases in learners' levels of achievement. This emphasis has been supported in recent years by public concerns about the issue of subject-matter learning in the schools.

- In active teaching, teachers play a central role and lead the class in the role of a (1) presenter of new information, (2) monitor of learner progress, (3) planner of opportunities for learners to apply what they have learned, and (4) re-teacher of content to learners who are confused.

- Active teachers are greatly concerned about the issue of matching their instruction to needs of individual learners. In achieving an appropriate match, they consider such things as the difficulty of the material relative to the individual learner's ability and the learner's level of interest in the content to be taught.

- Active teachers are very concerned about the issue of good lesson presentation. This involves actions designed to (1) stimulate and maintain learner interest, (2) present material systematically, (3) model expected behaviors and expected products of learning, (4) maintain an appropriate lesson pace, (5) ask questions skillfully, (6) provide opportunities for learners to practice what they have learned, and (7) monitor learners' progress.

- Research has established the importance of clarity as a teacher variable associated with learner achievement. Among dimensions of clarity are the teacher's verbal and nonverbal styles, lesson presentation style, and proficiency in providing cogent explanations.

- Effective teachers use class time productively. They make decisions related to allocated time, engaged time, and academic learning time.

- Teachers' expectations have an influence on how individual learners perform. Researchers have found that (1) teachers have certain behavioral expectations of learners, (2) teachers' behaviors toward learners vary in terms of what they believe that individual learners can do, (3) learners' self-concepts are affected by how they perceive themselves to be viewed by their teachers, and (4) teachers who are conscious of the impact of their expectations can monitor and adjust them in ways that can improve learners' performance.

- Teachers' questioning patterns often influence learning. Teachers tend to ask questions of two basic types: lower-level questions and higher-level questions.

Lower-level questions call on learners to recall specific items of previously introduced information. Higher-level questions require learners to use more complex thinking processes.

• Many observation systems are available that can be used to provide specific information to teachers about what goes on in their classrooms. Some of these approaches use time sampling, others use event sampling, and still others employ a combination of the two.

• Review and Discussion Questions

1. Is there research-based knowledge available today that pinpoints behaviors associated with effective teaching?
2. What criteria should be used in determining a teacher's relative effectiveness?
3. What are some general characteristics of active teaching?
4. What goes on during the task analysis phase of instructional planning?
5. What are some differences between motivation that occurs (a) before a learning sequence begins, (b) during a learning sequence, and (c) at the end of a learning sequence?
6. What are the steps in the Hunter-Russell model?
7. Why is the issue of clarity so important, and what are some dimensions of teacher clarity?
8. Is a teacher decision to increase the amount of (a) allocated time related to a given topic or (b) academic learning related to a given topic more likely to increase the overall performance of a class on a test related to the selected topic?
9. Research on the effect of asking higher-level and lower-level questions on learners' academic achievement has found mixed results. How might you explain these inconsistent findings?
10. What are some features of observation instruments based on (a) narrative approaches, (b) frequency counts, (c) coding systems, and (d) seating-chart systems?

• Ideas for Field Experiences, Projects, and Enrichment

1. Review ideas for gathering observational data. Select one category associated with teacher effectiveness that was introduced in this chapter. Visit a classroom and gather data related to this category using an observation system of your own design. You may wish to consider a scheme based on a narrative approach, frequency counts, a coding system, or a seating chart.
2. A thread that runs through much recent teacher-effectiveness research is the idea that effective behaviors are contextual. This means that a pattern that is effective with certain kinds of learners and for teaching certain levels of understanding or skills may not necessarily work well with other learners and for teaching other levels of understanding. With your instructor's guidance, review some research literature associated with the topic of direct instruction. Under what circumstances does this approach seem to work well? Under what circumstances has it been found to be less appropriate? Present your conclusions in the form of a brief oral report.
3. Some of the research on teacher effectiveness has produced results that have surprised some people, particularly when the discovered information has challenged some popu-

larly held beliefs. With your instructor's guidance, look up some research findings associated with teacher praise. Is teacher praise always good? Report your conclusions in the form of a short paper.

4. Today, teachers are increasingly getting involved with research in their own classrooms. Much of this research is directed at improving their own instruction. Review some articles in education journals (look for titles in such sources as the *Education Index*) that focus on the topic of the teacher as researcher. Then share with the rest of the class what you find out about the approaches teachers are taking to gather research about their own instruction and some of the things this research is revealing. (You might wish to look ahead to Chapter 14, "Teachers as Researchers.")

5. Prepare a list of source materials related to research data about effective teaching. Ask your instructor for some ideas to get you started. Combine your list with those prepared by others in your class. Eliminate common entries, produce a single composite list, and prepare copies for the files of all class members.

• References

Acheson, K. A., & Gall, M. (1992). *Techniques in the clinical supervision of teachers*. White Plains, NY: Longman.

Berliner, D. C. (1984). The half-full glass: A review of research on teaching. In P. L. Hosford (Ed.), *Using what we know about teaching* (pp. 51–77). Alexandria, VA: Association for Supervision and Curriculum Development.

Cazden, C. (1986). Classroom discourse. In M. Wittrock (Ed.), *Handbook of research on teaching* (3rd ed., pp. 432–463). New York: Macmillan.

Cooper, H. (1989). Synthesis of research on homework. *Educational Leadership, 47*(3), 85–91.

DeGarmo, C. (1903). *Interest in education: The doctrine of interest and its concrete applications*. New York: Macmillan.

Denton, J. J., Armstrong, D. G., & Savage, T. V. (1980). Matching events of instruction to objectives. *Theory into Practice, 19*(1), 10–14.

Finn, J. D. (1993). *School engagement and students at risk*. Washington, DC: National Center for Education Statistics, U.S. Department of Education.

Good, T. L., & Brophy, J. E. (1994). *Looking in classrooms* (6th ed.). New York: HarperCollins.

Goodlad, J. A. (1984). *A place called school*. New York: McGraw-Hill.

Heckman, P. E., Confer, C. B., & Hakim, D. C. (1994). Planting seeds: Understanding through investigation. *Educational Leadership, 51*(5), 36–39.

Hunter, M., & Russell, D. (1977). How can I plan more effective lessons? *Instructor, 87*(2), 74–75, 88.

Meyer, A. E. (1975). *Grandmasters of educational thought*. New York: McGraw-Hill.

Posner, R. S. (1987). Pacing and sequencing. In M. J. Dunken (Ed.), *The international encyclopedia of teaching and teacher education* (pp. 266–272). Oxford, England: Pergamon Press.

Ramsey, I., Gabbard, C., Clawson, K., Lee, L., & Henson, K. T. (1990). Questioning: An effective teaching method. *The Clearing House, 63*(9), 420–422.

Redfield, D., & Rousseau, E. (1981). A meta-analysis of experimental research on teacher questioning behavior. *Review of Educational Research, 18*(2), 237–245.

Rosenshine, B., & Stevens, R. (1986). Teaching functions. In M. Wittrock (Ed.), *Handbook of research on teaching* (3rd ed., pp. 376–391). New York: Macmillan.

Rowe, M. B. (1986). Wait time: Slowing down may be a way of speeding up. *Journal of Teacher Education, 37*(1), 43–50.

Tobin, K. (1987). The role of wait time in higher cognitive learning. *Review of Educational Research, 24*(1), 69–95.

Walker, V. N., & Chance, E. W. (1994/1995). National award winning teachers' exemplary instructional techniques and activities. *National Forum of Teacher Education Journal, 5*(l), 11–24.

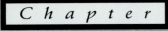
14

Teachers as
Researchers

OBJECTIVES

- Recognize that research can empower teachers.
- Describe several ways that action research benefits teachers.
- Explain how involvement with research changes teachers' behaviors toward students.
- Describe the transition that has occurred in how American teachers are involved with research.
- Contrast early teacher perceptions toward research with current teacher perceptions toward research.
- Identify steps followed in a typical teacher-research project.

Some teachers began using research in their classrooms as early as the beginning of the twentieth century (Lowery, 1908), but this practice did not spread for 50 years. In fact, early teacher research was done without much regard to bringing immediate improvement to teaching.

The few teachers who were associated with research participated as assistants to researchers. Many of them became involved only because they were forced to do so (Glatthorn, 1993). In many cases, these teachers had little or no communications with the researcher (Bain & Groseclose, 1979). Certainly, they were not included in selecting the problems to be studied. They permitted the researchers to use their classrooms, or they helped the researcher by collecting data. When gathered, the data were turned over to the researcher, often without the teacher even knowing the results (Atkin, 1989).

This early pattern began to change as early as the 1920s. During these years, John Dewey and others began arguing that teachers should study their own practices for the purpose of developing solutions to practical problems. In the late 1940s, the term *action research* was applied to these kinds of teacher investigations. Action research focused on problems encountered in the classrooms taught by the teachers who were the researchers rather than on problems of a more theoretical nature that were of greater interest to university-based researchers.

Today, research conducted by classroom teachers seeks to expand the teacher's role as an inquirer about the profession (Copper, 1990). This is done through systematic observation of classroom practices and instructional modification taken in response to findings of these research efforts. When we function as researchers, results can lead to general improvement of the curriculum, development of better inservice programs, and establishment of a knowledge base that can contribute to efforts to upgrade the quality of our schools (Johnson, 1993). Research we do as teachers can assist in our own professional development. Results give us valuable information we can use to self-monitor our instructional behaviors and modify them in directions that make sense in light of our research findings.

Even though teachers' interest in becoming more actively involved in classroom research is on the upswing, many teachers still do not function as researchers. In part, a disinclination of some teachers to pay serious attention to research findings or to conduct action research studies of their own may have resulted from a belief that teachers' actions had to have little direct influence on learners' levels of achievement. Home environments, genetic factors, and kinds of learning materials purchased by the school, for example, have been seen as variables having at least as much impact on learners' achievement as teachers. Although these things do have some influence on what people in our classrooms learn, recent careful scholarship has repeatedly shown that teachers are a key determiner of student academic success (Stake & Easley, 1978).

Effective teachers believe that learners are capable regardless of any less-than-optimal home and environmental conditions they may experience. When we set high goals for our learners, believe they can succeed, and design appropriate instructional experiences for them, prospects increase that they will do well.

BARRIERS TO RESEARCH BY TEACHERS

Some barriers continue to stand in the way of teachers who wish to do classroom research. For example, relatively few teacher preparation programs place much emphasis on research. Indeed, many beginning teachers know little about research findings in areas relevant to classroom practice, let alone details about how a teacher might initiate a classroom research project on his or her own. As a result, there has been a tendency for "teachers [to] ignore research and overestimate the value of personal experience" (Egbert, 1984, p. 14). In part, this perspective seems to result from (1) a general belief by teachers that research is too theoretical and superficial and (2) a professional work environment for teachers that is concrete and action oriented (Chattin-McNichols & Loeffler, 1989; Cuban, 1992). Time is also a factor. As Linda Darling-Hammond (1993) has pointed out, our schedules seldom provide time for research or, indeed, for planning of any type (Darling-Hammond, 1993).

Some teachers may have resisted personal involvement in classroom research because experimentation can lead to change. Change often brings discomfort. It is much less threatening for us to continue to do what we have always been doing and to avoid asking questions that might suggest the appropriateness of some modifications of usual ways of doing things.

Sometimes school administrators have discouraged experimentation. Principals who themselves have had little exposure to teachers' roles as researchers may believe that teachers are stepping out of their expected areas of responsibility when they commit time to planning and carrying out research investigations. Although they may not say so in as many words, such administrators send an implicit message that tells teachers to leave research to the academics because the teachers' job is to instruct members of their classes.

Happily, many administrators today have more enlightened views. Educational leadership programs encourage principals to expand roles of all of their staff members. In addition, the national movement to decentralize management of schools is making principals and teachers more accountable for planning and delivering instructional programs that are successful. This encourages experimentation as professionals in individual schools seek ways to better serve their own learner populations.

TEACHER RESEARCH

The kind of research activity that makes most sense given our interests and priorities as classroom teachers is *teacher research*. Teacher research is the more modern term for action research. As noted previously, there is a long tradition of action research in the schools, and interest in it is broadening. People entering the profession today are likely to find at least some individuals in their buildings who are active teacher researchers, and they will probably discover the school environment hospitable to research efforts they may wish to undertake themselves.

Teacher research has been defined in many ways. Most definitions center on the idea that teacher research refers to investigations that teachers conduct or co-

conduct in the classroom to improve their teaching. For example, Lytle and Cochran-Smith (1990) defined it as "systematic, intentional inquiry by teachers" (p. 83). McCutcheon and Jung (1990) suggest that it involves "inquiry teachers undertake to understand and improve their own practice" (p. 144). This definition identifies the researchers as teachers.

Teacher research has several specific advantages over traditional university-based research for us who teach. The following list enumerates some of these:

- The "problem" we select to identify is of our own choosing. It is relevant to our own learners and our own classroom.
- We do not seek findings that are necessarily generalizable to other settings. Our interest is in improving instruction or in providing some other kind of a benefit in our own setting of practice.
- Findings can give us a rationale we can use to make practical decisions. We may find that the results confirm that what we are doing is good. They may also suggest the appropriateness of trying alternative approaches.
- We frequently work with other teachers in conducting teacher research projects. These kinds of efforts can build a stronger sense of professional community.
- We typically undertake projects that require a fairly short time to complete. As a result, we do not need to wait months or even years to get the results and to act upon them.
- Since the results we get are based on local populations of learners, we gain data that can be very convincing when we need information to convince administrators, school board members, parents, and other community members about the need for changes.

BENEFITS TO TEACHERS

How can involvement in teacher research help us? What do we know about its effects? Why should we bother to make time for teacher research given the many other obligations we have to discharge as professional teachers? Interesting answers to these questions are beginning to emerge (Henson, 1996).

To begin with, there is evidence that teachers who have become active teacher researchers gain knowledge about research methodologies and their appropriateness as approaches to different kinds of problems. These individuals also tend to do more serious thinking about all of their own instructional practices than teachers who have not engaged in teacher research (Oja & Pine, 1989). Conducting teacher research also raises teachers' levels of awareness about the methods used and their effects on learning, and prompts teachers to develop an ongoing commitment to staying current (Stevens, Slanton, & Bunny, 1992; Sardo-Brown, 1992). Because our learners have varying learning styles, we need to employ a wide repertoire of teaching methods. Researchers have reported that through making teachers more aware, involvement with research leads teachers to develop a greater variety of teaching methods (Fullan, 1982; Dicker, 1990; Santa, 1990).

Are Kids in Teacher-Research Studies Just Guinea Pigs?

Seventeen years in the classroom is a long time. That's how long Moira McKenna has been working with her 3rd-graders. After so many years, some teachers lose their enthusiastic edge. But not Moira. She charges off for Van Buren Elementary each morning eager and ready to get to work. It wasn't always this way, however.

Five years ago, Moira told one of her friends, "I'm sure that alarm clock goes off earlier every day. I'm getting to the point that I just have to force myself to get up and get ready to go to work. I must be getting old."

Back then, Moira's work in the classroom didn't have the sharp professional edge that characterized her teaching in the early days. Whereas her work was adequate, she just didn't get pumped up much any more about what she was doing. Then her life changed.

A local teacher who had done a lot of research in her own classroom received an appointment as an adjunct professor. She organized a class called "The Teacher as Researcher" that was scheduled to meet on Thursday nights in one of the local schools. Moira needed a few more university credits to qualify for the next step on the salary schedule, and she enrolled. She headed off to the course expecting it to be a mildly interesting experience, but certainly nothing particularly special. She was wrong.

The instructor's experience included years of work "in the trenches" as a teacher, and she knew that teachers had little patience with a lot of educational research that seemed to have little practical relevance for their own classroom. Members of the group really perked up when the instructor started asking them to identify some problems they were having with kids in their own classrooms. She began explaining some of her own frustrations and how she had designed some simple research studies to help get at sources of some of the problems. After the first several classes, Moira found herself thinking, my God, this person is actually making sense. She's talking about doing something really practical. This is neat.

By the end of the course, Moira had initiated two separate research studies in her own classroom. One focused on helping her learners pay more attention to their spelling on their written assignments. The other looked at ways to get more pupils involved during classroom discussions. As a result of these projects, Moira made some changes, and she found that learners were spelling better on their papers and many more youngsters were participating during classroom discussions. Moira became a believer. She recognized the power of her own research to make her a more effective teacher, and she found her enthusiasm for the profession being rekindled.

As a result of her experiences, Moira has become an eloquent spokesperson for teachers as researchers. She has conducted many studies of her own. She has been invited to share some of her findings at meetings with other teachers. She has made numerous inservice presentations promoting the benefits of teacher research.

Teacher research can also provide us with interesting and important insights about what our learners know and think. One technique teacher researchers use to gather this kind of information is the *clinical interview*. This procedure is "specifically designed to elicit information in an accepting environment, one in which children feel comfortable sharing their beliefs and explanations, some not yet completely developed" (Flake, Kuhs, Donnelly, & Ebert,

Recently, Moira's work came to the attention of the education editor of the local newspaper. This person came to the school, interviewed Moira, and prepared a long feature article on her work. In the interview, Moira spoke about a research project she has in mind for the coming spring semester. She wants to study a new approach to developing writing skills that will require her class members to prepare many more written assignments as part of their science and mathematics lessons than have ever been required before.

Publication of the article netted Moira some wonderfully supportive comments from her principal and from other teachers in her building. The article also caught the eye of several parents of pupils in her class. One group of parents was not pleased at all. A spokesperson for this group, Mr. Ogden, went to a school board meeting. At the end of the regular agenda, the president of the board invited anyone in attendance to make a comment. Mr. Ogden's hand went up.

"You have the floor," said the president of the board.

"Thank you very much. I am here speaking on behalf of a group of parents of children who are in Moira McKenna's third grade classroom at Van Buren. We read the article in the paper about how she's going to try some unproved approach with our kids, beginning right after the first of the year.

"We strongly object to our children being used as guinea pigs. We're not talking about laboratory animals here. We're dealing with children's lives. These innocent youngsters have no right to avoid going to school. We think it is unfair and unethical for a teacher to use them as subjects in an experiment. We want this project stopped."

Members of the board listened attentively. At the conclusion of Mr. Ogden's remarks, the president commented, "Thank you for taking time to share concerns of your group with us this evening. Certainly everybody here is interested in doing what is right for the children. Be assured that this matter will be looked into."

What assumptions has Moira made about teacher research? What does she see as the purpose of this kind of activity? How might she react to the charge that she is setting up her learners to function as "guinea pigs"? What do we know about some of Moira's basic values? How are they reflected in the information we have here?

What priorities are implied by the comments of Mr. Ogden on behalf of the group of concerned parents? Are there some legitimate concerns here? Why might members of this group of parents have developed these feelings?

Is there any kind of reasonable middle ground the board could use in resolving this potential conflict? What roles, if any, should be played by other teachers, administrators, and other parents? How do you think Moira McKenna feels about the reaction of the complaining parents? Is she likely to consider this group as representative of parents, or will she conclude that these people have views that are not generally shared? How will she decide?

In the end, what do you think the school board will do? What might you do if you were Moira McKenna?

1995, p. 406). The process begins with some focus questions we teachers design that we feel will elicit responses that will reveal information about learners' preconceptions or patterns of thinking. Often these questions are revised after one or two youngsters have been interviewed, and it becomes apparent that either wording of the original questions needs to be modified or that other questions need to be asked.

Clinical interviews sometimes reveal that learners who we initially believe to have poor backgrounds in subjects we are interested in teaching know more than we thought they did. At other times, we uncover misinformation that we can correct as we teach. One of the authors when working with some young learners had occasion to display a large picture of a cow with a very prominent udder. One of the youngsters in all seriousness asked, "Which one of those neat spigots squirts out the ice cream?"

Participation in teacher research can make us seem more interesting to the people we teach. Nobody enjoys a boring teacher. Learners rarely work to their capacity when they see that their teachers are bored and tired. Involvement with research can revitalize us and keep us searching for more information about effective teaching methods (Sucher, 1990). Participation in teacher research encourages us to become career-long learners (Boyer, 1990; Brownlie, 1990).

Teachers who continue to be effective over many years in the classroom keep up with their fields. Being involved in teacher research helps us to stay informed. Investigations we undertake on our own prompt a broader interest in research findings of others (Doyle, 1990). This kind of activity can also help us become more sophisticated consumers of research conducted by others (Bellon, Bellon, & Blank, 1992). Involvement in research has been found to help teachers develop a deeper understanding of their fields (Atkin, 1989).

Another reason to get involved with teacher research studies is the effect that this involvement has on our abilities to reach our goals. Bennett (1993) found that involvement with research makes teachers more goal oriented, better problem solvers, and more confident in their own expertise. If we become involved, we are more likely to be aware of both our own patterns of behavior and the causes of those behaviors (Oberg, 1990).

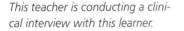

This teacher is conducting a clinical interview with this learner.

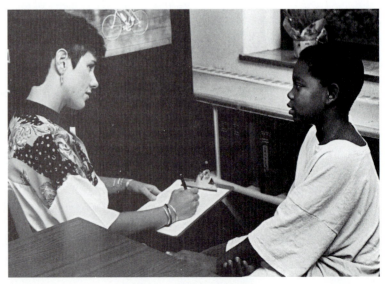

Participation in teacher research has also been found to have potential for changing our perceptions and attitudes. Several studies have found that those of us who engage in teacher research feel more positively about ourselves and our profession than colleagues who do no research (Carr & Kemmis, 1986; Boyer, 1990; Carson, 1990).

A summary of benefits of participation in teacher research was prepared by the Reading/Learning in Secondary Schools Subcommittee of the International Reading Association (1989). This group identified the following pluses for teachers who become involved in this kind of activity (1989):

- helps solve classroom problems
- encourages effective change
- revitalizes teachers
- empowers teachers to make decisions in their classrooms
- identifies effective teaching and learning methods
- promotes reflective teaching
- promotes ownership of effective practices
- verifies what methods work
- widens the range of teachers' professional skills
- provides a connection between instructional methods and results
- helps teachers apply research findings to their own classrooms
- enables teachers to become change agents

RESEARCH TRADITIONS

To understand some approaches to teacher research, we need at least a sketchy understanding of two major research traditions. The distinguished learning psychologist Jerome Bruner (1986) used the terms "top-down" and "bottom-up" to clarify some major features of each. The top-down position seeks broad explanatory principles. The purpose is to identify truths that are so powerful that they apply irrespective of any special local circumstances. This kind of research requires careful measurement of variables. Hence, the term *quantitative research* often is applied to top-down studies. Sometimes the top-down approach is said to be positivistic. Experiments in the sciences are examples of research that is associated with this tradition. There is also an experimental research tradition within education.

The bottom-up tradition, on the other hand, has a different set of operating assumptions. It places a heavy emphasis on differences in conditions in different places. The results of this kind of research are not "truths" that can be generalized to large numbers of other settings. Rather, they are insights that can shed light on circumstances associated with a particular context. Because of its emphasis on illuminating qualities associated with a particular context, the term *qualitative research* often is used to describe studies consistent with this tradition. Naturalistic and ethnographic studies that use techniques such as case studies are in the qualitative research tradition.

Today, we find large numbers of university-based researchers in education using both top-down and bottom-up designs to guide their inquiries. This was not always the case. A decade and more ago, the vast majority of educational researchers came out of a top-down orientation. Much of their work was what we call "process-product" research. The idea here is to identify specific things teachers do (processes) and then tie them to measures of pupil and student learning (products), often scores on tests. The purpose is to identify practices that "work" that can be replicated by other teachers in other schools.

Doing this kind of experimental work in schools often requires identification of distinct "experimental" and "control" groups of learners. These arrangements are difficult to make, and when this kind of research represented the majority of school-based inquiries, individual teachers found it hard to conduct research on their own. They simply lacked the resources, the time, and often even the interest to pursue investigations that required participation of learners beyond those in their own classrooms and that did not seem to promise results that would necessarily be particularly helpful to them in working with their own learners.

As bottom-up research gained new adherents among university-based educational researchers, however, the interest of teachers engaging in research activities in their own classrooms increased. This kind of research assumes that "teaching is a highly complex, context-specific activity in which differences across classrooms, schools, and communities are critically important" (Cochran-Smith & Lytle, 1990). Its purpose is to generate information that will lead to an enriched understanding of the specific context where the research took place. This could be a single school classroom. The focus of bottom-up research on a specific context and its intent to shed light on that context rather than to develop generalizations that are applicable to many other settings has made this orientation particularly attractive to teacher researchers. Although some teacher researchers do conduct experimental studies, it is fair to say that more of them conduct studies that are aligned with the bottom-up tradition.

Teacher researchers want to do more than simply "explain" what is going on in their classrooms. A defining feature of most teacher education research is that the researcher wishes to reflect upon what has been learned and to modify practices to solve a problem or to enhance learning. The intent is to make research knowledge a practical tool that can be used to make some kind of an improvement. For example, an elementary teacher may wish to know how several individual learners are reacting to role playing. The teacher may develop some initial questions to ask these learners, make arrangements to interview them (being prepared to modify questions, as appropriate), take notes on what they say, and consider some possible changes that might make the learners be more effective and more comfortable in subsequent role-playing activities.

A high school teacher, using an approach associated with the top-down, experimental tradition, may be interested in whether it is better to use questions as advance organizers before showing a videotape or whether it is better to use them after showing a videotape. Both arrangements can be tried, and the teacher can use results of a quiz over the content of the videotape lesson that featured questions before it was shown with results of a quiz over the lesson that featured questions after the tape was played.

As these examples illustrate, problems selected as subjects do not have to be strange or complex. Indeed, since the purpose is to provide information that will allow us to reflect on our practices and to modify them, as needed, the focus of some of the best teacher-research efforts is narrow and practical.

HOW TO BEGIN

Teacher research specialists Leslie Patterson, John Stansell, and Sharon Lee (1990) emphasize that questions that can serve as the focus for specific teacher research projects come from two basic sources: the classroom experience of the individual teacher and professional literature. As we work with our learners in our own classrooms, few days pass when we are not confronted with a problem, a concern, a challenge, or at least a minor vexation of some kind. These can lead to all kinds of questions with potential to serve as organizers for research. Here are some examples:

- Why did my learners like the unit on navigators but not the unit on pioneer life?
- Why do some members of my class get almost perfect scores on spelling tests and then misspell so many of the same words when I ask them to write something?
- What might members of my class do if I started to intersperse prompt questions throughout my discussions?
- If I give more essay tests, will this have any effect on how well members of my class do on standardized tests where they have to answer only multiple-choice questions?

Other good initial focus questions can come from articles in professional journals. For example, some researchers have found that learners who are asked higher-level questions (questions requiring them to use more sophisticated thinking processes) as part of their regular classroom instruction will do better on examinations that ask them to analyze issues. If we wanted to see whether the members of a class we are teaching might be helped to do better in analyzing issues if we were to ask more higher-level thinking questions when introducing new content, we could easily develop a focus question for a classroom research study. We might frame the question in this way: What will be the effect of interspersing frequent higher-level questions in lectures that will introduce new content on students' abilities to analyze issues?

Identifying a specific question begins the process of establishing a focus for teacher research. Even though the question is helpful, more is required before we will be able to proceed. Many questions do not suggest exactly what we need to be looking at. We must decide what to "look at" before we can proceed (Patterson et al., 1990). Suppose we had decided to use the following question to guide our research:

> What might members of my class do if I started to intersperse prompt questions throughout my discussions?

Some things we might "look at" include:

- the number of learners who are paying attention throughout the discussion (There may be changes over the period of time that I use prompt questions.)
- the nature of responses to questions that are asked (Responses may change in terms of their sophistication during the period of the research study.)
- participation in the discussion (Numbers of learners in the class who participate may change during the time I use prompt questions.)
- problem behaviors occurring during the discussion (Episodes of unacceptable classroom behavior may not stay the same during the period covered by the study.)

Once we have decided what to look at, we need to identify some things to "look for" (Patterson et al., 1990). We need to think about how any expected changes might reveal themselves. Sometimes it is useful to generate a list of behaviors to look for. These may be framed as short phrases or as questions. "Look-for" questions such as the following might be developed for the bulleted list of things to look at that was just introduced:

- How many learners indicate interest by looking at me during the discussion?
- How many hands are raised to volunteer information?
- What kinds of body language (nodding the head, frowning, smiling, other behaviors indicating that the learner is attending) suggest that learners are staying with the discussion?
- Are questions learners asked pertinent to the discussion?
- Do questions indicate that learners are following the logic of the discussion?
- What is the length of learner responses to questions? Are they giving me short one- or two-word answers, or are they making more extensive comments?
- As time goes by, do more learners give longer, more sophisticated answers?
- How many people are participating? Does this number increase as time goes by?
- How many times do I have to stop to handle a discipline problem? Do these incidents decrease in frequency as time goes by?

Once we have established an initial focus question and determined what we wish to look at and look for, we need to consider our data sources and our procedures for recording information. In the example we have been working with, our primary data source will be our personal observation of our learners as they participate in discussions. At some point, it might be appropriate to invite a colleague in to work as an observer. He or she might be able to record information about body language of learners and keep an accurate count of how many individuals participate in the discussions. Notes taken by this person would be another data source. Data sources used in a specific teacher research project will vary depending on the purpose and focus of the study.

Data in many teacher research studies is recorded in the form of "field notes" (Patterson et al., 1990). These are simply notes we write down about what has happened. Obviously we cannot do this at the same time we are teaching. These notes have to be written when time allows. There is no need to worry about capturing every detail. The intent is simply to take note of significant observations. Often the act of writing the field note prompts a recollection of important details. Part of their purpose is to make a record of what has happened, and part of their purpose is to stimulate us as the researcher to remember specific things that occurred (Patterson et al., 1990).

The data sources and our field notes tie directly back to our focus question, particularly as the focus question has been refined to make clear what it is we wish to look at and what it is we wish to look for. Figure 14-1 illustrates the relationship between the focus question and the data sources.

CONDUCTING RESEARCH: THE STEPS

Identifying a good focus for something we want to study is the first step of a sequence that can lead to a productive investigation. This sequence for planning and implementing an investigation is adapted from one initially developed by Leslie Patterson (1990):

1. establish a focus
2. identify an appropriate design
3. select, gather, and analyze data
4. prepare a report

The Focus

Some issues associated with refining the focus question were addressed in the discussion of how to begin in the previous section. Before we get to the point of iden-

This teacher is preparing field notes. The notes will provide a written record of what the teacher has observed.

Framing and Refining Research Questions   **Data Sources**

Step 1	Step 2	Step 3	Questions	Look At	Look For
How do kids respond to journal writing?	Do their written products change?	Do they become longer?	Entries longer?	Student journals	Number of words per entry
		Do they become more complex?	Entries more complex?	Student journals	Indices of grammatical, semantic complexity
		Do the topics and themes change?	Entries more varied?	Student journals	Number and variety of topics or themes
	Does their use of the writing process change?	Do they revise more than before?	More revision?	Journal writing	Instances of revision in process
				Student journals	Number, types, effectiveness of revisions
		Do they engage in any more prewriting?		Classroom talk	Informal interviews, conferences, class discussions, conversations
		Do they share their writing more? For what purposes?	More prewriting?	Journal writing	Instances of prewriting in process
	Do changes in journal writing show up in other writing?	Do changes show up in in-class writing assignments?	Writing shared?	Classroom talk	Informal interviews, conferences, class discussions, conversations
		Do changes show up in outside assignments?		Classroom talk	Informal interviews, conferences, class discussions, conversations
				Journal writing	Instances of sharing in process
		Do changes show up in any other writing?	Changes elsewhere?	Writing process (nonjournals)	Indicators of length, complexity, revision, prewriting, etc.
				Written products (nonjournals)	Indicators of length, complexity, etc.
				Writing process	Interviews with students, outside of class, other teachers

Figure 14-1

Refining the focus questions and pinpointing data sources

From *Teacher Research from Promise to Power* (pp. 12–13) by L. Patterson, J. C. Stansell, S. Lee, 1990, Katonah, NY: Richard C. Owens Publishers, Inc. Copyright © 1990 by Richard C. Owens Publishers, Inc. Reprinted with permission.

tifying the question, we need to think about some general categories of information that might be of interest to us. Leslie Patterson (1990) suggests that we must make decisions regarding:

- whether we want to focus on our whole class or just a few individuals
- whether we want to develop a "snapshot" of reality that brings into sharp focus reality at a particular time, or whether we want to gather information continuously over a longer time period, perhaps over the time a given unit is taught
- whether we are interested in the kinds of behaviors learners demonstrate in the classroom, or whether we are interested in the nature of the learning products (papers, scores on tests, and so forth) that learners produce
- whether we are interested in gathering information about what we do as teachers when interacting with learners, or whether our focus will be on what our learners are doing

The Design

Once we have established a clear focus, we need to think about the specific research approach we will take. At the most general level, we will need to decide whether we wish to use a top-down or a bottom-up approach. In part, this choice will depend on our own interests and priorities. If we are particularly interested in developing information that others may generalize to different settings, an experimental design associated with the top-down research tradition may make sense. On the other hand, if our primary intent is to solve a problem or simply to shed more light on a situation we are dealing with in our own classroom, a qualitative approach may make more sense. Because much teacher research seeks to solve problems of personal interest to the researcher, it is fair to say that more teacher research studies today use bottom-up qualitative designs rather than top-down quantitative designs.

The Data

The data sources we select will vary in terms of the kinds of information we need to respond to the focus we have established for our study. For example, if we are interested in how young people in our class respond during a discussion, our data sources may be pretty much limited to field notes we make after each discussion. These will include information about such issues as the number of learners who participated, names of those who participated, typical lengths of comments made by individuals who volunteered, appropriateness of their comments, number and sophistication of questions asked, and so forth. On the other hand, if our focus is on learners' writing abilities, we might identify examples of all kinds of learner work as important data sources.

Once we identify and gather data, we need to analyze this information. The specific procedures used will vary with the design we have chosen. Standard works on quantitative and qualitative design provide guidelines for doing this. Some excellent examples of the sorts of considerations that go into a well-designed qualitative study are included in a chapter by Leslie Patterson in Patterson et al. (1990, pp. 22–36, particularly pp. 29–33).

The Report

Summarized findings of our research can take many forms. One alternative might be for us to begin with the "look ats" we developed from our focus question. These can be used as major headings as we begin to describe specific things we observed, our analyses of these observations, and any actions we propose to take as a result. Teacher research ordinarily generates a tremendous amount of data. Field notes alone can go on for many pages if a study has been conducted over a considerable period of time. The volume of data allows opportunities to analyze and report information in many different kinds of ways.

For example, if we had gathered data during the project involving interjection of prompt questions during discussions, we could prepare reports on how different categories of our learners responded. There might be a report focusing on how our more academically talented people reacted to this change. Another could describe its impact on lower-ability learners. Reports could be generated describing the reaction of the class as a whole at different times, perhaps after one week, after four

This teacher is sharing teacher-research findings with a number of colleagues.

BOX 14-1

The Teacher as Researcher: Rita's Story

Initially, Rita's research topic centered on using games to make science fun. However, early in the project — during the August seminar days — she changed her topic to "exploring what happens when students use writing to learn science." The use of writing to learn in science class was new for Rita and was not widespread in the school system. Rita decided to try a different teaching strategy and examine what happened.

Two people contributed to Rita's topic selection. She admired another teacher researcher, Barbara, who taught English and was a consultant to the Northern Virginia Writing Project. The previous year, they had sometimes talked about writing instruction. Marian, a central office staff expert in teacher research and writing instruction, had distributed to the group two articles about teacher research and using writing to learn. During one of the seminar days, Rita found herself seated between Barbara and Marian and became involved in a conversation about writing in the content areas.

Rita's choice of topic was further influenced by her school's growing emphasis on writing in the content areas. Every teacher was required to assign a minimum of one piece of writing a quarter. Rita felt that although she met the requirement, writing was not really integrated into her teaching. That bothered her.

In comparison to the rest of the group, Rita defined her research topic early in the process, and this meant she was able to move quickly into establishing her data sources. First, she had her own research log. She designed writing assignments for her students and had them use logs to write about what they were learning in science. She also gave her students sample surveys. In addition, she had the data sources available to most content teachers: assignments, tests, and grades.

At one point, Rita counted more than 20 writing activities she had designed for her science classes. She targeted some of her underachieving students and began to look at their writing for their use of content vocabulary. As she looked at her data, she further refined her research question. The research topic began to reflect her interest in the vocabulary of science.

Rita quickly collected boxes of data and, like other teacher researchers, began to ask, What does all this tell me? At the suggestion of one of the central office staff members, she started her analysis by making a schematic web of her research project. This web provided structure for her to organize her research and draw some tentative conclusions. On a snowy day in February when schools were closed, she created an outline and turned to her data to document her findings.

Rita's research gave her another way to look at her students — through their writing. She found a new way to learn about their interests and to determine what they were learning. From her students' logs and the surveys, she learned that they were eager to share their writing and they felt that writing helped them to learn. The data also showed that when writing replaced the worksheets-after-the-film routine, students' interest and comprehension increased.

Rita's research influenced various aspects of her teaching. Her research report states that she no longer uses worksheets, she now gives essay tests instead of short-answer tests and, most importantly, she gives her students time to write.

Abridged from Nocerino, Mary Ann. (1993). A look at the process. *Teachers Are Researchers: Reflection and Action*, Leslie Patterson, Carol Minnick Santa, Kathy G. Short, and Karen Smith (Eds.), 86–91. Reprinted with permission of Mary Ann Nocerino and the International Reading Association.

weeks, and after six weeks of this kind of instruction. Still another report might provide a kind of narrative snapshot of a single day's instruction using the technique. The purpose of this option might be to help someone else sense the general flavor of the classroom when this technique was used.

Teacher research puts the teacher in charge. The final report, then, should mirror what we want to highlight. It gives us an opportunity to reflect on what we have observed, consider possible implications for our own teaching, and think seriously about changes we might want to make in the future. Ideally, preparing the report is part of our continuous development as reflective educators.

Teachers who are new to research react to the experience in different ways. Several years ago, some teachers in a single school in Virginia had an opportunity to enroll in a graduate seminar on teacher research and to undertake research projects of their own. A teacher named Rita was a member of this group. Rita's experiences as a novice teacher researcher are reported in Box 14-1.

• Key Ideas in Summary

- Some teachers began conducting research in their own classrooms as early as the beginning of the twentieth century. The interest in research is on the upswing today. In part, this results from more interest in qualitative research approaches. These approaches, with their focus on providing information relevant to a specific setting, have proved attractive to teachers who are more interested in developing solutions to problems they face in their own classrooms than in developing broadly applicable generalizations.

- Even though more teachers than ever are conducting research in their own classrooms, this by no means is something that all teachers do. Some teachers in the past have been disinclined to study what goes on in the classroom out of a conviction that home backgrounds of learners and other variables beyond the control of teachers had more impact on learners' achievement than anything teachers do.

- Relatively few teacher preparation programs place much emphasis on teachers' roles as researchers. In some places, school administrators have not been enthusiastic supporters of teacher research. However, this situation is tending to give way in many places to support for this kind of activity. In part, this has resulted from a trend to decentralize management of education, a phenomenon that has placed more responsibility for the success of school programs at the individual school level. This has given administrators and teachers in individual schools an incentive to research their practices to develop information that can be used to improve programs.

- Teacher research is directed at improving teaching. Typically, it is undertaken to address a problem or concern that is of personal importance to the researcher. Findings are usually not expected to be generalizable to other settings. Rather, they comprise a set of data that can be used as a basis for making decisions related to practice in the teacher's own instructional settings.

- Individuals who do teacher research perceive themselves to have more control over their professional lives than those who do not engage in this activity.

They develop an awareness of multiple approaches to instruction. They also develop important insights into how their learners think and act. Participation also tends to revitalize teachers and make them appear energetic and enthusiastic to their learners. These teachers tend to do a better job of keeping up with their professional fields than teachers who do not engage in teacher research.

- There are two major research traditions. People who associate with what Jerome Bruner calls the "top-down" tradition seek powerful explanatory principles that apply in many settings, regardless of different place-to-place conditions. On the other hand, individuals who associate with what Jerome Bruner styles the "bottom-up" tradition assume that differences from context to context are extremely important. Their research does not seek to generate widely applicable principles. Rather, it attempts to produce as much information as possible about a particular setting. Although some teacher research is conducted within each of these traditions, most today is bottom-up research.

- Focus questions teachers use for their research studies tend to come from two sources. Some come from their own classroom experiences. Others come from a careful reading of professional literature in education.

- A general sequence for conducting teacher research includes these steps: (1) establishing a focus; (2) identifying an appropriate design; (3) selecting, gathering, and analyzing data; and (4) preparing a report.

• Review and Discussion Questions

1. What is the history of teacher research in this country?
2. Why, historically, were some teachers reluctant to commit time to teacher research? How valid do you think their reasons were?
3. How is "teacher research" defined, and what are some of its general purposes?
4. What are some specific barriers teachers have faced who have been interested in doing teacher research? Some people argue that these barriers are not as important today as they once were. What do they base this opinion on? Do you agree with it? Why or why not?
5. It has been said that teacher research has some advantages over more traditional, university-based research. What are some of these claimed advantages?
6. How can involvement in teacher research lead to personal and professional pluses for teachers?
7. What are the distinguishing features of research associated with the top-down tradition and with the bottom-up position? Why do some people believe that research designs that come out of the bottom-up orientation are more attractive to teacher researchers than those that come out of the top-down orientation? Do you agree? Why or why not?
8. Where do focus questions used in teacher research come from?
9. Why is it important that a teacher researcher identify both what to look at and what to look for?
10. What are some general steps followed in a teacher research study, and what typically is done at each?

• Ideas for Field Experience Projects and Enrichment

1. Locate a teacher who is doing teacher research. (Your instructor may help you find someone.) Ask the teacher to explain the purpose of the project and the anticipated value of the study. Prepare an oral report for your class that describes what this teacher is doing.
2. Suppose you wanted to conduct a teacher research study of your own. Develop a focus question. Then, prepare a chart similar to the one depicted in Figure 14-1. Share it with your instructor and request a critique.
3. During an observation in a local school, identify some things you see that might suggest focus questions for teacher research studies. Prepare a short paper in which you describe four or five areas that might be researched, and suggest a possible focus question for each.
4. Using such resources as the *Education Index* and the catalog in your university library, prepare a bibliography listing a total of at least 20 articles and books that focus on teacher research. (Many of these will use the phrase "teacher as researcher" in the titles.) Prepare enough copies of your bibliography so everyone in your class can have one.
5. Read Chapter 4, "Teachers as Researchers," in the Association of Teacher Educators' *Handbook of Research on Teacher Education*, 2nd ed. (New York: Macmillan, 1996). Prepare a written and/or oral report for your class that highlights findings that you find interesting.

• References

Atkin, J. M. (1989). Can educational research keep pace with education reform? *Phi Delta Kappan, 71*(3), 200–205.

Bain, H. P., & Groseclose, J. R. (1979). The dissemination dilemma and a plan for uniting disseminators and practitioners. *Phi Delta Kappan, 61*(2), 101–103.

Bellon, J. J., Bellon, E. C., & Blank, M. A. (1992). *Teaching from a research knowledge base.* Upper Saddle River, NJ: Merrill.

Bennett, C. K. (1993). Teacher-researchers: All dressed up and no place to go. *Educational Leadership, 51*(2), 69–70.

Boyer, E. (1990). *Scholarship reconsidered: Priorities of the professorate.* Princeton, NJ: Carnegie Foundation for the Advancement of Teaching.

Brownlie, F. (1990). The door is open. Won't you come in? In M. W. Olson (Ed.), *Opening the door to educational research* (pp. 21–31). Newark, DE: International Reading Association.

Bruner, J. (1986). *Actual minds, possible worlds.* Cambridge, MA: Harvard University Press.

Carr, W., & Kemmis, S. (1986). *Becoming critical: Education, knowledge, and action research.* London: Falmer.

Carson, T. (1990). What kind of knowing is critical to action research? *Theory Into Practice, 29*(3), 167–173.

Chattin-McNichols, J., & Loeffler, M. H. (1989). Teachers as researchers: The first cycle of the teachers' research network. *Young Children, 44*(5), 20–27.

Cochran-Smith, M., & Lytle, S. L. (1990). Research on teaching and teacher research: The issues that divide. *Educational Researcher, 19*(3), 2–12.

Copper, L. R. (1990, April). *Teachers as researchers: Attitudes, opinions, and perceptions.* Paper presented at the Annual meeting of the American Educational Research Association, Boston. (ERIC Document Reproduction Service No. ED 322 130)

Cuban, L. (1992). Managing dilemmas while building professional communities. *Educational Researcher, 21*(1), 4–11.

Darling-Hammond, L. (1993). Reframing the school reform agenda: Developing capacity for school transformation. *Phi Delta Kappan, 74*(10), 752–761.

Dicker, M. (1990). Using action research to navigate an unfamiliar teaching assignment. *Theory Into Practice, 29*(3), 203–208.

Doyle, W. (1990). Themes in teacher education research. In W. R. Houston (Ed.), *Handbook of research on teacher education* (pp. 3–24). New York: Macmillan.

Egbert, R. L. (1984). The role of research in teacher education. In R. L. Egbert & M. M. Kluender (Eds.), *Using research to improve teacher education: The Nebraska Consortium* (pp. 9–21). Lincoln, NE: American Association of Colleges for Teacher Education.

Flake, C. L., Kuhs, T., Donnelly, A., & Ebert, C. (1995). Reinventing the role of teacher as researcher. *Phi Delta Kappan, 76*(5), 405–407.

Fullan, M. G. (1982). *The meaning of educational change*. New York: Teachers College Press.

Glatthorn, A. A. (1993). *Learning twice: An introduction to the methods of teaching*. New York: HarperCollins.

Henson, K. T. (1996). Teachers as researchers. In J. Sikula, T. Buttery, & E. Guyton (Eds.), *Handbook of research on teacher education* (pp. 53–64). New York: Macmillan.

Johnson, B. (1993, March). Teacher-as-researcher. *ERIC Digest*. Washington, DC: ERIC Clearinghouse on Teacher Education. (ERIC Document Reproduction Service No. ED 322 130)

Lowery, C. D. (1908). The relation of superintendents and principals to the training and professional improvement of their teachers. *Seventh yearbook of the National Society for the Study of Education, part one*. Chicago: University of Chicago Press.

Lytle, S. L., & Cochran-Smith, M. (1990). Learning from teacher research: A working topology. *Teachers College Record, 92*(1), 83–103.

McCutcheon, G., & Jung, B. (1990). Alternative perspectives on action research. *Theory Into Practice, 29*(3), 144–151.

Oberg, A. (1990). Methods and meanings in action research: The action research journal. *Theory Into Practice, 29*(3), 214–221.

Oja, S. N., & Pine, G. J. (1989). Collaborative action research: Teachers' states of development and school contexts. *Peabody Journal of Education, 64*(2), 96–115.

Patterson, L. (1990). Teaching, researching, and problem solving. In L. Patterson, J. C. Stansell, & S. Lee (Eds.), *Teacher research from promise to power* (pp. 22–36). Katonah, NY: Richard C. Owen Publishers.

Patterson, L., Stansell, J. C., & Lee, S. (1990). *Teacher research from promise to power*. Katonah, NY: Richard C. Owen Publishers.

Reading/Language in Secondary Schools Subcommittee of IRA. (1989). *Classroom action research: The teacher as researcher*. Newark, DE: International Reading Association.

Santa, C. M. (1990). Teaching as research. In M. W. Olson (Ed.), *Opening the door to classroom research* (pp. 64–76). Newark, DE: International Reading Association.

Sardo-Brown, D. (1992). Elementary teachers' perceptions of action research. *Action in Teacher Education, 14*(2), 55–59.

Stake, R. E., & Easley, J. A. (Eds.). (1978). Case studies in science education (Vol. 1). Urbana, IL: Center for instructional research and curriculum evaluation.

Stevens, K. B., Slanton, D. B., & Bunny, S. (1992). A collaborative research effort between public school and university faculty members. *Teacher Education and Special Education, 15*(1), 1–8.

Sucher, F. (1990). Involving school administrators in classroom research. In M. W. Olson (Ed.), *Opening the door to classroom research* (pp. 112–115). Newark, DE: International Reading Association.

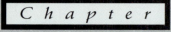

Chapter

15

Legal
Concerns
of Teachers

OBJECTIVES

- Identify legal issues associated with conditions of employment.
- Describe some conditions under which teachers have the right to due process.
- Explain some rights and responsibilities of teachers in areas associated with their personal lives outside of school.
- Point out major types of professional negligence.
- Describe kinds of responsibilities in reporting suspected child abuse.

Many things we do as teachers have the potential to lead to conflict. Today, more often than in the past, educators find themselves embroiled in legal disputes. Governmental authorities at all levels, social organizations, religious groups, business alliances, fraternal orders, and other bodies that draw people together often have an interest in some aspects of public education. People associated with these groups may have differing views regarding what teachers should do and about how schools should be run. When conflicts among these competing perspectives cannot be resolved in other ways, the courts become involved.

In our society, litigation is becoming more common in all aspects of life. As a prospective teacher, you need to have an understanding of some basic legal principles. To test your knowledge of some basic information in this area, respond to the following questions. What would you do if:

- you signed a teaching contract with a school district and then had a more lucrative contract offered to you by another district?
- you were told by your principal not to teach a controversial topic in your social studies or English class?
- your principal asked you not to report your suspicion that one of your learners was being subjected to child abuse?
- a parent objected to your using a particular literary selection in your class and threatened to bring legal charges if you persisted in using it?

Each of these questions raises an important legal issue. Each is an example of the kind of questions teachers face every day. Actions you might take in the absence of adequate knowledge could cost you your job, lead to the revocation of your teaching certificate, or even subject you to civil or criminal charges.

As you read this chapter, bear in mind several cautions. First of all, laws relevant to education and educators vary from state to state. There are also differences in how individual jurisdictions interpret and enforce these regulations. Finally, every case that is adjudicated is considered on its own merits. Since no two cases are exactly alike, it is difficult to make absolute predictions about what might happen in future cases dealing with issues that other courts have considered in the past.

CONDITIONS OF EMPLOYMENT

Teachers' Certification

Possession of a valid teaching certificate is a prerequisite for individuals seeking employment as a public school teacher. Certification is a function of state government. Each state has identified conditions that must be met by individuals seeking authorization to teach within its boundaries.

Although each state has its own certification requirements, this does not mean that a certified teacher who moves across a state line must start all over again. Most states have reciprocal certification agreements. This means that when someone has a teaching certificate from one state and wishes to teach in another, the second state will grant a certificate allowing the person to do so. The second state may require the teacher to take some specified courses within a given period of

Some legislators are responsible for establishing basic rules regarding certification of teachers.

time to maintain the new certificate. When this is done, these course requirements are not oppressive. Often, little is required beyond a course in the history or government of the new state.

There is no basic "right" to obtain a teaching certificate by means other than those specified in established state regulations. Once a certificate has been granted, the authority it grants may be changed by the issuing state agency. For example, the state may pass new regulations requiring certificate holders to take certain courses or to pass a competency test in order for their certificates to remain in force (Valente, 1994).

A teaching certificate is essentially a license to practice. It confers specific benefits. Holders are entitled to either a minimum salary mandated by the state or this salary plus any supplements provided for on the locally adopted teachers' salary schedule. The certificate provides the holder with "an assumption of competence." This means that any charges of incompetence made against the holder will receive serious consideration only if they are backed up with evidence that is compelling enough to demonstrate the error of the competence assumption.

A teaching certificate is almost always a prerequisite for a legally binding contract to teach. Individuals who have signed teaching contracts but have not possessed valid teaching certificates have in some cases been declared to be "volunteers" who have no right to any monetary compensation. The regulation in California is typical of those many states have regarding the connection between a teaching certificate and remuneration. The California Education Code requires all teachers to register their certificates within 60 days of their employment and declares that no salary can be paid to individuals whose certificates are not on file (California Teachers Association, 1992).

The Hiring Process

State and federal laws govern processes used in screening applicants for positions. Many regulations address the issue of discrimination in employment. For example, the Washington State Law Against Discrimination (RCW 49.60) makes it an unfair practice for an employer of eight or more people to use any form of application for employment or to make any inquiry in connection with prospective employment that expresses any limitation, specification, or discrimination as to age; sex; marital status; race; creed; national origin; color; the presence of sensory, mental, or physical handicap; or any intent to make any such limitation, specification, or discrimination, unless based upon a bona fide occupational qualification. In plain English, this statute means that questions asked of applicants must have a demonstrated relationship to the job. For example, a question regarding physical disability would not be legal unless such a disability would prevent the accomplishment of tasks required by the person to be awarded the position.

Most states have laws similar to the Washington statute. Such legislation restricts what school personnel can ask teacher candidates during interviews. Although practices vary from place to place, questions regarding marital status, pregnancy, age, and religious preferences generally cannot be asked.

Some laws, such as Title VII of the Civil Rights Act of 1964, apply to public as well as private educational institutions. Others concern only public institutions. This area of the law is complex. For example, if a particular condition can be demonstrated to hinder the ability of a person to teach or to interfere with the mission of the school, it may legally be included as a condition for employment. In other words, a private religious school can legally give preference to individuals with a particular religious affiliation if such affiliation is required for the school to fulfill its mission.

Teachers' Contracts

The contract is one of the most important documents we encounter as teachers. A contract spells out our salary and delineates other conditions of employment. This is a document we need to read carefully. Contracts are legally binding. They set forth our responsibility to the school district as well as the school district's responsibility to us.

As a rule, when one party to a contract breaks it, the other party is entitled to a legal remedy that provides compensation to the injured party for any damage the breach of contract has caused. For example, a teacher who fails to show up for work after signing a contract could be required to pay the school district the costs of finding a replacement (Fischer, Schimmel, & Kelly, 1987). It is not advisable for someone who has signed one contract to later sign another one and ignore the first. This puts the person in the position of being legally obligated to perform duties simultaneously in two places. Obviously, this cannot be done, and legal difficulties may arise if charges are initiated by the school district that finds itself without a teacher.

The issue of "oral contracts" sometimes comes up for discussion. A person who has applied for a teaching position may believe that a spoken offer from a personnel officer representing a school district constitutes a binding contract. It does not. The school board (sometimes known as the board of trustees or by some other title), the governing authority of a school district, is the only party that can legally bind the school district. To be legal, a teaching contract must be approved by the school board.

Since the approved written contract is the ultimate legal authority that delineates conditions of employment, the written version needs to be scrutinized closely to ensure that its provisions are consistent with what might have been presented orally at the conclusion of an interview. For example, if the interviewer stated that the regular salary would be increased by an additional $900 per year to compensate the teacher for bus supervision, this proviso must be included in the written contract. Otherwise, the school district is under no legal obligation to pay the additional money.

Testing for AIDS and Substance Abuse

Recent concerns about substance abuse and the spread of AIDS have led to proposals for universal drug and AIDS testing for teachers. Court decisions in this area suggest that tests of this type qualify as a form of search. To be legal, these searches must be consistent with guarantees outlined in the Fourth Amendment to the United States Constitution. This means that a school district must demonstrate a "compelling interest" in the results of any tests that have the potential to infringe on individuals' privacy rights. As an example, a district might be able to demonstrate a compelling interest if it could show potential harmful effects on learners of a teacher who was either using a controlled substance or who had AIDS. Proving this latter point to the satisfaction of a court of law might be difficult. To date, there is no evidence that AIDS is transmitted through the kinds of contacts that characterize usual teacher-learner interactions.

Tenure and Continuing Employment

Some people are attracted to teaching because they see it as providing a high degree of job security. In considering employment security as it relates to teaching, we need to understand some issues related to *tenure*.

Tenure gives teachers employment rights that cannot be altered at the whim of school officials. Simply put, it provides teachers with a right of employment for an indefinite period of time and allows for dismissal only for reasons specified by law. Many states have tenure laws for teachers. The pattern varies greatly from place to place. In some states, these laws apply to all school districts in the state. In others, states allow individual districts to choose whether or not to offer tenure contracts to teachers.

Tenure came about because of a belief in our society that an open exchange of ideas and free discussion of issues are core values. Tenure is designed to protect teachers from pressure groups who may wish to dismiss teachers because they do not agree with some ideas being taught in their classes. Tenure laws seek to promote an open exchange of ideas in the classroom and to keep good teachers in a district by guaranteeing them long-term employment.

Since tenure provides teachers with an expectation of continuing employment, it has been defined by the courts as a "property right" that qualifies for constitutional protection. This means that the contract of a tenured teacher cannot be violated without implementing full due process procedures.

In places where teachers can become tenured, they typically begin working for a probationary period (usually about three years) as a "nontenured" teacher. During this period, their contracts can be terminated at the end of each school year. The school board does not need to provide a reason for nonrenewal, nor are due process steps required. Teachers who complete a satisfactory, nontenured probationary period are then hired as "tenured" teachers.

In recent years, several state legislatures have discussed eliminating or modifying tenure laws. The argument made in support of this action is that tenure guarantees permanent employment and, hence, insulates incompetent teachers from dismissal. Some authorities claim this makes school reform difficult. They argue that teachers should not enjoy any more job security than people working in other occupational roles.

Whereas there may be some merit in these concerns, the arguments that tenure provides lifetime employment and that tenure protects incompetents are of questionable validity. In fact, tenure statutes typically outline a number of circumstances under which a tenured teacher can be removed. It is true, however, that the processes required may take time and may be costly. This is because the burden of proof falls on the school district that initiates the dismissal action. In one California case, it took eight years and an expenditure of over $300,000 in legal fees before one teacher had exhausted all of her legal remedies and was dismissed (Richardson, 1995).

A tenured teacher can be dismissed usually for reasons that fall within the following six categories:

1. *Incompetence:*   The conditions that have been used to dismiss teachers for incompetence include lack of knowledge, failure to adapt to new teaching methods, violation of school rules, lack of cooperation, persistent negligence, lack of ability to impart knowledge, physical mistreatment of learners, and failure to maintain discipline. Failure to maintain discipline is one of the most common causes for dismissal actions filed against tenured teachers.
2. *Incapacity:*   This standard includes any physical or mental condition that keeps a teacher from performing his or her assigned duties.
3. *Insubordination:*   This is most commonly applied to teachers who stubbornly and willfully violate reasonable school rules and policies. Usually a series of insubordinate acts are required to exercise dismissal.
4. *Conduct:*   This is a broad standard that can embrace behaviors as varied as insulting fellow teachers, espousing personal political causes in the classroom, taking time off without permission, and even shoplifting. Some specific instances where school districts have successfully dismissed teachers for inappropriate conduct have involved drinking to excess, serving alcohol to learners in the teacher's home, and telling wrestling team members to lie about their weights when registering for a tournament.

5. *Immorality:*   The courts have consistently ruled that moral fitness is a standard that teachers must meet. Dismissal actions related to this category may include such things as criminal activity, sexual misconduct, drug use, and dishonesty.

6. *Other causes:*   Many tenure laws provide for dismissal for a number of other reasons that include such things as intemperance, neglect of duty, cruelty, and willful misconduct.

As this list illustrates, there are many reasons a tenured teacher can be dismissed. A problem school districts face, however, is gathering sufficient evidence to convince a court of law that a dismissal action is justified. Clearly, it is much more difficult for school district officials to sustain a dismissal action against a tenured teacher than against a nontenured teacher.

PROFESSIONAL RIGHTS AND RESPONSIBILITIES

There are many areas where we can run into legal difficulty while performing our professional responsibilities as teachers. Because we are in a position to influence impressionable young people, questions have frequently come up before the courts that relate to the appropriate balance between the rights of professional educators and the obligations of our schools not to tread upon basic rights of learners and parents.

Curriculum and Instruction

What are our rights and responsibilities in assigning grades, choosing the content of the curriculum, using instructional materials, employing specific methods of instruction, and expressing personal and moral convictions in the classroom? All of these are issues that, from time to time, have come before the courts.

Grades

The courts have generally considered school officials to be uniquely qualified to judge the academic achievement of learners. They have been reluctant to overturn teachers' grading decisions unless there is overwhelming evidence that grades have been given for arbitrary, capricious, or bad-faith reasons. To avoid a possible charge of "arbitrary grading," we need to have clear grading standards, keep accurate records, and not lower grades as a punishment for nonacademic misbehavior.

Academic Freedom

Academic freedom refers to the idea that teachers and learners should be able to inquire in the classroom into any issue, even one that is highly controversial and unpopular. The courts have tended to support academic freedom as a core value that derives from the First Amendment to the United States Constitution. Academic freedom, however, does have limits. Problems sometimes arise when there is a conflict between our right as teachers to conduct our classrooms in a way consistent with our best professional judgments and the responsibility of the school district to ensure that the adopted curriculum is being taught.

In academic freedom cases, the courts generally have supported teachers' rights to introduce material that is relevant to the subject being taught, appropriate to the age and maturity levels of learners, and unlikely to interfere with the educational process. School boards, however, have been found to have the right to prohibit certain texts and materials, but they must provide reasons that are constitutionally reasonable and not based simply on a desire to avoid controversy or to promote particular religious or political views.

Academic freedom does not allow us to ignore the approved course of study and the assigned text, nor does it sanction discussions or materials that are not relevant to the subject we are supposed to be teaching. Several cases will illuminate this point.

In one case, an American history teacher used a simulation exercise that evoked strong learner responses on racial issues. Acting on the complaints of several parents, the school board told the teacher to stop using the exercise. When the teacher continued the simulation, the school board made a decision not to renew her contract. She took the issue to court. In its decision, the United States Fifth Circuit Court of Appeals ruled that the district had violated the teacher's First Amendment rights (*Kingsville Independent School District v. Cooper*, 1980).

In another case, an 11th-grade English teacher assigned a story to her class. Her principal and the associate superintendent described the story as "literary garbage" and advised her not to use it again. The teacher felt the piece was good literature, and she refused to follow the administrators' advice. Subsequently, she was dismissed. She took legal action against the school district, claiming that the dismissal action was an unconstitutional violation of her academic freedom rights. A federal court, ruling in favor of the teacher, found that the school board had failed to show that the assignment was inappropriate for 11th-graders or that its use had created a significant disruption of the educational process (*Parducci v. Rutland*, 1970).

Not all rulings have gone in favor of the teacher, however. Courts supported dismissal actions against (1) a teacher who continued to teach sex-related issues in a health class because he believed the topic was of great interest to learners, (2) an art teacher who actively promoted her religious beliefs in class and encouraged learners to attend meetings of her religious group, and (3) a mathematics teacher who encouraged learners to protest the presence of army recruiters on the school campus.

In summary, decisions related to what can be taught tend to be somewhat situation-specific. However, in general, we do have a right to deal with controversial topics that are relevant to what we are teaching. On the other hand, the door is not open for us to "just teach anything." What we teach needs to have some logical connection to the curriculum.

Reporting Suspected Child Abuse

Public concern for child abuse is growing. Today, all 50 states and the District of Columbia have laws that make mandatory the reporting of suspected instances of child abuse. Because we have prolonged contact with learners in our classrooms, we are deemed to be in a particularly good position to spot young people who have been abused. As a result, we have been designated as "mandatory reporters" of

How Free Is a Teacher to Choose Teaching Methods?

Todd Allenby teaches 9th-graders. One of his classes just isn't motivated. He thinks their written work this semester has been abysmal. Often all he gets is a page with the student's name and one or two barely coherent sentences. At the end of last week, he spent some time discussing his frustrations with Darcie Schwartz, another English teacher.

Darcie listened carefully and asked, "Are you letting them write what they want? I find most of my people won't give me much quantity unless they have a personal interest in the topic."

Todd thought about this idea over the weekend. On Monday, when this class filed in, he began with some general comments about how people can become frustrated when they have something personal to say and nobody listens. He went on to say that the next writing assignment was going to provide members of the class with an opportunity to really say what they want about any subject they want to talk about. He concluded by promising that these thoughts would reach a broad audience because he personally would see to it that every student's essay was copied and passed out to every member of the class. After a few preliminary questions, members of the class for the first time all year buckled down enthusiastically to do the assigned written work. Todd collected essays students had written at the end of the class period.

When Todd got home on Monday evening, he sat down to read through what these students had written. He was pleased to see that the essays were much longer than those he usually got and that some of the students were doing some serious thinking. However, about midway through the stack of papers, his pleasure turned to dismay. He began running into essays sprinkled with sexually explicit language. His stomach knotted up as he reflected on his promise to share all of the essays with members of the class.

Despite his concerns about the content of some of these materials, Todd decided that a promise was a promise. He made copies of all the essays and made sure that they were passed out to all students in the class. Two days later, he received a call to report to Duwayne

child abuse. Mandatory reporting laws place a legal obligation on us to report instances of suspected child abuse. A failure to do this can subject us to both civil and criminal penalties. In one state, the penal code provides that a failure to report child abuse by someone who reasonably should recognize it makes the party guilty of a misdemeanor that is punishable by six months in jail, a fine of $1,000, or both (California Teachers Association, 1992).

We do not need to have a high level of suspicion before reporting suspected child abuse. Terms often used in describing grounds for reporting suspected cases include phrases such as "reasonable grounds," "cause to believe," or "reasonable cause to believe." We do not need to fear retribution as a consequence of reporting a potential child abuse case. All states provide some form of protection from lawsuits for reports of child abuse that have been made in good faith.

Some states include a provision for the state to pay attorney's fees for a suit filed as a result of a teacher's report of suspected child abuse. Indeed, in most cases, the identity of the teacher making the report will not be known. Many statutes

Clark, the school principal. When he arrived at Mr. Clark's office, Todd noticed that copies of several of the student essays were spread over the top of his desk.

"Todd," began Mr. Clark, "what in the world were you thinking about? I mean, it is bad enough that these kids use this kind of language to begin with, but to go so far as to make copies and distribute them to others — that's just too much. Can you imagine what some of our parents are going to say when they find out a *teacher* has done this?"

"Look," replied Todd, "I'm not at all thrilled about some of the content of these things. But these kids did write something. For many of them, that's a first. And I *did* commit to make copies and pass them out. I felt I had to follow through to keep my credibility intact."

"That's a commitment you had no right to make. It put you in a position of agreeing to distribute just anything. That's not professional. In fact, it is not the kind of behavior we tolerate in this district. You need to know that this is a serious matter and that I am going to initiate an official complaint with the central administration. You'll be kept apprised of what is happening. Let me just tell you that this sort of thing could lead to an official dismissal hearing."

What is Todd Allenby's perspective on what has happened? What were his motives? How does he view "professionalism"? What were his objectives? Do you think his approach was reasonable, given what he wished to do?

How does the principal, Duwayne Clark, define professionalism in this case? In what ways is his conception different from Todd Allenby's?

What about the students? Are they likely to hold a teacher (or any other adult) to account if there is a breach of promise? Or, are there ways a promise might be broken that could be explained logically to the people to whom it had been made?

What are your personal thoughts about Todd Allenby's assignment and its consequences? Should teachers have unlimited academic freedom when it comes to making assignments? What sort of criteria should be applied in determining whether specific methods teachers use are "unprofessional"? What do you think the likely outcome in this case will be if the principal and the school district decide to move ahead with dismissal procedures? We don't know whether Todd Allenby is tenured or nontenured. Would his tenure status make any difference? If so, how?

afford anonymity to mandatory reporters. These regulations also often provide that these individuals may not be disciplined by their employer for reporting suspected instances of child abuse and may not be sued for any action they took in the process of reporting (Underwood, 1994). On the other hand, if it can be demonstrated that a teacher filed a report in bad faith for malicious reasons, he or she may face legal action.

Teachers' Tort Liability

A *tort* is defined as a civil as opposed to a criminal wrongdoing. Torts involve an injury against another person that resulted from a breach of legal duty. Settlements of tort disputes often conclude with the award of some kind of compensatory monetary damages to the injured party. Tort suits against teachers have been increasing in number. Today, many professional organizations offer group insurance designed to protect teachers from judgments that might be awarded to complainants in tort actions. Tort law differs from criminal law in that it is based on common law and the concept of fault or intent. In tort cases, as opposed to criminal cases, findings do not need to prove fault "beyond a reasonable doubt" (Valente, 1994).

We in the schools have a responsibility for the health and safety of members of our school community. If we are negligent in doing this, we may face lawsuits. Some questions that are relevant to injury-related suits against teachers include:

- Did the teacher have a duty of care under the law to avoid the injury?
- If so, was the duty breached?
- If a breach of legal duty occurred, was it the proximate cause of the injury?

In many states, the test that is applied to determine whether a teacher has a "duty of care" is whether the probability of injury could have been foreseen and how a reasonable person with similar training would have acted (Valente, 1994). Suits against teachers have tended to focus on a relatively small number of issues. These include the use of force in discipline, negligence, and malpractice.

Use of Force in Discipline

Many court cases have concerned the issue of teachers' rights to use force when disciplining learners. Physical punishment such as paddling has been a focus in many of these cases. In *Ingraham v. Wright* (1977), the United States Supreme Court ruled that teachers could use reasonable, but not excessive, force in disciplining a learner. In this decision, the High Court declared that corporal punishment in the classroom did not constitute "cruel and unusual punishment" and, hence, was not a violation of learners' constitutional rights.

The decision in *Ingraham v. Wright* left certain ambiguities. In particular, what is meant by the term "reasonable force"? The collective thinking of courts in cases where they have had to decide what should be considered in deciding when applied force is reasonable has led to the identification of several variables that often are used in making this determination. These include:

- the gravity of the misbehavior
- the age of the learner
- the gender and size of the learner
- the size of the person administering the punishment
- the implement used to administer the punishment
- the attitude or predisposition of the person administering the punishment

These variables suggest that the courts look carefully at circumstances surrounding the particular incident they are reviewing in making their decisions. For us as teachers, the pattern of decisions in use-of-force cases is a warning that says, Be careful.

Most rules relating to corporal punishment are state and local school district regulations. A few states prohibit all forms of corporal punishment. In other places, individual school districts have adopted a similar prohibition. Even where corporal punishment is permitted, there usually are strict guidelines regarding how it is to be administered.

Even if corporal punishment is permitted in a given jurisdiction, a teacher is not necessarily protected from legal action if a learner or a parent believes force used in administering it was not "reasonable." A teacher might also face legal action even if the force applied is regarded as reasonable, but it results in an aggravation of a learner's health or medical condition. This is true even if the teacher is unaware of this condition at the time punishment is administered.

In summary, corporal punishment is controversial and risky. Particularly at a time when there is so much concern about the growth in child abuse, we would be remiss not to take a stand against the use of corporal punishment. (Do we really want to be known as the profession that beats its clients?) The emotional, psychological, and legal risks of corporal punishment outweigh any claimed benefits. There are better ways to discipline learners. (You may want to review Chapter 3 for some more productive approaches to controlling learners' behavior.)

Negligence

Negligence is the failure to use reasonable care to prevent harm from coming to someone. There are three kinds of negligence: misfeasance, nonfeasance, and malfeasance.

Misfeasance occurs when a teacher acts unwisely or without taking proper safeguards. The teacher may have had a worthy motive but still have acted in a way that

Teachers and administrators regularly check playground equipment to ensure its safety. Legal liability problems can result if learners suffer injuries because equipment has not been properly maintained.

allowed harm to come to a learner. For example, a teacher of very young children might ask a child to carry a glass container from one location to another. If the child falls and is cut, the teacher could be charged with misfeasance. The courts might deem it improper for the teacher to have asked a very young child to perform this kind of a task. The probability of injury could have been foreseen, and the teacher's action established conditions that increased the likelihood that there might be an injury.

Nonfeasance is a failure to act. Cases involving teachers frequently revolve around things that happen when teachers are away from their assigned areas of responsibility. For example, a learner may be injured by another learner when the teacher has stepped out of the classroom. Or, there might be an injury to a learner on the playground that occurred when the teacher assigned to playground supervision failed to report for duty.

The determination of negligence in nonfeasance cases often turns on the issue of whether proper supervision could have prevented the injury and on whether the teacher's absence from the assigned duty station was justifiable. For example, if a learner were injured while the teacher left the classroom to extinguish a fire in a wastebasket in the lavatory across the hall, a court might well decide that this situation represented a reasonable cause for the teacher to be out of the classroom.

Malfeasance involves behavior that is undertaken deliberately and knowingly to harm someone else. Suppose a large, strong male teacher comes upon two boys fighting. One of these boys is a young man the teacher does not respect and whom he considers to be a troublemaker. The teacher could lose control and deliberately set out to hurt the boy he does not like as part of his effort to break up the fight. If the boy is injured, he might receive a favorable hearing in court proceedings brought against the teacher for malfeasance.

Malpractice

Even though such suits are not common, as teachers we need to know that malpractice complaints are sometimes brought against teachers. Among conditions that might lead to a malpractice suit against a teacher (Valente, 1994) are:

- a failure to bring learner achievement up to satisfactory levels
- an injury to the development of a learner because of lack of professional practice in testing, evaluating, or placing the learner
- a failure to act to protect a seriously threatened learner

Attempts to sue teachers for malpractice when learners' academic achievement levels have not been as high as complainants feel they should be have not received a warm reception in the nation's courts. Part of the difficulty involves clearly defining the limits of teachers' responsibilities to ensure learning. The courts have recognized that many variables other than the work of individual teachers have the potential to affect achievement levels. These range from home backgrounds of learners, motivational levels of learners, the nature and appropriateness of learning-support materials provided by the school, and the kinds of instructional resources provided to individual learners by members of their own families. Most

This teacher carefully monitors these students who are working with chemicals in the laboratory. This kind of professional attention protects teachers in the event of a negligence suit.

authorities do not look for much change in the reluctance of courts to support claims of malpractice against teachers whose learners do not do well on measures of academic achievement.

There have been a few successful malpractice suits brought against teachers who have not evaluated and placed learners properly. Successful suits of this kind must be supported by impeccable documentation. Nevertheless, the possibility exists for successful suits to be brought against teachers who are excessively careless in evaluating and placing learners.

There are varying circumstances in which a teacher might be charged with failing to provide adequate protection for a learner. For example, the teacher might fail to act when a learner suggests to the teacher that he or she is being threatened by other learners. If these threats are carried out and the learner is hurt, the courts might seriously consider a malpractice charge against the teacher. A death by suicide of a learner who provided information about his or her intentions to a teacher who failed to take any action might also be grounds for a successful malpractice suit brought by surviving relatives (Valente, 1994).

TEACHERS' CIVIL RIGHTS

Many years ago, few questioned the legitimacy of asking teachers to forgo some of their freedom of personal action as a condition of personal employment. In some places, teachers were forbidden to smoke. Many other districts insisted that teachers never consume alcohol. Still others required teachers to be regular participants in religious services. Today, few restrictions are placed on teachers' lives away from school. These issues occasionally do still come up, however, and court cases have centered on kinds of personal rights teachers ought to have.

Some people maintain that teachers are role models for impressionable learners. As such, they have a responsibility to behave more discretely and more suitably than "typical" citizens. If this is true, these individuals contend, then teachers' behavior both in and out of the classroom is a proper concern of school officials.

In cases that have been litigated, courts typically have ruled that teachers cannot be punished for exercising their constitutional rights. However, the United States Supreme Court has noted that the exercise of constitutional rights by public school teachers and administrators has to be balanced against the interests of the general public (Valente, 1994). In one case where the decision supported this view, a court declared that certain professions such as teaching impose limitations on personal actions that are not imposed on people in other occupations (*Board of Trustees of Compton Junior College District v. Stubblefield*, 1971).

In practice, when teachers have been dismissed because of actions in their personal lives, school districts have had to present convincing evidence that their behaviors were interfering with their abilities to function in the classroom. The impact of these behaviors on the ability to work positively with parents and other professionals also has received careful attention from judges in these cases.

Freedom of Association

There have been instances of teachers being dismissed for belonging to so-called radical organizations or even for being active in more conventional partisan politics. Others have either been dismissed or threatened with dismissal because a blood relationship to a school board member was discovered or because they married a school board member or a school administrator employed by the same district. Many teachers who have been dismissed for these reasons or who have been threatened with dismissal have gone to court to keep their jobs.

In general, courts have ruled that teachers cannot be dismissed simply because they belong to a controversial group unless there is evidence that they have supported illegal activities. In addition, courts have demanded that school districts prove that membership of teachers in these groups was detrimental to the functioning of the school (Valente, 1994).

The courts have almost uniformly ruled that teachers cannot be dismissed because of their political support of candidates for school boards or other elected offices or for participating personally in partisan political activities (including wearing political buttons in school). The line has been drawn, however, when teachers have attempted to indoctrinate learners. As with similar issues, the courts typically have considered whether a teacher's partisan political activities have seriously disrupted or impaired the instructional process (Fischer et al., 1987).

Personal Appearance

A number of court cases have centered on rights of school districts to impose dress and grooming standards for teachers. Decisions have reflected a mixed pattern. A line of reasoning found in some decisions holds that teachers do not have substantial constitutional rights in this area, and that school districts have the right to establish dress codes and grooming standards for teachers. A line of reasoning in other decisions has been that school districts' limitations on teachers' behaviors must be tied to the districts' responsibilities for ensuring an orderly educational environment. If dress codes and grooming standards cannot be shown to be necessary for the existence of an orderly educational environment, then such requirements cannot be defended (Valente, 1994). In recent years, most decisions seem to be following the first line of argument. More and more, courts are overturning grooming and dress standards only if (1) teachers have been able to prove the regulations are unreasonable or (2) teachers have been able to establish that grooming standards negatively affect matters associated with racial pride or academic freedom (Fischer et al., 1987).

Lifestyle Issues

Many issues related to teachers' rights to choose their own lifestyles have been litigated. Among these cases have been those concerning homosexuality, unmarried cohabitation, and rights of teachers to breast-feed their own infants in school. For the most part, the courts have maintained that teachers have a right to privacy and that school officials cannot take actions that infringe on this right. However, decisions in right-of-privacy cases have varied greatly depending on particular circumstances of individual cases. For example, some attempts to use homosexuality as grounds for dismissal have been upheld in situations where teachers publicly flaunted unconventional sexual conduct or lied about their sexual orientation when applying for their jobs (Valente, 1994). On the other hand, in many other cases, courts have rejected dismissal actions, noting that homosexuality cannot be used as a reason for dismissing a teacher unless it can be proved that this orientation clearly led to conduct that has impaired the teacher's ability to discharge his or her professional role.

A number of court cases have considered the legitimacy of dismissal actions taken against a teacher charged with unmarried cohabitation. In one such case, a teacher moved in with her boyfriend. Two months later, the school authorities told her she could either resign or be fired. Ten days after receiving this information, she married her boyfriend. Nevertheless, the school district initiated action to suspend her on the grounds of immorality. She challenged this decision in court. In its decision, the court upheld the rights of the teacher, noting that prior to the dismissal action, most people in the community had been unaware that she was living with her boyfriend. Furthermore, there was insufficient evidence to sustain the contention that the teacher's behavior had interfered with her effectiveness in the classroom (*Thompson v. Southwest School District*, 1980).

Immoral Conduct

Frequently, cases concerning alleged immoral or unprofessional conduct of teachers have come before the courts. Immorality, as noted earlier in this chapter, is included in many tenure laws as a justification for dismissing a tenured teacher. When teachers have been found to have acted in immoral ways, the courts have acted to support dismissal decisions. The difficulty in these cases has been in defining what constitutes immoral behavior. For example, unmarried cohabitation might be considered outrageous behavior in some places. In others, it might occasion little concern.

When they have dealt with immoral behavior cases, the courts have tended to look at how the teacher's behavior influenced both his or her standing in the community and his or her ability to teach. When the teacher's behavior has been seen to violate prevailing community standards and when it has resulted in widespread public outrage, the courts have generally supported dismissal decisions.

In general, the courts have been less tolerant of teachers who have been accused of immoral behavior involving learners than with immoral behavior involving adults. This has been particularly true in cases where sexual misconduct is one of the issues.

Criminal Conduct

Conviction or even indictment on a criminal charge can be the basis for teacher dismissal or denial or revocation of a teaching certificate. In several states, prospective teachers must reveal whether they have been convicted of a felony when they apply for a teaching certificate. Admission of such a conviction or failure to answer the question truthfully may be grounds for denial of a certificate to teach.

When cases involving dismissal or revocation of a teaching certificate because of a felony conviction are challenged, courts often weigh the seriousness of the offense in making their decisions. For example, in a Pennsylvania case, a teacher was dismissed because she had been convicted of shoplifting. The school district argued this was an immoral act. The court agreed and upheld the teacher's dismissal (*Lesley v. Oxford Area School District*, 1980).

However, in another case involving shoplifting, the outcome was different. In this instance, a school counselor had been convicted of shoplifting at a local mall. In its decision, the court indicated that the school district had failed to provide sufficient evidence demonstrating that this conviction established that this person was unfit to serve as a school counselor (*Golden v. Board of Education of the County of Harrison*, 1981).

Sometimes teachers who have been convicted of misdemeanors have faced dismissal actions. A teacher in Alaska was fired after being convicted of illegally diverting electricity to his house. The court upheld the dismissal, contending that the act was a form of theft and constituted moral turpitude (*Kenai Peninsula Borough of Education v. Brown*, 1984).

Freedom of Conscience

The separation of church and state and the role of religion in schools continue to be controversial. Some teachers may have religious views that conflict with those of parents and others in the community. Because learners have little personal choice about where they go to school and who teaches them, our society has frowned on teachers who attempt to impose their own religious beliefs on learners.

Some court cases involving teachers' religious views have been closely associated to subjects teachers were assigned to teach. In one situation, a teacher belonged to a religious group that opposed all references to patriotism and national symbols. She told her principal that she would not teach her learners any content that was designed to promote love of country. Further, she would not acknowledge such national holidays as Washington's Birthday.

In response to this situation, the principal, with the support of the school district administration, told the teacher she would have to follow the prescribed curriculum. The teacher challenged this decision. Ultimately, the case was considered by a federal court. It its decision, the court upheld the action of the school district, noting that the First Amendment to the United States Constitution does not provide a license for a teacher to teach a curriculum that is at variance with the one prescribed by the state. The court went on to say that whereas the teacher had a right to her own religious beliefs, she had no right to require others to submit to her views and, thereby, to be deprived of an ordinary part of their educational experience (*Palmer v. Board of Education of the City of Chicago*, 1980).

Another controversial issue relates to teachers' rights to be absent from school to observe religious holidays. For the most part, the courts have ruled that teachers do have a right to take leave for a religious holiday so long as their absence does not cause undue hardship on the school district. In other words, the amount of time taken off cannot be excessive. Whereas the courts have supported the principle that teachers have the right to ask for time away from their jobs to participate in religious holidays, they have also noted that school districts are under no obligation to pay for such leaves unless there are stipulations in teachers' contracts requiring such payments.

• Key Ideas in Summary

- Teacher certification is a function of state government. The certificate itself is essentially a license to practice. Individuals who accept a teaching position without the appropriate certificate may find that they are not eligible to receive a salary. State governments have the authority to change requirements for obtaining and retaining teaching certificates.

- Contracts are legally binding documents that place obligations on all parties who sign. In the case of teaching contracts, they typically involve two parties, a teacher and the employing school district. When a contract is broken, the injured party may be entitled to compensation.

- AIDS testing has been found to be a form of legal search. Hence, any form of AIDS testing must be consistent with constitutional protection associated with search. This means that a school district must demonstrate a "compelling interest" in the information before it can require people to take an AIDS test as a condition of employment.

- Free access to information and ideas has been deemed critical to the survival of a free society. Tenure laws were developed to protect teachers from arbitrary dismissal because some school patrons may not agree with some of their ideas. Contrary to popular opinion, tenure laws do not provide an unconditional lifetime guarantee of employment. These laws spell out specific conditions under which tenured teachers can be dismissed. These typically require that due process procedures be followed and that the school district initiating the action provide substantial proof of its allegations.

- For the most part, courts have been reluctant to interfere with professional decisions of teachers in such areas as grading. However, there have been instances where grading decisions have been overturned when complainants have demonstrated grades were awarded in an arbitrary or capricious manner.

- The courts typically have upheld teachers' rights to include course material in their classes that is relevant to topics they are teaching and that is appropriate for the age and maturity levels of their learners. However, school districts have the right to place some limits on materials that are used. For example, they can insist that materials pertain to the required curriculum. School districts cannot use unconstitutional reasons as grounds for censoring material.

- Some content about religion can be included in public school curricula. However, teachers may not promote or demean a particular religion or belief.

- Teachers and school officials are mandatory reporters of suspected child abuse. This means that they may be subject to criminal penalties that could include jail time or fines if they fail to report instances of suspected child abuse.

- A tort is a legal action that involves a suit by one individual against another for an injury that resulted because of a breach of legal duty. Torts in education often involve charges of teacher negligence or even malpractice. The three major categories of teacher negligence are nonfeasance, misfeasance, and malfeasance.

- The use of excessive force when disciplining learners is a common cause of suits against teachers. Whereas the United States Supreme Court has found that corporal punishment in schools does not constitute illegal "cruel and unusual punishment," some states now forbid the practice. At a time when people do not hesitate to sue and when there is much concern about child abuse, teachers need to consider other means of discipline.

- As do all citizens, teachers enjoy civil rights protection. However, because of their special relationship to impressionable youth, teachers' rights as individuals must be weighed against the right of the state to provide a proper education for its young people. This implies that in some instances, teachers may be held to higher standards of personal behavior than the public at large.

- Teachers' actions away from school may provide grounds for dismissal if these behaviors are found to impair their ability to discharge their professional responsibilities or if they pose a threat to the welfare of learners.

- Conviction or even indictment for a crime can lead to revocation of a teaching credential, dismissal, or both. Not all convictions have been supported by the courts as indications of adequate grounds for dismissing a teacher. On the other hand, in some jurisdictions, convictions even of misdemeanors have been upheld by the courts as adequate grounds for terminating a teacher's employment.

• Review and Discussion Questions

1. What are examples of issues that sometimes embroil teachers in legal actions?
2. What might be some consequences of signing a teaching contract and beginning to teach without a valid teaching certificate?
3. What is the legal status of an "oral teaching contract"?
4. What must a school district do to provide an adequate legal justification for requiring teachers and prospective teachers to be tested for substance abuse or AIDS?
5. Why have some states passed tenure laws, and what are some concerns critics of these laws have voiced?
6. Some people argue that once a teacher closes the door to the classroom, he or she has the legal right to say anything to learners. Are there truly no limitations on teachers' academic freedom?
7. What kinds of protection are there for teachers who discharge their responsibilities as mandatory reporters in suspected child abuse cases?
8. What are some common categories of negligence, and what are some things teachers can do to avoid litigation associated with each?
9. Why do some people argue that the negatives associated with corporal punishment far outweigh any positives?
10. Why have some people argued that teachers should be held to higher standards of moral conduct than typical citizens? Do you agree with this position? Why or why not?

• Ideas for Field Experiences, Projects, and Enrichment

1. Investigate the requirements for teacher certification in your state. Are different types of certificates available? If so, what are the qualifications for each? How does a person go about applying for a certificate? How long does it take to get the certificate once all application materials have been completed? How long is a certificate good for? Are there special requirements that must be met by holders of teaching certificates to maintain their validity? Report your findings to your class.
2. Interview a representative of a local teachers' association or a local school administrator regarding teaching contracts and conditions of employment. How does this person feel about issues such as tenure, arrangements for teachers to take off a certain number of personal business days each year, provisions for sick leave, and so forth? If several others in your class interview different people, share findings with the class as a whole.
3. Look through some back issues of newspapers or educational journals for articles focusing on teachers' legal problems. (*Phi Delta Kappan*, a leading journal in education, includes a feature on a legal issue of concern to educators in every issue.) Share these materials with your class. Identify legal principles discussed in the articles you read. As a group, think about how these problems might have been avoided. Were you surprised by any of the situations that resulted in these legal difficulties? If so, which ones, and why?
4. Organize a debate on the topic: "Resolved that tenure laws impede efforts to achieve meaningful reform of public education."
5. Many state teachers' organizations produce information about state laws and regulations that relate to legal concerns of teachers. Obtain a copy of some of this material. Compare some of the legal requirements in your state with some of the ideas introduced in this chapter. What are some differences and similarities? Share your findings with your instructor.

• References

Board of Trustees of Compton Junior College District v. Stubblefield, 94 Cal. Rptr. 318, 321 (Cal. Ct. App. 1971).

California Teachers Association. (1992). *Guide to school law.* Burlingame, CA: Author.

Fischer, L., Schimmel, D., & Kelly, C. (1987). *Teachers and the law* (2nd ed.). New York: Longman.

Golden v. Board of Education of the County of Harrison, 285 S.E.2nd 665 (W.Va. 1981).

Ingraham v. Wright, 430 U.S. 651 (1977).

Kenai Peninsula Borough of Education v. Brown, 691 P.2d 1034 (Alaska 1984).

Kingsville Independent School District v. Cooper, 611 F.2d 1109 (5th Cir. 1980).

Lesley v. Oxford Area School District, 420 A2d 764 (Pa. Commw. Ct. 1980).

Palmer v. Board of Education of the City of Chicago, 603 F.2d 1271 (7th Cir. 1979), cert denied, 444 U.S. 1026 (1980).

Parducci v. Rutland, 316 F. Supp. 352 (N.D. Ala. 1970).

Richardson, J. (1995, March 1). Critics target state teacher-tenure laws. *Education Week,* pp. 1, 13.

Thompson v. Southwest School District, 483 F. Supp. 1170 (W.D. Mo. 1980).

Underwood, J. (Ed.). (1994). Child abuse. *The Schools and the Courts, 20*(1), 1027–1028.

Valente, W. (1994). *Law in the schools* (3rd ed.). New York: Macmillan.

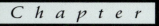
Professional Groups

OBJECTIVES

- Identify basic orientations of the National Education Association and the American Federation of Teachers.

- Describe the historical development of the National Education Association and the American Federation of Teachers.

- Point out some arguments both supporting and opposing the idea that teachers are *professionals*.

- Differentiate between *sanctions* and *strikes*.

- Describe how actions of teachers' organizations have enlarged roles teachers play in making educational policy.

- Identify some teachers' specialty organizations that seek to improve the teaching of certain subjects and age groups.

There are two types of teachers' professional organizations: general organizations and specialty organizations. The two largest general organizations, the National Education Association and the American Federation of Teachers, seek members from among teachers at all grade levels and across all subjects. The specialty organizations focus their attention on groups of teachers who are interested in certain subject areas or specific categories of learners. Both general and specialty organizations either have active student affiliates or welcome students as regular members.

WHY BECOME INVOLVED?

Specific benefits that come from membership in a professional organization vary somewhat from group to group. However, some common benefits are those associated with networking with other teachers and sharing information.

Networking

A major advantage of working in an occupation such as teaching is personal control over much of what is done each day. We have more latitude to make decisions about what we do to discharge our responsibilities than many others in the work force. Because of the nature of what we do, we often do not come into much direct contact with other teachers during the teaching day. In the past, this situation has sometimes inhibited teachers from taking full advantage of the autonomy they enjoy (Henson, in press). By affiliating with professional groups, we grow to appreciate common bonds that draw together all who teach. This can build confidence that translates into more willingness to take advantage of the autonomy we have as classroom teachers.

Sharing Information

Teachers who belong to teacher organizations have access to information through several channels. These include annual meetings, workshops, journals, and newsletters. Membership also allows us opportunities to come into personal contact with other teachers. These contacts can help us gain insights from others who can encourage us to try new approaches in working with our learners (Cornell & Farkas, 1995).

GENERAL ORGANIZATIONS

One of the biggest changes in education over the past 100 years has been the emergence of a view of teaching as permanent rather than temporary employment. Throughout most of the nineteenth century, teachers were required to have little formal training. They were poorly paid. Almost no one considered teaching to be an occupation that would provide someone with a fulfilling, lifelong career. Teaching was seen as a fallback occupation that could tide a person over until something better came along. Today, many of us who teach perceive ourselves as being occupationally permanent. This perception has been important in building support for large general organizations to respond to teachers' needs.

In part, interest in large national teachers' associations has been prompted by the growth in the size of school districts. This growth trend has been in evidence since the early years of this century. Consolidation of districts into larger units has produced some economies of operation. At the same time, it has tended to distance teachers from central office administrators. Teachers' organizations have provided a vehicle for giving a collective voice to teachers who sometimes have felt isolated from district-level decision makers. The organizations have functioned as conduits to transmit teachers' concerns to school policymakers.

Over the years, several organizations have attempted to attract a nationwide membership of teachers. Today, the two largest groups by far are the National Education Association and the American Federation of Teachers.

The National Education Association (NEA)

The National Education Association (NEA), boasting more than two million members, is the largest teachers' organization in the country. It traces its roots back to the National Teachers' Association, formed as long ago as 1857 (Hesson & Weeks, 1987). In the 1870s, the National Teachers' Association merged with the National Association of School Superintendents and the American Normal School Association to become the National Educational Association (Donley, 1976). Some years later, the word *Educational* was shortened to *Education*.

In its early years, the National Education Association (NEA) was little concerned with teachers' benefits, in part because many of its most active and influential members were administrators, not teachers. (Today, administrators do not belong to the NEA.) A widespread belief that teaching was a "calling," almost in a religious sense, and thus it was not proper for teachers to evidence too much concern about financial rewards and working conditions also contributed to the lack of concern for their welfare on the part of the NEA.

The NEA became much more attuned to compensation issues after World War II. Low salaries had driven many teachers to seek other work. In response to this situation, the NEA began lobbying legislatures and taking other actions to apprise the public of the teachers' plight. Among these efforts were attempts to get school district leaders to sign agreements calling for formal negotiation between teachers' organization representatives and school board representatives on issues pertaining to salaries and working conditions.

During this post–Word War II period, the NEA leadership was reluctant to use strikes as a policy weapon. To many NEA members, strikes were too closely associated with organized labor. The NEA's view of teachers as "professionals" did not square with the use of strikes as a bargaining tool. Instead, the NEA preferred to pressure states and school districts to do right by teachers by threatening or actually imposing sanctions. *Sanctions* involve the deliberate dissemination of adverse information about a district or group of districts to the entire national community of educators. Their purpose is to use negative publicity as a means of bringing pressure on school officials to improve conditions for teachers.

Teachers from all grade levels attend a session at a national convention of the National Education Association.

Concerns about the effectiveness of sanctions eventually led the NEA to acknowledge the strike as a legitimate bargaining weapon for teachers. By the late 1960s, teachers' strikes had become a predictable early fall event. This pattern continues today.

The NEA's membership has demonstrated great growth throughout most of this century. In part, this growth has resulted from the organization's successful push for unification. *Unification* means that a teacher may not select membership in a local NEA affiliate, a state NEA affiliate, or the NEA itself without simultaneously joining all three groups. All states are now unified. This has produced a tremendous gain in the total income of the NEA, and it has turned the group into a potent national political lobby.

Philosophically, the NEA takes the position that teachers have much in common with members of the learned professions, such as medicine and law. Like doctors and lawyers, teachers go through a specialized preparation program. Typically, the state certifies their competence. (In a few places, there are exceptions, such as some charter schools that are not required to hire teachers with state-issued certificates.) As is the case with doctors and lawyers, teachers usually are charged with

BOX
16-1

Teachers' Strikes

Should teachers go on strike? This question has led to heated exchanges between people who support strikes and people who are against them. Individuals opposed to strikes frequently argue that they undermine the image of teachers. Some fear that teachers' strikes will alienate middle- and upper-class citizens, who have traditionally been extremely supportive of public education. This could well translate into a reduction in their support of funding for the public schools.

Supporters of strikes as an appropriate weapon often argue that most people are indifferent to the many pressures teachers face. As evidence, they point out the conflicting obligations legislatures have placed on teachers. For example, teachers are expected to turn out learners who perform better than ever with little or no increases in funding for the schools. Although the public may say improvements in working conditions are needed, there is little evidence that much real action has occurred when teachers have been unwilling to strike.

What Do You Think?

1. Do strike actions threaten teachers' credibility with parents and other influential people in the community? Why or why not?
2. Is the issue of whether teachers should strike something that may be answered yes in some school districts and no in others, depending on the general attitude of the particular community toward this kind of action?
3. Have you or any members of your family been involved in a strike, particularly one involving public schools? What were reactions of various groups of people who were involved?
4. What is your personal feeling about the issue of teacher strikes? Are there some experiences you have had that led you to adopt your position on this issue?

maintaining their level of competence by participating actively in self-improvement programs and by pursuing advanced study. A code of professional ethics guides teachers' behavior.

This view of the nature of teaching has led the NEA to push hard for programs designed to give teachers more control over their professional lives. Many of these efforts have sought to increase teachers involvement in governance. *Governance* is a broad term, but it generally implies that teachers should have substantive input into profession-related decisions such as training teachers, hiring teachers, determining course content, selecting learning materials, and identifying appropriate instructional methods.

Today, the NEA is an organization run by and for classroom teachers. Its publication arm, legal services operation, research division, and other components are all oriented toward serving teachers' interests. For further information about the NEA and its programs, write to:

National Education Association
1201 16th Street, NW
Washington, DC 20036

The American Federation of Teachers (AFT)

The American Federation of Teachers (AFT), a union affiliated with the AFL-CIO, has never enjoyed the numerical strength of the NEA, but it still has had a great impact on teaching. Much of its influence is explained by the concentration of AFT membership in large cities. Teachers' benefits packages won through AFT action in such places as Chicago and New York have influenced teacher groups throughout the country. Because the smaller AFT has always had the potential to chip away at the membership of the much larger NEA, the NEA has become more aggressive in its pursuit of better conditions for teachers. In the absence of a competing AFT, it is doubtful that the NEA would have embraced strikes as a legitimate bargaining weapon as early as it did.

The AFT has always been strongest in areas where organized labor has enjoyed wide support. This accounts for the group's distinctively urban flavor. The organization traces its beginnings to Chicago, where the Chicago Teachers Federation was organized in the late 1890s. A meeting of the Chicago union and others from industrialized parts of the upper Midwest resulted in the establishment of the American Federation of Teachers in 1916.

From the beginning, the AFT differed from the NEA in two ways. First, it sought as members people who were classroom teachers. The AFT was never dominated by university people or administrators. Second, the AFT focused heavily on winning benefits for teachers right from the beginning. Although the same has been true of the NEA in recent years, in its early days, the NEA was concerned with educational issues that ranged well beyond obtaining benefits for teachers.

The AFT views teachers differently than does the NEA. As the AFT sees them, teachers are more like employees of large corporations than like lawyers and doctors. One reason supporting this view is that teachers do not go through a lengthy professional preparation program that extends multiple years beyond the award of the baccalaureate degree. Another rationale for this position is that many studies have revealed that teachers do not have a social status as high as lawyers or doctors. Perhaps the key point undergirding this perspective is that large numbers of lawyers and doctors are self-employed, whereas nearly all teachers work for an institution. In many cases, school systems are large, and teachers have little personal contact with those who are responsible for their continued employment. This, it is argued, makes teachers similar in many respects to employees of large corporations. Given this situation, the AFT believes that teachers need a strong organization that can counterbalance the potential for often distant administrative power to be exercised arbitrarily.

The AFT's perception of teaching has led it to be concerned about winning noticeable improvements in teachers' salaries and working conditions. The AFT has generally been less concerned than the NEA with increasing teachers' responsibilities for educational governance. The AFT position has been that there are two classes of educators: administrators, who represent management, and teachers, who represent labor. The interests of the two groups are fundamentally different. Therefore, the role of an organization representing teachers should be to maximize the benefits for teachers and restrict arbitrary administrative power. The AFT acknowledges the right of administrators to manage what has been negotiated so long as what is done is consistent with the formally adopted agreements. When administrative management is seen to be inconsistent with the agreements, a pattern of teachers' organization–administrator arbitration (based on traditional labor-management practices) is considered to be the most productive approach to resolving the problem.

For further information about the AFT and its programs, write to:

American Federation of Teachers
555 New Jersey Avenue, NW
Washington, DC 20001

The NEA and AFT: Prospects

Chances are good that the NEA and AFT will continue to be visible participants in American education. Three pressures seem destined to continue to be felt by teachers: (1) rising public expectations for public schools, (2) increased demand for cost containment in education, and (3) legally mandated changes directed at school curricula. In response to these pressures, those of us who teach will likely feel an ongoing need to make our feelings known through major teacher organizations.

With regard to rising expectations, we in education find ourselves confronted by public concerns about mediocre learner performances on standardized tests. We share concerns about levels of academic achievement, but we also recognize that how well our learners do on these tests is only partly a result of the quality of what is provided at school. For example, teachers have little control over the amount of time parents allow their children to watch television instead of working on school assignments. Comments on issues of this kind from professional groups enlightened the general public on issues that are beyond teachers' direct control.

Cost-containment issues are of concern to those of us who teach as well as to other citizens. We, too, pay taxes. At the same time, we sometimes find ourselves caught between pressures to improve learners' performance and pressures to spend less money to get the job done. Professional groups can help bring this incompatibility to the public's attention.

Legally mandated changes place great strains on teachers in certain areas. This is particularly true when legislatures ask us to teach content we have not been trained to teach. Some years ago, elementary teachers in California found themselves required to teach Spanish, a language with whom few were familiar. A recent Kentucky law requires teachers to introduce consumer- or economics-related content into their instructional program. Few have had formal academic training in this kind of content. Professional teachers' groups have important roles to play, particularly when mandates seem to place teachers in a position of being evaluated on their knowledge of newly mandated subject matter, on their ability to teach newly mandated subject matter, or on both their knowledge of and their ability to teach newly mandated subject matter.

Today, both the NEA and AFT carefully monitor proposals that have the potential to affect their members' professional lives. For example, today both groups are studying carefully the evolving national certification program being developed under the leadership of the National Board for Professional Teaching Standards. (For more information about this issue, see Chapter 1.) Both organizations are particularly wary of any attempts that might be made to require national certification and to undercut the legitimacy of certificates issued by the individual states.

The influence of the NEA, the AFT, and their local affiliates varies greatly from place to place. In some parts of the country, representatives of teachers' groups have no legal right to negotiate for teachers' benefits. But they do have an influence even under these conditions. The organizations articulate views at school board meetings, through contacts with influential local decision makers, and in other ways on such issues as teachers' salaries and working conditions.

Clearly, the influence of actions of general teacher professional groups is more discernible in parts of the country where these organizations have a legal authority to represent teachers' interests when salaries and working conditions are negotiated. In these areas, the local affiliate of the NEA or AFT (or sometimes another group not connected with either of these national organizations) is designated as the official bargaining agent for teachers. Although teachers usually are free to belong to the organization of their choice, for pragmatic reasons, many choose to affiliate with the group that has been designated as the official bargaining agent. Since representatives of this group actually negotiate agreements affecting teaching conditions, many teachers want to belong so they can have a voice in shaping positions that will be presented by those representing teachers' interests.

THE SPECIALTY ORGANIZATIONS

We educators are great believers in professional improvement. This interest is reflected in the dozens of specialty organizations that have been formed, at least in part, out of a desire to establish forums where those of us with particular kinds of learners or with special subject matter interests can exchange information and learn about promising new approaches.

Most of these groups have large annual meetings that draw together educators from throughout the country. Many also sponsor regional and state meetings. Some have local affiliates that provide opportunities for educators with common interests to get together frequently to share ideas.

Specialty groups often have arrangements that allow college and university students who are preparing to become teachers to join at reduced rates. Many of these groups also publish excellent professional journals. These are good sources for up-to-date research findings and for information about innovative teaching practices.

Subsections that follow provide basic information about some of the specialty groups that serve teachers. This listing is by no means comprehensive, but it does suggest the wide range of concerns that are addressed by specialty groups in education. The following organizations are discussed:

- American Alliance for Health, Physical Education, Recreation, and Dance (AAHPERD)
- American Vocational Association (AVA)

Critical Incident

Pressure to Join a Teachers' Organization

Leonard Stephenson is in his first year of teaching biology at Rutherford Hayes Senior High School, which enrolls about 2,000 students from the West Markley School District. He is one of 80 teachers in the school.

The West Markley School District has recognized a local teachers' organization as the official bargaining agent for the district's teachers. Its representatives sit down with representatives of the local school board each year to negotiate issues related to salaries and working conditions.

The building representative for the local teachers, Sarana McPartland, has been actively encouraging Leonard to join the group. She has made frequent mention of the point that 78 of the building's 80 teachers are members, and has suggested that some teachers who pay dues might not feel kindly toward a teacher who enjoys the benefits of negotiated agreements without paying dues and affiliating with the teachers' organization. She has also noted to Leonard that the district allows member teachers to pay the annual teachers' organization dues as a monthly payroll deduction.

Leonard has no real problem with the amount of the dues, but he does have some philosophical concerns about membership. He knows that some of the local organization leaders have actively talked about the possibility of a teachers' strike if negotiations with the school board do not go well. Also troublesome to Leonard is that some of the organization's publications always seem to paint administrators as villains who are out to exploit teachers.

Leonard believes that the students are being overlooked in the whole process. He is concerned that the teachers' organization needlessly interferes with cooperative efforts of teachers and administrators to meet students' needs. He is afraid that joining the teachers' organization will signal his approval of the breakdown of teacher-administrator cooperation. Sarana has told him that she will be coming by again this afternoon and wants a definite answer to her invitation to join the group.

What are some values reflected in the position taken by Sarana McPartland? How do these square with some of Leonard's bedrock beliefs? What are some implications of these values for how Sarana and Leonard might define "acting appropriately"? Have you ever found yourself in a situation where it has been assumed that you will conform to the expectations of others that are at odds with some of your own personal convictions? How did you resolve the situation?

In this case, what should Leonard do next? Are there some others he might consult? If so, who might they be? What problems might result if he decides not to join the organization? What might happen if he does decide to join? Is there a reasonable compromise that might be worked out?

- Association for Childhood Education International (ACEI)
- Business Professionals of America (BPA)
- Council on Exceptional Children (CEC)
- International Council for Computers in Education (ICCE)
- International Reading Association (IRA)
- Music Teachers National Association (MTNA)
- National Art Education Association (NAEA)

Teachers often form affiliations with groups sharing interests in certain parts of the overall school program. These teachers are attending a session sponsored by the National Council of Teachers of English.

- National Association for Gifted Children (NAGC)
- National Business Education Association (NBEA)
- National Conference on Parent Involvement (NCPI)
- National Council for the Social Studies (NCSS)
- National Council of Teachers of English (NCTE)
- National Council of Teachers of Mathematics (NCTM)
- National Science Teachers Association (NSTA)

American Alliance for Health, Physical Education, Recreation, and Dance (AAHPERD)

This large national group embraces individuals with interests in health, physical education, recreation, and dance. Membership includes elementary and secondary school teachers, school administrators, college and university professors, and others who share an interest in the group's work. Student memberships are available.

AAHPERD sponsors the publication of several journals. The *Journal of Physical Education, Recreation, and Dance* is published nine times each year. *Health Education* appears six times a year. Members are informed about ongoing activities through the group's monthly publication, *Update*. Research results are reported in *Research Quarterly for Exercise and Sport*. For information about this group, write to:

American Alliance for Health, Physical Education, Recreation, and Dance
1900 Association Drive
Reston, VA 22091

American Vocational Association (AVA)

This large association has 57 state affiliates of teachers, supervisors, administrators, and others with interests in improving vocational, technical, and practical arts education. It supports a monthly publication, *Vocational Education Journal*. This journal publishes articles about trends affecting the workplace and programs that prepare learners to enter the work force. In addition to this monthly publication, AVA also publishes *Update: The Newspaper for Vocational Educators*. This newspaper keeps members apprised of association news as well as information about employment opportunities. AVA invites college and university students who are preparing to teach to join. For further information about this group, write to:

American Vocational Education Association
1410 King Street
Alexandria, VA 22314

Association for Childhood Education International (ACEI)

The Association for Childhood Education International has about 200 chapters scattered throughout the country. Its members are particularly concerned about the development of children from infancy through early adolescence. There are special divisions within the organization that focus, respectively, on (1) infancy, (2) early childhood, and (3) later childhood and early adolescence. Student memberships are encouraged.

ACEI publishes a journal for its general membership entitled *Childhood Education* five times a year. The group also publishes the *Journal of Research in Childhood Education*, which includes reports of research on child development topics. For information about this group, write to:

Association for Childhood Education International
11141 Georgia Avenue, Suite 200
Wheaton, MD 20202

Business Professionals of America (BPA)

Business Professionals of America is a 51,000-member association for people interested in business and office education. It seeks to develop interest in the American business system and office operations within the framework of vocational education programs. The group publishes a quarterly newsletter, *Advisor's Bulletin*, as well as a quarterly journal, *Communiqué*. For information about this group, write to:

Business Professionals of America
5454 Cleveland Avenue
Columbus, OH 43231

Council on Exceptional Children (CEC)

The Council on Exceptional Children is dedicated to promoting better educational programs for gifted learners and learners with disabilities. Membership includes teachers, administrators, parents, university-based professionals, and others interested in the group's work. Membership is open to students.

CED publishes two major journals. *Exceptional Children* appears six times a year, and *Teaching Exceptional Children* is published quarterly. For information about this group, write to:

Council for Exceptional Children
1920 Association Drive
Reston, VA 22091

International Council for Computers in Education (ICCE)

As its name suggests, the International Council for Computers in Education seeks to serve the interests of people who are committed to making more effective use of computers in schools. Membership is available to students.

ICCE produces two regular publications. *The Computing Teacher* is issued nine times each year, and the *SIG Bulletin* appears quarterly. For information about this group, write to:

International Council for Computers in Education
University of Oregon
1787 Agate Street
Eugene, OR 97403

International Reading Association (IRA)

The International Reading Association, with about 90,000 members, is one of the nation's largest education specialty groups. There are 1,200 local chapters scattered throughout the country. IRA's membership includes regular classroom teachers, reading specialists and consultants, administrators, educational researchers, librarians, and others interested in promoting reading. Student memberships are available.

IRA publishes several journals. *Reading Teacher*, published nine times a year, contains articles of primary interest to people who want to improve reading instruction in elementary schools. The *Journal of Reading*, also published nine times a year, focuses on the theory and practice of reading as applied to middle schools, junior and senior high schools, and adult learning situations. *Reading Research Quar-*

terly, appearing four times a year, is devoted to disseminating the work of reading researchers. IRA also publishes a Spanish-language quarterly, *Lectura y Vida*. For information about this group, write to:

International Reading Association
800 Barksdale Road
P.O. Box 8139
Newark, DE 19714

Music Teachers National Association (MTNA)

The Music Teachers National Association has chapters throughout the country. Members include music teachers in the schools (elementary, secondary, and higher education) and music teachers with private tutoring practices. The group is dedicated to improving music instruction, performance, and understanding. Membership is open to students.

MTNA sponsors several publications. *The American Music Teacher* appears bimonthly, and the *Directory of Nationally Certified Teachers* is an annual volume. For information about this group, write to:

Music Teachers National Association
2113 Carew Tower
Cincinnati, OH 45202

National Art Education Association (NAEA)

The National Art Education Association is the leading national professional group for art teachers. It is dedicated to improving visual-arts instruction in the schools. Members include teachers, administrators, and others with a direct connection to art education in the schools. Special memberships are available for students who are preparing to be art teachers.

NAEA publishes several journals. *Art Education* and *NAEA News* appear bimonthly. A research journal, *Studies in Art Education*, is published four times a year. For information about this group, write to:

National Art Education Association
1916 Association Drive
Reston, VA 22091

National Association for Gifted Children (NAGC)

The National Association for Gifted Children promotes the interests of parents and educators who are concerned about school programs for gifted learners. The group conducts training sessions for parents and educators and lobbies at the national and state levels for better programs for the gifted. Membership is open to all who support the organization's objectives. Student members are welcome.

NAGC has one major publication, *Gifted Education*, which appears four times a year. For information about this group, write to:

National Association for Gifted Education
4175 Lovell Road, Suite 140
Circle Pines, MN 55014

National Business Education Association (NBEA)

The 18,000 members of the National Business Education Association include secondary and postsecondary teachers of business subjects. The group has a total of 54 state and local affiliates scattered throughout the nation. It publishes a quarterly journal entitled *Business Education Forum*. This publication includes articles covering accounting, business principles and economics, communication, information processing, marketing, and other business-related subjects. For further information about this group, write to:

National Business Education Association
1914 Association Drive
Reston, VA 22091

National Conference on Parent Involvement (NCPI)

The National Conference on Parent Involvement includes parents, teachers, community workers, and others interested in promoting higher levels of parental involvement in schools. Among other things, the association provides information to members on possible implications of existing and pending legislation for parental involvement. For information about this group, write to:

National Conference on Parent Involvement
579 W. Iroquois
Pontiac, MI 48341

National Council for the Social Studies (NCSS)

The National Council for the Social Studies is the largest national group for educators with interests in history and the social sciences. State and local affiliates are located throughout the country. Student memberships are encouraged.

NCSS publishes several journals. The group's most widely circulated publication is *Social Education*, which appears seven times each year. It contains articles focusing on all aspects of teaching and learning social studies content in grades K through 12. *Social Studies and the Young Learner* is published four times a year. Its articles focus on classroom activities, curriculum content, and other information about teaching social studies to elementary school learners. *Theory and Research in Social Education* is a quarterly journal that reports research related to social studies education. For information about this group, write to:

National Council for the Social Studies
3501 Newark Street, NW
Washington, DC 20016

National Council of Teachers of English (NCTE)

The National Council of Teachers of English has chapters in each state, as well as a large number of local affiliates. NCTE seeks to improve the quality of English language and English literature instruction. Membership is open to individuals who teach language arts and English at any level. Special memberships are available for students who wish to join.

NCTE sponsors several journals. *Language Arts*, published eight times a year, is a journal for elementary school teachers and administrators. *English Journal*, also published eight times a year, serves interests of middle school, junior high school, and senior high school teachers of literature, language, and composition. A quarterly journal, *Research in the Teaching of English*, reports results of research in the teaching and learning of English. For information about this group, write to:

National Council of Teachers of English
1111 Kenyon Road
Urbana, IL 61801

National Council of Teachers of Mathematics (NCTM)

The National Council of Teachers of Mathematics has more than 200 state and local chapters throughout the nation. It is dedicated to improving mathematics instruction in the schools. Members include elementary and secondary teachers and others interested in furthering the organization's objectives. Student memberships are available.

NCTM publishes several journals. The *Arithmetic Teacher*, published nine times each year, is for people interested in improving mathematics instruction in elementary schools. The *Mathematics Teacher*, also published nine times a year, serves mathematics teachers at the secondary level and in two-year colleges. Research in mathematics education is reported five times each year in the *Journal for Research in Mathematics Education*. For information about this group, write to:

National Council of Teachers of Mathematics
1906 Association Drive
Reston, VA 22091

National Science Teachers Association (NSTA)

The National Science Teachers Association is the nation's largest group of educators with interests in improving science instruction in the schools. NSTA has affiliates throughout the country. Members include elementary and secondary school teachers, administrators, university-based science educators and scientists, and others committed to the group's mission. Student memberships are encouraged.

NSTA publishes journals for particular groups of science educators. *Science and Children*, published eight times a year, is for elementary school teachers and administrators. *Science Scope*, issued five times a year, provides information about teaching science that is particularly relevant for teachers and learners in middle schools and junior high schools. *The Science Teacher*, published nine times each year, serves the interests of junior and senior high school science educators. The *Journal of College Science Teaching* focuses on issues of concern to science instructors in higher-education settings. For information about this group, write to:

National Science Teachers Association
1742 Connecticut Avenue, NW
Washington, DC 20009

All of these organization draw much of their membership from among our nation's teachers. There are other kinds of specialty organizations in education as well. Some of them are directed at school administrators. Others serve interests of school boards. Still others are comprised primarily of college and university professors with interests in teacher education.

We believe that affiliation with one or more of the specialty groups that are of particular interest to teachers makes sense for college and university students who are preparing for careers in education. Local and regional meetings offer opportunities to meet and learn from teachers already in the field. Additionally, publications sponsored by these groups are outstanding information sources about innovative approaches to classroom instruction. Finally, joining a specialty group can build a sense of community. For example, if you are interested in teaching science, you may find only a few others with a similar interest in some of your methods courses. But if you start attending meetings of a local chapter of the NSTA, you may come into contact with dozens of people who are enthusiastic about their roles as science teachers.

On many campuses, there are student chapters of the larger teacher specialty groups. If there are none on your campus, you might want to establish one. The first step is to find a faculty person who will serve as the group's sponsor. Many of the national groups are eager to help campus-based chapters get started. You may wish to write to the national office of the relevant group for specific information.

• Key Ideas in Summary

- Two types of organizations draw large numbers of members from the ranks of teachers: general organizations and specialty organizations. General organizations focus on issues of interest to the profession as a whole. Specialty organizations promote narrower interests, for example, interests of teachers concerned about certain categories of learners or about teaching certain subjects.

- The nation's largest teachers' organization is the NEA, with more than two million members. It traces its roots to the middle of the nineteenth century when its forerunner, the National Teachers Association, was formed. In its early days, the NEA included both teachers and administrators; today, it is an organization for teachers only.

- The NEA has tended to view teachers as professionals who have much in common with members of other professions such as law and medicine. This view has led the NEA to push hard to increase teachers' involvement in educational governance, that is, having input into decisions regarding such things as teacher training, teacher hiring, course content, selection of instructional materials, and identification of instructional methodologies.

- The AFT has always been smaller than the NEA. This group is affiliated with the AFL-CIO, and its major membership strength has always been in the nation's largest urban areas. The AFT grew out of the Chicago Teachers' Federation, a group organized in 1890.

- The AFT tends to perceive teachers differently than does the NEA. It sees teachers as more like employees of large corporations than like professionals such as doctors and lawyers. The AFT believes that the primary need of teachers is to have an organization that will defend their interests against sometimes distant administrative authority. This view has led the AFT to be less interested in the general issue of governance than the NEA, concentrating instead on winning economic benefits and improved working conditions for teachers.

- There are many specialty organizations that serve teachers' interests. These groups focus either on concerns related to certain categories of learners (e.g., gifted learners or very young learners) or on concerns related to certain subject matter areas (e.g., social studies, English, mathematics, physical education, and so forth).

- The specialty organizations generally publish journals that help bind together their national membership. Among other things, these publications report promising classroom practices, new developments in curriculum, and findings of researchers.

- Most specialty organizations for teachers welcome memberships from college and university students who are preparing to go into teaching. Memberships afford an opportunity for prospective teachers to come into direct contact with people working in settings similar to those where they hope to work once they complete their certification programs.

• Review and Discussion Questions

1. How would you describe differences in purposes of general organizations and specialty organizations?

2. What are some changes that have occurred over the past century that have encouraged the growth of such groups as the NEA and the AFT? Do present trends suggest to you that membership of these groups will increase or decrease over the next quarter century?

3. How do you explain the reluctance of early leaders of the NEA to evidence much concern about benefits for teachers? In what ways has the organization changed from its first years to today?
4. Today, the NEA does not include administrators. What do you see as some pluses and minuses of building a major organization around a membership solely of teachers?
5. What are some differences in how the NEA and the AFT view the roles of teachers?
6. There continues to be much debate in the profession about the desirability of the strike as a legitimate weapon for teachers to use in pursuit of their objectives. What are your views on this issue, and why do you feel this way?
7. All things considered, are teachers better served by the existence of two large national teachers' organizations, the NEA and the AFT, or would they be better served if there were only one such group? Why do you think so?
8. What are some examples of teachers' organizations that are dedicated to serving the special interests of particular kinds of learners or of educators who are strongly committed to teaching certain subjects? Some people argue that these groups tend to segregate teachers into their own specialty groups and that education would be better off if teachers with varied interests and teaching specialties all belonged to a common organization. What are your feelings on this issue?
9. What are some periodicals produced by specialty organizations in education, and which groups publish them?
10. What potential advantages might there be for a college or university student interested in becoming a teacher to join a local unit (perhaps a campus-based chapter) of a specialty organization?

• Ideas for Field Experiences, Projects, and Enrichment

1. Invite a representative from a local unit of either the AFT or the NEA to visit your class. (If both organizations are active in your area, consider inviting representatives from each.) Ask the representative(s) to comment on particular services these organizations provide for their members. Inquire about activities at the local level and lobbying at the state and national levels.
2. Ask representatives from central administrative offices of local school districts to come to your class. Invite these visitors to comment on the nature of their relationships with local affiliates of groups such as the NEA or the AFT.
3. With the assistance of your instructor, learn whether teachers in your state are obligated to join either the NEA or the AFT. (There may well be place-to-place differences in your state.) Share your findings with others in your class.
4. Organize a group of four or five people in your class to investigate some of the publications produced by specialty groups in education. Assign each person to look at issues of a different publication. Make a report to your class in which you address such issues as:
   • general kinds of articles contained in the publications
   • relative emphases on practical, how-to information and more theoretical, research-oriented information
   • your views about whether information in each journal would be helpful to a beginning teacher
5. Attend a meeting of a local affiliate of an educational specialty group. Pick one that focuses on areas that are of interest to you. Take notes on what you observe, and share findings with others in your class.

• References

Cornell, A., & Farkas, P. R. (1995). Professional associations: What value? *Educational Media International*, 32(1), 44–46.

Donley, M. O., Jr. (1976). *Power to the teacher: How America's educators became militant*. Bloomington: Indiana University Press.

Henson, K. T. (in press). *Instructional supervision*. New York: HarperCollins.

Hesson, R. R., & Weeks, T. H. (1987). *Introduction to education*. New York: Macmillan.

361